OUT OF THE NIGHTMARE

RECOVERY FROM DEPRESSION

AND

SUICIDAL PAIN

Out of the Nightmare

Recovery from Depression and Suicidal Pain

David L. Conroy, Ph.D.

New Liberty Press
New York

New Liberty Press
Box 6598, 909 Third Avenue
New York NY 10150-1904

Library of Congress Cataloging in Publication Data

Conroy, David L., 1946-
        Out of the Nightmare : recovery from depression
        and suicidal pain
    / David L. Conroy. --
        p. 364.
        Includes bibliographical references and index
        1. Suicide. 2. Suicidal Behavior--Treatment. Suicide--Social
aspects. 4. Depression, Mental. 4. Depression, Mental--Treatment.
I. Title.

RC569   1991   616.85'8445   90-63398
                              QBI90-21

ISBN 1-879204-00-2

10 9 8 7 6 5 4 3 2

To Fanny Semiglia

CONTENTS

PREFACE

Cultural mythology and psychiatric theory have jointly created an oppressive ideology that judges the suicidal as being morally bad and mentally inferior. This combined ideology is a Hydra-headed monster. It is an omnipresent part of the external world, and its tentacles have a stranglehold within the private hell of suicidal pain. Our present conception of suicide is a morass of interconnected and interdependent prejudice; we must isolate and cauterize each source of venom and infection. This is a laborious task, there are no shortcuts that are quick, neat, or elegant.

The Hydra of Greek mythology had nine heads, one of which was immortal and could not be destroyed by any means. The social prejudice against the suicidal is similar; it is inherently rooted in basic parts of human nature, and, to some degree, will always be with us. If this oppressive force is to be kept at bay, we must have new conceptual resources. *Out of the Nightmare* advances the aggregate pain theory of suicide. This approach is not an esoteric theory of psychiatry; it can be understood and used by anyone. From a new conception of what suicide is, and an analysis of how the non-suicidal defensively respond to their fears about suicide, we can develop a unified program for suicide prevention (including suicide self-prevention), suicide postvention, recovery from depression, public education, the integration of suicide prevention into other areas of public health, and a sounder and less prejudiced basis for scientific inquiry.

Much of this book is polemical. I believe it is helpful to distinguish sharply between various positions. Secondly, I am not an emotionally disengaged observer: I suffered from depression and suicidal pain for 10 years. Though I studied the academic literature and pursued the available forms of therapy, I found little relief. In the years since then I have come to recognize that there are vast areas of the experience of depression and suicidal pain that are simply unmentioned by theorists on these subjects. I hope that my inquiries into fear, envy, shame, self-pity, powerlessness, and other neglected topics will provide academic researchers with an impetus for more formal studies.

I once invited a social worker from a rape crisis program to speak to a training class for a suicide hotline. I asked her why she emphasized the necessity for *repeatedly* telling the rape survivor, "You're not to blame. It's not your fault this happened." She explained that the harmful effects of internalized forms of the blame-the-victim prejudice cannot be undone easily or quickly. I believe that a similar process is at work in those of us who become victims of depression and suicidal pain. The cultural prejudices that we apply to ourselves make us suffer more, and suffer longer. This added pain causes some of us to die.

During the past seven years I have listened to hundreds of suicidal and depressed people, suicide attempters, and relatives, friends and caregivers of suicide victims. These people came from all walks of life in New York City. I have been left with the conviction that the suicidal, as a group, whether or not their pain ultimately causes them to die, are mentally and morally average in the same way that victims of heart disease, diabetes, and sprained ankles are mentally and morally average. Our culture's predominant assessment of the character of suicidal people is negative: weak-willed, selfish, manipulative. There is a small counterstrain that makes positive assertions: suicide is courageous or honorable, or suicide tends to happen to people who are creative or intelligent. I believe that these assessments respond to the emotional needs of the assessors, not to the actual qualities of the assessed. The thesis that the suicidal are simply average people, of course, also responds to need: the need to counteract the twin demons of self-loathing and grandiosity, the need to recover from shame and self-pity, the need to reduce stigma, aversion and loneliness.

Though my purposes are entirely practical, three chapters and parts of others are devoted to theoretical issues. My work in public education has convinced me that the practical demands of suicide prevention require general theories about suicide that are entirely based in the terminology of ordinary language. The task of this book is to construct one such theory, and argue for its plausibility and utility.

I am grateful to Hilda Margaret Bailey for her patient suggestions on an earlier draft of the manuscript. Masculine singular pronouns have been used to refer to hypothetical suicidal individuals as a matter of simplicity; readers may substitute feminine pronouns or expressions such as "he or she".

CHAPTER ONE

VOLITION AND SUICIDE

Introduction

Suicide is not chosen; it happens when pain exceeds resources for coping with pain. As in other forms of death, the victim of suicide dies if enough trauma is suffered or if life support systems are withdrawn or give out. An analogy to suicide is to imagine weights being piled onto a person's shoulders. Regardless of physical, emotional, or moral qualities, the person will eventually collapse. None of us is invulnerable to suicide; it is directly caused by unbearable pain. Two types of suicide, those that occur without an observable precipitating event and those that are precipitated by a "straw that breaks the back," are not mysterious when viewed from the involuntarist perspective. Precarious structures can collapse under small increases in stress, and support mechanisms can weaken over time.

The position that suicide is something people choose is the prevalent view of our culture and of our theorists on suicide. My critique of this position begins by pointing out that in its simplest formulation it is obviously false. I go on to argue that there is a more reasonable formulation of voluntarism, but this interpretation does not have better empirical support than the involuntarist position.

The simple version of voluntarism holds that each of us is potentially immune to suicide; we can choose not to do it no matter what. Suicide is always a matter of choice. An unstated assumption of this view is

There are no unbearable pains.

Every human being has sufficient will power to tolerate any level of pain for any length of time. This position has only to be stated to be recognized as absurd. Absurd or not, we would like it to be true. In a tacit and unarticulated way, it is a basic part of our culture's mythology of suicide and believed by nearly everyone.

A second version of voluntarism would agree that most of us, at least, are theoretically vulnerable to involuntary suicide. This position would go on to claim that such suicides rarely or never happen: people choose suicide when the pain gets really bad, but before it reaches the level of complete intolerability. Defenders of this position might point out that the kinds of unhappiness that lead to suicide are things that other people are able to survive. Suicides have options, and elect death instead. This version of voluntarism is the claim that the pains that are factors in suicide are bearable, therefore suicide is by choice.[1]

The position that suicide happens when pain is really bad, but the person could still elect courses of action other than suicide, is denied by involuntarism. Involuntarism holds that whatever level of pain the suicide occurred at simply was that person's level of unbearability. The fact that many people suffer as much or more pain than a suicide does not show that the suicide was voluntary. Most of us have cardiovascular systems that can withstand 60 years of stress. Some of us do not, and suffer premature heart attacks. The heart attacks are not voluntary, the people who have them simply have bodily systems that are weaker than average. There are thousands of variables in our capacities to suffer pain and to withstand pain. It should not be surprising that individuals vary greatly in these respects.

Given the current state of scientific method, the two positions:

1. Nearly all suicides happen when pain is bearable.

2. Nearly all suicides happen when pain is not bearable.

are impossible to evaluate definitively. We do not know how to measure the kinds of pain that contribute to suicide, or how to measure our resources for coping with pain. We do not know how to examine a corpse to determine if the pre-attempt level of pain was greater (or less) than coping resources. Even in ordinary behavior, the extent of our volitional capacities is uncertain and controversial. It seems to us that some of the events of our lives — buying a newspaper — are voluntary, and that others — catching a cold — are involuntary. But later on we sometimes feel that initial self-judgments of voluntarism or the opposite were wrong. We realize that actions we thought were freely chosen had causal factors of which we were unaware, or that things we thought we did not create were really things we were trying to bring about. Some "mind over matter" theorists argue that our range of choice is greater than we believe; other positions — behaviorism, for example — argue that our idea of freedom is a complete delusion. I am not an advocate for any systematic view on freedom of the will. I claim only that one class of events — most suicides — that are thought to be voluntary, should actually be regarded as involuntary. Besides an examination of problems with how the voluntarists have formulated their position, I try to analyze the needs and fears that underlie the universal belief that suicide is voluntary. This judgment is not made by the suicides themselves; they are all dead. It is made by the non-suicidal, and its role in their lives is not that of a factual statement. Its purpose is moral: it says that no one but the suicide is to blame for the death. Though I appear to be trying to replace one factual view with another factual view, I am, in large part, asking that we change our moral perspective. In some areas of inquiry it is reasonable to adopt the policy "If you can't reach a definitive conclusion, withhold judgment." Suicide is not one of those areas. Because nearly everyone believes 1., we have a cultural mythology that oppresses the suicidal. The mythology adds to their pain, makes it harder for them to get help, and greatly contributes to suicide. Abandoning 1. in favor of 2. is not only empirically reasonable; it will save lives and reduce suffering.

Two qualifications need to be added. The first is that the claim that suicide is involuntary applies only to suicide that results from personal despair. Suicides by political terrorists, spies who take poison, soldiers in acts of war, political protesters, sacrificers of self for others, and ritual suicides of culture or religion may well be voluntary. Some instances of what is called "rational suicide" — situations in which someone prefers death to the final stages of terminal illness — also may be voluntary. Secondly, the position advanced here, the aggregate pain theory, is not the view that suicide is involuntarily caused by insanity. Many suicides are not in obvious ways victims of recognized mental illnesses. The large majority of people with mental illnesses do not commit suicide. "Insanity," by itself, does not explain why suicide happens. Since both the suicidal and the victims of mental illness suffer from similar stigmas and taboos, an "involuntary by cause of insanity" theory would do little to engender a more compassionate social environment.

The Myth of Unimpaired Volition

Virtually all writers on suicide agree that the cognitive operations of the suicidal are severely impaired. Shneidman describes this as

> ...a narrowing of the mind's content, a truncating of the capacity to see viable options which would ordinarily occur to the mind, (1985, p. 35)

He later writes

> This fact, that suicide is committed by individuals who are in a special constricted condition, leads us to suggest that one should never commit suicide while disturbed. It is not a thing to do while not in one's best mind. Never kill yourself when you are suicidal. It takes a mind capable of scanning a range of options greater than two to make a decision as important as taking one's life. (p. 139)

In part this view is correct: suicidal pain does cause cognitive impairment. In two other respects this view is very odd. The "special constricted condition" seems itself to be constricted: once it decreases the number of options to two it stops constricting. Shneidman gives no reason for this limitation. The second oddity is the assumption that while the person's cognitive abilities can be drastically curtailed, his volitional capacities remain entirely intact. Though the capacity to conceive options becomes limited, the ability to elect one or another is as unfettered as ever.[2] Evidence does not support the view that the volitional capacities of the suicidal are unimpaired. Freedom of the will is constrained by many conditions associated with suicide: alcoholism, drug addiction, profound grief, physical illness, depression, anxiety disorders, schizophrenia, paranoia, and eating disorders. These conditions limit power of choice in both physical behavior and mental activity. The human capacity for choice is not a magical entity; it is subject to the same material influences as the rest of our capacities. If someone suffers enough pain and abuse, his volitional capacities will diminish to nothing.

Self-assessments of the power of choice, "I could go on living like this; I just don't want to," are no better as evidence for volitional capacity than self-assessments of cognitive capacity. Some suicidal people say, "I understand my situation. I see things very clearly," and go on to provide very inaccurate accounts of the hopelessness of their situations. People with other self-destructive conditions are notorious for practicing denial on their powerlessness: "I can quit anytime I want; I just choose not to." The belief that suicide is a matter of choosing life over death is analogous to a brave claim by someone who was about to be tortured, "No matter what happens, I won't talk." The sincerity of the belief does not guarantee its truth. The real functions of "I understand my situation. I'm in control of my situation," are to cope with fear and pain. Like many coping mechanisms of the desperate, these illusions are double edged. On one hand, they are self-fulfilling. A poor understanding is cognitively better than incoherence. A sense of no self-control is terrifying; a belief in control can reduce the terror and thereby increase volitional capacity. On the other hand, the belief, "I can always choose not to do it," is not conducive to early entry into a recovery program.

The myth of unimpaired volition provides support for the "snap out of it" abuse inflicted on the suicidal. "Snap out of it," presupposes that people are completely free to alter instantly their emotional conditions. Common observation shows that this is not true; people in profound pain do not have this power. To insist that people do the impossible is cruelty; it adds to suicidal pain.

Abandoning the idol of voluntarism, the view that the mind always has power over suicide, is not as frightening as it first seems. Virtually all suicides result from conditions that develop over time. Rejecting voluntarism means rejecting the myth that suicide prevention is a last minute activity. It enjoins the sensible policy that people should be educated to give and get help sooner rather than later.

The Myth of the Something More

After a suicide one often hears a comment of the form

> He couldn't have committed suicide over problems x, y,
> and z. That's just not enough. There must have been
> something more we didn't know about.

There probably are cases where something like the "something more" exists. But the belief in the something more is held by a great many survivors of a suicide victim, particularly non-family members, and yet precipitating causes that might count as this extra factor rarely come to light. The prevalence of the belief in the something more is due to denial: we do not want to believe that human beings — the victim, ourselves, those close to us — are so susceptible to suicide that it can be caused just by problems x, y, and z. We may want to think well of the deceased: surely he could have withstood x, y, and z. We want to avoid blame: the way we interacted with the person could not have been a cause, it must be something else. Not believing in the something more means reducing our conception of what it takes to cause suicide; it means seeing ourselves as weaker than we would like.

The myth of the something more is an artificial means to create distance between ourselves and the victim. This may help us adjust to the shock of the event, but it also has some negative consequences. It insinuates a secret vice in the individual and a secret shame in the family. This adds to the pain of the immediate survivors, and contributes to their difficulty in regaining normal social relations. The myth helps prolong a common "stuck" position of many survivors: brooding at length and depth in search of the cause of the death. The myth makes it more difficult for suicide prevention activities to begin sooner rather than later. The myth of the something more implies that problems x, y, and z are not enough to justify asking for help and not enough to justify giving help. It causes us to overlook the debilitating long-term effects of substance abuse, chronic stress, and mental and physical illness. To an external observer someone's life may not seem to change, but inwardly the senses of powerlessness, hopelessness, frustration, and impatience can grow. The fact that a specific group of problems was not enough to cause suicide at one time does not mean that it is not enough at a later time.

A version of the myth of the something more is part of the support for the "just wants attention" myth for attempters and considerers. We do not want to believe that their problems are enough to cause an attempt or a preoccupation with suicidal feelings and ideation, so we postulate a "something more." In this case the something more is the ulterior motive of attention and manipulation. Since the accused have no way to prove themselves innocent of the ulterior motive, as completers have no way to prove themselves innocent of secret vices, they (or their memories) suffer a stain that can never be removed. Such accusations are not only groundless, they are abusive. Giving up the myth of the something more means giving up a small source of help for the non-suicidal, and gaining a great deal in our overall approach to suicide prevention and postvention.

The Projection of Volition

It is natural for the non-suicidal to believe that suicide is voluntary. As individuals and as a species we prefer to have robust senses of our own powers. We are pleased by the idea that we are masters of our destinies. Positions that suggest that free will is less than what we think it is have always been met with hostility.

Our strongest fear is the fear of our death. The belief that suicide cannot happen unless it is chosen helps to reduce this anxiety. The human capacity to practice denial on death is immense. Belief in the afterlife is part of this denial, and denial is evident in people whose behavior is conducive to cancer, emphysema, heart disease, cirrhosis, AIDS, and accidental death. We fear death, we fear particular kinds of death, and denial on the risk of suicide is part of a complex system of anxiety-reducing beliefs. "No matter how much I suffer, suicide cannot happen unless I choose it," is analogous to "No matter how much I smoke, cancer won't happen." The suicidal are sometimes accused of being infantile, but the proposition that every human being, no matter how great the pain, can just say no to suicide is itself tinged with childish omnipotence. Beliefs such as these are not based on evidence, they are caused by fear.

We project our own psychological condition onto the suicidal. For suicide to happen to someone who was not suffering suicidal despair, it would have to be a voluntary action. Such an act would realize the intention of the victim; it would require the "oomph" that is said to be courage or guts. In our imaginations, at least, this is what we assume happens with heroes who sacrifice themselves so that others may live. Our projection of voluntarism in these cases may be correct. But heroes and non-suicidal ordinary people are in different psychological conditions than those who suffer suicidal pain. Suicidal pain includes the feeling that one has lost all capacity to effect emotional change. The agony is excruciating and looks as if it will never end. There is the feeling of having been beaten down for a very long time. There are feelings of agitation, emptiness, and incoherence. "Snap out of it and get on with your life," sounds like a demand to high jump ten feet. There is no validity to using the deliberative or volitional capacities of the heroic or the ordinary as models for the mind of the suicidal.

The word "ambivalence" is often used to describe the suicidal person; it is said that a part of him wants life and a part wants death. (This, for example, is the position of Farberow, 1967, p. 385. I shall argue in subsequent chapters that half of this position — the claim that the suicidal want death — is a mistake.) The model of ambivalence is also a false projection from the ordinary life situation of being torn between two alternatives. The suicidal do teeter between life and death; but the forces buffeting them are non-volitional and non-intentional.

I have discussed my views on our powerlessness over suicidal pain with the survivors of a suicide victim, and the reaction is often polite reserve. They want to think well of the deceased, and, like the survivors of someone with a terminal illness, they do not want to perceive their loved one as lacking strength to keep up the fight. Some survivors see the suicide as a courageous act. To regard suicide as an act requiring "oomph", rather than as an event caused by enfeeblement, has significant coping benefits for the survivor. It is difficult to criticize this position, since survivors are entitled to their viewpoints and coping strategies. For the purposes of this book, however, two problems need to be mentioned. The first is that the cause of suicide prevention is not well served by perceiving suicide as a courageous, and therefore positive, action. The second is that once our illusions are cast aside and we accept vulnerability to suicide as a human weakness, the involuntarist position is a basis for stronger personal and social action. Our current attitudes are pathetically weak. The myth of voluntarism has paralyzed us into believing that it is hopeless to try to prevent suicide. To regard suicide as an event caused by an excess of pain over coping resources enables us to recognize that effective action can be taken against it.

Other Self-destructive Behaviors

For several decades scientific and social opinion has been evolving in directions that reduce belief in the volitional component of destructive behaviors such as alcoholism, drug abuse, self-mutilation, gambling, anorexia, and bulimia. One step in this process was recently reported in *The New York Times*:

> Evidence is mounting that for biological reasons the millions of people who continue to smoke are more intractable and their problems more profound than the millions who have given up smoking, said Dr. Ovide Pomerleau, a psychiatrist specializing in nicotine research at the University of Michigan.
>
> It appears that many smokers have a genetic predisposition to the addiction and that they smoke "to maintain optimal brain function," he said, adding that it is not a question of moral fiber. In other words, individual biological makeup may determine how people respond to nicotine; some can take it or leave it, while others, once exposed to the drug, cannot seem to live without it. Doctors say one of the main unanswered questions in nicotine research is what these biological factors are. (June 9, 1988.)

Articles such as these appear with regularity on every issue except suicide. Some focus on biological predisposition, some on experiences of early childhood. Still others point out that the behavior of Americans of all ages is influenced by thousands of messages telling us that emotional problems are to be solved by quick fixes. These three influences, nature, nurture, and social environment, are not things for which we are responsible. They affect our behavior, and, as the nicotine article indicates, they affect different people differently. In most cases the power of choice decreases as the activity increases in its self-destructiveness. People in the early stages of alcoholism, for example, are more able to have periods of dryness or reduced drinking. We no longer assume that will power and moral choice are the factors of primary importance in other types of self-destructive behavior; why should we continue to do so in the case of suicide?

At what point does the capacity for voluntary action end and involuntary behavior begin? I don't know. Recovering substance abusers talk about an "invisible line," the point at which they crossed from being heavy users to being addicts. They do not know where in their life histories this happened, but they do know that at one time they were one and at a later time they were the other. The transition is real, even if a date cannot be fixed.

The Suicidal Crisis Is Not Chosen

Some of our attitudes about the volitional component in suicide are applied to the circumstances leading up to the crisis. "You got yourself into this mess," is a common opinion about someone who is suicidal. Menninger reflects the view of many professionals: "For we know that the individual always, in a measure, creates his own environment, and thus the suicidal person must in some way help to create the very thing from which, in suicide, he takes flight." (1966, p. 18) Secondly, we have a cultural prejudice that holds that people who suffer pain or remain in pain do so because of personal failings. If they had more will power or more common sense they would not be in their sorry condition. By acts of will they could end their suffering and stop being a nuisance to us. These are not accurate points of view. In their discussions with a suicidal person, most counselors focus 95 percent of the conversation on areas that they believe are within the volitional range of their client. In some sense this is understandable, but it leaves us with the distorted view that 95 percent of his condition is his responsibility. It might be more accurate to say that personal volition explains five percent of his condition. We do not choose inherited capacities to avoid pain, or our early childhood experiences, or traumatic experiences, or the impact of education or culture on the development of personal resources, or the lack of social resources, or the large extent to which cultural mythology contributes to suicidal pain. Most of the agony of the suicidal person is due to factors far beyond his control.

In cancer, heart disease, and alcoholism, two people can have the same behaviors and environmental experiences, and one get the disease and the other not. The difference is not that one person chose the disease and the other chose not to get the disease, but innate biological factors. Why should we assume that suicide is different? Two people have the same experiences and only one becomes suicidal — why should he have the added pain of moral reproach? We do get angry at alcoholics and at cancer victims who smoked, but some cancer victims never smoked and some alcoholics report alcoholic behavior from the first drink. These people had greater than average vulnerability. The group that has perhaps the greatest vulnerability to suicidal thoughts and feelings are the children of completed suicides. Whether this vulnerability is innate or acquired is beside the point of this chapter; they did not choose their condition. Being suicidal is like most other life-threatening conditions: many suicidal people did little or nothing by way of abnormal volitional behavior to put themselves in their condition. To be subjected to pain that threatens to exceed coping resources is not something that people choose.

The subsequent point is that if the conditions that cause suicidal feelings and ideation are not chosen, then how can we regard it as volitional if death occurs to a percentage of the people who are in this condition? If a group of people are placed in any other life-threatening circumstance, a certain percentage of them will die. The fact that some live and some die has little to do with choice; why should suicide be different?

Attempters and Considerers

The voluntarists define suicide as an act in which the victim forms the intention to die, and then wills into existence an action designed to realize his intention. This view of suicide leaves considerers and low-lethal attempters in an undefined limbo. They say they are suicidal, but they do not have the intentions and volitions of those who are "really" suicidal. Therefore, they must have other intentions, motives, and goals. They are pretending to be something they are not; they are phonies, deceivers, manipulators. By default, considerers and low-lethal attempters must live in a social climate of suspicion, defensiveness, hostility, and efforts to prove and deny seriousness of suicide risk. The value of this climate for the purposes of recovery is zero. It is a barrier to progress in individual treatment, in social policy, and in public education. "He isn't serious, he just wants attention," is a blight on the suicide prevention landscape, yet it is directly sanctioned by the voluntarist conception of suicide.

On the involuntarist view these kinds of differences between fatal and non-fatal suicidal conditions do not exist. Suicide is no different from many other life-threatening conditions: what determines who lives and who dies is the extent of the trauma in relation to the extent of the coping resources. The interpretation we should give to sub-lethal behaviors and to reports of suicidal feelings is not that they are false and deceptive. "I can't stand this pain anymore"; "I'm in horrible pain. I can't go on"; and "I want to go to sleep and never wake up," are honest reports of the suicidal condition: pain threatens to exceed resources for coping with it. We should not regard attempts as "unsuccessful" since they are not acts chosen to achieve a goal. Attempts for the suicidal are like binges for the alcoholic or scab-picking for the self-mutilator; given their condition at that moment they could not do otherwise. Attempts, of course, are not even "attempts," much less "unsuccessful attempts." "Involuntary self-injuring event" is a more accurate description. "Considerers" is unfortunately also inaccurate: the ruminations of suicidal people are efforts to organize and discharge pain, they are not analogous to what we do in ordinary life when we deliberate about possible courses of action.

Just as involuntarism does not require prejudicial distinctions between fatal and non-fatal suicidal conditions, it applies equally to both children and adults. Most books and papers on theory about suicide omit mention of suicidal behavior among children. Theory and social mythology hold that suicide is voluntary, and the victim should be blamed. Is it plausible to apply this view to child considerers, attempters, and completers? In one case a five-year old in Queens was discovered trying to hang himself. A few weeks earlier he had been playing in the house with a sibling when a heavy piece of furniture fell and accidentally killed his two-year old brother. In this case the major factor was bereavement; school counselors have told me of other cases in which the suicidal child was a victim of various forms of abuse. The cousin of a 15-year old girl who had hung herself told me that the victim had suffered seven years of sexual abuse from both her stepfather and her stepbrother. The volitional theory entails moral judgments that we hesitate to apply to children; this should cause us to question the extent to which the theory should be applied to adults.

Volitonal Aspects

An objection that might be raised against the involuntarist theory is that a few completed suicides seemed unusually calm during the day or two prior to their deaths. Suicide warning sign lists often contain the sentence, "Depression that seems to lift for no apparent reason is cause for concern." This phenomenon is usually described as "someone who has made up his mind."

Involuntarism readily admits that these people may believe they are going to be suicides. But believing that something is going to happen to you is not the same as causing it to happen by choice. As is common in terminal illness, a number of AIDS patients I knew reached a point where they no longer fought the illness. This transition was often described by caregivers, relatives and other patients as "giving up." We need to ask if this transition really is as voluntary as the description implies. Do human beings have an infinite amount of energy with which to resist death? It is kinder and more accurate to say that they fought until they had no more fight left in them. After the transition, signs of psychological exertion and anxiety disappear, and are replaced by calmness and peacefulness. These patients may stop taking medications, except for pain killers, and make less effort to eat nutritiously. They may believe that death is going to happen, but this does not mean that they have chosen it. "Given out" is a term that describes their situation equally well.

It is not surprising that some suicides exhibit a pattern of behavior that can be observed prior to many other types of death. The transition is not chosen; it is an event that happens to the person. In some cases the transition may not even be "giving out," much less "giving up," or "has already made up his mind," but an involuntary transition to an alternative coping strategy. If struggling does not work, maybe not struggling will be an improvement. A few of the AIDS patients who became passive and weak did go on to regain strength and return to a better level of health. In the case of suicide it is not unusual to hear anecdotal accounts of the calm before the death. What is not heard about, but has been related to me on several occasions, is an instance of someone who accepted the belief that suicide was imminent, experienced a reduction in stress, and then the attempt did not occur.

A related objection is that some of the behavior of some suicides shortly before their deaths clearly is voluntary. They make out wills, say goodbye, wear particular clothing. What is not clear, however, is the inference from the voluntary nature of these acts to the voluntary nature of suicide itself. There is no inconsistency in the view that the acutely suicidal are at liberty in some of their affairs, and yet are losing their power to choose whether or not they remain alive. People who believe they are going to die by illness still remain capable of volitional behavior in other matters. The alcoholic can choose his brand and choose what clothes he wears when he drinks it; what he cannot choose is whether or not he drinks. To be able to choose small things is not incompatible with not being able to choose larger things.

A Dark Cloud

Some of the verbal behavior of suicidal people seems to support the view that suicide is voluntary and intentional: "I want to go to sleep and never wake up," "By Mother's Day I am going to join my [deceased] mother," "This is a bad world. The [fifteenth floor] window is open. I don't want to live in this world and I don't want my baby to live in it either," "I'm going to permanently check out." It is not difficult to provide alternative explanations for these kinds of statements which leave them compatible with the involuntarist thesis. The first, of course, is to see them as cries for help, rather than statements of intention. One could argue that these statements themselves are involuntary responses to suicidal pain. A second point is that our cultural concept of suicide is that it is voluntary and intentional; most, or all, of the suicidal person's beliefs about suicide are socially acquired; so he naturally uses the language of volition and intention. Even if his nightmarish sense of powerlessness causes him to doubt these beliefs, he knows that if he is to communicate with others he will have to use terminology that they understand and accept. For most audiences of these statements, the language of passivity is less acceptable than the language of volition. A fourth factor is that the suicidal feel powerless over their pain, this is frightening, and the terminology is an attempt to cope with their fear.

A phenomenon not much discussed by volitional theorists is that some suicidal people largely, and others intermittently, speak of their suicide as an ominous thing that looms over them. They refer to it as an event that may or may not happen, and over which they have little or no control: "I'm afraid something bad is going to happen," "I don't know if it's going to happen." Their psychological reality is that they feel passive with respect to the event of their suicide. These types of remarks are some evidence for the involuntarist position. It would be a fallacy, of course, to try to draw a stronger conclusion. Involuntarist ideation and verbal behavior does not prove involuntarism any more than their counterparts prove that suicide is voluntary. A voluntarist might argue that these remarks are alternative (and voluntary) ways of asking for help, and that the suicidal person has sensed that this particular listener might be more responsive to passive rather than active language. Verbal behavior provides evidence for and against both positions.

Access to the Means

An objection to the thesis that suicide happens when pain exceeds resources is that suicide also requires access to the means. We can imagine situations where pain becomes extreme, yet suicide does not happen because of the unavailability of a firearm or high building. I believe, however, that the simple formulation of the position still holds. The unavailability of the means, or the ignorance of how to use them, can be understood as coping resources.

Counselors for the suicidal often hear accounts of guns being given to someone else for safekeeping, pills being flushed down the toilet, and insistences that others drive for fear of what might happen. The disposition for this behavior, and for behavior that avoids the initial acquisition of the means, is a resource that helps people endure pain without dying. A variable in the coping resources of individuals is the willingness of relatives and friends to restrict access to the means. In New York City laws prohibit the sale of handguns and enjoin the installation of window guards in apartments that contain children. (These guards are not just for accidental falls; on a number of occasions city counselors have told me about cases of suicidal children aged six and under.) A coping resource for people who must endure the pain of being in jail is the policy that requires their belts and shoelaces to be impounded. Involuntary confinement in a psychiatric ward is a service provided by the community to help people survive a suicidal crisis. A less tangible but very real resource is the strong and effective social sentiment against the dissemination of information about practical techniques for suicide. It is not an accident that our resources for enduring pain include extensive restrictions on access to the means of suicide. This is part of the written and unwritten social contract, and it is something that human beings have a disposition to provide for themselves and others. It is a resource on the side of life, and obviously an area in which we can improve.

CHAPTER TWO

MENTAL AND MORAL
INTERPRETATIONS OF SUICIDE

He's Different

The existing theories of suicide claim that there are mental and moral differences between the suicide and everyone else. Only the suicide makes a voluntary decision to bring about his death. He sees death as a solution; his act has an intention, a goal, a purpose had by no other. He wants to escape, to reject, to revenge, to seize power and control. His action is an affirmation that there is a better alternative in death than he could find in life. He makes a moral statement: he is unworthy of us, we are unworthy of him, life itself is not worth living.

None of these are true. The morals, motives, and intentions of the suicide are in no way different from ours. The only distinguishing feature of the suicide is the relationship between his pain and his coping resources. Besides being false, these doctrines are profoundly harmful to suicidal people. The horrors of suicidal pain include the growing sense of estrangement between oneself and the rest of humanity. These positions add to that pain. Two other parts of suicidal pain are prejudice and stigma. The outstanding characteristic of prejudice and stigma is that they are grounded in alleged basic differences between the in-group and the out-group:

> The prejudiced person invariably explains his negative
> attitudes in terms of some objectionable quality that
> marks the despised group. The group as a whole is
> alleged to have a bad odor, an inferior brain, a sly,
> aggressive, or lazy nature. (Allport, 1954, p. 85)

Compare the latter three of these characteristics with some of the
alleged objectionable qualities of the suicidal: manipulative, selfish,
rejecting, vengeful, failure to use will power to snap out of it and get on
with their lives. The psychological dynamic of prejudice — put down
someone else so you can feel better about yourself — cannot work unless
there is a way to distinguish morally and mentally between "us" and
"them". Modern theory on suicide is the bedrock of the social
oppression of the suicidal. This oppression adds to their pain and
deprives them of coping resources. These doctrines cause suicide. They
are intellectual versions of the historical practice of refusing the
suicide burial in the church graveyard; they say, "He's different. He's
not one of us. He doesn't belong here."

A second basic feature of current theory about suicide is that it locates
the entirety of the problem within the skull of the victim. The things
that are said to be causally responsible for suicide are choices, conscious
and unconscious motives, intentions, purposes. It is because of these
mental entities that suicide is said to have a meaning: escape, revenge,
or affirmation. Given this theoretical background it is not surprising
that an otherwise excellent recent book on survivors begins:

> ...we do not believe in ascribing "responsibility" for
> suicide to anyone other than the victim. The failure to
> choose life is the failure of the deceased, not of the
> survivors. (Dunne, 1987 p. xvi, preface by Edward J.
> Dunne and Karen Dunne-Maxim.)

Involuntarism agrees that the survivors should not be blamed, but
blame the victim is not our best alternative. Current theory supports
two basic purposes of the mythology of suicide: deny personal
vulnerability and deny social complicity. If the causes of suicide are
bad things in the victim, then none of the causes are in the outside
world. Suicide prevention, on these theories, means changing the
suicidal; we do not have to change at all. Modern theory on suicide does

not accommodate the fact that the suicidal person's pain is made worse by society's negative views about suicide and by the victim's internalization of those views. Read the works by Shneidman, Hendin, Maris, Litman, Maltsberger, and Beck. This is a component of suicidal pain they never discuss; they pretend it does not exist.

The "bad thought" theories of suicide receive uncritical acceptance because they help the non-suicidal cope with *their* fears and anxieties. Prejudice in suicide, as with prejudice everywhere, has its roots in unconscious and self-interested efforts to cope with personal insecurity. If he is different from us, then we are different from him. The assumption of a gap between him and us is a comfort that helps us repress awareness of our fear of our own suicide. When we deny social complicity in suicidal pain we help ourselves feel better. The price, of course, is that we make the suicidal feel worse.

Intention

> ... the psychological key to defining suicide is intention, (Litman, 1987, p. 85)

> ... suicide ... is the consciously intended act of self-inflicted cessation. (Shneidman, 1985, p. 206)

> Minimally, suicide means self killing; it is an overt, explicit act in which an individual *intentionally* ends his or her own life.

> ... all suicides die self-intended deaths ... (Maris, 1981, p. 5, and 1986, p. vi.)

> These criteria are based upon a definition of suicide as "death arising from an act inflicted upon oneself with the intent to kill oneself." (Rosenberg, 1988, p. 1445)

Litman's discussions of the nature of intention include:

> The noun "intention" indicates stretching out of the mind, or psychological exertion for a purpose, to an end.

> ... suicide certification requires that persons committing self-destructive actions have it in mind that the

actions will result in their deaths, within the limits of predictability.

... a person must have a certain minimal degree of intact volition and thinking ability, and understanding of cause and effect, in order to produce fatal self-inflicted injuries. (1987, pp. 86 & 90)

To some degree, then, the suicidal act had purposefulness, with a goal in mind, and there were elements of choice. (1984, p. 94)

The involuntarist theory does not require that suicides be aware that the events that are happening to them will result in their death. Extreme pain makes thinking difficult, and sometimes causes delusional beliefs about reality. It is surely correct, though, that most suicides believe that their death will soon occur. Understanding and awareness, however, are only part of intention. Prisoners on death row or non-suicidal terminal cancer patients may believe that they are going to die, but they do not have the intention of dying because they are not performing psychological exertions or acts of will that try to realize death as a goal. Intention requires not only a conception of the end, but a willingness to exert oneself to bring about that end. This is "wanting to die"; the voluntarists believe that suicides have it:

In suicide there must be some willing, some formal purpose, some conceptualized goal, some striving in relation to some conflict. (Shneidman, 1985, p. 128)

The concept of suicide requires that the self-destructive action has, at least as one of its purposes or goals, the death of the person. (Litman, 1987, p. 86)

Involuntarism denies that suicides wish to die. I shall argue in this chapter, and in parts of subsequent chapters and the Appendix, that we do not have sufficient evidence for the view that suicides desire death, and that an adequate theory of suicide does not require that we make this stigmatizing assumption. This assumption has broad practical significance: if we follow the intentionalists and believe that the suicidal person is full of negative desires, how can we help but have negative attitudes toward him? The aggregate pain view provides us with a completely different conceptual framework for the suicidal crisis: as long as someone is still alive, it means that his resources exceed his pain. This is a positive image both for the person and for his relatives, friends, and counselors. It does not put his condition in a morally negative light.

Is "having suicide in mind" evidence of wanting to die? Some evidence *against* this position comes from one of the great contributions of Shneidman and his co-workers. They successfully and correctly taught us that expressions of suicidal thoughts to other people are "cries for help." The real meaning of "I want to die," when said to a friend or counselor, is "I want to live." The theorists regard the utterance of "I want to die," in such circumstances as an intentional act; its goal is to obtain help and thereby remain alive. The way intentionalists explain this situation is to claim that considerers and low-lethal attempters have the intention to live, and that completers have the intention to die. The intentionalist position thus warrants negative judgments about anyone with a suicidal condition. Completers have the stigma of the "bad thought" that separates them morally from the rest of humanity, and considerers and attempters are open to the characterization of "not serious, manipulators, deceivers." The view that people are driven to suicide by pain that is literally overwhelming does not need to assume the existence of a desire to die. Completers still have the desire for life, just as the man who collapses under an unbearable weight still has, at the moment of collapse, his desire to remain standing.

It is helpful to look at good intentions. Drug addicts trying to recover often have them, but trying to stay clean in a drug environment is virtually impossible. Good intentions are overwhelmed by pain and the absence of pain-coping resources. In these circumstances the addiction itself suffices to explain the relapse; we do not need to assume that the addict had the same intentions he had when he began using drugs.

The Solution Theory

> Suicide is always available as an option for persons who have problems in life that they consider to be insoluble by any behavior other than suicide. The purpose in suicide is to resolve problems of living that

are causing a great deal of pain and distress. (Litman, 1987, p. 86)

Every suicide has as its purpose the seeking of a solution to some perceived problem. To understand what a suicide is about, one has to know the problem that it was intended to solve. (Shneidman, 1985, p. 129)

... suicide is largely *rational*. Suicide is at least an effective means of resolving common life problems. (Maris, 1981, p. 290)

The spy who swallows the poison capsule and the hero who falls on the hand grenade use their deaths to solve problems. Some solution suicides exist, and some cases of what is called "rational" suicide by the terminally ill may fall into this category as well. For 99 percent of all suicides, however, this theory is harmful and false. If the weight on the shoulders analogy is correct, the solution theory is absurd. Unbearable stress causes people to collapse, regardless of their beliefs about collapsing being a solution for their problems.

For anyone who does public education work in the prevention of suicide, the idea of using the concept "suicide is a solution," is one that sticks in the gut. A resource for coping with suicidal pain is the general social belief that it is not desirable that suicide happen. There is some validity to associationist psychology, and to associate the words "suicide" and "solution" undermines the influence of social disapproval. Defenders of the solution theory might reply that for the purposes of public education we should associate "suicide" with "poor solution" or "the worst solution." This still has the problem of associating the two concepts, and uses a framework that negatively judges the suicidal.[1]

We use rational argumentation in ordinary life to dissuade people we know from taking actions we deem ill-advised. To point out unnoticed consequences of present situations, or to suggest better alternatives, will often immediately cause people to change their minds. Telling a prospective purchaser of software, "That product has poor documentation, is a memory hog, and crashes if you forget to give it the commands in the right order," will have a direct effect on his thinking and behavior. As all hotline workers have found out, this approach never works when applied to the suicidal. "Your suicide will cause your relatives a lot more pain than you realize," "Most people who suffer terrible depression, depression so bad it seems hopeless, eventually do recover and regain the enjoyment of life," and "Valium users with longer-term dependencies than yours have found ways to stop," simply do not have the same result that analogous statements have in discussions of the problems of ordinary life.[2] "Problem solving" with the acutely suicidal does not work because problem solving is a false model for the nature of their mental activity.

Suicidal people do sometimes say, "It's the only solution." Many ruminate about their problems, reach the view that their future contains nothing but unrelenting pain, and think or say, "If I commit suicide, I won't have to suffer any more." But simply having the idea, "Suicide is a solution," does not mean that the idea is a motive for action. Sometimes people with advanced terminal illnesses express the idea that death is a solution. For the terminally ill to have this idea does not mean that it is a motive or goal, or that their death is voluntary. In this regard the suicidal and the terminally ill are alike; "death is a solution," is not a motive for future action, but a way to cope with current pain.

The imposition of a rational structure on the suicidal nightmare reduces confusion and fear, and provides senses of understanding and control. Far more people reach the condition of "rational hopelessness" than attempt suicide. For these people, the poor understanding derived from illogical operations on a skewed evidence base may be better than the confusion and turmoil of no understanding at all. The perception of suicide as a solution is not just a personal coping device, it also helps in dealing with others. It provides a framework for communication and conversation within which the non-suicidal are able to respond. For many suicidal people, "I'm entitled to feel this bad," is a precondition for "I'm entitled to ask for help"; for many counselors, "He's entitled to feel this bad," is a precondition for "He's entitled to be given help." This is why the suicidal resist problem solving. It adds to their pain by belittling their needs, and it threatens to undermine the coping resources of understanding and access to help. In crisis situations rational argumentation does not reduce pain; "problem solving" is not a solution.

Satisfaction of Need

A companion to the solution theory is the view that suicide is an action that is intended to satisfy human need. Involuntarism agrees with part of this position: the suicidal are in need. They need relief from pain, and they have specific needs for such things as love, companionship, security, and physical health. Shneidman's practical recommendation on this issue is completely reasonable:

> The clinical rule is: Address the frustrated needs and the suicide will not occur. In general, the goal of psychotherapy is to decrease the patient's psychological discomfort. One way to operationalize this task is to focus on thwarted needs. (1985, p. 127)

What is objectionable is the inference from the observation that frustrated needs are part of suicidal pain to the theoretical assertion that suicide is an act that satisfies needs:

> In order to understand suicide in this kind of context, we are required to ask a much broader question, which, I believe, is the key: What purposes do most human acts, in general, intend to accomplish? ... human acts are intended to satisfy a variety of human *needs*. (p. 126)

Viewing suicide as the satisfaction of need confuses the satisfaction of a need with the termination of neediness. The way to *satisfy* a need for shoes is to give someone shoes, not to cut off his feet. A need is satisfied only if the thing needed is provided. Needs for companionship and relief from pain are satisfied only by companionship and relief from pain. Just because death ends the existence of need does not mean that death satisfies need. All people near death have needs; it does not follow that death occurs because they want to satisfy those needs. "He was in pain because of frustrated needs," is perfectly compatible with "His suicide happened because his pain exceeded his resources"; we do not have to use "He choose his suicide because he wanted to satisfy his needs," as an explanation. To view the suicidal as needy people may be helpful in clinical work (provided one has an accurate and unprejudiced view of their needs), but the position that suicide satisfies needs has negative utility in public education. Associating the idea of "suicide" with "satisfies needs" is no better than associating it with "solution".

Meanings

"Means", as it used in statements involving suicide, sometimes means causal connection:

a. The rise in teen suicide means that Americans put too much pressure on their young.

b. His suicide meant weeks of emotional upheaval for the patients and staff.

Sometimes it is used prescriptively:

c. The high rate of geriatric suicide means we should improve conditions for the elderly.

d. His suicide means the hospital should review its policy for issuing passes.

These types of sentences may be true. Very different senses of "means" are those that claim that suicide is an act of communication, an act of escape, rebirth, rejection, or revenge, or an act that in symbolic form is the murder of someone else. Some writers try to find a meaning that is common to all suicides, others divide suicide into a few categories with distinct meanings (Maris, 1981, p. xix, and p. 290: "The most common objectives of the suicides we have known and/or studied have been *to escape* (pain, unhappiness, hopelessness, etc.) or *to act aggressively* against another person or situation."), and still others believe that each suicide has a distinct meaning (Hillman, 1964, p. 41: "... suicide is one of the human possibilities. Death can be chosen. The meaning of this choice is different according to the circumstances and the individual. ... An analyst is concerned with the individual meaning of a suicide, which is not given in classifications." Alvarez, 1971, p. xiv: "... suicide means different things to different people at different times."). Those who believe suicide has meaning in these senses assert statements such as:

e. His suicide meant he hated himself.

f. His suicide meant he rejected us.

g. His suicide makes the statement: "The pain you suffer as the result of my suicide is my revenge for the way you treated me." (f. and g., as versions of the meaning theory, are discussed in detail in Chapter 9.)

h. His suicide meant he felt life was not worth living.

i. His suicide meant he felt that in death he could find a better alternative than he could find in life. (An effort to find positive meanings for suicide is in the work of Robert Jay Lifton: "... our concept of suicide as the destruction of the self on behalf of a larger principle, of a quest for meaning. ... the powerful theme of suicide as self-completion, as the only means of appropriately locating oneself in the 'design' of the cosmos. This theme is present in every suicide, however agonizing or demeaning the circumstances. The act of suicide is an expression of formative process, even as it ends that process in the individual." (1979, pp. 251-2, and see Lifton, 1974, pp. 88-90 & 1987, pp. 220-30)

The involuntarist believes that these statements are false not because suicide has some other meaning, but because it has no meaning of this type at all. Suicide, like heart attacks and accidents, is not an action; therefore it is not an act of communication or revenge or any other kind of act. A pedestrian killed by a falling construction beam may die believing life is not worth living, hating his family, or wishing to escape to a better life. But his death means none of these things. He died because his body was crushed by a force it could not withstand; no mental attribute he had at the time of his death is his last message to the world. Suicides, victims of overwhelming pain, die with all kinds of beliefs, emotions, attitudes, and values. Death is not something they choose, and these beliefs and attitudes, *themselves things distorted by massive pain*, are simply what they are; they are not some sort of special communication.

The meaning theory of suicide is not just false; it is harmful. Most of these theories add to the pain of survivors. Try to imagine what it is like to survive the suicide of a loved one, and to live in a culture that believes that suicide is an act of rejection and vengeance by someone who really wanted to murder someone else. The meaning theories that do not directly inflict more pain on survivors do nothing to support their capacities to cope with pain. They describe suicide as an escape or a search for a better alternative, or they say it means that this person believed life was not worth living. These ideas do nothing to reduce vulnerability. Meaning theories establish a climate for suicide prevention that is defensive, hostile, fearful, and argumentative. Meaning theories abet romanticism and glorification.

Each of the meanings is a something more. We do not want to believe that pain alone can cause suicide, so we add on the concepts of escape, reunion, rejection, and aggression. These imply volition, intention, and moral agency. These are bad things that exist entirely within the person who has them; without these bad things suicide would not happen. Some of the meanings suggest an additional feature: they blame the family as well as the victim. (Scapegoating the family is also a form of denial on social complicity, and is discussed in Chapter 9.) The meanings mean nothing about the suicidal, but they do mean things about the non-suicidal who invent them and project them back onto the victim. The event of suicide is deeply disturbing to us. Meanings provide sense for an event that seems senseless. They give us rules of behavior — wariness and caution — to use in dealing with the suicidal. Frustrated rage is common among survivors; five weeks after the death, the father of a suicide told me, "If I could get my hands on him, I'd kill him." Our anger gets a small measure of relief by being projected onto the victim. His alleged anger at us is a license that permits us to talk about our anger toward him. Meanings are ostensibly causes or motives for suicide; in reality they are coping devices for the non-suicidal. Meanings are phony as explanations. A desire for vengeance explains an act of vengeance, but since people satisfy this desire all the time without committing suicide, it does not suffice as a reason for suicide. "He used his death to say something about us," really means "We need to say something about his death, something that gives us a feeling of power and control over it."

Death Fantasies of the Suicidal

"They'll be sorry at my funeral," and ideas of peace, escape, and personal change are common among suicidal people. Herbert Hendin lists seven psychodynamic constellations he found in suicidal hospital patients in the United States and Scandinavia: retaliation for abandonment, omnipotent mastery over death, retroflexed murder (Freud's theory of anger turned inward), reunion, rebirth, self-punishment and atonement, and feelings of already being dead. (Hendin, 1965, pp. 19-29. See also Maltsberger, 1985, p. 125: "Fantasies such as these ... may be powerful motives to self-destruction." & pp. 47-48, 87-88; and Maltsberger, 1980; and, for a Jungian perspective, Hillman, p. 51: "... to understand a suicide we need to know what mythic fantasy is being enacted.")

These concepts, and combinations of them, are found in the mental life of many suicidal people. What the involuntarist objects to is the way these phenomena are to be interpreted. Hendin and other theorists see these concepts as motives or goals for suicide; involuntarism sees them simply as efforts to cope with the pain that the individual is experiencing in the present moment. On the voluntarist theory, suicide is an action and needs a motive. On the involuntarist theory, suicide is not an action, cannot have a motive, and the mental phenomena regarded as motives must be given an alternative explanation.

Grandiose fantasies are usually due to frustrated needs for attention, care, respect, and love. Suicidal people are especially frustrated in these areas; the funeral fantasy is a common way to discharge the pain, and to provide something that is insufficiently available in reality. This type of fantasy is often had by people who are not suicidal. Since it does not function in the lives of the non-suicidal as a motive, we might ask why it should be regarded as a motive in the suicidal. Secondly, the funeral fantasizer usually imagines himself as somehow being there to observe the mourners' reactions. This and other fantasies contain elements of denial — we somehow continue to exist after dying. As we all do, the suicidal fear death (see Chapter 4) and react with denial; the fantasies are similar to the "get religion" phenomenon among people who fear that death (by any means) is close. The fear of death is a source of pain distinct from frustrated needs and adds the immortality component to the fantasies. The "afterlife" is itself a pain-coping construct; fantasies that use it are specific efforts to cope with pain.

Both the suicidal and the non-suicidal are often angry with others. One way to discharge this anger is to fantasize about violent revenge. The insults of daily life often cause fantasies of revenge to flare up and quickly subside. The people with these fantasies usually do not act on them; they are not motives or goals. They are involuntary responses to perceived insult — ways of coping with rage. The suicidal, whether or not they attempt, suffer tremendous and persistent pain and anger. That this pain should find its way into their fantasies and dreams is no surprise. This ideation is not a motive for action; it is an alternative to action. Fantasizing about suicide is an effort to delay or avoid suicide, not the activity of formulating a motive, goal, or intention. Fantasies doubtlessly succeed in preventing many attempts. Whether or not they can be recommended as coping mechanisms to the suicidal is an open question.[3] There must be some benefit, or they would not exist; and they are potentially a source of self-knowledge. On the other hand, simply being obsessed by fantasies increases isolation and does not lead to positive change.

Seeing the fantasies as efforts to cope with pain, rather than as motives, helps to explain a broader range of suicidal ideation. Hendin includes in his list the feeling of already being dead, which in some degree is common among the acutely suicidal, yet it is hard to see how this, as opposed to a reunion fantasy, can be characterized as a motive for a suicide attempt. It is quite easy, however, to see it as a coping mechanism. As horrible as this feeling is, it is less terrifying than uncontrollable anxiety and agitation. It wards off a yet more painful condition, and thereby wards off suicide as well.

Some psychoanalysts regard these fantasies as reversions to similar fantasies that the suicidal person had as an infant or child. Even in people who are not suicidal, great pain can cause behavior to revert to childish forms of expression. Fantasies of reunion, rebirth, and retribution may have helped us cope with pain when we were children, and help us cope with pain now. Children and the suicidal have strong feelings of powerlessness; fantasies of action and mastery help them manage the pain this causes. Undifferentiated and chaotic pain is more painful and frightening than pain that is organized and coherent. Fantasy is a way to articulate pain, discharge it, and reduce it. It is not surprising that suicidal people should attempt to reuse something that helped them once before.

An example of a delusional fantasy in a suicidal person, though it was not specifically about death, was that of an HIV-positive man in his late forties. Besides other activities pertaining to the epidemic, he did volunteer work with hospitalized AIDS patients in the later stages of the disease. The patients were in a unit that was designated for "long-term care", but, at that stage in the development of treatment procedures, the terms were not very long. While some patients died slowly and gradually, others died suddenly and unexpectedly. A patient might be ambulatory and relatively healthy one day, and then succumb to a secondary illness within 24 to 48 hours. On top of all of their problems, the unexpected deaths added greatly to the fear and insecurity of other relatively healthy patients. The volunteer was cheerful, dedicated, and caring, but in time he became increasingly agitated and frustrated over all aspects of the AIDS epidemic. He experienced fatigue and other symptoms that caused him to worry over his own medications and treatment. His time and his emotions became increasingly bound up with the patients on the hospital unit. Late one night he tried to take several patients out of the hospital, hospital security guards were called, and they prevented him from throwing himself in the river. He had developed the delusional ideas that all those affected by the disease were in the process of uniting, they would be visited and blessed by Mother Teresa, this combined force would acquire enough political power to effect dramatic change in the priorities of government, and a cure for the disease would be realized. This delusion originated from massive fear, from needs for acceptance and approval, from feelings of powerlessness and hopelessness. It was an involuntary and desperate effort to ward off pain and to stay alive. It is natural that people such as this man should resist efforts to have their delusions "corrected"; the condition is something that helps them cope with terror. As happens in the development of a suicidal crisis, an increase in pain led to an increased dependence on a coping resource, in this case, his volunteer activity. Unfortunately, a resource that is positive at one level of dependence may become less so at an increased level. During his recovery from his crisis, the volunteer abided by a program requirement that his involvement with the patients be on a more modest level.

The Death Instinct

> After long doubts and vacillations we have decided to assume the existence of only two basic instincts, *Eros* and *the destructive instinct*. ... The aim of the first of these basic instincts is to establish ever greater unities

and to preserve them thus — in short, to bind together; the aim of the second, on the contrary, is to undo connections and so to destroy things. We may suppose that the final aim of the destructive instinct is to reduce living things to an inorganic state. For this reason we also call it the *death instinct*. (Freud, 1949, p. 20. Freud's position is endorsed by Menninger: "... the best theory to account for all the known facts is Freud's hypothesis of a death instinct," 1966, p. 71; and by Litman: "My experience is in agreement with Freud's general schematic view. Deep down, there is a suicidal trend in all of us.", 1967 p. 339. See also Hillman, p. 11 (preface to 1976 edition) and pp. 73-74.)

The death instinct is a something more. Given a strong desire for life, behavior to the contrary seems inexplicable unless we hypothesize the existence of an additional entity that explains such behavior. The question — How could this be? — that is asked of the phenomenon of self-destructive behavior can also be asked of the hypothesized death instinct. A universal death instinct does not seem compatible with our beliefs about the theory of evolution. Its existence is even more puzzling than the phenomenon it is designed to explain. The pain exceeds pain-coping resources theory does not require the assumption of entities beyond those of normal science.

The implausibility of the death instinct is only part of the reason why this theory has not been popularly received. A second factor is its implication that each of us is potentially vulnerable to suicide. For a different reason, involuntarism shares this view: each of us can be done in by unbearable pain.

Aside from being unnecessary, the death instinct theory endorses the cultural myth that suicide is caused by forces that are entirely within the breast of the victim. If the key factor in suicide is the death instinct, then we need not look for social causes of suicidal pain.

The death instinct has been used to explain a range of self-destructive behavior that is broader than suicide, but it is not clear that this hypothesis is necessary. Victims of many health-damaging disorders report that they find themselves in positions of personal anguish where they could not do otherwise:

> They found that the compulsion to continue with
> promiscuous sex or to return over and over to a
> destructive relationship could not be controlled by will-
> power alone. ... Unlike normal persons, who seek love
> and sex to fill normal needs, addicts use them to lessen
> the pain that comes from problems in other areas of
> life. ("An Introduction to Sex and Love Addicts
> Anonymous", The Augustine Fellowship)

Self-destructive behaviors do not exist because there is a force within
us that tries to hasten our return to an inorganic state; they exist because
they provide short-term relief from pain that threatens to become
intolerable.

In *Totem and Taboo* Freud argues that "... a thing forbidden with the
greatest emphasis must be a thing that is desired." (p. 69) If this
principle is true, then the social prohibitions against suicide would be
strong evidence for the existence of the death instinct. This principle
may be plausible for the forbidden acts of incest and murder, but in
general form it is very dubious. Our taboos on contact with people with
infectious diseases can be explained simply as a result of the desire to
stay alive, not as based upon a desire to acquire the disease. In Freudian
terms, Eros suffices as an explanatory principle for the prohibitions
against suicide.

Romance and Drama

Movies, television, and literature often portray suicide in a romantic
manner. In life it never has this quality. The themes of romance are
usually interwoven with ideas of escape, affirmation, reunion, rebirth,
and peace. All of these imply continued existence and deny the finality
of death. These ideas help the non-suicidal cope with fears of death;
they do not correspond to anything we know about reality. Suicide in
fiction is dramatic: it begins stories, ends stories, and provides turning
points in stories. It satisfies plot line needs for authors and
psychological needs for audiences. As parts of dramatic structures,
suicides take on meaning and significance. Actual suicides, as with
other types of death, simply happen. They are not parts of organized

sequences of events that have coherent and psychologically satisfying beginnings, middles, and ends.

Most people who get suicidal feelings do not attempt or commit suicide, or have a single positive experience that propels them back to normal life. Their conditions usually do not have a climax, let alone a climax-building momentum and structure. Yet the influence of romance and drama on our ideas about suicide encourages the suicidal, and those around them, to look for a concluding experience that will purge them once and for all of uncomfortable feelings. Such events rarely or never happen.

The dramatic view of suicide has no practical benefits. It models help-seeking behavior that is dramatic, rather than behavior used for other health problems. This helps perpetuate the myth that the suicidal are phony and manipulative. The dramatic model encourages gambling-with-death and rescue scenarios. It adds tension and anxiety to a situation that already has more than it needs. The idea that suicide and its prevention are dramatic activities does nothing to encourage early help-seeking and help-giving behavior. Substance abuse programs have made progress away from the skid row stereotype that inhibits efforts at early intervention. We need to try to do the same in suicide prevention.

The interpretation of suicidal situations as glorious, romantic, and dramatic is a coping device for the non-suicidal. Involvement with people who consider, attempt, or complete suicide is profoundly disturbing. To perceive these events as parts of dramatic scenarios gives them coherence and intelligibility, and enables us to organize our fear, shock, and pain into a familiar structure. The dramatic conception of suicide may be better than none at all, but it is not the best that we can do.

The Romantic Crisis Theory

A different type of moral position in suicide is a romantic view that holds that suicidal crises are good for people. The crisis is an opportunity to make an authentic choice between life and death. Authentic choices are good things; we should morally approve of both the decision to remain alive and the decision to end life. Authentic choices reveal the true self and promote self-knowledge.

This position has one distinct benefit: the people who hold it are willing to give a suicidal person levels of acceptance, sympathy, and respect he is unlikely to find anywhere else. "You are a good person no matter how your crisis turns out," is a necessary attitude in suicide prevention.

In other respects, however, the romantic crisis theory has many drawbacks. As with any other human experience, suffering suicidal pain does cause people to learn things about themselves. Is what they learn worth the price they have to pay? Victims of AIDS, assault, and drunk drivers learn a good deal about themselves and the world, but no one has claimed that this knowledge is so wonderful that everyone should get it by first-hand experience. Most acutely suicidal people become so, in part, because of alcoholism, drug addiction, eating disorders, depression, manic-depression, schizophrenia, paranoia, panic disorders, physical abuse, sexual abuse, the death or terminal illness of a loved one, disabling injuries or illnesses, or losses that accompany aging. Talk to people in these conditions. Ask yourself if they have attained such great levels of self-awareness that you want to have the condition as well. All these conditions bring with them psychological impairments that render their victims *less* able to accurately perceive themselves and the rest of the world. Perhaps the romantic crisis theorist would reply that since suicide deals directly with death, the experience of being suicidal will yield unique and profound insights that will not be gained merely by having the conditions associated with suicide. I have talked with hundreds of suicidal people; some of them had one or more of the above conditions, others had none of these conditions. None of these people said, "I'm glad this is happening to me. I'm learning wonderful things about myself." An example of a suicidal person who might lack the above conditions is a lonely woman who meets a charming guy. She gives him her love, she loans him several thousand dollars, and then he stops seeing her and does not repay the money. There are things that this woman can learn from this experience. But does the woman who suffers this experience and is not suicidal learn *less* than the woman who does become suicidal? How does the additional pain convert into additional knowledge, additional knowledge that makes the additional pain worth having? And this *is* the romantic crisis theory; the more pain you suffer, the closer you get to suicide, the better it is for you. On hotlines, in counseling, and sometimes in ordinary life we have opportunities to talk with suicidal people, and to people during and after suicide attempts. We can read the notes of completed suicides and talk with their survivors about their last days alive. There is no evidence that these people had an interest in authenticity, or that they learned anything that made the experience worthwhile. They were simply poor souls trapped in horror and terror.

An aspect of real life suicide, as opposed to the single ordeal fantasy of the romantics, is that being suicidal is something that often recurs again and again; some people attempt suicide many times, and some people suffer suicidal feelings and ideation on a daily basis for years. The chronically and recurrently suicidal have learning experiences not had by the non-suicidal, or by those who have had a single short-term siege of suicidality. What they learn from being beaten down by suicidal pain is what it is like to be beaten down by suicidal pain. Talk with people who have beaten down by pain for years. Ask them what wonderful things they learned from their experience, and if they recommend it for everyone.

A second claim of the romantic view of suicide is that in a suicidal crisis the real person is revealed. Hillman, for example, argues that it is "... needed to separate from the collective flow of life and to discover individuality." (p. 64) The real self, however, is a dubious concept. The experiences of becoming suicidal, of inheriting a million dollars, of becoming a parent, and of being offered a bribe are all opportunities to discover hitherto unnoticed aspects of the self. Why is any one of these more real than any other? Review the list of conditions associated with suicide. Are people with these conditions more real or individual or authentic than people who lack them? Most people, at some point in their lives, have thoughts of suicide. By doing so, they may become more like the majority, not less.[4] Make a list of people you know who have had periods of being profoundly suicidal or have had an attempt, and make a second list of people who have never had a siege of suicidal pain. Are the people in the first group more real or more individual than those in the second group?

A topic undiscussed by Hillman or other advocates of the romantic crisis theory is the aftermath of real life suicide. Romantics believe in the right of anyone at anytime to commit suicide. They usually justify this position by appeal to the principle that someone should be free to do as he likes as long as his action does not harm others. But this principle does not justify the right to suicide. Suicide harms others. It harms them a lot. It causes survivors deep and lasting pain. A consistent romantic crisis theorist might acknowledge this fact and still hold that people have a right to suicide. This theorist sees the suffering of the survivors as a good thing: it provides the survivors themselves with opportunities for authentic choices and enables them to lead lives of greater individuality. This is a fantasy. The overwhelming majority of survivors do not have lives that are on the whole better because they lost a child or spouse or parent or sibling to suicide. The horror of suicide, especially the lasting trauma for child survivors, is not something that can be witnessed and approved of by any rational person.

The romantic crisis theory confuses the legitimate and invaluable coping strategy of finding positive aspects in negative situations with the absurd view that any situation that has any positive part is positive on the whole. The fact that we can find something good in almost any bad event does not mean that what happened was good.

The practical disadvantages of the romantic view of suicide are many. Since it believes that the closer people get to suicide, the better it is for them, it does not encourage early suicide prevention measures.[5] Romantics believe it is best to be alone with one's pain. They encourage keeping the secret and discourage the development of support systems for the suicidal and those who know of their condition. Romanticism generally encourages a passive attitude toward suffering and the risk of suffering. It does nothing to encourage education and research in the prevention of suicide. It does not encourage the implementation of measures to relieve pain or provide coping resources during a crisis.

The benefits of the romantic crisis theory are for those who believe it, not for the people it is supposedly about. Since the theory holds that suicide is always a matter of choice, it calms personal fears of suicidal death. If suicide is a private and individual moral crisis, then we can continue to avoid the acknowledgment of the social contribution to suicidal pain, and we can practice denial on the social responsibility for the prevention of suicide. As with romantic attitudes about poverty and mental illness, romantic attitudes about suicide structure the experience of someone else's misfortune in a way that reduces pain for the perceiver. If we see human suffering and can find a way to tell ourselves, "It's good that they suffer," then we feel better. The history of our civilization shows that we take pleasure at being spectators at the ordeals of others. It is not surprising that we should try to establish the same relationship in our experience of someone's suicidal condition. Romanticism, however, is a false model. It causes us to minimize the scope of the problem, to imagine beneficial things the situation does not have, and to deny uncomfortable things it does have.

One of the mechanisms involved in romanticism is envy. It is uncomfortable for us to consider the situation of someone who is less well off. We may try to repress awareness of his envy for us is by finding something in his situation that we can envy. Many AIDS patients, for example, have terrible problems with lack of appetite due to the disease and to their medications. Their body weight may go from 160 pounds to under a 100 pounds in a few months. It is common for overweight caregivers to envy the fact that they refuse food. (Caregivers can even imagine that this is voluntary.) A second type of envy is for experiences we have not had. We have an innate curiosity for experience, and we are inclined to feel inferior to those who have experienced things that we have not. They have something we lack, and even if it is on the whole it is an undesirable experience, we may still recognize (or imagine) desirable parts and become envious. If our envy is strong enough, we may confuse the desirability of the part with the desirability of the whole.

Theory and Practice Out of Joint

Theoretical discussions of suicide often include observations such as:

> In our day to day therapy of suicidal crises we pay little
> attention to theory, particularly such deep abstractions
> as the death instinct. (Litman, 1967, p. 342)

The mental and moral interpretation of suicide is indeed not useful in work with the suicidal. "Use more will power"; "Your ideas are morally wrong"; and "Suicide is a solution," get nowhere in counseling or in public education because they are worse than useless, they are harmful. What is disturbing is that none of the literature on suicide, academic or popular, is willing to acknowledge and discuss this deep incompatibility between theory and practice.

The voluntarist theories tell us that the problem of suicide lies with the ideation and morals of the victim. This suggests that our initial response should be to try to change the things that are wrong: the intentions, the values, the idea that suicide is a solution, the fantasy about what death is like. Since this never works, theorists end their books by advising counselors not to use their theory:

> Experience has taught us the important fact that it is neither possible nor practical in an individual who is highly lethal and highly perturbed to attempt to deal with the lethality directly, either by moral suasion, confrontatory interpretations, exhortation, or whatever. (It does not work any better in suicide than it does in alcoholism.) The most effective way to reduce elevated lethality is by doing so indirectly; that is, by reducing the elevated perturbation. Reduce the person's anguish, tension, and pain and his level of lethality will concomitantly come down, for it is the elevated perturbation that fuels the elevated lethality. (Shneidman, 1985, p. 230)

Involuntarism agrees with this completely. Dealing directly with the content of suicidal ideation (what Shneidman refers to as "lethality") is useless. Reducing pain is what works, and if we do that the ideation also subsides. What then is the point of defining suicide in terms of the ideation? Even worse, what is the point of claiming that it is the ideation that is causally responsible for the suicide? If we have a theory that is not at odds with practice, then we cannot help but be more effective in the actual work of suicide prevention.

The mental and moral definitions of suicide do not serve the purposes of crisis intervention, counseling, education, medicine, or science. Besides falsely assuming that all types of suicide have the common mental structure of motive, intention, and volition, they also reflect and reinforce cultural prejudice.[6] Such definitions only add more pain to the agony of lonely and despairing souls. The real basis of these definitions is the needs of the non-suicidal: to feel morally superior, to use the suicidal as scapegoats, to protect themselves from uncomfortable feelings of vulnerability and complicity. The desire to find mental and moral qualities that separate the suicidal from the rest of us has the appearance of scientific inquiry; actually it has the unconscious motives of the primitive pathology of stigma and taboo. Allegations of mental and moral inferiority in other people is an unhealthy way for us to respond to our fears of vulnerability and complicity. We need theories that will help the suicidal feel better, not worse. We need theories that acknowledge that the suicidal person is as much a part of humanity as anyone else.

The view that suicide happens when pain exceeds pain-coping resources is more useful for the suicidal, their relatives and friends, their counselors, and their survivors. It gives anyone with any level of education a clear idea of what to do in a crisis. It does not add more pain on top of existing pain. It does not reinforce the myth that suicide prevention is a last minute activity. It strips suicide of romance, of attractiveness, of denial.

The involuntarist theory is more scientific than the views it seeks to replace. "Free will", "intention", "motive", "unconscious", "choice", "affirmation that death is a better alternative", "perceived as a solution", "his responsibility", and "unwillingness to accept the terms of the human condition" are hardly testable scientific conditions. A view of suicide that is non-moral, less private, and less mental is one that is more amenable to scientific inquiry.

CHAPTER THREE

MORAL JUDGMENTS

Unfair Moral Judgments

Social disapproval adds pain from sources outside the suicidal person, and adds pain from socially created private demons. All of us — the suicidal, the pre-suicidal, the post-suicidal, the relatives, friends, and counselors of the suicidal — grew up with and continue to be affected by these negative attitudes. They deter early presentations for help, retard therapeutic progress, and discourage continuation with treatment. They create an atmosphere of mutual defensiveness and reciprocated hostility. Until stigma and prejudice are reduced, until suicide is removed from the arena of moral judgment, little progress in suicide prevention will be possible. The argument of this chapter is not that it is wrong to make moral judgments per se; "Arson for profit is wrong," and "Promoting health is good," are true statements. Its limited claim is that many particular judgments commonly made about the suicidal contain mistakes of fact, unproven assumptions, and misjudgments about morality. These judgments are false and harmful.

Recognizing the unfairness of the judgments against the suicidal is only part of our task. We must learn more about the role these judgments have in the lives of the people who make them. These judgments oppress; to fight oppression we need to reach an understanding of its dynamics. The first step in oppression is separation. The social invention of the moral inferiority of the suicidal separates us from them, and puts us in the superior position. If they are bad, selfish, and weak, then we are the opposite. If they are to blame, then we are not.

As with all moral scapegoats, we deny the suicidal self-worth so we can preserve it for ourselves. We have pent-up feelings about suicide; these judgments license their discharge. Since other aspects of the mythology of suicide hold that the ones who are going to do it cannot be stopped, and the ones who talk about it are not going to do it, we can freely ventilate hostility and moral revulsion without fear that we have increased the risk of suicide.

Moral oppression supports the stigma of suicide and justifies social aversion — the desire to avoid the physical or emotional presence of the despised object. Who wishes to associate with people who have been stereotyped as selfish, self-centered, and manipulative? One of the few positive statements made about people in suicidal pain is "The good man sucks it up." This statement is not about the "good man." It is about us; it says we don't want to see it, we don't want to hear about it, and we don't want to think about it. The victim of suicidal pain has been prejudged by himself and by his society as weak, selfish, and foolish; he knows that other people abhor him and his condition. When we are up close to suicidal pain, moral judgments help discharge the anger and fear of the immediate situation. We are angry at the turmoil we have been placed in and are afraid of blame and guilt. When we are at a distance, our moral posture denies social as well as individual complicity in suicidal pain and helps us cope with fears of our own suicides. The scapegoat represents a vulnerable and disowned part of ourselves. The end result is cruelty and abuse.

Will Power

It is sometimes said that the problem with suicides and the suicidal is that they fail to use their will power. People in pain should grit their teeth and ride it out. Or better, they should get their act together and get on with their lives.

This view of suicide has considerable social economy. Suicide prevention is purely a matter for the individual in despair. Completed suicides and the prolongation of suicidal pain are due to shortcomings in the individual, not in anyone or anything else. Society and significant others are under no moral obligation to do anything, and since the suicidal are unwilling to to help themselves, there is not much practical point in trying to do anything anyway. This suicide prevention strategy — tell people to use their will power — helps the non-suicidal feel much better. If someone we know is in chronic pain, his condition causes us to feel uncomfortable and frustrated. It is an unpleasant nuisance, a burden, and a continuing reminder of our own vulnerability. The will-power theory gives us license to discharge our negative feelings by morally reviling our acquaintance. This hostility causes him more pain, and it creates a moral climate in which everyone he encounters will regard him as a malingerer and a weakling, but if he used his will power he could overcome these things as well.

One of the sad features of this position is that it is believed by many of the suicidal as well. Like all of us, they grew up believing that only the morally inferior cannot get out of their own pain. The suicidal can remain alone with their pain for a long time because they believe that is what good people (i.e., people with will power) should do. Yet their pain may get no better, despite repeated efforts at self-improvement. Their internal evidence for the belief that they have will power, the fact that they have ridden it out for a period of time, begins to get contradicted by evidence that they lack will power: they have been unable to get their act together and get out of their condition. The dissonance of these contradictory conceptions of will power adds to their confusion and torment.

This approach to suicide prevention ignores the fact that established and successful programs for other self-destructive conditions have all rejected the will-power theory. In the 1930s the founders of Alcoholics Anonymous wrote:

> The fact is that most alcoholics, for reasons yet obscure,
> have lost the power of choice in drink. Our so-called will
> power becomes practically non-existent. (1976, p. 24)

In treatment programs the various addictive and compulsive behaviors are regarded as diseases, diseases that get progressively worse regardless of will's efforts to arrest and reverse them. As the A. A. quotation indicates, with time the inner sense of having will power deteriorates. This inner sense of having the "oomph" of will power is something that non-suicidal people have. We use it to make phone calls we "really don't want to make," we use it to avoid dessert if we are on a diet. Whatever this "oomph" is, it is highly uncertain in its results. Tens of millions of people have tried to use will power to endure the pain and discomfort of nicotine withdrawal. For many, it was not enough. Does it make any sense to recommend will power as our method of choice in suicide prevention?

Assume for the moment that will power exists. Its capacity for altering human behavior is not only unpredictable within individuals and variable from one person to another, but it is also finite. Though someone with will power may have more stamina than someone who lacks it, the stamina is not infinite. To suppose otherwise is magical thinking. Even if will power exists, even if it can be enhanced by education and training, it is still no guarantee of freedom from suicide risk. It is also unclear that will power is always a positive coping resource. People who use will power to ride it out may end up watching their lives get worse because they do not get outside help. Will power may just help workaholics, for example, dig themselves into a deeper hole. In conversations, the suicidal will often express the attitude of "I've been struggling for a long time." There is no reason to suppose that suicidal people are not already using all the will power they have. "Use will power," if it has any value at all, can only be used for people not in massive pain. When said to the suicidal, "use will power," is like flogging an already exhausted horse.

Will power is often suggested as a solution for the problem of being beset by suicidal feelings and ideation. Considerers are admonished to "Stop it." But these thoughts and feelings are involuntary. Despair, grief, and depression are not things that people can simply stop, any more than someone can will an end to a toothache or the pain of withdrawal. Acutely suicidal people have lost all sense of having power over their pain. To tell them to magically acquire will power is like asking a crippled person to race against a champion. It does not help them do the thing in question; it just makes them feel worse.

"Just use will power," in suicide prevention is analogous to "Just say no," in drug abuse prevention. The latter reflects a pleasant fantasy: the drug problem can be ended by admonishing children to refuse invitations to use drugs. This is a drug prevention strategy that is adapted to the needs and interests of the people doing the admonishing, not to the needs of the population at risk. It implies that all we need to do to correct the drug problem is make changes in users and potential users — we do not have to do anything to change ourselves or our society. And we do not have to spend any money to do it.

The drug problem is the fault of the people who lack will power; no complicity belongs elsewhere.

Weak

A negative judgment made about suicides is that they are weak. Use the following thought experiment to consider the fairness of this charge. Take 100 average Americans, aged four and up, who come from all walks of life and have varying degrees of physical well-being. Begin piling weights onto their shoulders and ask them to hold out for as long as possible. Eventually 49 of the people will collapse. In some sense, these people are weak. They have below average strength. Is it fair, however, to condemn them morally for collapsing, to sneeringly pronounce the word "weakling"?

This is what suicide is like. People have varying capacities for coping with pain. Some people who die by suicide have weaker than average pain-coping resources. This does not mean that their weakness is a sort for which they ought to be morally condemned. Some people's bones are more brittle than others; some people are more susceptible to cancer and heart disease. These people have weaknesses, but not of the sort that makes them bad people.

If we continue with the experiment, eventually even the strongest person will collapse. This is also what suicide is like. People with greater than average pain-coping resources will become suicides if the pain is great enough. Is there even justification for the claim, "Suicides as individuals have weaker than average personal capacities for coping with pain,"? In the United States older males have the highest rate for completed suicide. Many of these men have spent a lifetime believing, "As an individual, I am stronger than average." Let us suppose for a moment that this belief is true. This self-image, coupled with an acceptance of the myth "the suicidal are weak," and an awareness of the other stigmas of suicide, can deter such men from seeking help and from establishing and maintaining a social network that can be used to cope with pain. Just because an individual is stronger than average, it does not follow that in the entirety of his pain-coping resources he is stronger than average. It does not follow that suicides, as individuals, are weaker than average.

A charge that is even more unfair is that people with thoughts of suicide are weak. Post-considerers, people who were once beset by suicidal thoughts and feelings and then recovered, may have stronger than average pain-coping resources. Some of the formerly suicidal suffered years of depression, loneliness, and agony — pain that is beyond the ken of people who have never been suicidal. That they should suffer a life-threatening condition and recover is not evidence that they are weak. People who find themselves lost in the wilderness, or at sea, and survive despite suffering and hardship are regarded as admirable and heroic. People trying to survive the ordeals of the inner landscape receive only contempt and aversion.

Hostility for suicides, attempters, and considerers on grounds of weakness has no basis in reality. What basis it has is entirely within the minds of their judges. Saying someone else is weak has the tacit suggestion that the speaker is strong. It means that the speaker is afraid that his own resources for coping with pain may not be adequate. We put others down so that we can bolster our own insecurities.

Selfish

The suicidal are often charged with being selfish. Is this accurate? Is it fair?

The accusation of selfishness, when applied to the suicidal, has a different meaning than it does in normal discourse. This criticism is not made by the sort of social moralists who claim that business interests are selfish, or that politicians and television evangelists are hypocritically self-interested. If we review the lives of suicides we knew or hear accounts about in survivor groups, we immediately recognize that they were not people who had out of the ordinary appetites for the standard goals of the selfish and greedy: money, power, social position, material things. There is no evidence that shows that suicides and the suicidal, as a group, have greater avarice than the rest of the population.

The suicidal are said to be greedy or selfish in psychological and neurotic senses. On this view, completers regard escape, revenge, or the end of their pain as more important than the suffering that their suicide will cause their survivors. Attempters and considerers are said to want more love, care, attention, and time than is due to them.

The view that the suicidal are selfish in some psychological sense is held by many average citizens and virtually all mental health professionals. Both the population of suicidal people and the population of non-suicidal people contain members who had greater than average self-centeredness from childhood or adolescence until their deaths (by whatever means). Is psychological selfishness, *as a life-long character trait*, more likely to be found in the suicidal than in the non-suicidal? There is no scientific evidence to support the view that people who complete, attempt, or consider suicide are inherently more selfish than other people. No studies have ever been done on this subject; the myth has continued unchallenged. If you listen to the lives of suicidal people as described by themselves or their survivors, it is evident that they were more or less normal people until they developed the conditions that led to their being suicidal. The behavior characterized as selfish did not begin (and for many, it never does begin) until their pain reached critical proportions. The behavior that causes all suicidal people to be characterized as selfish is manifested only by some of them, and then only when they are suffering from the conditions that cause them to be suicidal.

When people in great pain do things to get attention and care it is not selfish; it is normal and natural. If a loved one of yours were in pain, you would want him to do whatever it took to get help. The suicidal did not create the social conditions of ignorance, stigma, and prejudice; they did not create the conditions under which they view their own suffering through a fog of false beliefs and false values; they did not create conditions which make it nearly impossible for them to understand what is happening to them, and to know what they ought to do about it; they did not create social conditions that produce hostility wherever they turn. It is grossly unfair to criticize people for their behavior in these circumstances. "Inconsiderate" is part of the selfishness criticism. But the suicidal are human beings, not disembodied spirits. Being in great pain directly causes them to push for their needs, and makes it difficult for them to recognize and respond to the needs of others.

When we criticize the suicidal for being selfish, we are actually criticizing them for not enduring their pain with grace and good manners. These are nice qualities; we may be correct to reproach average citizens for not having them. But to expect everyone in pain to have them is unrealistic. Bearing pain quietly is what moralists call a supererogatory act — an act that is above the call of duty. Expecting *everyone* who is suicidal to behave in a way that is morally above average is simply abusive.

Selfishness requires the capacity to do otherwise. Normally we are free to be selfish, egalitarian or altruistic, but excruciating pain causes our range of options to dwindle to few and none. *Some* AIDS patients exhibit the same kind of demanding behavior as *some* suicidal people. The level of demand is usually a function of the level of pain, not of moral deficiency. The behavior diminishes when the pain is reduced, and the environment becomes more supportive. (Though with AIDS patients, at least, it may take a few weeks before the behavior catches up with the relief from suffering.) "Selfishness" is a prejudice with a self-perpetuating mechanism. Suicidal people know that prejudice is going to make it harder for them to get help and support. As elsewhere, awareness that what is needed is going to be in short supply causes people to seek it ever more urgently.

Among professionals the stereotype of selfishness and self-centeredness is based upon how a very small part of the suicidal population interacts, for a very small part of their lives, with a very small part of the general population — psychotherapists. Is this a fair basis on which to prejudge an entire group? This is a stereotype that does not fit many suicidal people at any point in their lives, and does not fit nearly all suicidal people for the periods of their lives in which they are not wracked with pain. The stereotype ignores the fact that most suicidal people, despite their pain, continue to go through the motions of most of ordinary life in ways that are morally average. The prejudice also ignores or belittles altruistic behavior related to suicide. In New York City many family systems are under tremendous stress. Suicidal people from such families often say "I have not told so-and-so [about my suicidal thoughts] because she already has all the problems she can cope with." Regardless of family circumstances, the desire to avoid bringing shame and stigma on the family is a common reason for not seeking help. It is easy, and unfair, to say that these reasons are disguised selfishness. Prejudice and stigma are real, and do cause families to suffer embarrassment and shame; sometimes family members are at the limit of what they can cope with.

The thoughts and behavior of suicidal people can become excessive. The HIV-positive man mentioned in Chapter Two became excessively involved in his volunteer work. His ideas moved beyond fantasy — a coping resource of ordinary life — into temporary delusion. I participated in a workshop held by the City Corrections Department after it had experienced an unusually high number of employee suicides. Staff counselors said that one of the warning signs was the type of reason that officers gave for volunteering for overtime, holidays, and weekends. While one type of officer would say that he was saving for a vacation or a down payment on a car, a different type would say, 'I broke up with my boyfriend, I need something to fill up my time." "Selfish" is not a word that comes to mind in describing the behavior in these types of cases. Some suicidal people, however, do make excessive demands on the time and energy of other people. When we see this behavior — and react to it emotionally — we can feel the urge to explain it and judge it as selfish. An alternative explanation is to argue that to be suicidal means to be in pain and to have one's inner and outer resources for coping with pain to be at the brink of exhaustion. It is natural that people in these crises should manifest abnormal and excessive demands on any available resource. These demands are not evidence of moral inferiority, they are evidence of the desire for life. And, unfortunately, in many cases the excessive demand can soon lead to more pain and fewer resources.

"He should have known how much pain this would cause us," is often expressed at support group meetings for surviving relatives and friends. Since I believe that suicidal people basically do care about their relatives as much as everyone does, I believe that public education about the problems and suffering of survivors will encourage suicidal people to seek help sooner and will reduce the incidence of suicide. Is their current ignorance on this something for which the suicidal are responsible? Suicidal people are part of the general public, and the general public has a very inadequate idea of the suffering that suicide causes survivors. Most suicides cannot help but know very little about the emotional consequences of suicide. This is partly due to general ignorance, partly because their pain blinds and distorts their perception of reality, and partly because only the people who suffer this loss really know what the pain is like.

Just Wants Attention, Isn't Serious

The question "Was he serious, or did he just want attention?" prejudges all suicidal people as falling into either

Category A: on the verge of death

or

Category B: not suicidal, but use "suicide" to try to get attention for problems that are not serious.

At any given time, only a small percentage of the people with suicidal feelings are in Category A. *None* of the others are in Category B. People with suicidal feelings are suicidal, period. Category B is populated by people who are not suicidal, claim to be suicidal, and have no serious problems. It is unlikely that Category B is empty, but clear instances of it are very rare. False claims to suicidal feelings are made, for example, by people who want to use psychiatric wards for shelter during cold weather. How many of these people have no problems that need serious assistance? At a minimum they need shelter. This is not just wanting attention. The existence of this type of behavior by people who are *not* suicidal is no grounds for having negative attitudes toward people who *are* suicidal. The non-suicidal focus on the behavior of a small part of *their* population and use it to abuse the suicidal.

This has analogues in other types of prejudice. Every year, in every suburban high school in the country, stories are whispered about someone at some other school who falsely claimed to be a member of a minority group to gain admission to a college. Is there any doubt that this discharges hostility and envy, and reflects anxiety that one's own needs will not be met? The ostensible target of anger is the person who falsely represents himself, but the real target of anger in both cases is the person who really is suicidal or really is a member of a disadvantaged group. The whisperers cannot quite bring themselves to criticize the people they really resent, so they attack the person who falsely represents himself. Public assistance is similar: what is hated are all recipients of welfare, but what is openly attacked are the "chiselers." The prejudiced person imagines that most or all recipients of public aid are in this category. In suburban America "welfare recipient" and "welfare cheat" are synonymous. In reality most people on welfare are children or have disabilities. The forms of prejudice repeat themselves with unfailing regularity: will power is also a popular anti-poverty theory.

"Just wants attention" ventilates a sense of unfairness:

Mary: job problem, boyfriend problem, suicidal

Jane: job problem, boyfriend problem, not suicidal

Mary gets more attention and care than Jane, and has done nothing in the sense of individual virtuous activity to deserve it. What we need to keep in mind is the medical model: if the two women had all the same environmental experiences and one got cancer and the other did not, we would not begrudge the victim her extra care.

To put every member of

Category C: having suicidal feelings and ideation but not currently on the verge of death.

into Category B is false and harmful. It is an injustice to deny an appropriate level of assistance to people who need it. In contemporary America a red flag for this type injustice is the word "just". The myth that suicide prevention is a last minute activity, the theory that the key concepts in suicide are intention and volition, the claim that what separates attempters from completers are differences in personality — all provide a license to use low-lethal attempters and considerers as punching bags for our hostility. "Just wants attention" says that when people in Category C ask for help in preventing their suicides, they are asking for more help than they need and for more help than they are entitled. Misrepresenting ourselves so we can get something to which we are not entitled is morally wrong. This is misbehavior, and misbehavior deserves a punitive response. The just deserts of the person who just wants attention are pain, embarrassment, and humiliation. He and others like him need to be discouraged from scaring us with their exaggerated claims.

In ordinary life, if we continuously hate someone, some thing, or some group, we will habitually make a negative remark each time the person, subject, or group is mentioned. Bêtes noires are invariably recipients of knee-jerk derogations. For many people, including professionals, the suicidal are bêtes noires, and "just wants attention" is their compulsive put-down. As with similar comments about other bêtes noires, it tells us more about the attitudes and needs of the speaker than it does about its ostensible subject. The utterers of "just wants attention" have chronic needs to distance themselves from the suicidal and to discharge hostility.

The prejudice "just wants attention" discourages presentations for help, discourages early presentations, and discourages straightforward presentations. The corollaries to this myth — "The ones who are serious don't talk about it," and "It's the ones you'd never suspect," leave us with the suicide prevention principle: "We'll take you seriously insofar as you try to keep your condition hidden from us." Is it any wonder that so many cries for help include requests for secrecy? The ultimate causes for this behavior lie not with the person in pain, but with the world he is trying to get to respond to his needs.

Suicidal feelings, like a lump on the breast or blood in the urine, are serious. They say that pain is threatening to exceed coping resources. Most suicidal people have conditions, such as depression, substance abuse, bereavement, or physical illness, that are independently worthy of serious assistance. Moreover, as is indicated by the myth of the something more, the apparent absence of these conditions does not mean that suicidal feelings should not be taken seriously.

The origins of the impulses to remain alive are primitive, pre-cognitive, pre-volitional. These impulses sometimes manifest themselves in ways that are disturbing, alienating, and frightening. Given our cultural attitudes about suicide, it is normal for the non-suicidal to respond with defensiveness and suspicion. We project onto the suicidal person a cognitive structure he does not have, a cognitive structure that serves our needs. To belittle and minimize his problems as "not serious, just wants attention" reduces our anxiety and discharges our negative feelings. It helps us feel better and causes him to feel worse.

Unfortunately, the suicidal do not recognize "just wants attention" as a prejudice that has its basis in the fears of other people. They interpret it as not caring, as saying, "We care about whether you continue to exist because we might get blamed for your death; otherwise the quality of your life is not worth serious concern." The prejudice reinforces the self-perception "I'm not worth caring about." This is why the real goal of suicide prevention must be the relief of suffering in all people with suicidal feelings. To limit our assistance to people who are on the verge of death just makes the disregarded feel worse, and get worse.

Infantile

One of the derogations against some acutely suicidal people is that they are infantile. This behavior exists, but it can also be found among the elderly, and sufferers of critical medical conditions and other types of great pain. It is not uncommon among very ill AIDS patients. It is neither accurate, nor fair, nor useful to regard this condition as voluntary and deserving moral reproach. If adults in great pain have run out of other coping options, they may find themselves doing uncharacteristic things to try to get relief for their pain. Infantilism is one example of types of uncharacteristic behavior that may occur during suicidal crises. This behavior may be a reversion to coping strategies that were used early in life; at that time it probably got some results. We respond negatively because infantilism is unpleasant to deal with, and because it strikes inner chords that cause us to feel uncomfortable. We have to keep in mind that the behavior is not voluntary, it is caused by pain. "Infantile needs of the suicidal" is not an accurate expression. The underlying needs that require a response are needs that all adults have (or, more precisely, are needs had by people of the chronological age of the victim), even if the manner of expressing neediness is infantile. Shneidman's advice

> The way to save a suicidal person is to cater to that individual's infantile and realistic idiosyncratic needs.

> A psychotherapist can try to decrease the elevated perturbation of a highly suicidal person by doing almost everything possible to cater to the infantile idiosyncrasies, the dependency needs, ... (1985, pp. 228 & 231)

prejudices counselors against the person and against the relationship they have to the person. Responding to adult needs that happen to be expressed in infantile ways is not "catering"; it is not different from any other aspect of the therapeutic response.

Blame the Victim

Whether the issue is rape, incest, substance abuse, mental illness, crime, or suicide, "Blame the victim" is a popular policy. When people do things that are wrong, they deserve punishment. "Blame the victim" helps dish out this punishment by adding pain on top of the pain the victims already have. "Blame the victim" abets another goal of this campaign for social justice; by deterring victims from seeking out ways to reduce their pain, it protects those not in the wrong from having their lives disturbed by these unpleasant people. More power to us if we can internalize "It's your own fault," into the minds of the victims; the inner torment of guilt is their just desert. Anyone who denies that "blame the victim" adds pain on pain should talk to someone whose depression has been successfully treated as an organically based problem: "What a relief, I thought it was my fault." To blame suicides for their failure to choose life, to blame the suicidal for becoming suicidal, and to blame them for remaining suicidal, all have the marvelous economy of denying that the fault lies anywhere else. The alternative to the mono-fault theory — dump all the blame in one place — should not be distributive fault: hand some out to all parties. To dilute the feeling of being at fault does not make its sting less bitter, and still leaves plenty of unnecessary pain, defensiveness, estrangement and hostility. The aggregate pain theory advocates a no-fault approach to suicide.

If you are the friend or counselor of someone who is suicidal, ask yourself if the person's prior patterns of moral behavior were much different than those of ten other people of similar age and background. The sequences of events leading to suicidal conditions rarely contain nothing but acts of voluntary and intentional self-malevolence. They contain the actions of ordinary people grappling with the problems of ordinary lives.

"If you are not happy, it is because something is wrong with you," is a widespread and deeply entrenched part of American social consciousness. A part of the reason for this can be found by attending the meetings and reading the literature of the Twelve-Step self-help groups for people raised in a families that had alcoholism, drug abuse, gambling, eating disorders, incest, child abuse, workaholism, mental illness, criminal behavior, or were otherwise dysfunctional. Perhaps 50 percent of all American families qualify. An outstanding characteristic of these families is denial: nothing is wrong. The residents of these homes, during and after the time they live there, suffer a lot of pain. "Don't talk about being in pain," is a rule the family member obeys with other family members, and with people outside the family. The price of disobedience to this rule is more pain. Since family members deny that the pain exists, they deny that it has the causes that it has — the problems of the parents or grandparents, the disease of alcoholism, the family rules that repeat from one generation to the next. Children have a natural tendencies to blame themselves and to feel responsible for problems in the family; this is not discouraged in a family system of denial. Children in dysfunctional families cannot help but acquire the belief that their pain is due to inadequacies within themselves. They apply this belief to themselves, they apply it to other people (i.e., other people's problems are due to faults within the individual), and when they become parents, their children acquire it as well. When anyone becomes suicidal, the self is to blame.

A Prejudice about Pain

Human beings do not respond in a uniform manner to loss and trauma. Being victimized by sexual assault, losing a job or relationship, and enduring a death in the family will affect different people differently. Some suffer longer and more intensely than others. Unfortunately, people whose suffering is greater than average are often singled out in ordinary life and by professionals as "having something wrong with them." (This is an aspect of a more general prejudice: anyone in any kind of emotional pain or unhappiness, regardless of precipitating event, has some personal inadequacy.) This charge is usually inaccurate and always lacking in compassion. The basis is not evidence; there are no scientific studies that support the claim that "greater than average sufferers" have higher incidences of moral inferiority than "less than average sufferers." Its real source is usually the uncomfortable feelings that the other person's suffering arouse in the person making the charge. The prejudice reduces the discomfort of those who hold it; it increases the pain of those who are its victims.

The prejudice does not specify if the "something wrong" is a defect of innate physical nature, upbringing, or moral character. The victim of the prejudice is supposed to be able to figure that out for himself; if he cannot, then he has yet another thing wrong with him. His original pain is compounded by the pain of insult and the pain of confusion.

The variability of mourning rituals across different cultures shows that how much pain is "appropriate" for a given traumatic event is socially defined. American culture defines low and short-lived amounts of pain as appropriate. This decreases our willingness to seek help, increases isolation, and increases the pain of self-judgment. This is one of the basic vicious circles of suicide: the more pain you get, the more pain you get. The additional pain and further reduction of pain-coping resources has social causes; it is not due to personal failings. "If you are not happy, something is wrong with you," is a not a diagnostic maxim; it is a license for social abuse. Our moral imperative — people ought to suffer in ways that are convenient for others — makes suffering hurt more and last longer. The suicidal cannot help but strive to comply with the demand of this imperative; they are less powerful than the non-suicidal, and their own non-suicidal past and their hopes for recovery cause them to share the norms of their oppressors.

A popular version of this prejudice is "You didn't choose the bad thing that happened to you, but you can choose how you respond to it." No matter what bad thing or combination of bad things happen to you, you can always by an act of will be completely unaffected. If you are bothered by the bad thing, it is because of an inadequacy in you. This is a fantasy. This does not acknowledge that people have their volitional capacities limited by age, disease, and the painful condition or trauma itself. It imagines that human volition is a magical entity that can will complete non-reaction — or any other reaction — to the most horrible events imaginable. We would be happier if we gave up the belief, "If you're not happy it is because something is wrong with you."

Distrust and Suspicion

The view that the suicidal are manipulative should be rejected: "selfish" and "just want attention" are unfounded myths. The natural consequence of the myth of manipulativeness is that counselors should respond to suicidal presentations with an attitude of distrust and suspicion. This attitude is prejudice, similar to an attitude that is common in racial and ethnic prejudice:

> Throughout history and all over the world one of the commonest accusations against out-groups is that they are dishonest, tricky, sneaky. (Allport, p. 150)

Individual holders of this prejudice may have had little contact with members of the groups in question, or have had contacts that did little to provide evidence for the prejudice. They may engage in distorted reasoning by judging an entire group on the basis of one incident with one individual. No studies have ever been done to find out if completers, attempters, or considerers have greater or lesser than average levels of honesty and sincerity. No studies support the view that counselors should begin interviews with distrust and suspicion. These prejudices remain strong and persistent, however, because the fears behind them are strong and persistent. Human beings adopt defensive postures at the drop of a hat, and, once in them, are stubborn about staying in them.

There would be no in-group/out-group structure in suicide unless there were some elements that contributed to the unity of at least one of these groups. Prejudices generally help individuals bond together; when we find someone who shares our fears and our aversions, we find a measure of acceptance, and an ally against the thing that is feared. Among caregivers, "manipulative" may go beyond the usual binding function of prejudice to become what Allport characterized as a "social entrance ticket." During a talk I gave for a group of medical students, who were beginning their residency program at a large city hospital, two staff physicians turned to the students and emphatically asserted that all suicidal people were manipulative. Even if they had wished to, the students were hardly in a situation that tolerated disagreement with their supervisors. The suicidal are not oblivious to the shared nature of the prejudices against them. This awareness increases their sense of isolation, and is part of the source for the universal form of one of their common complaints, "Everyone hates me." Suicidal people reciprocate the fallacy of over-generalization, and, in help-seeking situations, are usually suspicious of people they have not yet met.

CHAPTER FOUR

FEAR

A major deficiency of academic theory about suicide is the lack of attention it gives to the immense fearfulness of suicidal people. The mental and moral view of suicide cannot do otherwise: it is explicitly committed to defining suicide in terms of intention, motive, goal and volition, and it is implicitly committed to sustaining our denial on the social causes of suicidal pain. In stereotype the suicidal person acts: he forms an intention to die and thereafter is unstoppable, or he commits aggressive non-fatal acts to get attention and manipulate others. Fearfulness does not fit this stereotype and so fearfulness is ignored. Reality is different. The suicidal, like all fearful people, are defensive creatures. Many are socially isolated; many keep their feelings and thoughts hidden for as long as they can; many adopt the self-help strategy of "do nothing, ride it out"; many back away from any situation that threatens them with more pain. These conditions inhibit recovery and consequently are part of the cause of suicide. The social prejudice that causes these fears is vile and contemptible. We can improve our understanding of suicide simply by enumerating and examining these fears.

A. DIRECT INSULT

1. verbal abuse: selfish, stupid, foolish, manipulator, attention getter, crybaby, sick, wacko, psycho, nut.

2. moral abuse: sinful, your fault, morally deficient.

3. labeled as failure, loser, inadequate, defective, anti-social, family hater.

4. stigmatized as mental patient, crazy, suicidal.

5. branded with shortcomings in psychological makeup: narcissistic, dependent personality, immature, weak character, no will power.

6. ridicule, teasing.

7. belittlement of self and problems.

8. moral or social condescension.

9. being ignored.

10. reactions of anger and hostility.

11. being passed along from counselor to counselor, agency to agency.

12. rejection, avoidance, shunning.

13. increased isolation and estrangement.

14. loss of confidence in one's judgment, character, and dependability.

B. LOSSES OF CONFIDENTIALITY

1. disclosure of one's situation to family, friends, neighbors, co-workers, employer, fellow students, teachers.

2. being a subject of gossip and rumor.

3. school, job, medical, insurance, legal, or newspaper record of one's condition.

4. future personal embarrassment, having a prior suicidal condition thrown in one's face.

5. future discrimination in gaining, continuing, or advancing in school or job situations.

C. MATERIAL CONSEQUENCES

1. suspension from school or work.

2. suicidal victims of child abuse, domestic violence, and elder abuse fear the perpetrator will find out that they have sought help and inflict additional abuse. (Victims of child abuse often present suicidal feelings to school staff members. In New York City, Board of Education regulations require that parents be notified if their children are at risk of suicide, regardless of the situation at home.)

3. police custody.

4. involuntary institutionalization. [1]

5. financial cost of treatment.

6. financial or other forms of exploitation by caregivers.

D. FEARS ASSOCIATED WITH BELIEFS ABOUT RELIGION AND THE AFTERLIFE

E. HARM TO OTHERS

1. bringing shame and stigma upon the family.

2. having the knowledge of one's crisis be an additional burden on family members.

3. causing fear and anxiety for confidants, putting these people in difficult situations with difficult choices.

F. PERSONAL WORRIES

1. having feelings of embarrassment and shame caused by admissions of failure, weakness, or inability to cope and prosper.

2. afraid of being seen to be afraid.

3. having to discuss intimate problems.

4. "someone (or everyone) will find out how bad I am."

5. the lid of the emotional volcano will come off.

6. loss of self-control.

7. loss of sanity. (Even F. 6. and F. 7. have social causes; most of us grow up ignorant of what most suicidal people are really like, and we are acquainted only with horror movie and tabloid stereotypes.)

8. loss of ability to make oneself understood to others.

9. more disappointment and frustration: efforts to get relief from pain will be unsuccessful, and personal senses of hopelessness and powerlessness will increase.

10. pain will never end.

G. COERCION

1. being asked to look at things one doesn't want to look at.

2. being asked to do things one doesn't want to do: change relationships, behavior, beliefs, identity, values.

3. being asked to do too much, too soon.

4. being pressured to do things.

5. being threatened to do things.

6. the loss of self-esteem that comes with giving in to pressure.

H. THE NAMELESS FEARS

Many fears, of all sorts and of both the suicidal and the non-suicidal, are of things that can be easily identified and categorized: a fear that the boss will get angry at us, a fear of being assaulted, a fear that a child will say something that causes us to be embarrassed. People with mental illness and substance abuse problems, however, often live with an obscure awareness of anxieties that do not seem to have names or fit into categories. "I was afraid all the time, but of what I couldn't tell you." Members of Alcoholics Anonymous call these dreadful apprehensions "the nameless fears."

This concept is helpful to keep in mind when working with children and adolescents. They are not as far along as adults in learning to apply words to feelings and in being able to adapt feelings to words. When we do not have a name for something, it is unknown, and the unknown is frightening. To be able to apply a common word to a feeling means knowing that other people can have similar experiences. Not being able to find a label increases the sense of estrangement and isolation. Someone who tries to talk about experiences for which he cannot find words is open to ridicule, belittlement, and condescension. Painful feelings that remain bottled up are liable to find expression in non-verbal self-destructive behavior.

Almost all of the fears listed above are fears of more pain, fears that have social causes, fears that deter people from seeking help, fears that are reasonable to have, and fears that are themselves causes of additional pain and anxiety. It is painful to be suicidal. By being suicidal, people have many fears that the non-suicidal do not have; this makes being suicidal yet more painful. The suicidal continuously live with the threat of receiving more pain from social sources. The threat of pain is the essence of stress, and this stress is additional pain. The fears simultaneously add to pain and also act as resources to protect their victims from getting more pain. How much better would it be not to have all these fears of socially inflicted pain!?! Reduce these pains, reduce the fears of these pains, and we can greatly reduce completed suicide and the suffering of suicidal people.

I. FEAR OF DEATH AND FEAR OF SUICIDAL DEATH

An adequate inventory of the fears of the suicidal needs to include not only the fears that deter them from getting help, but also fears that deter them from committing suicide. These fears are rarely addressed as such in writings on suicide, partly because of the prejudice that the suicidal are somehow fundamentally different from the rest of us. The neglect of this aspect of the psychology of suicide is also due to the false view that the suicide is someone who desires his death. The fear of death and the fear of suicidal death are strong and important; they are major reasons why 90 percent of all people with suicidal feelings do not make highly lethal attempts.

All of us, including the suicidal, fear death. The fear of death is the subject of many books; I shall not discuss it except to claim that the suicidal have it. This fear does not go away just because someone becomes so full of pain that he cannot stand life any longer. In everyday life, non-suicidal people are usually not consciously aware of their fear of death. But not being consciously aware of the existence of the fear does not mean that the fear, at some preconscious level, is not present as a basic part of their personalities. The fact that some people near death, by any means, report that they are not experiencing this fear does not mean that it has become non-existent and non-influential at pre-conscious levels. The fear of death is a built-in resource for coping with pain and tragedy. The fear of death, and the fear of each kind of death, including suicide, have strong evolutionary value. We are born with these fears, and no matter how we die, we never lose any of them. These fears are such an entrenched and basic part of all of us that it is folly to assume that the kinds of events that lead up to suicide cause them to disappear. (Chapter 11, page 270 describes cases in which the fear became conscious while highly lethal attempts were in progress.) People who recover from suicidal crises do not have to relearn the fear of death; it continues to be there all along. It is just unfortunately the case that sometimes pain gets so great that it overwhelms the fear of death and our other pain-coping resources.

Different people have different levels of fear for different types of death: fire, drowning, disease, accident, choking, suffocation, freezing, poisoning, stabbing, etc. Some fear dying while they are awake more than dying while asleep. Some fear dying alone more than dying with others present. Death by suicide also has a place within our individual hierarchy of ways to die. Some might rank it last, others might prefer it over incapacitating disease. The fear of suicidal death is something we all have, and something on which we practice particularly strong denial. We can readily admit to a fear of dying by almost any other means, but the stigma of suicide keeps us from admitting any fear that it might happen to us. This denial is part of why we believe suicide is voluntary, why we tacitly assent to the omnipotent assumption that no pain is too great to force us to be suicides. We are afraid of suicide, afraid of losing our volitional capacities, and afraid of immense pain.

Fear and the Means of Suicide

It becomes easier to recognize our fear of suicide when we realize that just as we can personally order our preferences in types of death, we can also rank our preferences in the means of suicide: shooting, hanging, jumping, drowning, burning, poisoning, suffocating, stabbing, electrocution, victim precipitated "homicide", apparent "accident". If asked, the non-suicidal can make a ranking, and this, of course, need not be the ranking they would give if they were on the brink of suicide. Many of the suicidal think about the means quite a bit. The means of suicide of which they have the least fear and the easiest access becomes the weakest link in a chain of fears that helps keep them alive. Each of these means carries its own set of fears: amount of pain, scars, paralysis, partial disability, brain damage, bodily organ damage, disfigurement of corpse, probability of autopsy. These are frightening considerations for the suicidal and non-suicidal alike.

Intentionalists believe that suicide results from the desire for death, and believe that the means of suicide represent particular types of desire. Freud writes:

> That the various means of suicide can represent sexual
> wish-fulfilments has long been known to all analysts.
> (To poison oneself = to become pregnant; to drown = to
> bear a child; to throw oneself from a height = to be
> delivered of a child.) (1970, p. 149, footnote 9)

Hendin also sees means as resulting from desire:

> For many suicidal individuals, choosing the means of
> their suicide is integral to their use of suicide as a form
> of control. ... Some suicides use their control over how
> they choose to die to express feelings about why they
> want to die. (1982, pp. 148 & 149)

On the involuntarist theory neither the event nor the means is chosen or desired. Just as the event is not an act, the means is not a method. Suicide happens when pain exceeds coping resources, and the means is the least feared of those available. An example Hendin gives to support his view is actually better as evidence for the least fear theory of the means:

> One woman who tried many times to kill herself with
> pills before doing so was being truthful when she told
> her doctor, who was concerned about her being on a high
> floor of a hospital, that she could never jump, because
> she was afraid of heights. (p. 148.)

Hendin suggests that suicides with multiple methods may reveal multiple motives. (p. 149.) The involuntarist theory does not believe that multiple means has this type of significance. In a suicide that took place several years ago, the victim swallowed fully lethal poison and then called someone else. While on the phone the pain of the poisoning became extreme and he then hung himself. The only explanation necessary for the hanging, as well as the poisoning, is that suicide is an involuntary response to overwhelming pain. (And, in the early part of conversation, the victim expressed the desire to live and gave the person he called the information necessary to call for an ambulance, which arrived too late. The victim died wanting to live.)

The means have no meaning, at least not in the sense of sexual wish-fulfillment, control, communication, aggression, or desire for escape. The only meaning in Hendin's example is that the woman had greater fear of suicide by jumping than she had of suicide by pills. When the least feared means is not available, the use of a more feared means requires a greater level of pain. This is not a volitional process: we do not choose the different levels of fear we have for suicide by different means, any more than we choose the fears we have in other areas of our lives. Fear is a better hypothesis to explain means than wish-fulfilment, and it is less stigmatizing: it does not require that we assume that the suicide is mentally or morally different from the rest of us. The types of suicide — gunshot, jumping, poisoning — and the types of cancer — lung, brain, skin — are no different: each of us has individual levels of vulnerability to each of the different types.

The fears of the suicidal include not only the fears associated with the attempt, but also fears of the afterlife and fears for the shame, stigma, and hardship for the survivors. Though these factors are ignored in most discussions of suicide, they help explain why most suicidal people do not make lethal attempts. The fear of suicidal death increases pain-coping capacity, even though, as death gets near, it also increases anxiety, turmoil, and pain.

CHAPTER FIVE

PAIN

No Single Pain — No Single Resource

In one sense the cause of suicide is simple: overwhelming pain. This overwhelming pain, however, is the aggregate of thousands of pains. Any hurt that we have ever suffered, if it remains consciously or unconsciously lodged within us, can contribute to suicide. This may range from being an incest victim 50 years ago, to losing a job 10 years ago, to having a car battery stolen yesterday. The pains come from everywhere: ill-health, family, peers, school, work, community, caregivers. For each suicide there was a finite point at which this aggregate became too much. Although "The straw that broke the back," is frequently an accurate metaphor, no one pain is ever *the* cause of suicide. Suicidal pain is decomposable into thousands of pains, and nearly all of these pains are decomposable into painful constituents. Sexual abuse, job loss, and personal theft each have numerous painful constituents. The search for the single cause is a fundamentally wrongheaded approach to the understanding and prevention of suicide.

It is inaccurate to say simply that pain causes suicide, since a level of pain that is lethal for one person may not be lethal for someone with greater resources. Similarly, deficiency in resources cannot be regarded as the cause of suicide, since two people may have equal resources and unequal pain. Our resources may also come from everywhere; even such trivial distractions as going to a movie can contribute to coping with suicidal pain.

In a discussion of an attempted suicide, Freud singles out three motives as essential factors for the attempt. The first was conscious, the latter two unconscious:

> ... the explanation she gave of the immediate reasons determining her resolution sounded quite plausible. ... In her despair at having thus lost her loved one for ever, she wanted to put an end to herself. The analysis, however, was able to disclose another and deeper interpretation behind the one she gave, which was confirmed by the evidence of her own dreams. The attempted suicide was, as might have been expected, determined by two other motives besides the one she gave: it was a "punishment-fulfilment" (self-punishment), and a wish-fulfilment. As a wish-fulfilment it signified the attainment of the very wish which, when frustrated, had driven her into homosexuality — namely, the wish to have a child by her father, ... From the point of view of self-punishment the girl's action shows us that she had developed in her unconscious strong death-wishes against one or other of her parents: perhaps against her father, out of revenge for impeding her love, but more likely, also against her mother when she was pregnant with the little brother. For analysis has explained the enigma of suicide in the following way: probably no one finds the mental energy required to kill himself unless, in the first place, he is in doing this at the same time killing an object with whom he has identified, and, in the second place, is turning against himself a death-wish which had been directed against someone else. Nor need the regular discovery of these unconscious death-wishes in those who have attempted suicide surprise us as strange (any more than it need make an impression as confirming our deductions), since the unconscious of all human beings is full enough of such death-wishes, even against those we love. ... Lastly, a discovery that several quite different motives, all of great strength, must have co-operated to make such a

deed possible is only in accord with what we should
expect. (1970, pp. 148-150. See also Litman, 1967, p. 338,
and Shneidman, 1985, pp. 211-12. In later writings
Freud advanced the death instinct hypothesis as an
additional factor in suicide.)

This way of analyzing suicide is incomplete and impractical. For an
involuntarist the three factors are types of pain, not motives. Assuming
the existence of these three pains — disappointment in love,
unconscious frustrations over not having a child by the father,
unconscious anger at the parents turned inward — does not explain
suicide. Other young women suffer these pains and do not attempt
suicide. In fact, to explain why *this* attempt occurred and attempts did
not occur to other people who had these three factors, we would have to
list *other* pains (and/or deficiencies of coping resources). From this
perspective, these *other* factors could lay claim to the title "the cause".
No single factor, such as the third Freud mentions, or short list of
factors, is ever the cause of suicide. Given the immense permutations
possible on human pain and on our coping resources, we must regard the
total causal conditions of each suicide as completely individual.

Defenders of the single cause (or small number of causes) approach
may object that some pains are more important than others.
Involuntarism denies this; other than being quantitatively more
painful, no pain is more important than any other. Consider, as an
example, unconscious anger toward one's parents. Psychoanalysts argue
that it is a major factor in suicide since all suicidal people have it. But
the constant conjunction of this pain and the suicidal feelings does not
prove that this anger is *the*, or the most important, cause of suicide.
Everyone has unconscious anger toward his parents, and not everyone is
suicidal. All suicidal people, and, indeed, all people, have unconscious
love for their parents. Should we say that unconscious parental love is
the cause of suicide? The response to this is that only the suicidal and
the severely depressed have great unconscious anger toward their
parents, and it is this huge anger that is the pre-eminent cause of
suicide. This is the huge pain of clinical depression. Is this huge pain
the cause, or the pre-eminent cause of suicide? First, severe depression
is not one thing, it is decomposable into thousands of pains. The next
chapter argues that psychoanalysis has given a very incomplete
analysis of depression; it contains other painful emotions besides anger.

Secondly, it still does not suffice as a cause of suicide. Two people can have this huge pain in equal amounts, yet their suicidal behavior may vary according to the presence or absence of coping resources and other types of pain. Thirdly, unconscious anger toward one's parents is said to be the primary cause of depression, but perhaps it is itself, in part at least, merely an effect of pain unrelated to one's parents. Consider the man who yells at his children because of problems at work. Directing anger at loved ones who are not responsible for the anger is a common human tendency. Why is it implausible to assume that someone else, instead of venting his anger at his children, unconsciously directs it at parental introjects? (Analysis claims that the depressed person, at an unconscious level, identifies with each of his parents. Anger at them, turned inward, becomes anger at the self.) Were this person to become suicidal he would have a lot of unconscious anger toward his parents, but the unconscious anger would not be the cause of his condition. "Bottled up anger is the cause of depression and suicide," is an inaccurate theory. Bottling up anger is like the ride-it-out method of suicide prevention, a coping strategy with uncertain results. Unconscious mental activity, like every other human process, helps us cope with the demands of life; it is not a reservoir for the original causes of suicide. If anger at family members is not entirely an original cause of suicide, but is in part derivative of original causes, then we can approach depression and suicide in therapy with less defensiveness and hostility. If we reduce anger at the world by coming to an improved understanding of the social causes of depression and suicidal pain, we may concomitantly reduce anger at parental introjects and reduce depression.

Suicidal pain finds expression in dreams and in other operations of the mind that are not directly accessible to consciousness. Psychoanalysis can assist us in understanding these matters. There is no reason to suppose, however, that any special significance should be given to these aspects of suicidal pain. Psychoanalysts single out certain manifestations of suicidal pain, to which they alone have access, and claim that these are the crucial elements in suicide. This has become a part of the modern mythology of suicidal pain: it has elements that have special importance, and are accessible to only a few highly trained individuals who use complex and esoteric doctrines to provide therapeutic response to that pain. This view of suicide is supported both by the doctrines of psychoanalysis and by the desire of the non-suicidal general community to maintain its distance from the suicidal. "Leave it to the experts," is a comfort to non-suicidal non-experts. But access to psychoanalysis is an impossibility for 95 percent of all suicidal people. Most of them are aware of the myth that only analysis can reveal the real source of their pain, and for these people the myth just adds to their despair. The myth is false. No pain is more important than any other pain, and most pains of the suicidal are the pains of ordinary life. Most of the resources for coping with those pains are the resources of ordinary life. There is no practical advantage to the assumption that the pains that are the most difficult to gain access to are the most important.

The pains that cause suicide do not come from just one place, they come from everywhere. This means that we should abandon the idea of responding to a suicidal person with a single resource. No individual, the suicidal person himself, a friend, a therapist, or individual discipline, such as the mental health profession, can hope to have a complete understanding of suicidal pain. Some theorists, notably Shneidman, assert that suicide prevention should be an interdisciplinary activity. Their theories, however, do not support this viewpoint, since they hold that suicide has key elements that are the proper province only of trained psychologists. As long as we have these theories, workers in every other area of human pain will be frightened of suicide and unwilling to work with the suicidal. And "interdisciplinary", of course, still limits the range of resources to persons with some type of special expertise. But in suicide, no pain, apart from the amount of painfulness, is more significant than any other pain. Counselors for bereavement, substance abuse, eating disorders, aging, social injustice, crime victimization, physical disabilities, gambling, debting, sexual identity, rape, incest, child abuse, and domestic violence can all respond effectively to suicidal pain. The suicidal have as much right to ask for help from these counselors (and these counselors have just as much an obligation to respond to such requests) as they do from mental health counselors. Workers outside the mental health profession routinely refuse to assist the suicidal on the grounds that "We're not equipped to deal with that." But there is no special "that" to suicide. In fact, substance abuse problems, bereavement issues, and crisis aspects of other problems have to be addressed before it is possible to make any progress on mental health problems. Suicidal pain includes not only a broad range of problems dealt with by trained counselors, it also includes the pains of ordinary life. Problems at school, on the job, and at home may all be factors in suicide. The aggregate pain theory does not advocate a "leave it to the experts" approach to suicide prevention. Ordinary people can do a lot to reduce the pains of ordinary life. "Leave it to the experts," is a groundless rationalization for social stigma and aversion; it deprives the suicidal of resources they need to stay alive. An approach that recognizes the significance of ordinary pains and ordinary pain-coping resources may help relieve one of the vicious circle problems that arise in work with the suicidal. In crisis situations there is often an interactive escalation of fear between the suicidal person and his acquaintances: "I'm not enough to cope with this," is felt by each person, and each person senses this fear in others. If the various parties recognize that there are many areas in which they can act effectively to reduce pain, then there is less likelihood that this fear will increase to panic proportions.

Recovery From Suicidal Pain

The theoretical view that suicide has a single or a few key components has not been lost on cultural mythology. Many suicidal people believe or half believe that if they could just discover the one or a few great insights, then they would have immediate and wonderful recovery. The corollary to this belief is the view that as long as the great insights have not been found, nothing substantial can be done to promote recovery. Acceptance of this pair of beliefs is a recipe for prolonged agony.

This limited view of the nature of recovery is akin to the common tendency to focus on a single aspect of suicidal pain. A single problem, the loss of a girlfriend or the death of a loved one, is perceived by the suicidal and those around him as the make or break issue: either the person will adjust to the loss, the lost thing will somehow be regained, or the suicide will occur. This approach fails to recognize other painful aspects of the person's life that can be given aid, and it usually takes an all-or-nothing attitude to the particular problem. The particular problem itself is never a single entity. Though large parts of the pain are often not be immediately reducible, there are always smaller aspects that can be helped. The aggregate pain approach provides opportunities for a large number and variety of people to provide care. Suicidal pain has thousands of components, and most of these pains can be reduced. The suicidal condition is one that tells you "Recovery is an impossible hope." Yet more than 90 percent of the people who get this condition do recover, and most of them get recovery on a step-by-step incremental basis.

The tendency to focus on a single problem or a few problems is an aspect of the "tunnel vision" psychology that many writers have noted is very common in suicidal people. A helpful way to view suicidal pain is not just in terms of major problems of life or underlying psychodynamics, but also as including pains that can be put into a conjunction such as the following:

I hurt,
I am alone,
nobody cares,
no one understands,
I am losing my ability to make myself understood,
I am powerless to change my present situation, and
my pain will always be there in the future.

Each of these is had by just about all suicidal people. Each of these feelings, for the person who has it, looks as if it will always be there. What is hard to see, both for the suicidal and for counselors and acquaintances, is that each of these pains is decomposable into many components, and many of these components can have their painfulness reduced in both the short- and long-term. Moreover, each of these pains has, as part of its cause, the social oppression of the suicidal.

"No one understands," for example, is equivalent to a long conjunction of the form, "Person A does not understand and person B does not understand and ... ." Each conjunct is decomposable into "A has some understanding of the job problem and A has little understanding of the home problem and A does not know about the health problem and ... ." An analysis of "No one understands," quickly becomes very complex. To be in pain is bad, to not have one's pain understood is even worse. *What is not understood* — the aggregate of suicidal pain and its relationship to one's resources — is an enormously complicated entity. The opportunities for making improvements in how the pain is understood are considerable. Increasing the understanding had by others and by oneself can decrease the pain of not being understood. The single cause myth unfortunately fosters the belief that understanding is an all-or-nothing enterprise.

The confusion of suicidal pain is neglected and important subject. Being confused about why one is in such a horrible situation is itself painful. To honestly say to others, "I don't know why I'm in so much pain," is likely to provoke a pain-increasing response. Pain that is not specific and identifiable is subject to scepticism and belittlement. If you do not know the cause of your pain, then you are judged by yourself and others to have two inadequacies: the pain, and the inability to figure out the cause of your pain. Confused pain is not less pain, or less real pain; it is actually more pain because of the prejudice against it.

Psychoanalysis has an explanation for this confusion that is partly correct. We often do repress awareness of anger toward loved ones. When a depressed person ruminates on the causes of his unhappiness, he does not see this repressed anger, and hence he is ignorant of some of the causes of his pain. But the social myths of suicide are not part of the analytical views on repression, and they cause us to be unaware of the social causes of suicidal pain. Social myth exists because the non-suicidal wish to deny personal vulnerability and wish to deny social complicity. As we grow up we absorb the false beliefs engendered by these two forms of denial, and these false beliefs obscure our efforts to understand the causes of our pain. It does not require psychoanalysis to unravel much of the confusion about the causes of suicidal pain.

An understanding problem of a different sort is with the individual's personal conceptions of his pain-coping resources. The involuntarist criterion for suicide is not "pain exceeds the person's conception of his pain-coping resources." Different people may over or under estimate their capacities for tolerating pain. As long as we remain alive, we never do know the minimum amount of pain necessary to kill us. (This is true even of survivors of highly lethal attempts. During later periods of their lives, they may have greater or lesser levels of coping resources.) Sometimes people who have never attempted suicide assert, "If that ever happened to me I would kill myself," but its speakers do not know whether it is true. Many people have the "that" happen to them, for example, testing positive for the presence of the HIV antibody, and a few commit suicide, and most do not. The rule in dealing with all traumatic experiences is to provide support in every way possible, reduce pain, and give the person time. Working with people in the aftermath of traumatic experiences provides overwhelming evidence that those who have not suffered these experiences have very inadequate ideas about what the pain is like, and about human resources for coping with pain. The prejudices about pain discussed in Chapter 3, which are abetted by this ignorance, find expression in just about every type of trauma: they add pain and subtract resources.

Giving up the view that suicide is caused by one or a few factors will help us recognize a further feature of suicidal pain: it changes over time. Some people suffer from chronic or recurrent suicidal feelings. On the aggregate pain model, it is a mistake to regard this as continuously or recurrently the same situation. Over time fresh insults are added to the aggregate and some older pains may become less painful. Old resources are lost or deteriorate, new ones are found. Lasting pains we suffer from traumatic events may wax and wane for the rest of our lives. In many cases there are therapeutic things we can do to come to terms with aspects of major losses, but there is no guarantee that a subsequent painful event will not revive memories of an earlier one.

Suicidal Pain and Psychological Pain

...the common stimulus of suicide is unendurable psychological pain, (Shneidman, 1985, p. 215)

...the patient finds himself in an intolerable affective state, flooded with emotional pain... (Maltsberger, 1986, p. 2)

A problem with current theory is that it limits suicidal pain to psychological pain. This limitation is false. Problems in physical health are very common factors in completed, attempted, and considered suicides. The psychological approach has two major drawbacks. The first is that it supports prejudice. In the popular imagination "psychological pain" carries the taints of "not real" and "all in the head," and is a pain that has secondary status. Our social norms make psychological pain more vulnerable to ridicule and belittlement than physical pain. Definitions of suicidal pain that limit it to psychological pain make the part of the pain that *is* psychological even worse. The second drawback is that it encourages counselors to address only psychological issues and give secondary consideration to reductions in physical pain. Since the suicidal condition is believed to be caused by mental and moral inferiority, and most physical problems are not stigmatized in this way, then the physical suffering cannot be "the" cause of suicide. "Treat physical suffering," is rarely mentioned as a priority in any book on suicide. This policy has no utility. It is not unusual for seriously ill AIDS patients to have periods of suicidal feelings. They have both physical and psychological pain, and suicidal periods are usually concurrent with an increase in pain of both types. Relief from physical suffering invariably brings the suicidal period to an end. The reduction of physical pain shows care, control, understanding, and is a powerful direct means of preventing suicide. "Reduce physical pain" should be an *obvious* direct consequence of any theory of suicide.

The aggregate pain approach does not distinguish between types of pain. It regards physical pain and resources for coping with physical pain as important as any other kind of pain or coping resource. We underestimate the possibility of reducing pain and the intensity of suicidal feelings by attending to concerns with physical well-being. This applies not just to problems such as sleep disorders, that current theory regards as sometimes physical and sometimes psychological, but also to problems that are obviously physical, and even to problems that are comparatively small. Such a policy reduces suffering, gains time, and provides unmistakable evidence of concern. Anyone who works with physically ill people knows that small improvements in physical health can bring significant change in emotional condition.

Maltsberger's *Suicide Risk* is an example of the bias against taking a direct, sincere, and serious approach to physical health problems in the suicidal. In a brief passage he cites three studies that show "... *most* of the patients who commit suicide are physically sick; many have serious illnesses." He then says, "From the psychodynamic point of view, this is not difficult to understand. Physical illness is very likely to interfere with every class of sustaining resources on which a suicide vulnerable individual may rely." (p.70) Maltsberger believes that suicidal people have a lifelong mental inferiority that causes them to rely excessively on external supports. (see Chapter 12) This mental inferiority causes the person to "give up on himself" when the external supports are no longer available. Since the "real" cause of suicide is the excessive dependence on external supports, Maltsberger's clinical recommendations do not include "Take action on complaints of physical pain and illness." His actual recommendations on this subject are "We may also learn to what extent the patient will use ill health to claim special attention and care from others whom he feels might otherwise be indifferent to him."(p. 118) and "Is there evidence of hypochondriasis ...?"(p. 142) When suicidal people plead for relief from physical illness and suffering, Maltsberger advises that we examine their behavior to see what can be learned about their mental inferiority.

The evidence is that physical suffering is a large part of the problem of suicide. Besides interfering with external supports, it directly adds to suicidal pain. There are no studies that show that completers, attempters, or considerers are more likely to suffer from hypochondria than the general public. Yet our leading text on psychiatric interviews with the suicidal warns clinicians to be alert for signs of manipulation and attention seeking in dealing with complaints of physical illness. This is pure prejudice. It de-emphasizes the role of physical pain in suicide, and discredits attempts by sufferers to get help. The suicidal, like the rest of us, want to avoid the label "hypochondriac"; this advice deters them from asking for help with physical problems.

Physical Examination

Essays on suicide must advise a thorough physical examination for anyone suffering from depression. Depression has been linked to a very wide variety of physical conditions that includes such things as hepatitis, mononucleosis, thyroid problems, nutritional deficiencies, food allergies, and vision problems. It is sometimes caused by birth control pills, medications for blood pressure and heart disease, combinations of medications, changes in tolerance for dosage levels of medications, and withdrawal from medications. Undiagnosed learning disabilities may contribute to depression in young people. In this situation there is the stress of trying to compensate for the disability, and school problems lead to family and social problems. Medical conditions often cause depression; depression in turn, because of its stress, anxiety, and behavioral changes, is a high risk period for physical illness.

Though many people have found relief from depression in proper diagnosis and treatment for physical conditions, others have not. And, unfortunately, many providers of medical care do not have enlightened attitudes about mental illness. If an examination does not turn up a physical basis for the depression, many doctors display an attitude of "You have wasted my time and your money. It's all in your head. Go see a shrink." They may insinuate that the patient is a hypochondriac, or is looking for a physical alibi for a problem that has its basis in moral weakness. The dynamics of this reaction are transparent: something is wrong with the patient, the physician did not find the cause and provide the cure, so some frustration gets ventilated on the patient. This reaction is factually incorrect and practically despicable. It is totally rational for a depressed person to request a physical examination:

> That a wide variety of organic dysfunctions and biological illnesses can effectively "masquerade" as functional psychiatric disturbance is known and documented in the literature, yet all too frequently this possibility is neglected by mental health practitioners of all disciplines. (Struve, 1986, p. 55)

Negative results from an examination do not mean there is no physical basis for depression. Few examinations test for all the physical causes that have been linked to depression, and new connections between physiological problems and depression are regularly reported. Since the suffering of depression is great, and can last indefinitely, a physical examination is not a waste of time.

Negative results from a physical examination add two more pains: hope for relief is disappointed and the patient is marked by the stigma of mental illness. The sequence of insinuations: "It's not physical, it's not real, it's phony, the patient is a phony," and the fact that they come from an authority figure greatly increase the pain of depression. It is appalling that this behavior occurs when people are just beginning to enter the world of mental healthcare. The legitimate fear of getting this reaction deters people from seeking initial physical examinations, and from seeking examinations for areas not covered in the first examination.

Biochemical Imbalance

The psychological theory of the mental illnesses of depression and schizophrenia believes that they are largely or entirely a matter of such things as early childhood experiences and moral, developmental, adaptational, and cognitive deficiencies. The biochemical theory believes that mental health problems are primarily caused by dysfunctions in brain chemistry. The former approach stresses the need for psychotherapy; the latter believes that the best hope for progress lies with such treatments as anti-depressant medications and electroshock. Many mental health professionals embrace both; they believe that biochemical factors and problems in interpersonal relationships can individually and conjointly cause mental illness. In their current states of development both approaches have been successful in treating some people and unsuccessful with others. Even professionals who strongly tend to one approach or the other may recommend pursuing both types of treatment programs in recovery.

It is thought that imbalances in brain chemistry may originate in two ways. The first is that we are born with an imbalance, or that we are born with a disposition to develop an imbalance at a stage of life such as puberty, childbirth, or old age. The second possible cause of biochemical imbalances are external factors such as poor nutrition, toxins in the environment, stress, or trauma. The stresses and traumas may include all the problems of living that are treated by conventional psychotherapy or by programs for substance abuse, bereavement, or assault. Just as there is uncertainty over the extent to which depression is mental or physical, there is uncertainty in both the mental and physical camps over how much is innate and how much is acquired. Given a broad view of the causes of biochemical imbalance (i.e., the imbalance can be triggered by any event in life), the aggregate pain theory is compatible with the position that the biochemical imbalances in turn cause their victim to experience depression. A theory that regards socially induced pain and physical pain as direct causes of depression and suicide is actually more compatible with the biochemical hypothesis than are the mental and moral interpretations. Chronic fear means chronic stress, and physical pain may have physiological effects on our emotional capacities.

It is important to recognize, however, that the position that stresses (i.e., pain and the lack of resources for coping for pain) of every sort —

social, psychological, physical — can cause biochemical imbalances, and these imbalances in turn can cause depression, does not mean that anti-depressant medications should always be our method of choice for the treatment of depression. If the social stress is physical, sexual, or emotional abuse, the way to treat the depression is to stop the abuse. Unfortunately, advocates of the biochemical treatment of depression have gone along with the view of academic theory and popular culture that the problem is entirely within the skull of the victim. Enthusiasm for biochemical treatment and research is partly due to the fact that it helps perpetuate the myth that suicide and depression should be treated by changing the victim, not by changing ourselves. As long as we have a narrow view of the causes of biochemical imbalance, such as limiting it to innate genetic defects, we can practice denial on the social complicity in the causation of suicide. The narrow view does nothing to help reduce pain and increase resources for the millions of people whose problems do not respond to medications. It also deprives us of an opportunity for progress in a much broader area for social reform. The dynamics behind the oppression of the suicidal is similar to the dynamics of other forms of injustice; progress in one area can support progress in other areas.

This interpretation of the biochemical hypothesis in terms of the aggregate pain theory is analogous to the treatment it gets from other theorists:

> ... it is not unreasonable to speculate that persons who suffer emotional injuries in childhood not only may later prove vulnerable to despair, but, as a consequence of early traumatization, may when despairing secrete such substances. At present we do not know whether the coincidence of these spinal metabolites and states of despair reflects the operation of inheritance or trauma; possibly both are involved.

> ... or in the event the child is unable for biochemical or other reasons to complete the task of introjecting a loving superego. (Maltsberger, 1986, pp. 2 & 14)

But which hypothesis is more plausible: one that limits itself to deficiencies that result from inheritance or childhood trauma, or one that says that the deficiencies may have a much broader range of causes?

Even if we accept the view that biochemical imbalances may contribute to depression and suicide, it is a mistake to assume that the biochemical aspect of the problem is entirely within the victim. It is also partly within the physiological makeup of the people around the suicide. If a student goes to a counselor and says, "I'm suicidal," the counselor's biochemistry will be altered in ways that are different than if the student had said, "I need the form for the school sports exam." This alteration of biochemistry affects the counselor's behavior; this alteration of behavior causes changes in the student's biochemistry; the change in the student's biochemistry causes further changes in the counselor's behavior — and so on. Why has the biochemistry field studied only the biochemistry of the victim? It pretends that the anxiety and aversion of the non-suicidal have no causal role in suicide. The same point can be made about the approach that seeks to reduce much of our behavior to our genes. If behavior is genetically predisposed, then it seems reasonable to suppose that we have a genetic predisposition to help children with broken limbs, and a genetic aversion to people in suicidal pain. On this theory, the genes of the non-suicidal positively affect the mortality rate of children, and negatively affect the mortality rate of the suicidal. Isn't this also part of the problem of suicide?

Biochemistry has been advanced as an approach that will help us reduce our moral contempt for the suicidal. What has not been recognized is that it also could have a beneficial effect in the opposite direction. Just as we have anger toward the suicidal, they often have anger toward us. If the suicidal can see our fear and aversion as involuntary, then they can approach us for help with less defensiveness and hostility. One way in which victims of abuse learn to cope with the harm inflicted upon them is to see their perpetrators' behavior as involuntary, as something for which neither the perpetrator nor the victim is responsible. To regard the cause of the social abuse of the suicidal by the non-suicidal as genetic or biochemical (as opposed to having purely social causes) is not a pleasant thought, but as a hypothesis it cannot be ruled out. And, just because it is a genetic trait of the majority does not mean that it is morally legitimate, or that we ought do nothing to resist its effects.

CHAPTER SIX

DEPRESSION

The most important and influential work on depression is Freud's essay "Mourning and Melancholia". Freud argued that depression is best understood as a form of anger turned inward:

> If one listens patiently to the many and various self-accusations of the melancholiac, one cannot in the end avoid the impression that often the most violent of them are hardly at all applicable to the patient himself, but that with insignificant modifications they do fit someone else, some person whom the patient loves, has loved or ought to love. This conjecture is confirmed every time one examines the facts. So we get the key to the clinical picture — by perceiving that the self-reproaches are reproaches against a loved object which has been shifted on to the patient's own ego. (1957, p. 130)

Anger turned inward is the most important factor in suicide:

> ... we have long known that no neurotic harbors thoughts of suicide which are not murderous impulses against others redirected upon himself, (p. 133)

The psychoanalytic explanation for the mechanisms of this process are technical and complex. It involves the view that the depressed person unconsciously identifies with the person or persons at whom the original anger is directed, conscious anger at these persons is prohibited, and the result is that one part of the self directs rage at another part of the self. This continues to be the prevailing view in psychoanalysis: "The primitive superego forces the aggression around against the self, inexorably sentencing the patient who wishes to kill a beloved person to die by his own hand." (Maltsberger, 1986, p. 33. See also Maltsberger, 1980, p. 70: "The hating introject, poorly integrated and always alien in some degree, calls out for execution of the evil self.") Our concern is not with the technical aspects of this position, but only with the claim that depression and suicide are wholly or primarily caused by anger toward present and past love objects turned inward. From the aggregate pain perspective, this theory is incomplete and misleading. Anger turned inward may be a significant factor in many cases of depression. Depression, however, has other components; these include envy, self-pity, and shame. These emotional conditions have been neglected in analyses of depression and suicide because they have social dimensions not had by the kinds of anger Freud discusses. On the psychoanalytical model the causes of depression and suicide begin and end with the victim and his immediate family. The root of the problem does not even exist in the victim's present circumstances, but in his experiences in early childhood. This view holds that the world outside the family and other intimates makes no contribution to the pain that results in depression and suicide. This is one reason why psychoanalysis has been such an influential and enduring theory; it supports and is supported by the need of the larger culture to deny social complicity in the causation of suicidal pain.

The following sections present brief analyses of envy, shame, self-pity, and grandiosity as they exist in depressed people. These conditions are components of suicidal pain, and they cannot be understood without considering the depressed person's relations to the larger community. Much of the pain in depression does involve anger, but depression also essentially involves a number of other conditions besides anger. I do not believe that our limited understanding of depression puts us in a position where we can say that any one of these conditions is more important than any other. The conditions themselves are causally interactive. Conscious and unconscious anger, for example, may be fueled by the repression of feelings of envy and shame. The anger at loved ones, which psychoanalysts regard as the original cause of depression, may in part derive from painful conditions that originate outside the family. Two examples may clarify this. A woman who loses a husband that she loves may originally be angry at the loss of love and secondarily envious of women who still have their husbands. This experience of envy may breed more anger. A girl who feels her school clothing is not the equal of that of her peers will experience envy and shame first, and then anger at her parents for being unable or unwilling to provide her with the clothing she desires. This in turn may cause her envy of the other girls' clothes to broaden to envy of the other girls' family situations. There is not one painful emotion in depression, but a host of painful emotions that painfully interact.

This has the appearance of being a depressing view of depression: besides anger, the victim is burdened with other painful emotions as well. Actually this is a hopeful theory. It provides sufferers and their counselors with a larger range of opportunities for understanding and progress. The depressed are often in stuck positions, and frequently are unable to recognize and identify their feelings of anger. Parts of their self-pity, shame, and envy may be much more accessible. The position that depression is not simply a problem of self and family can reduce stigma and resistance. Suicidal people feel that they have run out of options for coping with pain. If we abandon our theoretically constricted vision of suicidal pain, we can provide people with a greater number of options in recovery.

ENVY

Envy has two aspects. In its primary sense envy is the experience of pain when we see that someone else has something desirable that we lack. We practice a good deal of semi-conscious denial on this type of envy: it often involves the recognition that someone else is better and that we are inferior. Envy is also the experience of pleasure when the person who has that desirable quality suffers misfortune. This experience tends to be privately acknowledged and publicly stifled or disguised. The feeling is often discharged as an expression of pity for the person's loss.

1. The depressed and the suicidal envy other people's enjoyment of life. Ordinary non-depressed people experience the discomfort of envy when they see a couple who have just fallen in love. We infrequently have this pain since we infrequently see the display of mutual affection that arouses it. The suicidal experience a similar kind of pain when they see the non-depressed enjoying the pleasures of ordinary life, and they see that all the time. Regardless of one's view of the original causes of depression — biochemical imbalance, cognitive distortions, anger turned inward, or aggregate pain — one cannot deny that people in that condition are bound to experience profound envy. A depressed person is prone to believe "Every part of my life is bad." We can safely infer that in every part of this person's life, he has massive envy for what others have. Even if his material possessions equal his peers, he does not get the same enjoyment from them. The depressed person's envy, of course, is much greater for the non-material blessings of life. These not only include love and friendship, but the freedom and power that the non-depressed have to take action to resolve problems in living. The suicidal have lost this capacity, and they envy those who still have it.

2. A great deal of suicidal pain is comparative. In counseling it is not uncommon to listen to one person complain because he lacks qualities a, b, and c; and then listen to someone who has a, b, and c complain because he lacks d, e, and f. A seasonal variation in the incidence rate for completed suicide is that it rises in the spring. Envy is a better explanation for this phenomenon than anger. The depressed person sees that others have become happier during this period, and it increases his own pain. A precipitating factor in several completed suicides with which I am familiar was the happy recent marriage of a sibling or close friend. The increased pain was not due to personal loss, but to the gain of someone else.

It would be interesting to see a study of envy that compared different age groups. People of all ages, of course, are affected by envy. But one has only to spend time listening to older people, who have the highest incidence rate for completed suicide, to realize how strongly and persistently problems with envy pervade their thinking. Adolescents and post-adolescents, who have the highest incidence rate for suicide attempts, are struggling to learn how to cope with their own feelings of envy and how to respond to feelings of envy that other people have toward them. The problems of adolescence — peer pressure, parental pressure, achievement of independence from the family — are inextricably bound up with personal and parental feelings of envy.

Theorists with reductionist tendencies might be tempted by two types of moves. The first is to reduce all forms of envy to one form. This would reduce envy of health, prosperity, and friendship to envy of being loved (or of being lovable or of being approved of) and then reduce all forms of envy of being loved to envy of being loved by one's parents.[1] A second step would argue that envy has its hostile aspects, and then claim that it is really a form of anger. This reductionist position is that all envy, somehow, is really anger at family members. This position would point out that envy involving family relationships is a powerful force in our lives and surely interacts with envy as it extends out to the larger community. In organizations the envy and hostility of sibling rivalries are often replicated. But what is to be gained by claiming that all envy is really anger over not being loved when someone else is being loved? This claim denies the obvious fact that the subjective experiences of anger and envy are very different. They are plainly two emotions, not one. The practical utility of the reduction of envy to anger, or of all forms of envy to one form, is limited. In some cases, such as the organizational example, it can be helpful to find links between one's childhood and one's current situation. And in decomposing pain it is helpful to be sensitive to ways in which anger may contribute to envy and vice versa. But to assume automatically that all forms of envy are really one form of anger deprives victims of depression and their counselors of access to potentially fatal pain. Reductionism necessitates complex theoretical principles to justify the reduction. As these principles grow more esoteric, the number of people able to implement them in counseling diminishes. If counselors or the depressed themselves are unable to determine how a particular feeling of envy in current circumstances is related to anger toward one's parents, then they are likely to discount or not even recognize the extent to which it contributes to depression and suicide risk. On the aggregate pain model the important steps are to identify and deal with individual current pains. To find connections between these and other pains is a helpful but secondary task. At a level of social policy, there is no evidence that the complex theoretical reductions that characterize psychoanalysis provide that theory with greater usefulness in public health.

3. Depressed people and others with low self-esteem have difficulty in recognizing and coping with situations in which *they* are the objects of envy. In discussing anonymous people with the label "depressed" or "suicidal," we may mistakenly assume that no one would envy them. But nearly all suicides have some or even many valued personal qualities: intelligence, youth, jobs, material assets, a pension, homes, children, education, physical skills, physical attractiveness. Nearly all are or have been on the receiving end of envy.

Envy gets expressed in negative attitudes and behavior, including the behavior that studiously pretends envy is non-existent. If we perceive it accurately, being envied is evidence for a positive view of ourselves. But depressed people have such low self-esteem that they see only the hostility and indifference — being envied makes them feel worse instead of better. The other aspect of envy — malicious delight in another's misery — may be a source of pain if the person's condition has recently deteriorated. The person is likely to be aware of negative feeling, but fail to recognize that it stems from feelings of personal inferiority that are had by the envier. Instead he perceives the negative attitude as confirming "I'm worthless. I'm a failure."

4. Envy is a major factor behind the poor relationship that exists between the suicidal and the non-suicidal. His envy of us is painful for him, and our awareness of his envy is painful for us. Just as we try to be modest about our material advantages when we are around the poor, we may avoid flaunting our enjoyment of life when we are around the depressed. This is not altruistic behavior; it is not done to avoid causing the suicidal more envy and hence more pain. It is done to minimize feelings of guilt, which are often experienced by the better off in any situation involving unequals. It is also done simply because awareness of the envy of others is painful in itself. At some level we know that our happiness causes him pain, but since this is painful for us we rigorously repress awareness of this idea. That our happiness causes suicide is not a happy thought. It is one reason why we theoretically and culturally practice so much denial on the interpersonal nature of suicidal pain. It is painful for the envier and the envied to be with each other, so the envier isolates. This deprives him of coping resources and increases the probability of suicide.

Envy is part of the force behind the "just wants attention" myth. Suicidal people get a type of attention that says, "We want you to live." The non-suicidal are envious, no one has directly said this about them. People who obey the unwritten rule, "Don't talk about your pain," are envious of those who seek help. They are envious of the attention, and angry that they got no praise for following the rule. They feel that it is unfair that the rule breaker is rewarded. The management of *this* problem, being an object of envy and anger for having sought help, may place an additional burden on the help seeker.

The attitudes of many affluent people toward poverty, "It's not so bad and they could get out of it if they wanted to," have as part of their basis the uncomfortable feelings engendered by being in the envied position. The perception of inequality is painful; we often dissemble to reduce the perceived disparity. This is an exact analogue to the denial, belittlement and minimization — "Your problems really aren't that bad," — that frequently occur in counseling the suicidal. In both poverty and suicide we have the same hostile social attitude: it's your fault you are in this situation and you should be able to get out of it without seeking special and favored attention.

This type of analogy helps us see the relationship between envy and hostility a bit more clearly. Wherever there is a situation of enviers and envied — disparities of wealth, social status, physical health, educational level — there is invariably hostility. The depressed and the non-depressed, the mentally ill and the mentally healthy, and the suicidal and the non-suicidal are simply three special cases of this general relationship. Is our understanding of these situations improved by dropping the middle term in "inequality breeds envy, and envy breeds hostility"? The gain to be had by not including envy in our analysis of the plight of the suicidal, by claiming it is reducible to anger, is that it spares the non-suicidal awareness of how much they contribute to suicidal pain.

5. In the United States envy is governed by different social norms than anger. "I'm angry at Jones"; "Jones is angry at me"; and "You are angry at Smith," have a level of social acceptability that similar utterances concerning envy do not. Feelings of anger are more easily discharged, feelings of envy are not. Social norms require that we repress, or at least pretend unawareness, of both aspects of envy in ourselves and in others. This is a general social phenomena that occurs in all situations, not just those related to suicide and depression. This

general cultural denial of envy makes it additionally difficult for the suicidal and their counselors to recognize problems in coping with the pain of envy. It is uncomfortable for them to discuss their own inequalities, and consequently it is difficult for them to discuss the problems that the suicidal have with envy outside the counseling situation.

6. Our culture values fame, youth, power, wealth, beauty, and social status; the people who have it are objects of envy. It is not surprising that we should give such attention to the suicides of celebrities and teenagers from affluent communities. This is partly due to the malicious delight aspect of envy.

SHAME

We experience the pain of guilt when we believe that a specific part of our behavior is morally wrong. We may feel guilty for cheating on our taxes, or for not doing anything to help the homeless. Shame is a painful feeling about identity, rather than about a particular action. If my country does something I believe is wrong, I feel ashamed to be an American. Some people who are single are ashamed to be unmarried. If someone feels badly about the kind of person he is, as opposed to some specific act he has or has not done, he feels ashamed. An occurrence of the feeling of shame requires both the negative attitude about oneself and the real or potential exposure of one's shortcoming to others.[2]

1. Writers on depression and suicide have not recognized the extent to which shame shrouds the world of the depressed. Shame casts a pall on every experience and every attempt to look at the self. The issues that can cause feelings of shame are nearly endless: social class, economic status, housing, clothes, physical appearance, education, sexuality, areas of talent and skill, marital situations, health, problems with family and friends, and career achievement. The suicidal believe "My life is bad in every area," and it invariably follows that in every area they experience shame. Most of these pains are lacks, and each instance of self-consciousness of the lack brings a renewed feeling of shame.

Each area of our lives has a shame history: situations in the past when we felt shame, situations that cause us current feelings of shame when we remember them. One writer (Schneider, 1977, pp. 22-4) claims that feelings of shame are unexpected and cause an image of oneself to be broken. This view is too narrow. Someone who believes that his clothing is shabby or that he is overweight may be able to predict correctly feelings of shame every time he goes out in public. The depressed are especially liable to develop entrenched images of themselves as having shameful qualities. These self-images modify behavior; the depressed adapt themselves to living patterns that avoid or minimize awarenesses of feelings of shame. These coping strategies reduce pain in the short run, and usually increase it in the long run. Fear of feelings of shame is something that regulates nearly every aspect of the behavior of the depressed and non-depressed alike. Shame is a penalty for failure to maintain standards, and the standards are usually socially created norms.

The depressed and the suicidal are often lonely and inhibited. Discussions of inhibition in this context usually emphasize fear of rejection. But what is often a larger factor is the fear of fresh instances of shame. Someone who invites a guest into living conditions that he feels are shameful will feel shame whether or not his guest has a negative reaction to the conditions in the home. For the depressed nearly all aspects of the self are shameful, and each time an aspect of the self is exposed, they feel a fresh stab of shame, regardless of the reactions of others. The suicidal lead shame-drenched lives.

2. The circles of shame are vicious. Painful feelings of shame help cause people to be depressed and suicidal, these in turn become shameful aspects of the self. Being angry does not necessarily cause more anger, being envious does not necessarily cause more envy (though once we envy, we can also envy someone else's lack of envy), but, in our culture at least, shame (and envy and self-pity) are things to be ashamed about. The two common feelings of suicide are hopelessness and powerlessness; each is shameful, and this additional experience of shame adds pain on pain. A man who despairs because he feels his prospects of having a family are hopeless also feels he will never lose the feeling of shame over being wifeless and childless. To be powerless to change one's life in ways that others can is cause to feel ashamed of one's powerlessness.

3. The pain of people with a lot of shame is not made easier by general denial on the significance of shame in American culture and American suicide. Suicides of shame are said to characterize rigid cultures, where losing face is an important concept. We are less inhibited, and socially and economically mobile. But pretending shame does not exist does not make it go away; it is a basic part of human nature. In the United States it is an unnoticed and unacknowledged aspect of nearly every suicide.

Though it was not recognized as such, shame was a factor in the suicide of a friend and former roommate of mine in college. His suicide was a great shock to all of us. He was popular and had a loving, intact family. There was no substance abuse or obvious mental health problem. We talked a few weeks before his death and I congratulated him on having completed a six month tour of duty in the Marine Reserve Program. His response surprised me. He said he was disappointed, he had joined the Marines because he thought it would make a man out of him, and yet, "On the inside, I'm still the same weak guy I always was." I had not thought he was a weak person before he joined the Marines, and certainly not afterwards. But the feeling that he "wasn't a man" caused him to feel ashamed, as he did about dropping out of school a year earlier with poor grades, as he did about playing B football in high school instead of varsity, as he did about surfing seven foot waves instead of twelve foot waves, as he did about a gambling loss the day before his death. He went out with great looking girls, and in this regard had the advantage over myself and most of our friends; yet he would feel bad because there were still prettier girls with whom he could not get dates. As the reader can surmise, he was a classic example of a normal person who has the mistaken belief, "In every area of my life, I am inadequate." This thinking pattern, no level of achievement is good enough, is very common. At the time of his death he was back in school and getting good grades, but discounted that because the new school was a junior college. This type of chronic self-criticism causes pain; but besides anger, the pain includes envy, shame, and self-pity. Psychoanalysts are right in claiming that some of the self-criticisms of some depressed people are really disguised complaints about other people. But some complaints are about the self. Shame, feeling bad about who we are, is a primary source of the self-loathing in depression.

4. Shame is part of the comparative nature of suicidal pain. Some people will feel ashamed unless they get average grades in school, some will feel ashamed unless they get better than average grades, some can avoid shame only if they get the highest marks. Perfectionism often psychologically presents itself as an attempt to comply with an abstract ideal, but this is part of the denial of shame. The norms that cause pain when we do not live up to them are culturally created entities. We repress awareness of their source, and regard the norms as impersonal ideals. Perfectionism is actually an effort to be as good as or better than other people. Perfectionists, and all those susceptible to shame, measure themselves by socially defined goals. If they come up short, they feel shame. The sad part is that if they succeed, the only payoff is an avoidance of shame. Shame-bound people who avoid shame get a positive emotional payoff of, ... well ..., nothing. When envious people compete for a prize, the winner at least gets the malicious pleasure of seeing a rival lose.

A start toward relieving the feelings of shame to which perfectionists are vulnerable is to recognize that perfectionism is often abusive. If a child is always expected to be more than he is, to do better than he is capable of doing, he is liable to become extremely unhappy: "I never measure up." If he internalizes these values, then as an adult he will have high expectations for himself and others. This becomes child abuse when he practices it on his own children, self-abuse when he practices it on himself. It is not uncommon to hear people say with pride, "I have high standards." If the standards manifest themselves in abusive behavior, there is nothing to be prideful about. For the depressed the sense of having high standards can be a negative coping mechanism. It gives the person who has it a feeling of self-worth, but in the longer run engenders self-loathing.

5. One way to shame people is with accusations of immaturity. "Grow up. You should be ashamed of yourself," is widely used in the moral education of young people in the United States. This injunction is used by adults for any behavior that is disturbing or violates family or social norms. Though we do not publicly talk about shame, it is used to mold the personality of virtually every person in our country. Like "Snap out of it"; "Grow up," says that immediate personal transformation is possible and desirable. The demand to become instantaneously more mature is impossible, and, because of its

impossibility, abusive. The injunction's real purpose is compliance, not the development of maturity. Compliance can be done immediately, and will be rewarded with approval. The real content of "Grow up. You should be ashamed of yourself," is "Shut up. Stuff your feelings. Do not disturb others. Do not be a child. Be obedient." It is an axiom of contemporary family therapy that children who are not allowed to be children usually grow up to be limited and dysfunctional as adults. The conclusion is inescapable: "Grow up," stunts emotional growth.

It is more for practical than theoretical reasons that I resist the position of Maris (1981, Chapter 3) and Hillman (p. 73) that the primary cause of suicide is the accumulation of developmental deficits or incomplete transformations. Life transitions are significant in the causation of suicide, and often do leave us with lasting pain and with deficiencies in coping resources. But suicide involves other pains and coping problems (e.g. trauma, social prejudice against the suicidal) that cannot easily be fit into this model. An example is an older teenage boy who attempted suicide twice. His problems included the transition from adolescence to adulthood and the developmental issue of separation from the family. But they also included the father's leaving the home when he was very young, an accident a few years later that left him with a disability that in turn caused educational and social problems, being in a street incident where a friend was shot and left paralyzed, and the difficulties of life in a very poor section of New York City. These pain and coping resource issues are outside the normal problems of personal development.

The problem with the positions of Maris and Hillman is that in contemporary America "developmental deficit" and "You should be ashamed of yourself," are inextricably associated. It is impossible for us to think of the first without also thinking of the second. "Developmental deficit" in colloquial terms is "immaturity," and immaturity, since no one cares to see that it is usually caused by non-voluntary conditions outside the self, is regarded as a shameful condition. The norm of our culture is that developmental problems are the moral fault of the person who has them. This doctrine is false. All children and at least most adults do not have developmental deficits because of problems within them, but because of problems that exist in the outside world. "Oral fixation" can be regarded as a problem in personal development; is it the moral fault of people who were emotionally deprived as children? Most addicts in New York start drinking and drugging when they are adolescents. When they begin recovery programs they still have adolescent personality traits. This is an incomplete transformation, but the real shame lies with the social circumstances of their childhoods.

During transitions children, teenagers, adults, and the elderly are liable to suffer both more pain and reduced resources. "Unwilling or unable to make the transition" is a blame-the-victim position. In nearly every case the additional difficulties have causes that lie outside the person. Yet in nearly every instance the victim is blamed by others and is expected to blame himself for "his" problem. The accumulated sense of shame adds pain on pain.

6. The position that mental illness and substance abuse are diseases has had a beneficial effect on removing these conditions from the arena of moral judgment. From the standpoint of the self, the value of these positions is that they reduce the pain of shame. Involuntarism hopes to make a similar contribution toward changing the social idea that it is shameful to be suicidal.

SELF-PITY

A barrier to progress in the treatment of depression and the prevention of suicide is the unpopularity of pity as a subject matter for intellectual and scientific inquiry. Pity toward oneself is nearly always a component of suicidal pain; we need to learn all we can about its structure and dynamics. The absence of theory about pity is peculiar; more peculiar yet is the way self-pity is usually dealt with in counseling practice: clients and patients are verbally rapped on the knuckles and told "Don't do it." Most counselors with this policy on self-pity also hold the view that the way to deal with bad feelings is to get them out and look at them. This contradiction can only retard efforts toward recovery.

1. The principal feeling in pity is the experience of sorrow at the recognition of another's suffering. Pity is not without some virtues: it takes us outside of absorption with our own affairs, it gives us a larger appreciation for the experiences of others, it may motivate us to take action to relieve hardship, and we may find solace for our own

suffering. Pity is a basic part of human nature. The common methods by which we express pity in our culture — phone calls to telethons, furtively giving a quarter to a panhandler — provide us with emotional outlets that are shallow and brief. We pay a cultural and personal price for the repression of this emotion, and for not finding healthier and more constructive ways to express it.

2. Historically, a basic part of pity is the relationship of condescension: if x pities y, then x believes he is better than y. When we pity a person, we pity a condition, such as homelessness or disability, that causes him suffering; his pitifulness means that he is worse off than ourselves. A common theme of drama is to take larger than life characters we would ordinarily envy and show them to be pitiful, so that we can have a feeling of superiority over them.

Community based fund raising drives in the United States often exploit the sense of social inequality that is part of pity. Benefactors of such campaigns are regarded and self-regarded as being above average in intellect, education, sophistication, affluence, and virtue. This reason for responding to appeals to aid the unfortunate, that you will have the pleasant feeling of superiority, is very different from two others. The first is based on self-interest: invest in drug programs and crime that affects you will be reduced. The second proceeds from a concept of human rights: all children have a right to decent housing. These types of appeals — the indigent have a right to aid, or it is in your interest to help them — are not part of pity. Pity does not imply that the pitied have a practical or moral right to our aid. Indeed, assistance motivated by pity is *not* obligatory or self-interested. Actions done from pity are morally above the call of duty. To act out of pity not only implies that one is better than the recipient, it also implies that one is morally better than those who have the means but do not contribute.

Both the advantages and the shortcomings of this approach are clear. The community appeal based on pity does raise money and the money is used for worthy causes. But in the longer view it could be argued that these charitable activities prop up an inadequate social system and inhibit social progress. The neediest members of the community have their demands for justice placated by the unearned gifts of charity, not by social services that adequately provide for basic human needs in education, nutrition, healthcare, and housing. To parallel the problems of the relationship between the suicidal and the non-suicidal, how can we hope for a long-term reduction of suffering if we employ mechanisms that depend upon moral and social distinctions between the in-group and the out-group?

3. Besides being given or withheld, pity can be accepted or rejected. Pity's acceptance will be discussed below. Pity's rejection is common in our culture. "I don't want your pity," may mean "I'm not inferior"; "I'm not your inferior"; "You're not superior"; "You're not my superior." Sometimes pity is rejected not on the basis of disagreement about superiority/inferiority issues, but because the object of pity claims that he is not suffering as his pitiers suppose. He may say his condition is not causing him pain, or that his suffering is primarily due to social prejudice concerning the condition, and secondarily due to the condition itself.

4. Pity is reserved for major misfortunes. We may pity people because they are orphans, because they have been sexually assaulted, or because they had a son die in war. We do not pity people, except in sarcasm, for losing a dress at the dry cleaners, for having a car battery stolen, for stubbing a toe.

5. Pity implies that neither the pitier nor the pitied is responsible for the suffering. If I cause an accident that injures someone else, I feel guilt, not pity. I will feel pity toward the person only if I had no involvement in the events leading to his suffering. My heart goes out to children who live in welfare hotels; their situation is no fault of their own. When I read that someone on Wall Street has been sentenced to prison for insider trading, I may feel the malicious side of envy, but my sentiments are pitiless. The objects of pity are people to whom fate has been cruel. They did not cause their suffering and they are helpless to do anything about it. Two ways in which we withhold pity are belittlement and denial of powerlessness. We issue sarcastic "poor babies" if someone seems to be asking for pity for a problem that seems to be too small to justify it, and we ignore the pleas of healthy-looking beggars because we feel their poverty is their own fault, and they could change if they applied themselves.

6. Pity says I'm not. If x pities y for condition c, then x lacks c. If y accepts or asks for x's pity, y acknowledges that x does not have c. I may ask for sympathy from a fellow sufferer, but I don't expect pity.

7. Pity has its pleasures. It enables us to feel that we are better than others. To see unfortunates as being at the mercy of events beyond their control gives us the feelings of freedom and powerfulness. This positive feeling, that we are not helpless, is what we experience when we take action to relieve their suffering. Pity puts some distance between ourselves and those who have suffered losses to which we are vulnerable; it allays fears and anxieties. We feel glad it has not happened to us. If we feel pity after the misfortune has occurred, then we were not to blame for the conditions that led to it. And pity is a "we" activity, something families and social groups can enjoy together. The fact that pity makes us feel better is the source of one of its disquieting aspects; we are sometimes aware of an uncomfortable suspicion that we are exploiting the suffering of others for our own benefit.

Though pity is something that is better to give than receive, receiving does have its benefits. The first is a sense of validation. To be pitied is to be told that you and your pain are real, that you are not alone, that you are worthy of attention. Pity may not be the nicest form of attention, but it is better than none at all. To be pitied is to be told that your condition is not your fault, and that you did not deserve it. Since your suffering is also not the fault of the pitier, it means that at least some part of the universe is not conspiring against you. And pity provides hope. Someone does not suffer as I do. Someone freer, more powerful, and more knowing may be able to take action that will improve my situation. In our personal lives, in social situations, and in public life we are besieged with requests to take pity on unfortunates. Arousing pity gets results. (It also evokes resentment. Since there are more requests than we can respond to, we dissemble with "Why me, I didn't cause this problem"; "It's not really that bad"; "They could help themselves if they wanted to"; "Others are better able to help, I've got problems of my own"; and "Nothing I can do will matter, It's pointless for me to get involved." Pity's susceptibility to manipulation and abuse contributes to the widespread contempt we have for it. Some of our suspicion is based on reality, but much of its energy comes from the familiar prejudice that members of the out-group are to be regarded with suspicion.) To be pitied is to have one's sorrow shared by someone who may be in a position to reduce one's pain. It is better than nothing at all. The frequently heard (and false) expression, "Self-pity is a worthless emotion," causes us to overlook the important and complex roles that pity has in the economy of ordinary life.

8. It is not difficult to see why pity, even without the abusive appeals for it, is unpopular within American culture. We wish to deny the existence of suffering, deny vulnerability to loss, deny the existence of social classes, deny limitations on personal power and freedom. Our culture is publicly committed to egalitarianism. This makes pity, and consequently self-pity, an unpleasant topic in conversation and in therapy. "Feeling sorry" for others is derided as a sign of weakness, an inhibition on narcissistic devotion to self-improvement. (One of the alleged advantages of dedicated self-improvement is that it sets a good example for the pitiful.) But every form of repression has its price. We lack clear, socially acceptable, constructive, and healthy ways to discharge our sorrow at the sufferings of others.

9. *Self-pity* is not reserved for major misfortune. We can pity ourselves for losses, disappointments, and limitations of every sort. We do not pity others for not having a date on Saturday night, for losing twenty dollars, or for being five feet six inches tall instead of six feet, but we can do it to ourselves in a big way. One reason for this disparity is that pity's strength varies according to our proximity to the suffering. My feelings are strong if I learn that someone I know has AIDS, less if someone I know tells me about a person with AIDS that he knows, and less yet for an account of a person with AIDS that I read about in the newspaper. My own misfortunes, over much smaller events, can cause me greater levels of pain than my awareness of these three tragedies. Our recognition of our own suffering is much more vivid than our appreciation for the suffering of others. This disparity explains why self-pitiers are the objects of sarcasm and belittlement: their misfortune is not large enough to arouse pity in others. (It may, however, arouse sympathy from fellow sufferers.) Self-pitiers can get resentful after being rebuked, and with some justification. Their misfortunes are often not enough to satisfy publicly accepted criteria for being pitied, but it is possible that their critics would suffer self-pity if the misfortunes happened to them.

10. Self-pity has an aura of futility. There is a useful purpose in presenting ourselves to others as being pitiful: we may get some help for our suffering. A self-presentation of pitifulness seems to be redundant; how can I help myself more than I can already help myself?

11. Self-pity entails a false view of the self. In self-pity, as in normal pity, we are more aware of the suffering that is the object of our feeling than we are aware of our act of pitying. Since our own suffering is felt intensely, we are not aware that in pitying ourselves there is a part of us that is saying "I'm not ... " and "I'm better than ... " Losses or disappointments related to social status frequently precipitate episodes of self-pity, and it is the part of us that does not want to accept the loss or disappointment that pities the part of us that suffers. By pitying the fact that we have suffered the fate of the inferior, the part that wants to be in the superior position hangs on to its existence and hangs on to the values and standards appropriate to its station. Consciously we know we have lost self-esteem and self-image, at some unconscious level we can retain them. This denial and distancing helps us cope with pain. Self-pity says "I'm a better person than what I am." This attitude is often seen in the depressed.

The part of us that receives self-pity contributes to the deception. The existence of pity implies that the sufferer is helpless; he is not responsible for causing his agony and he is powerless to change it. Just as some angers are righteous angers, self-pity often has a sense of righteousness. Others may have caused the pain, fate may have been cruel, but I'm not blameworthy. Besides being free of guilt, the self-pitier has the comfort of believing nothing he can do will improve the situation. If we are to go forward in life, losses require that we make changes in ourselves and/or our environment so that we can progress into an improved condition. A part of us fears these changes and self-pity enables us to resist making them. We see our plight as being like that of the starving child in a desolate third world country; we are powerless to improve things, so there is no point in trying. Whereas receiving pity may mobilize some assistance for ourselves, being self-pitied contributes to inertia and stagnation. When we present ourselves to others as being pitiful, we want help. When we maintain a pitiful posture toward ourselves, we may snarlingly reject outside help. Self-pity is a coping mechanism for the fear of change.

It is important to recognize that these feelings — I'm not responsible, it's forces beyond my control — are accepted by both the part that pities and the part that accepts pity. These feelings reduce pain in the short run. As with shock and denial, self-pity has a certain usefulness in coping with loss. Like denial, self-pity can seem absurd to outsiders.

People stay in self-pity because it reduces some pain and the contradictory parts of it are not accessible to consciousness.

Self-pitiers often have a sense of self-esteem that relies heavily on being better than others. If they don't feel "I'm better than ... " they don't feel good. When they fall on hard times, they fall hard. To like oneself in a way that does not depend on comparative judgments is a difficult concept for self-pitiers. What they have is not so much a false view of the self, but a false method of judging the self.

12. Self-pity is a part of normal psychology; it will be helpful to locate it as it can occur in ordinary life. The Kubler-Ross theory of bereavement holds that patients with terminal illnesses may go through a five stage process prior to death: denial, anger, bargaining, depression, and acceptance. (Kubler-Ross, 1969) The stages of this process, which may not be orderly, occur not just to people before death, but also characterize human response after death, and before and after losses of all sorts. Our reactions to divorce, losing a job, or moving from one state to another are likely to include at least several of these stages. The theory holds that each of these stages has a useful purpose, and we go through them as part of an overall process that is healthy and constructive. This theory has been criticized in some of its details, but its overall structure of decomposing grief into a number of components has helped a great many people.

(Pitying and grieving are different activities and about different kinds of objects. Grief is over loss, something that no longer exists. Pity is over suffering, something that exists and looks as if it will continue to exist. When I move to a new town I grieve the loss of old friends and pity myself for my current state of friendlessness.)

My argument is that self-pity is an important part of depression, and, on the Kubler-Ross model, depression is an inevitable part of the process of life. After a loss we suffer. At a certain point, we become aware of our suffering. One kind of awareness of a lack produces shame. Another type of awareness of a lack produces envy. A third type of awareness — comparing ourselves to what we were or would have liked to have been — produces self-pity. A fourth type of awareness of suffering produces anger. When we have these four kinds of awareness of our suffering, and practice denial on parts of them, we have depression. If depression is a normal reaction to loss, then each of its components is a normal and inevitable part of ordinary life. The relative amounts of each factor in depression and in grief will vary according to the individual and the circumstances. Given our cultural prejudices, it is inevitable that grievers of a suicide victim will suffer more shame than grievers of someone who died of pneumonia in old age. If we lose a parent when we are young we are likely to suffer much more envy than if we lose a parent when we are old. Grievers who compare themselves before their loss to themselves after their loss will suffer self-pity. These three reactions to death are inevitable; people do not choose to have them. Envy, shame, and self-pity are normal reactions to suffering. All three are culturally shameful, so we practice denial on them. Denial on pain, which is a more accurate description that "turned inward," is a major cause of depression.

13. Normal pity is the feeling of sorrow upon learning of the suffering of another. For us to reflect on our own troubles and have no emotional reaction would be very strange. Just as we can be involuntarily moved to pity someone else, self-pity can be an involuntary response to an awareness of our own problems. Self-pity is part of the natural world. It is present in bereavement, in all forms of mental illness and substance abuse, in the aftermath of illness, accident, and trauma, in people who suffer the losses of aging, and in all people who are suicidal. Verbal rebukes and a deprecating attitude toward self-pity increase pain, decrease coping resources, and make recovery longer and more difficult.

Severe self-pity is not something in which one "indulges." "Indulges" is a moral term: it implies the freedom to do otherwise. Normal people indulge in chocolate cake or a few too many drinks on New Year's Eve. Alcoholics and bulimics do not overindulge; their diseases cause them to chronically or periodically overconsume. Without a recovery program, they have no alternative. The chronic or periodic self-pity of depression is the same. It happens when people have massive pain and do not have alternative ways to cope with it. This kind of self-pity is not an indulgence, it is an involuntary reaction of the desperate.

In the short run self-pity can be a useful coping resource. However, just as relying on being pitied may not be the best way to get one's needs met, self-pity can devolve from being a normal response to loss into a negative coping mechanism. In the long run, self-pity can become habitual, addictive, compulsive. Like drugs, alcohol, gambling, shopping binges, and sexual promiscuity, self-pity can become a palliative that is repeatedly applied to chronically and progressively worsening problems. It is a coping mechanism that, in the long-term, can make things worse rather than better. Healthy ways of dealing with pain are not learned; alienation from others increases. As the pain increases, use of the coping mechanism becomes automatic and deeply entrenched. The longer it goes on, the harder it is to get out of it.

The stance of self-pity is the same stance from which grandiose fantasy develops as a second negative coping mechanism. Fantasies of power, happiness, approval, and adventure are ways to cope with stress, boredom, insecurity, and pain. In modest amounts fantasy is a nice part of normal life. But it can be also used as a way to cope with suffering, and it too can become habitual, addictive, compulsive. Comparing fantasy to reality provides fresh fuel for the engines of self-pity. The longer reality remains unpleasant, the more hopeless it seems, and the more heavily the sufferer relies on self-pity and grandiose fantasy as pain-coping devices. Little mental energy is left for constructive tasks that might bring genuine improvement.

14. Even though at an unconscious level self-pity contains the pleasurable feeling of "I'm better than this," it is consciously the pain of "poor me." It is a pain on top of the painful things for which one pities oneself. Two more pains are then added: society's moral disapproval of self-pity and the victim's internalization of that disapproval. This disapproval is unfair; self-pity is a natural and involuntary response to loss. It is no less of a healthy coping mechanism than the other components of grief. The prejudice against self-pitiers that expresses itself in sneering contempt has the same structure as similar prejudices against other out groups: disowned fear of our own vulnerability. Fear of vulnerability to self-pity is sometimes coped with by an indignant claim to be invulnerable: "I'm *not* a self-pitier." Because the extra pains of moral disapproval are unfair, self-pitiers actually do merit pity: they suffer unjust social cruelty that they did not bring upon themselves. We should feel sorry for people who feel sorry for themselves.

15. Self-pity in ordinary life passes by itself in a few moments, hours, or days. Self-pity caused by profound loss may take much longer to dissipate. The self-pity that is part of chronic depression or suicidal ideation should not be left to heal itself; that happy day may never come. As with other aspects of depression, we need to overcome denial, obtain insight, reduce pain, replace poor coping mechanisms with better

ones, and develop an awareness for early warning signs of relapse. Overcoming self-pity means letting go, sometimes painfully, of ideas that are not working, and trudging toward a better future.

The part of us that pities is the self we once were, or once thought we could have been. This part provides a sense of hope, but it is a sense of hope that lives in the past. It sounds cruel, but overcoming self-pity means killing the hope that is hopeless. An example of this is in the literature and support groups for adult children of alcoholics and other types of dysfunctional families. The people who join these groups pity themselves for not getting adequate parenting when they were children. As children they desperately hoped that somehow their families could be made whole and happy, and elements of this hope are carried into adulthood. They may find themselves once again in dysfunctional families where they try to "solve" the original problem. Overcoming denial means accepting that they are never going to get the parenting they once hoped for, and that the original family is never going to become what they would like it to be. As they let go of old ideas, their grief for their loss becomes unfrozen and they are able to move forward. Self-pity over these issues lessens, and they learn better ways to cope with their pain.

GRANDIOSITY

The depressed are often subject to grandiose ideation and desire. Some psychologists suggest that depression and grandiosity are in some ways mirrors of each other, both being types of "narcissistic disturbances." There doubtlessly is some connection between compulsively thinking you are worse than others and compulsively imagining you are their better. Grandiosity and depression are both partly caused by conscious and unconscious feelings of not receiving enough care, attention, and respect. These feelings are often legitimate. Positive attention is a human need. Depressed people can usually find periods of their lives when they did not get appreciation that was needed and deserved. After the onset of depression, victims then suffer reduced respect and attention. This in turn causes grandiosity and depression to get still worse. Grandiose ideation is a pain-coping strategy; reality is or has been deficient in respect and attention, and fantasy provides what is lacking in the outside world. The admiration received in fantasy has to be extreme; it must compensate for the fact that its pleasure is counterfeit and lasts only as long as the fantasy. Grandiosity contains the "I'm better than this," of self-pity, it contains envy, and when it ends, it ends with feelings of shame.

Grandiosity is caused not just by lack of positive attention in the victim's immediate environment, but also by the social oppression suffered for being suicidal or depressed. Grandiosity is frequently a consequence of prejudice:

> In real life the despised person may not find the gratification of status. But ... In his dreams he is strong, handsome, wealthy. He has grand clothes, social position, influence, and the cars he drives are powerful. Daydreams are a common response to deprivation. (Allport, p. 147)

Allport does not mention that this particular result of prejudice becomes a reason for heaping yet more abuse upon the oppressed. "Grandiose" and "living in a fantasy world" are used as epithets of scorn and ridicule. Social prejudice causes increased levels of grandiosity. Increased grandiosity causes its victims to suffer yet more social disapproval.

Social disapproval of the grandiosity of the depressed is unfair for two reasons. First, this type of grandiosity is an involuntary response to personal and social pain. Second, the real force behind social disapproval of grandiosity is not due to any negative social consequences that follow from someone's grandiose fantasy, but because grandiosity arouses two negative feelings in the non-grandiose. The grandiosity of depression is on a continuum with normal daydreaming, and when we revile it, we revile a disowned and vulnerable part of ourselves. The shame that concludes episodes of grandiosity involves the pain of comparing fantasy to reality, and the pain caused by the internalization of the social norm that says grandiosity is shameful. This second negative feeling explains why there is a stronger social sanction against expressing grandiose ideation and feelings then there is against parallel expressions concerning depression. It is harder to say, "I have tendencies toward grandiosity," than it is to say, "I have periods of depression." For most of us, at least, it is less uncomfortable to talk with someone who believes he is worse than us than it is to talk to someone who believes he is our better. The resentment expressed by "Who does he think he is?" indicates that the grandiose affront us in a way the depressed do not.

Grandiosity negatively interacts with the other components of depression. Like self-pity that becomes chronic, what is initially an apparently harmless coping mechanism ends up adding pain on pain. The shame attached to grandiosity makes it hard to talk about in counseling and in ordinary life. To not talk about grandiosity deprives us of a window of access to the pain that causes depression and windows of access to the shame, envy, self-pity, and anger with which grandiosity interacts. We can reduce the pain of the suicidal by reducing the unfair social disapproval of grandiosity. Grandiosity in the suicidal can be seen as a cry for help: in a distinct way it directly tells us to improve real life resources for attention and care.

Grandiosity expresses itself not just in private fantasy but also in attitudes and beliefs about oneself vis-à-vis the rest of the human community. Many suicidal people believe that their situation is so difficult, complex, profound, and unique that few mortals have the cognitive resources to provide them with assistance. Ordinary human beings have nothing to offer them. This feeling — "I'm better. I'm special. No one sees the things that are really important more clearly than I," — is a pain-coping strategy. The belief "I'm better than the average person," helps people of all ages and all emotional conditions feel better about themselves. We acquire it from the family and from the "We're better," of peers, schools, professional affiliation, and social class. In ordinary life the feeling is pleasurable and greatly helps to reduce personal and social anxieties. Any time in life that we find ourselves in an uncomfortable social situation, we can quickly move to the aloof position of "I'm better than these people," and start feeling better immediately. As the depressed and the suicidal decline from ordinary life into their private horrors, they use their pain-coping resources with increasing levels of desperation and compulsion. "Me and my problems are ordinary," is, at whatever level they are at, always more painful than "I'm a superior sort of person and so are my problems." These people resist the idea that ordinary people can understand their problems because it involves admitting that they have ordinary problems, and hence, are ordinary people themselves. Grandiosity also contributes to a form of denial that helps cause depression: events that cause pain to lesser people cannot hurt me.

This type of grandiosity rules out ninety-nine percent of the population as a pain-coping resource and is a major cause of suicide. People with "terminal uniqueness" resist all suggestions for treatment programs, and compulsively faultfind if placed in programs they believe are beneath them. The arcane theories of psychiatry, of course, do nothing to dispel the grandiose delusion of "ordinary people can't help me." Grandiosity is abetted by popular views about the romance of suicide and by romantically inclined suicide literature. Hillman's rhapsodies about the greater individuality of the suicidal sustain rather than reduce a significant factor in suicidal pain.

Involuntarism, however, argues that it is the accumulated and aggregated pains of ordinary life and the deficiency of ordinary pain-coping resources that cause suicide. Suicidal pain is decomposable into thousands of ordinary pains that are no different than those suffered by billions of other people. Whatever the pain aggregate is, large parts of it are perfectly intelligible to the average citizen. The actions that average people take to cope with their problems are actions that the suicidal can take to cope with theirs.

The "We're better," sentiment that many groups have is a pleasurable feeling. It is a feeling that entails "I'm better." When believers of "I'm better," suffer depression, they also suffer grandiosity. Since the pain, stigma, and shame of depression contribute to separation from the group, this type of grandiosity leads to strong feelings of loneliness. The grandiose, of course, regard their loneliness as having noble and other grandiose qualities, but loneliness is simply loneliness; there is nothing noble or grand about it. Though this loneliness is no more voluntary than any other aspect of depression, the grandiose do not see it that way. Since they have exaggerated conceptions of their volitional capacities, as they do about other parts of the self, they are especially vulnerable to the "It's your own fault," internal and external criticisms of their depression and their loneliness. Depression and grandiosity contribute to group disaffiliation, and group disaffiliation in turn adds pain, reduces resources, and thereby contributes to suicide.

Decomposing Depression

One of the painful components of depression is the sense of confusion, uncertainty, and self-ignorance that is expressed by the thought, "What's going on with me? Why am I in so much pain?" To read about technically complex theories in psychiatry or brain physiology usually does little to help relieve this distressing condition. I believe that a good way for someone to reach a personal understanding of his depression is to make a list of things about which he is envious, ashamed, self-pitying, angry, guilty, and worried. The entries on the list may take the form "I'm envious of so-and-so who has u, ... I'm ashamed of v, ... I pity myself for w, ... I am angry with so-and-so for x, ... I feel guilty about y, ... I'm worried about z." The list should include things that are small and trivial. It should include the past, especially the period during the onset of the depression, as well as the present. Some areas to consider are family, friends, romance, sex, health, physical appearance, money, work, housing, transportation, education, recreation.

This is a painful chore. It is hard to get started and hard to keep going. You will probably wish to spread it out over several days or weeks. Thoroughness is a good goal, but it is unlikely, and unnecessary, that a depressed person will be able to self-identify quickly and completely all the objects of these unpleasant feelings.

In contemporary America denial has become a general purpose concept that is both easier to use than the complex concepts of psychiatry and, for the purposes of understanding depression, more accurate. We deny awareness of part or all of a painful idea or emotion because at some unconscious level we believe that this denial is less painful than its alternative. Depressed people (and to a lesser degree, everyone else) practice denial not just on anger toward loved ones, but also on painful feelings in all aspects of their lives. Unarticulated resentment, envy, and self-pity about job or housing situations can be regarded simply as what they are; we do not have to trace them back to early childhood to find out their real meaning.

Denial causes depressed people to be unaware of much of their envy, shame, self-pity, anger, guilt and anxiety.[3] If we take a broader view of the causes of depression, and do not restrict it to just a few forms of anger or guilt, we can provide the depressed and their counselors with a greater range of treatment options. What we are envious of can be easier to recognize than what we angry about; shame can be easier to talk about than guilt. Denial, which in severe depression is rigid and strong, can be broken down gradually. Much of the denial has a structure that is no more complex than the phenomenon of pain on pain. We avoid acknowledging envy because doing so would cause two pains: the envy and the feeling that it is shameful to be envious.

A severe form of depression involves an inner experience of profound depersonalization. Victims report to counselors that they feel like empty robots and that, as far as they can tell, they have no feelings at all. Though these statements are honest efforts to describe a horribly barren emotional life, they unfortunately usually provoke a scornful response, "Of course you've got feelings. Everybody has feelings." Since denial is rigidly involuntary in severe depression, this type of response is unfair and adds pain on pain.

The first emotional reaction to overcoming denial on bad feelings, and to decomposing the pain into its numerous components, is likely to be strong anxiety. The turmoil of anxiety can be more uncomfortable than the deadness of depression, and is part of the reason why depressed people stay in depressed conditions. This anxiety does not last forever, and it is a sign of progress and change. An underlying factor in this turmoil is that the chronic depressive has to find a new non-depressed identity. This is more apparent on the broader view of depression. Anger and guilt involve specific actions in which the self has wronged the world or the world has wronged the self. But shame, self-pity and grandiosity involve basic senses of the kind of person we are, have been, or wish to be. To leave an old identity is frightening. It is in important to keep in mind that the transition is gradual; the decomposition of the pain of depression is not a dramatic insight approach. It takes a long time for entrenched ideas to fade away. Personal change is slow. Decomposing the pain of depression is not intended to be a single coping resource: any depressed person making out these lists is advised to make use of some type of supportive counseling.

Normalization

If the large and obscure thing of depression is decomposed into many specific things, then the perplexity over the question "Why am I in so much pain?' tends to dissipate. Decomposition locates the depressed person's pain with real objects in the real world. There is nothing mysterious about being envious of people with blond hair, or being angry with how you were treated on a job ten years ago. A benefit to decomposition is its normalization effect. The severely depressed often believe "I am just too weird. I am inherently defective. I will never be normal." Complex psychiatric theories do nothing to discourage this belief. Yet just about every individual element of a suicidal person's pain is something that is had by other people. People with suicidal pain are in a condition that the average person does not have for most of his life. But their pain is nothing more than a larger than average aggregate of ordinary pains. Depressed people will cease being depressed if we reduce their ordinary pains and supply them with ordinary coping resources. Depressed people are simply ordinary people with greater than average amounts of normal pain and/or less than average amounts of normal pain-coping resources.

Once the list is in progress, the person can review it and ask himself two questions: "How important is this for my happiness?" and "What modest steps can I take to reduce the pain that this feeling is causing me?" The pain of some of these feelings will lessen as soon as they are held up to the light of day. Plenty of people with blond hair are unhappy, and there are plenty of happy people who are not blonds. Given our culture's ideals of beauty, blonds have an edge in attractiveness, but it is not one that makes or breaks happiness. Most of us have many modest steps we can take to improve physical attractiveness; taking these steps will in small ways reduce the pain that envy of other people's attractiveness causes us. The person who envies wealth and pities himself for being chronically broke will realize that some of his pain can be reduced if he saves up and maintains a small bank balance. People who normally have a thousand dollars in the bank, or normally have on hand several changes of clean clothes, will normally have different states of mind than those who do not.

Some things on the list, initially at least, will leave the depressed person feeling stumped; the item is important to happiness and nothing can be done to reduce its pain. An example might be "I pity myself because my father died when I was a child." The strategy is to let these go for the present, and to focus in the beginning on the easiest and most manageable feelings. Concentrating attention on the many areas where progress can be made will itself lessen the painful obsessions with major problems. Work in areas that are amenable to change will bring significant relief from the pain of depression. Modest steps that can help with difficult areas — in our example it might be joining a bereavement group, or volunteer work with a child who also lost a parent — may begin to suggest themselves as the person gains confidence and experience with pain reduction activities.

Depression and the various stages of suicidal ideation and behavior occur when certain pain thresholds are breached. With time, pain can be reduced and on-going coping resources added so that victims may remain under these thresholds. The major pains of life cannot be made to vanish magically, but as the painfulness of some of their components are reduced, and as some of the pain on pain phenomena are reduced, the massive pain of depression will eventually lift. Some pain will still be left. I lost 10 years of my life, from age 25 to age 35, to chronic severe suicidal depression. I did not attempt suicide, but I thought about it nearly every day, and some days it was about all I thought about. That 10 year nightmare was the largest pain of my life, and it still causes me pain. I still feel some shame in talking about it in some situations even in general terms; some aspects are shameful to talk about it almost any situation. I still have envy for people who are enjoying that period of their lives. I still feel some self-pity; it was a horror I did not deserve. Each of these pains is complex; when you envy someone the enjoyment of 10 years of life, you envy a lot of things. The nightmare is fortunately over, I have not suffered depression for a number of years. I have worked to gradually reduce envy, shame, self-pity, fear, anger, guilt, and anxiety. My coping resources are stronger. I have even partly given up the belief that it was a "lost" 10 years, since I recognize that many good things did happen to me during that period.

Overcoming denial, admitting and then accepting that one has a painful condition, reduces part of the hurt. The energy that goes into denial is released, and the condition is regarded with less shame. Acceptance of pain provides a sense of having a more accurate and less fearful grasp of reality. Acceptance of parts of oneself means being able to see others more clearly: to recognize that others have a problem with envy helps reduce the pain of recognizing it in oneself. Denial is a coping device of ordinary life that has gone awry in depression. It works to reduce pain in the short run, but when it becomes blindly compulsive it can keep us trapped in perpetually painful conditions. When we are in a stuck position, the only way out may be to accept some of the pains that cause the condition. We have developed unhealthy mental and physical habits; we need to gradually replace them with healthier habits.

A place to begin changing habits is with anxiety. Pick out some small things on your list of worries and take action to reduce the discomfort they cause. We live in a culture where many people believe that it is not good to "let things get to you." (This is usually said when your worry is starting to annoy someone else — the speaker's solution to his discomfort at your anxiety is to tell you that it is good for you to repress your feeling.) This strategy of denial may work sometimes for some people, but if you have depression it is not working for you. You will suffer less pain if you improve your ability to recognize stressful situations, and your habits about responding to them.

One form of denial is "I don't care." "I don't care," reduces the pains of envy and shame. Acutely suicidal people may involuntarily find themselves with an "I don't care," attitude about their continued existence. They have lost the ability to reduce their pain, they are frustrated at their powerlessness to improve their condition, they are very afraid. In this context not caring about whether one lives or dies is an effort to reduce pain. It does have some very limited ability to do this, as it does when used in smaller situations. ("A dent in my new car? Oh well, no big deal. It still runs fine.") As with other coping resources, "I don't care," may be harmless in small doses in some situations, but when it becomes compulsive and desperate it turns into a negative coping mechanism. It is a habit like any other, and with time it can be turned around.

To repress self-pity does not help; it is a normal part of our emotional response to loss, and leads on to a next stage. Getting out of self-pity means recognizing both a certain level of grandiosity in the part that is doing the pitying, and also an element of magical thinking in the unconscious belief that somehow the injustice can be instantly righted, and all the pain can be made non-existent. The things we pity ourselves for can be seen as wants in the past or present. We can identify the type of want — health, family, housing — and take small steps to improve our current situations in some of these areas.

Guilt is an unpleasant emotion. It can contribute to the bewilderment and depersonalization of depression when we practice denial on both its large and small instances. As religion recognizes, acts of atonement are direct ways to reduce the pain that guilt causes. You can do something good for the person or thing you believe you have wronged, or, if that person or thing is not accessible, you can do some good for some worthy recipient in your present environment. This does not make the sense of guilt instantly vanish, but over time it does make it less painful. The post-act of atonement pain is less than the pre-act of atonement pain.

Depressed people are prone to relapses of depressive feelings. Giving up the single cause approach to depression and suicide provides us with a very different approach to the problem of vulnerability to relapses. The relapses are often caused by resurgences of envy, resentment, self-pity and anxiety. The broader approach to depression can be quite effective as a self-monitoring method to identify what is happening and what can be done when a recurrence threatens. The formerly depressed need to continue working on recovery in every painful area of their lives, not just on a single factor.

Religion often recommends constructive involvement with people who are less well off as a coping resource for personal despair. This advice is never found in theoretical books on the psychology, biochemistry, cognitive distortions, or romantic individuality of depression and suicide. Given these views on the causes of depression — anger turned inward, serotonin deficit, defective logic, incomplete transformations — there is no reason to suppose that working with others would be helpful. An analysis of depression that includes envy, self-pity, and shame makes it apparent why religion is correct, and the therapeutic prescriptions of contemporary theory are incomplete. Depressed people need to learn new ways to cope with all aspects of the pains of envy, self-pity, and shame, and working with people who are less fortunate is a practical and effective way to do this. It provides depressed people with more accurate views of themselves and the world, it improves habits of behavior, and it leads to a reordering of personal and social values. To become a pain-coping resource for others is a uniquely valuable educational experience. Working with others is not easy, and results do not come quickly, but it is effective and lasting. Depression, grandiosity, envy, shame, self-pity, anger turned inward, anxiety, and denial are all lonely ways to try to cope with pain. Working with others is an alternative.

The method of decomposition is not a temporary band-aid. It breaks down denial, processes pent-up ugly feelings, changes habits, and serves as a warning system for relapses. In time these strategies at pain reduction become habitual, and thereby become a basic part of the person's coping resources. The aggregate pain approach to depression in the individual is a lot like its approach to suicide prevention in society as a whole: chip away on any available front.

All of the components and mechanisms of depression are involuntary efforts to avoid more pain. For non-depressed people these mechanisms are simply ways to avoid pain. For the depressed these mechanisms avoid pain in the short run and become self-defeating in the longer term; they end up adding pain on pain. There is nothing bad in the depressed or the suicidal. With all of their being, they are doing the best they can to stay alive.

CHAPTER SEVEN

GROUNDWORK FOR RECOVERY:

PART I

Most Suicides are Self-Prevented

One and four-tenths percent of all deaths are officially recorded as suicides. An allowance for underreporting would put the actual suicide rate at two percent of all deaths. Let us estimate that an additional 10 percent of all Americans have made at least one suicide attempt, and that 20 percent more have had at least one period of strong suicidal feeling and ideation at some point during their lifetimes.[1] This means that roughly six percent of all *suicidal* people die by suicide. Ninety-four percent of all suicidal people do not become suicides. Many completers, attempters, and considerers suffer their feelings chronically or recurrently. If, on average, individuals in each of these categories is suicidal for a total of 100 days in each of their lives, then the odds of becoming a suicide during any 24-hour period of suicidal pain are six in 10,000. What happened to prevent the suicides from occurring during the other 9,994 days? On a few days suicide did not happen because a highly lethal attempt (i.e., a jump from a high bridge) did not result in death. On a few days there were suicide attempts where death was averted by the unprompted (i.e., the victim did not call for an ambulance or arrange to be discovered) intervention of other parties. On a few other days suicide risk was substantially lowered by periods of commitment that were either involuntary or strongly coerced. (This is the situation where the person is told that he either voluntarily commits himself or procedures to have him involuntarily committed will be initiated.) However, on at least 9000 of those days, the suicidal person either relied entirely upon himself, or made some use of family, friends, self-help literature, support groups, counselors, or uncoerced voluntary commitment. Since these latter situations involve at least the acquiescence of the suicidal person, we must conclude that at least 90 percent of the time suicide is largely self-prevented. In these cases suicide does not happen because personal resources successfully resist pain that threatens to overwhelm.

One might suppose that researchers into suicide would spend a good deal of time studying how people prevent their own suicides. There would be a large body of popular and professional literature that identified suicide self-prevention techniques, evaluated their effectiveness, considered ways to improve them, and tried to communicate the appropriate information to anyone who might need it. This research and education would prevent completed and attempted suicides and would reduce the suffering of suicidal people. You will look in vain for this literature.

The idea of giving a role in suicide prevention to that most disgraceful and incompetent of all human beings, the suicidal person himself, seems too ridiculous even to consider. He is someone bent on murder. Or reunion with the dead. Or manipulation and attention. He is a sinner, a moral inferior. He is structurally defective, permanently unreliable and untrustworthy. He is maladapted and developmentally deficient. He desires death, not life.

Reality is otherwise. By both passive and active means, suicidal people use the entirety of their being to avoid death. How they go about doing this is completely unresearched. In every other area of public health we have positive social attitudes, public education, and research on self-help recovery efforts. Formal and informal advice is immediately available to anyone who wants to quit smoking, drinking, drugging, or overeating. Vast public education programs help us prevent heart disease and cancer. Measures to protect oneself from physical assaults, and from occupational or automobile accidents, are regarded as normal.

The suicide self-prevention measures listed below are intended to either reduce pain, increase resources, or both. Since most are discussed more extensively in earlier and later sections of this book, listing them here appears to be repetitive and pedantic. But look at the other books on suicide listed in the bibliography; you will see that they include few or none of these suggestions.

1. See medical personnel for any problems in physical health. This will give some suicidal people a significant reduction in pain, some will receive minor relief, and some will find no relief. Members of the latter group have done nothing wrong; they deserve credit for initiating action on the side of life.

2. Educate yourself to overcome denial and to seek assistance for problems that seem to be unrelated to suicidal feelings and ideation. If drugs, alcohol, gambling, debting, eating disorders, sleep disorders, bereavement, problems in sexuality, crime victimization, or abuse that is physical, sexual, or emotional are part of your life, then they are part of the pain that causes you to be suicidal. If someone in your family has these problems, or had them when you were a child, then that is also part of your pain. It is very common for people in support groups for these problems to talk about suicidal feelings. Members get relief from pain, and recovery from suicidal conditions. Denial tells you that these things are not part of your basic problem, but, if they receive treatment, you will find that your basic problem has melted away.

3. Remove the means. Detoxify your home.

4. Seek help sooner, directly, and persistently. Recovery from all problems in health is easier and quicker if treatment begins sooner. There are no mind readers. Your unhappiness is something that most people would prefer not to see. Since society has stronger aversion for emotional problems than it does for physical problems, you will have to exert stronger than normal efforts to get help.

5. "I don't care," or "I don't care if I live or die," are common attitudes among the suicidal. We fail to recognize that these attitudes are pain-coping strategies. Consciously caring about pain that apparently cannot be reduced leads to frustration, disappointment, conflicts with others; these add to the existing pain. "I don't care," is often a way to block awareness of the real sources of one's pain. Counselors see "I don't care," as sullen hostility; the suicidal may see it as further evidence for negative beliefs about the self. Utterances of "I don't care if I live or die," are cries for help, and are part of the struggle to stay alive. Consciously not caring is indicative of caring at an unconscious level.

6. The American Psychiatric Association estimates that during any six month period 9.4 million Americans will suffer from depression. Millions upon millions more suffer from alcoholism, drug addiction and schizophrenia. Many more are victims of manic-depression, paranoia, anorexia, bulimia, domestic violence, incest, or rape. Divorce and separation cause horrible suffering for millions. Still millions more are hurt badly by bereavement, retirement and the loss of physical health. Is it unrealistic to estimate that each year nine million Americans suffer strong suicidal feelings? Each of these people feels "My pain is hopeless. No one else has ever suffered as I have. No one else has ever looked at a future that has such impossible odds for feeling better." The number of official completed suicides each year is about 31,000; the number of actual suicides is perhaps 45,000. By dividing 45,000 into nine million, we get the result that if you are suicidal, your chances of committing suicide this year are about 1 in 200. Some of the 199 survivors are people who will still be in pain at the end of the year. A smaller number will be in pain two years later, and a still smaller number three years later. If 6 percent of all suicidal people die by suicide, then 11 more of the 199 survivors will eventually become suicides. A few other suicidal people, unrecovered from suicidal pain, will die by other means. The great majority will find recovery. Cognitively you cannot help but believe, "I am permanently frozen in horrible pain." This is what depression is; there is no reason why you should feel otherwise. But you can at least begin to accept the fact that the odds are in your favor. Millions of people who have felt suicidal misery have recovered.

7. Recognize that everything in your emotional and cognitive makeup is on the side of life. Anxiety, feelings of numbness and deadness, disturbing dreams and fantasies, and tiredness result from things your body does to help keep you alive.

8. Some books on depression and suicide say that the crisis often simply passes with time, the person did nothing to help bring about recovery. Someone who believed this might argue that these suicides were not self-prevented, since the person apparently took no positive action. In many situations, however, doing nothing is doing something. Not drinking, not drugging, not eating too much, and not smoking are not always doing nothing. The struggle to avoid suicide includes considering and rejecting plans, getting rid of or not acquiring the means,

and postponing the date. In the depressed a great deal of what passes for ordinary life is really suicide prevention behavior: taking on extra work, "geographic" changes in jobs and living arrangements, negative coping mechanisms that provide brief respite. Suicidal people continuously engage in lonely and unappreciated struggles to keep themselves alive. I once knew a city employee who suffered from chronic depression. She began many conversations with "I want to go to sleep and never wake up." She hated her job, and she hated the lonely hours at home. Each day, on her way home from work, she would spend an hour sitting in a neighborhood coffee shop. That hour in the coffee shop was a suicide prevention activity. People in suicidal pain are dedicated suicide preventionists. All of their behavior is determined by their effort to keep the pain from getting worse.

9. Your pain is not your fault. People do not choose the events and conditions that cause them to be suicidal.

10. The negative moral judgments that others make about the suicidal are not valid. As with other forms of prejudice, these judgments say things only about the people who make them. Learning to recognize the forms of social abuse that are inflicted upon the suicidal is a step toward a reduction in your suffering.

11. Recognize the extent to which your internalization of social prejudice adds to your pain and fear. A vivid instance of the internalization of prejudice against the mentally ill occurred to a college freshman who told a counselor that he was having suicidal thoughts. He was then involuntarily taken to a hospital psychiatric ward and held overnight. The next day, back at school, "I thought I was stigmatized for life. I thought people would be able to tell I was a mental patient just by looking at me." The intense feeling, "Others can tell I am x just by looking at me," is a common reaction had by victims of stigmatized events. Its immediate sources are entirely from within, its ultimate origins are entirely from without.

12. The negative behavior you encounter is not something you cause or deserve. The people you try to get help from may be irrational, unpredictable, abusive, hostile, or paralyzed with fear. They may challenge you to go ahead and kill yourself. These ideas were inculcated into them when they were children and reinforced by parents, teachers, peers, and the media. Try to remember that becoming

morally judgmental about their behavior will usually get you nowhere. In many areas of their lives these people are usually decent citizens; their behavior is an involuntary response to their own emotional needs.

13. Insist on respect and better treatment. The real human rights issue is not the right to die, but the right to an equitable share of public resources on the side of life. The inequitable social distribution of pain-coping resources is a major cause of suicide.

14. Learning to accept imperfections in others is a step toward accepting them in yourself. No person or organization that works with the suicidal is immune to mistakes or shortcomings. Since we suffer from hundreds of years of ignorance and prejudice, our behavior in dealing with suicide is liable to be markedly worse than it is in many other areas. You will have to accept the imperfections of others even while they are locked into the imperfection of delusional perfectionism. An outstanding characteristic of untreated suicidophobia is denial: "We don't have that problem here. If there is a problem it must be with [delete the one that applies to the speaker] the school, family, peers, therapist, news media," or "If you don't get better it is because something is wrong with you, not us."

15. Anger and rage at the unfair treatment of the suicidal may discharge some of the pain in the short run, but in the longer-term, chronic bitterness is not conducive to recovery. We need to develop a no-fault approach to suicide.

16. Educate yourself about bereavement after completed suicide.

17. Recognize that recovery is genuine, even though the world pretends it never happens.

18. More of your life history than you realize has gone into your pain; it is not likely that recovery will come quickly. A step toward developing patience with yourself is to reject the impatience that others have toward you.

19. Understanding is possible and brings progress; it develops in piecemeal fashion.

20. Help others with their pain.

Bad Reactions

If you seek help for being suicidal, you may get

1. ignored, no apparent reaction at all.

2. verbal or non-verbal cues that the subject of suicide is not to be discussed.

3. told to go elsewhere; the organization or individual has a "no suicidals" policy.

4. "cover my ass" treatment: people whose main priority is to protect their own interests.

5. a quick referral to somewhere else.

6. quickly sent packing with advice or solutions that are sure to work.

7. told that suicide is a personal choice you should make on your own; the person you have turned to does not believe in interfering.

8. challenged to go ahead and kill yourself.

9. suspicion about your moral character.

10. told that you are self-centered and manipulative.

11. an argument: your ideas are morally wrong.

12. told that you are angry at others and want to cause them pain.

13. hostility and rejection for your thoughts and emotions.

14. belittlement of you and your problems.

15. denial on parts of your pain.

16. told that your problems are not enough for you to commit suicide.

17. someone who insists that someone else they once knew, who did not commit suicide, had the same problems that you have.

18. frequent and strong interruptions.

19. someone who is quickly fed up and frustrated with you.

20. told to immediately change your feelings.

21. pressure to start feeling better within the next thirty minutes.

All of these are parts of the other person's efforts to cope with his own fears and emotional discomfort. *They are responses to his problems, not yours.* Suicidal people are prone to interpret all negative behavior toward them as evidence that confirms the beliefs, "I'm worthless. Nobody cares. Everyone hates me. Some basic things are permanently wrong with me." *None* of the bad reactions is evidence for these propositions. These reactions say things only about the person manifesting the negative behavior; they say nothing about you. Dedicated self-reproachers may think, "I must be completely incompetent. I can't even select good people to try to get help from. Or maybe the bad reactions occurred because I mismanaged my half of the conversation." These are not valid inferences. People who may be compassionate and patient in dealing with many of life's problems can become frightened and defensive when asked to respond to suicidal feelings. The bad reactions are coping measures that help them feel better, and cause you to feel worse.

Your request for help did not cause these reactions. The causal history of these reactions goes back centuries. It includes a great deal of faulty teaching in the other person's developmental history. If you turned to a healthcare professional the odds are much better than fifty-fifty that he received zero formal training in suicide prevention. The training provided for the few who get it usually consists of a single fifty minute lecture that covers some statistics, a brief review of Durkheim and Freud, a discussion of suicide among teenagers, and a list of the warning signs. Your counselor's teachers dealt with suicide either by silence or superficiality. *They* were afraid that if they talked about it, somebody might commit suicide and then they would feel terrible. They were very frightened of suicide. Their fear was transmitted to your counselor. This is a main reason why he reacts with fear at your request for help, and why he responds so badly. The reactions are bad, but the person is not. Given the causal history of his ideas and feelings about suicide, he cannot behave otherwise.

Inaccurate Views of the Self and Others

Suicidal people invariably have a number of false beliefs about themselves and others. Though some of these ideas help keep them alive, others add pain or decrease resources. All of the ideas have some basis in the real world; they are either partly true or are derived from our culture's mythology of suicide. To attempt to change these ideas during an acute crisis is usually futile, but it can be helpful to address them as part of a recovery program. Many of these perceptions are not easily abandoned, particularly if they have been held for a long time.

1. I must be crazy.

This belief is usually an inference from a general premise that anyone with suicidal thoughts and feelings must be crazy. This general statement is not true. The real meaning of suicidal thoughts and feelings is "My pain is threatening to exceed my pain-coping resources." This condition says nothing about having or lacking sanity and has no pejorative connotations. It could happen to anyone and could be precipitated by thousands of different factors. Part of the pain and loss of pain-coping resources may involve mental illness; but it may not: not all mentally ill people are suicidal and not all suicidal people are mentally ill. Moreover, the popular conception of craziness is having delusional beliefs about reality, and most suicidal people do not suffer from these beliefs. Some people with delusional beliefs are at risk of suicide, but they make up a small percentage of the total number of completed suicides. People with depression, which is what most suicidal people suffer from, are usually lucid and rational. They say they are depressed because they hate their jobs, they are lonely, the doctors cannot cure their back pain. These things are all true and are all causes of their misery. Depressed people may have inaccurate senses of self-esteem, but so do many people who are not depressed. Having suicidal feelings does not mean that you are crazy, and does not mean that others should treat you as a "crazy person." If they do, it is because of their own false beliefs about suicide.

2. It's futile to try and get help.

Studies have been done of rape victims who did not report the crime to the police and did not go to medical providers for treatment. Reasons given for not coming forward included fear of stigma, prejudice, and hostility; a belief that the community lacked resources that might help; and desires to deny the event of the crime and to minimize its impact. Suicidal people have similar feelings, and with similar degrees of justification. Some people do recover without outside assistance. Some people seek help and get none, or worse, get more pain than what they already have.

There are, however, millions of people who were strongly suicidal, sought and received compassionate assistance, and currently enjoy normal life. Part of the problem is that suicidal people, like everyone else, tend to think in stereotypes: "they" don't care, "they" are all selfish and self-involved, "they" don't want to be bothered. But they are not a "they", they are individuals. The "they" stereotype is also an ingredient in a pain-coping stance that is common among the suicidal: "I'm good and the rest of the world is bad." This belief is an effort to explain pain and vulnerability to pain. It helps to prop up self-esteem. It discharges hostility. Suicidal pain is debilitating; the oversimplification by stereotype is an economical way to organize reality. Though the suicidal offer the "them" stereotype as a cause for their pain and as evidence for the hopelessness of their situation, it serves also to justify staying alive. It says "I'm not worthless. I have unique value." But it is not true that the world is a monolith of evil, or that all of "them" are full of fear, hostility, and prejudice. " 'They' are all bad," is an involuntary response to pain. In the short-term it helps cope; in the long run it deprives its victims of useful resources.

3. Negative Self-Image

I'm worthless. I'm a failure. I'm a loser. I'm unlovable. I'm worse off than anyone else. My situation is hopeless.

These ideas are normal parts of the condition of being suicidal. However, if you listen to accounts given by the survivors of a suicide victim, you will listen to the stories of people for whom these statements were not true. Some suicides were in declining health or had been given a terminal diagnosis, but even in these cases the relatives and friends felt death was premature; their loved one still had much to live for. Other victims had suffered disappointments in relationships and finances. But in these and other areas they had also had successes, and could reasonably hope to succeed again in the future. None were worthless, none were unlovable.

The misery of having these beliefs is compounded when they affect attitude and behavior. "I'm worthless," becomes "I'm not worth helping." "I'm hopeless," becomes "Social resources are better spent on people who can get some good out of them." These attitudes are as false as the judgments on which they are based. The suicidal have as much right to the assistance of others as anyone else. The probability that they will benefit from the assistance is excellent: people with strong suicidal feelings have much higher recovery rates than alcoholics from alcoholism and drug addicts from drug addiction. Even though suicidal people have the strong feeling that "I can't be helped," many do make good use of social resources during successful recoveries. It takes time, but the strong belief in these propositions gradually fades.

4. Questionable Values

I'm suicidal because I don't have x, because I'm not good enough at y, because I can't meet expectation z. A great many suicidal people find themselves in situations where they believe that they cannot be happy unless such and such happens, and such and such has not happened and is not likely to happen. Whatever it is, a special job, a marriage, the approval of one's family, there are millions of happy people who do not have it. One difference is that these millions of happy people do not have a value system that depends upon the possession of that thing for their happiness.

Thousands, perhaps millions, of suicidal people have been in this dilemma and recovered. Sometimes they got the valued thing and felt better. Sometimes they got the thing and were still unhappy. More often they got their pain reduced by other means, were no longer suicidal, and slowly realized that the thing they had been so desperate about was not really essential for their happiness.

5. Not all of the pain is private grief

A large part of the pain of being suicidal is due not just to private and personal disappointments, but also to negative attitudes that the non-suicidal have toward the suicidal and to the victim's internalizations of those attitudes. This additional pain is especially immobilizing. It prevents people from getting and giving help; it says "He's different"; "He's manipulative"; "His pain is his fault. He got himself into this situation; he should get himself out of it." The suicidal ruminate exclusively on their private woes because they live in a culture that says private woes are the sole cause of suicide. If they can see that not all of their pain is their fault, then they will be in less pain.

6. Who Am I?

It is unlikely that the suicidal person and the people he turns to for help are likely to agree on how much pain he is in, how hopeless his situation is, or how powerless he is over that situation. Both will have inaccurate views about the latter two questions, and counselors usually have inaccurate views about the first. This creates something of a dilemma; your perceptions of yourself are untrustworthy, and so are those of the people around you. So whom do you trust?

From a standpoint of self-knowledge, suicidal people have nowhere to go but up. The way they currently perceive themselves and others is full of falsehood, illusion, ignorance, and incoherence. In recovery they can reach self-conceptions that are new, stronger, more satisfying and contain unexpected elements.

7. The rest of the world is in one place, and I'm in another place.

The sense of profound estrangement from humanity is one of the most bone-chilling aspects of the suicidal condition. At any one time in the United States, there are hundreds of thousands of people who have it. Reports of having had it are frequent in support groups for every type of pain. The place you are at is a place where millions are or have been; and a place from which millions have recovered.

On the aggregate pain approach, the sense of estrangement is partly justified; the suicidal are different from the rest of the population in that their pain is closer to exceeding their resources. But this situation is on a continuum with ordinary life, there are no fundamental differences between the suicidal and others. The sense of estrangement is caused partly by the internal and external effects of an estranging mythology; partly by the psychological effects of extreme pain: depersonalization, numbness, "terminal uniqueness", grandiosity, extreme fear; and partly by the social effects of extreme pain: it adversely affects both our ability to have social intercourse with others and their willingness to spend time with us.

8. Depressed people see the world without illusions; they have a more accurate view of reality.

Depressed people sometimes arrive at this belief on their own, and sometimes from hearing about psychology experiments that claim to support this position. Ordinary people as well as optimists look at parts of reality with selective vision and rose-colored glasses. The human capacity for self-deception on the positive side is universal. Depressed people, with their negative view of reality, notice instances of this and see that there are aspects of life that they see more clearly than do other people. It does not follow, though, that they see *all* aspects of reality with greater accuracy. Using depression as an epistemological methodology has a price: you get a more accurate view of some parts of the world, and a less accurate view of other parts. Depressed people who believe they see the world with clearer vision are apt to say, "The world is a miserable place. I am the only good person in it," or "The world is a miserable place. I am the worst person in it." The first sentence has an element of truth. Non-suicidal people go through daily life simply not seeing a lot of the misery and suffering that are right in front of them. The second sentences are uttered or thought by thousands of depressed people every day. The lives of most of these of these people, if viewed from the outside at least, are morally indistinguishable from the lives of millions of fellow citizens.

Discounting

A universal belief among the suicidal is that their pain, anguish, and despair will never go away. "For as far as I can see, nothing but pain." A universal problem in suicide prevention is that the suicidal discount the assurances of others that there is light at the end of the tunnel. Discounting has several causes.

The suicidal often believe that the world is bad, that people in general are bad, or that the self is bad. They believe they see the world more accurately than others, and may even say, "It's because I see the world as it is that I am so unhappy." On being told that a therapy program can help them feel better, they infer that the program will indoctrinate them to have more positive but false views about reality. For these suicidal people, a sense of personal integrity is one of the few good feelings they have about themselves. This sense of integrity is a coping resource. Since it helps them to stay alive, they cling to it tenaciously. It is entirely natural for depressed people to reject suggestions that they perceive the world differently; to respond, "I

128 Out of the Nightmare

don't want to do it and it won't work anyway." Their belief that they cannot help but view the world as they do is partly accurate; the sense of integrity is an involuntary coping mechanism. Some counselors deride the sense of integrity as being grandiose, "You *alone* see the world correctly?" This response shows a lack of understanding for the desperation of the depressed. The aggregate pain theory does not ask the suicidal to develop a pollyanna view of the world or of other people. To develop a fuller appreciation for some bad things about reality can be a helpful step toward recovery. However, the aggregate pain theory, *much* more than any other theory, asks the suicidal person to have a kinder view about himself. There is nothing bad in him. He is simply an average person with a greater than average amount of pain.

Two other causes of discounting are the beliefs "No one understands my situation," and "My situation is unique." The depressed will look to others to see if their pain is understood; if they see a lack of understanding of any part of their pain, they will discount any expression of hopefulness. The premise for the discounting seems reasonable: How can someone who fails to understand an emotional condition be able to make a credible prediction about its future? While this form of discounting charges others with false understanding, the second charges them with a false analogy. "Other people with your problems have gotten better, so will you," assumes that the problems of the suicidal person are identical with those of the recovered persons. The suicidal person can easily reject this by finding differences between his situation and theirs. Or he can simply reason that if they have recovered and he has not, then there must be some essential difference between him and them. Or he can break the analogy in another way: It is true that some people with my problem recovered, but it is also true that some people with my problem committed suicide. How can the predictor of recovery be sure that I am not really in the latter group?

The aggregate pain theory readily accepts the premises of the discounter. The pain history and coping-resource history of each individual are completely unique. Your situation is identical with no one else's. No single person, including you, is ever going to understand completely all of your pain. This would require learning a very large amount of information about your childhood and about the history of your family for several generations. A great deal of this information is unobtainable. It would require a knowledge of principles of psychology, physiology, and sociology that exceeds anything that will be available in our lifetimes. It requires that one person have all the information, know all the relevant scientific principles, and also have practical experience in bereavement, mental illness, substance abuse, aging, divorce, child abuse and every other area of human pain that has ever affected you, or anyone with whom you have been involved. This is impossible. No one is ever going to understand fully your pain. If we return to the analogy, we can see that uniqueness and lack of complete understanding are no barrier to recovery. Lots of people have recovered from suicidal pain, even though their pain was also unique and fully understood by no one. Though each aggregate of suicidal pain is unique, nearly all of the components are shared with other people. Some components may be untreatable by current methods, but many others can have their painfulness significantly reduced. Some of the components may be incomprehensible because of lack of information, lack of scientific knowledge, or lack of the availability of anyone with the appropriate experience. Many other components of the pain, however, are capable of being fully or partly understood by the self or others. Everyone who does recover does so with his condition only partly understood; if full understanding were required, no one would ever recover. If you embark on a broad search for understanding, you will gain bits and pieces from a variety of sources. For most components of your pain there are people who have increased their understanding and found ways to reduce their suffering. Since there is hope that part of your suffering may be reduced, there is hope that the total aggregate may be reduced. If this happens, the suicidal feelings will pass.

Alcohol and Drug Abuse

Many studies have shown that alcohol abuse is involved in one-third to one-half of all completed suicides. A recent study in San Diego investigated 133 suicides of people under the age of 30 and found evidence of drug abuse in 88 cases, 66 percent. The same study examined 150 suicides of people over 30 and found evidence of drug abuse in 39 instances, 26 percent. More than half of the suicides in both age groups involved alcohol abuse. (Rich, 1986)

1. The transition from use to abuse in drinking and drugging often begins when the substance is used as a solution for other problems: anxiety in

social situations, stress at work, insomnia, disappointments, physical pain. In these contexts, the substance is a coping resource that provides short-term relief from pain and discomfort. The pattern of seeking short-term relief may continue, if the old problems do not go away or new ones are added. Healthier ways to cope with pain do not get learned.

2. Over time psychological dependence develops into physical dependence. As drugs and alcohol become a bigger part of the person's life, everything else shrinks. Relations with family and friends usually change for the worse. Many substance abusers eventually find themselves with lifestyles or behavior that they regarded with disapproval at earlier points of their lives. As their pool of personal and social pain-coping resources diminishes, they become increasingly dependent upon the substance. "Blot out pain with booze or drugs," becomes an ingrained and involuntary response. Substance abusers develop chronically low self-esteem; this is chronically painful, and it requires chronic substance abuse to blot out. Every problem the person has, especially the three other major co-factors of suicide: mental illness, physical illness, and bereavement, is made worse by alcohol and drugs. Because of their increased pain and decreased resources, substance abusers are more likely to develop suicidal conditions, and less likely to recover.

3. Most substance abusers will tell you that the substance is not their problem. This is denial. They have a disease that tells them that they do not have a disease. Alcoholism and drug addiction are diseases that affect the entire family. Their roots often go back several generations, and always go forward several generations. Denial, and the other dislocations caused by substance abuse, profoundly affect everyone related to the victim.

4. Recovery from suicidal feelings and ideation requires that treatment for substance abuse be a priority. If a person has a number of problems, and on the aggregate pain model there always are many factors that contribute to suicidal pain, it is difficult to make progress on any of them until the substance abuse problem is addressed. Recovery is easier the sooner it is begun. The first weeks or months of recovery can welcome the substance abuser to reality with some brutal pain. Old coping resources are gone and new ones are yet to be acquired. Like the person

trying to recover from depression, the recovering substance abuser may have periods during which his emotions and his cognitions tell him it is hopeless. Staying clean and sober during these periods will eventually make the person stronger, even if it does not seem that way when he is in them.

5. Millions of people have found recovery in professional programs and the non-professional support groups of Alcoholics Anonymous and Narcotics Anonymous. Affiliated programs provide assistance for people whose pain includes being a relative or friend of a substance abuser.

Those interested in the role of non-professional substance abuse support groups in the prevention of suicide should read the case history in Chapter 10. "Tough Love" and "The victim himself must call for assistance," are suggestions advanced by these groups for dealing with the active substance abuser. These suggestions can be useful if the victim is simply a substance abuser, but if he is also suicidal, they are ill-advised.

"Attempts Get It Out of Your System"

A widely held belief is that an attempt can get "it" out of the system of a suicidal person. The myth does not specify what the "it" is, or how "it" leaves the system. Presumably, the meaning of the myth is that suicide attempts discharge stress, anxiety, and pain. The people who advance this view often point out that some attempters are in a less painful condition in the short-term, and in the longer run some are never suicidal again. Though it is not stated quite so baldly, this amounts to the position that suicide attempts are good for your health. This position is not correct. Even when the attempter believes that the means are not lethal or harmful, the attempt can cause lasting bodily damage or death. Some people do attempt once and never again, but others attempt several times. Various studies indicate that 5 percent to 10 percent of all attempters subsequently become completers, and 35 percent to 40 percent of all completed suicides made prior attempts. A prior attempt is the single-event risk factor most strongly associated with completed suicide. Suicide attempts cause pain, often harm health, and have a poor track record as suicide prevention measures. The stigma of suicide causes attempters to suffer lasting feelings of shame and contributes to their alienation from others. Our cultural and scientific inattention to the processes of recovery are one reason for the perpetuation of this myth. Suicidal people may not know that, just as there are many attempts for every completion, there are many people with strong suicidal feelings and ideation for each person who attempts. A minority of strong considerers become self-injurers. This means that recovery can be achieved without the allegedly beneficial effects of an attempt. The "It gets it out of their system," myth deprives considerers of more accurate information about attempted suicide; this information, since it places attempts in a less desirable light, is a resource on the side of life.

Though little research has been done on the subject, it appears that attempted suicide can develop into a repetitive pattern that is similar to other self-destructive behaviors. I once spoke with a woman whose daughter had made more than thirty suicide attempts. The role of the attempts in the daughter's life seemed to be not unlike the repeated cuttings and burnings of self-mutilators. Self-injurers report that they recurrently find themselves in emotional conditions that they cannot tolerate, and the self-destructive behavior gets them out of that condition. For a few hours they suffer less pain, but the morning after brings feelings of shame, guilt and physical suffering. (Usually, however, suicide attempters do not get the temporary relief or numbness had by self-mutilators. Self-poisoners, for example, often become nauseated and suffer severe abdominal pain.) If others learn of the self-injuring behavior, the victim suffers social disapproval. If the behavior is kept secret, the victim suffers feelings of isolation and alienation. The "it" not only does not leave the victim's system, it becomes more firmly entrenched as a negative coping mechanism.

The "It gets it out of their system," belief is persistent, despite the fact that it does not correspond to fact, common sense, or practical utility. The myth persists because of its psychological benefits for the non-suicidal: it provides them with relief from stress, anxiety, and pain. "It's out of his system," entails "We don't have to worry anymore." The myth that says we do not have to worry after an attempt is an analogue to the one that says we do not have to worry beforehand: "The ones who talk about it aren't really serious." The myth directly reduces anxiety by claiming that there is no reason for anxiety; it indirectly reduces stress by providing organization and coherence for the jumble of feelings we have about attempted suicide. Confusion is a source of pain, and a false model at least reduces some of our discomfort. A further benefit of the myth is that it supports the more general myth that the causes of suicidal behavior are entirely within the victim.

The myth is dangerous after an attempt because it does not encourage the victim and those around him to pursue and continue with programs of recovery. The myth is dangerous before possible attempts because it does not encourage acquaintances to take action on the side of life. Acquaintances may consciously believe the myth as it applies to the victim, and subconsciously believe that the attempt will give *them* relief from *their* uncomfortable feelings. "Once he attempts it will get the stress and anxiety out of our systems," is not a valid belief for the acquaintances. If the attempt causes death or lasting harm, they will suffer for a long time. If the attempt does not cause permanent physical damage, they are soon likely to develop somewhat different feelings of stress and anxiety: "Will he do it again? With more lethal means?" The suicide attempt of a loved one has a poor track record as a means of providing lasting emotional relief for relatives and friends. The best way for acquaintances to respond to their own emotional needs is to become involved on the side of life as soon as possible.

The Myth of the Inner Light

Science, medicine, and psychiatry believe that suicide is caused by the presence of something negative: a deformed superego, distorted thinking patterns, developmental deficits, biochemical imbalances. The aggregate pain approach regards each of these as a theory about a part of the victim's pain. The myth of the inner light focuses on reasons for living; it says that suicide is caused by the absence of a particular positive coping resource. Reasons for living help people withstand the pain of a suicidal crisis, and may also provide direction for a program of recovery. The inner light is often religious in nature, though it can also be such things as a sense of obligation to others or a hope for a prosperous future. Inner lights are an important resource in the prevention of suicide. A vivid example was at a talk I gave to a group of foster parents on Staten Island. Near the end of the talk, an older man in the front row removed his cap, revealing an indentation and several inches of scar tissue at the hairline on the left side of his forehead. He said that seven years earlier he had shot himself. He had not been leading a good sort of life, and reached a point where he could not stand to stay alive any longer. He tried to reach out to people he knew, but was unable to get a response that made things better. After the attempt, he said, "I found religion." Religion, in its cognitive, emotional, and social functions, has historically been an immense coping resource. Theologians perform a valuable service for many people by giving sermons, and writing books and articles, that develop and adapt concepts of the inner light for succeeding generations.

Though the inner light approach has surely had its successes in the prevention of suicide, it has severe limitations. As with the romantic attitude toward suicide, an approach that advocates only "give people something inspiring to help them endure pain," does not always discourage a passive attitude toward suffering and the reduction of pain. The myth of the inner light says nothing about bringing other types of pain-coping resources to bear on the situation. Many suicides, at some point in their lives, received educations in reasons for living; for these people the inner light was not enough. While some people in despair seek religious guidance, others shun it completely. As a single policy for suicide prevention, the inner light is not enough.

Besides its limitations as a suicide prevention policy, the inner light makes a significant negative contribution to the mythology of suicide. Since it locates the cause of the problem within the victim, it says by implication that none of the problem is in us. The inner light hope for the suicidal is in reality a selfish hope of the non-suicidal that the problem can be made to go away, without our having to change ourselves or our world. As with all aspects of the mythology of suicide, the price of reducing the discomfort of the non-suicidal is an increase in pain for those who are suicidal. At any given moment, thousands of despairing souls are rummaging about for "reasons for living"; if they do not find any, their despair increases.

Human beings, like all animate creatures, do not need reasons for living to stay alive. Billions of people would not have much to say if they were asked to articulate their reasons for living. This does not prevent them from leading normal lives. The myth of the inner light not only causes suicidal people additional pain if they cannot find reasons for living, it also deprives them of coping resources. In the public imagination, giving people reasons for living is the way to prevent suicide. Anyone who feels he is unable to come up with good reasons for someone else to stay alive, will be afraid to become involved with someone who is suicidal. This fear is common in the non-suicidal, and is quite complex. It is the fear simply of being in an uncomfortable situation and not having anything to say. It is the fear that not being able to provide the reasons will confirm the victim's growing suspicion that he has no good reasons for staying alive. It is the fear that not being able to find reasons for someone else will cause one to wonder if there are good reasons for the self to stay alive.

The myth of the inner light adds pain and subtracts coping resources for many suicidal people. Though inner lights can be valuable at an individual level, the social myth of the inner light needs to be extinguished. Suicidal crises are resolved by reducing pain, increasing resources, or both. In some cases the increased resources may include the discovery of a reason for living, but in many cases it will not. Not having reasons for living is not a barrier to staying alive, or to helping someone else stay alive.

A culture that accepts the reasons-for-living mythology is bound to be confused by the suicides of people who appear to have everything to live for. Our culture values wealth and youth, so the suicides of people with these qualities are mysterious. Conversely, the non-suicidal are often mystified by the non-suicides of people who appear to lack many of the things we value. But possession of these qualities is no guarantee that pain will not exceed resources, nor does their absence mean that suicide is probable.

It's OK to Tell Someone

Most of us, if we suffer an unstigmatized problem in physical health, will go directly to an appropriate healthcare provider and state the nature of our problem as clearly and as accurately as we can. If we do not get a good response, we either strongly insist on proper treatment, or immediately go somewhere else. Unfortunately, most people with suicidal feelings and ideation do not behave this way. Most of their reluctance to seek help, and their inability to do it effectively and promptly, is due to the fear that seeking help will cause their pain to be increased rather than reduced. Some of this reluctance, however, is also due to the suicidal person's belief that his seeking help will cause pain, discomfort, inconvenience, and perhaps even harm to the other person.

It is natural that the suicidal should have this belief. "Don't be a drag," is a social convention. "Always be positive," and "In this organization you are either part of the problem or part of the solution," are rules espoused by many schools and social service facilities. "I don't want to hear about other people's problems," is an attitude most of us have some of the time, and some of us have all of the time.

Despite massive social discouragement, you have not done a bad thing if you have asked someone to help you with your pain. You have a need and a right to make this request. To ask for help violates the social taboo "Don't talk about it," but it is not harmful to society; the world does not need more suicides. You are not doing something harmful to the person in whom you confide. To help a suicidal person through a period of despair is a rewarding experience. It expands appreciation of life, teaches humility, and helps us to learn about the samenesses and differences of other people. It is not fun or comfortable, but afterwards there are no regrets about having done it. Though they are not material, the rewards are still real.

Many people, including professional counselors, are unable or unwilling to talk with the suicidal or the depressed. There are also many people who are willing to help. If you use some judgment you can reduce the risk of a negative response. A good way to begin the conversation is to say, "You seem like someone who might be able to listen and understand and have some patience. There are some things that are causing me a lot of pain." Most people regard themselves as above average in sensitivity, compassion, and understanding; your appeal to this improves your chances of a positive response, and you have also let the person know that you have something serious to talk about. Soon afterwards, you can say, "I'm in terrible pain. I'm having thoughts of suicide." The earlier you do this in the conversation, the better able the other person will be to respond to your needs. Words like these have been said to hundreds of thousands of people. The experience caused virtually all of them to feel anxious and to have a rush of adrenaline, but it did them no harm. When automobile accident victims arrive at a hospital emergency room the staff members experience stress. They are not worse people for it. Healthcare workers and counselors cannot effectively help someone unless they have an accurate view of his situation. Hopefully, knowledge of the severity of your pain will motivate them to take extra steps to get you assistance.

It is common for considerers to get bad reactions when they ask for help. The person to whom they appeal may be a good friend or a good counselor for other purposes, but simply have a lot of fear and ignorance about suicide. Bad reactions are due to problems in him, not in you. Imagine how you would react if you went to an eye doctor and told him you had a vision problem, and, without an examination, were shown the door and told you were just an attention seeker? The rational response is "This person has a problem. I'm going to try someone else." A second common situation is that the considerer gets a good response from the first person to whom he turns, and then that person gets a bad reaction when he reaches out to others. Some New York City school counselors, for example, receive less than zero support and cooperation from their principals or outside service providers. The most common negative attitude in this situation is "not serious." This says the suicidal person has illegitimately asked for help, and that the counselor has unnecessarily overresponded. These reactions hurt more because they come from higher level authorities and because they cause pain to more than one person. One of the problems in suicide prevention is that the more you do to get help, or the more that is done to get you help, the more likely you are to suffer pain-causing bad reactions. It has to be repeated: none of these responses means you are doing a bad thing by asking for help. This is true even if the people you turn to *insist* that you are trying to harm them: "You got us upset. You are trying to manipulate us. You want to bring shame on the family and school." Taking action to prevent your own suicide is none of these things. By getting help sooner, rather than later, you are doing something that benefits these people. When "I'm suicidal. I need help," is responded to with "He's threatening suicide," the "threat" concept has been added to the situation by the person who interprets the help-seeking behavior as a threat; it is not there in the original request. Threatening people is harmful and wrong, but asking for help is not a threat. Someone with dizziness and shortness of breath may, in an impersonal sense, be threatened by a heart attack. But if he tells a doctor about these symptoms, he is not threatening the doctor with a heart attack.

Stigmatized Options

A problem in the development of a recovery program is that many of
the conditions associated with suicide are themselves objects of social
prejudice and stigma. Just as some programs for these conditions may
have aversion toward the suicidal, the suicidal person, and his
intimates, who fear more pain for their loved one and fear stigma by
association for themselves, may have aversion toward programs that
can provide genuine help. This reciprocated aversion, of course, is
partly due to mutual ignorance. The suicidal person's aversion for
programs in mental health, substance abuse, or the actions of filing for
bankruptcy or applying for disability benefits, is unfortunately normal.
His ignorance and prejudice have social causes and reduce his access to
these resources. The prejudice and stigma associated with these
conditions or situations is painful, and fear of more pain is legitimate.
Suicidal people are not sure if they "really have that problem," in
which case they fear suffering the stigma without finding recovery,
and do not know that many people who gain recovery in these programs
consider the added stigma a relatively small price to pay. Good
recovery programs include procedures and assistance for coping with the
problems of anonymity and confidentiality.

Flirting with Getting Help

Flirting is a useful model for understanding the help-seeking
behavior of many suicidal people. A few flirters make obvious
overtures to a great many people, but most of us, when we flirt, do so
toward only one or two acquaintances who we think might respond. We
are afraid of rejection. We transmit ambiguous and disguised messages
that are designed to be noticed only by the intended recipient. If he or
she chooses to respond negatively, the rejection can be done in a face
saving manner. Third parties need never know that the advance was
made or spurned, and sometimes the flirter and the intended can
continue their previous non-intimate relationship under the pretense
that the incident never occurred. Most flirters are in a state of anxiety
until they get a response. If they fail to get one quickly, they will
terminate their anxiety by dropping the overture, and resume behavior
that does not express romantic interest. Behavior designed to encourage

others to initiate flirtation, such as making one's appearance more appealing, is also part of the social conventions of flirtation.

Many of the conventions of flirtation are designed to minimize risk of pain for both parties. Rejection hurts, and public rejection hurts even more. For most of us, it also painful to do the rejecting. Since it is less painful to reject privately than it is to reject publicly, flirting is a mutually acceptable form of communication. An important aspect of flirting is that it expresses and asks for interest that is tentative and conditional. Flirters reserve the right to become rejecters, once they have acquired more information about their intended. The same right is had by those who have responded to an initial flirtation. A public show of emotional interest, neediness, or responsiveness is an embarrassment that flirtation avoids.

Help-seeking behavior by the suicidal is often concealed from family members, neighbors, co-workers, fellow students, and the general community. The reason for this concealment is fear of more pain. The suicidal may select one or a few people from among his circle of acquaintances, someone he perceives to be more caring, more willing to be protective of his confidentiality, or more knowledgeable about pain-coping resources, and present that person with an ambiguous or disguised message. These messages can be non-verbal, including changes in appearance or behavior that hope to elicit overtures from others, and they can be statements such as "I can't go on. I want to go to sleep and never wake up. You won't have to worry about me anymore. I'm going away on a real long trip." Suicidal people may "fish" in various social environments with increasingly overt behavior until someone responds. This has greater risk for more pain, since help-seeking behavior that is less explicit is easier to dissemble, if the wrong person responds, or if the intended responds in a way that threatens to bring more pain. If the overture is rejected, the concealed nature of the overture enables both parties to avoid some of the pain of explicit rejection. They can both pretend that nothing significant happened and continue their previous relationship. There are two respects in which ordinary flirtation and suicidal help-seeking flirtation differ. In both situations the message recipient may not respond because he simply does not see the overture for what it is, or because he is so surprised, anxious, or ill-prepared that he cannot provide a timely response. In ordinary life flirters may recognize this (or even interpret a negative response as a non-response), and not regard the lack of positive response as reflecting badly upon themselves. Depression deprives its victims of this alternative. The suicidal help seeker always interprets a lack of response as further evidence for the belief, "I am not worth caring about." The second difference is that, in the case of suicide, both parties clumsily grope in a situation that lacks the unstated but commonly known conventions of romance. Neither party has a clear idea of what engagement in continued and more explicit communication will bring. This uncertainty adds more fear to an already fearful situation.

A conclusion we should draw from this is that while flirtation may be fine for romance, for public health it leaves a lot to be desired. People should be able to seek help for suicidal conditions in the same way they seek help for broken legs. This requires that we reduce the fear of rejection and additional pain by doing what it takes to effect a complete change in public attitudes about suicide. Since this is not going to be achieved in the near future, as an intermediate step we can recognize the positive aspects of the flirtation model. For both parties it helps normalize and destigmatize suicidal help-seeking behavior. The disguise and ambiguity is part of a rational strategy to minimize and ultimately reduce pain. Flirtation is a helpful concept for public education. I use this analogy in talks with various groups; audiences readily see it as a way to recognize, understand, and accept help-seeking behavior. It is a concept that legitimizes a compassionate response and it provides an alternative to the "threat" interpretation of help-seeking overtures. The flirtation model goes beyond the "cry for help" model in that it provides an understanding of the behavior of both the help seeker and the potential help giver. It can help people better understand what is going on in themselves and in others, and encourages more direct overtures and responses. The flirtation model requires that we recognize the fears that all of us have about involvement in suicidal situations. It enables potential help givers to have positive images of themselves. "Why is this person doing this thing to me?" can be replaced by "This person has a positive attitude toward me." It enables help seekers to interpret non-responses in a non-negative way.

Riding It Out

"Ride it out" is the coping strategy that says that the best way to survive the situation is to do nothing. Any action will either be wasted effort, or will make things worse. People who ride it out do not take action to either change themselves or to change their environment; they put their efforts into simply trying to endure. The going has gotten tough; they hang on and hope that eventually the pain will somehow subside. The strategies "Do nothing," "Say nothing," and even "Resist change," are profound parts of how individuals, organizations, and entire cultures respond to suicide.[2]

Public education about suicide prevention emphasizes that 80 percent of completed suicides did things in the weeks or months prior to their deaths to let others know that they were in a lot of pain. This emphasis is necessary to counteract the myth that "The ones who talk about it aren't serious." This approach tends to neglect the problems of non-presentations, delayed presentations, and non-persistent presentations. "Ride it out," is a strategy used, or partly used, by many completed suicides.

We must begin by recognizing that it is entirely natural that the suicidal should try to ride it out. Riding it out is a legitimate coping strategy of normal life. Each of us has problems that seem for the time being, at least, to be intractable. Our lives are full of petty annoyances about which we are able or willing to do little or nothing. We hope that without our taking action either the environment will change, or somehow we will get used to the problem and be bothered by it less. We believe that our time and energy are better spent elsewhere. At times, our cognitive judgment that effort is futile restrains an emotional demand to "Do something." Even if the nuisance never goes away, we cannot say that the ride-it-out strategy has failed. Because we did nothing about the nuisance we were able to make greater progress in other areas. The suicidal have fewer than average resources with which to manage greater amounts of pain. It is understandable that they should adopt ride-it-out strategies on a greater range of problems than do people in ordinary life. Besides having a greater need to avoid wasted effort, the suicidal have a greater need to avoid making their pain worse. Their fear that asking for help risks adding to their pain is legitimate. Though "ride it out" fails for thousands of people every year, it doubtlessly succeeds for many others. They say nothing, do nothing, and eventually get relief from their pain.

Riding it out, however, has several disadvantages:

1. It accepts the myth that any amount of pain is endurable for any length of time. Thousands of completed suicides have disproven this myth.

2. Riding out ordinary problems in ordinary life does not cause us loss of volitional capacity. Our positive coping abilities remain active in other areas and continue to be available to us. Suicidal pain, however, usually involves negative coping mechanisms and vicious circle problems. As the pain continues, these get worse, and our volitional powers deteriorate. Riding it out risks having suicidal pain become chronic pain, and chronic pain, even without additional factors, weakens us mentally and physically.

3. Riding it out is commonly used by people who do not want to admit that they have problems. This makes the abandonment of riding it out difficult, since doing so requires admitting one's original problems plus the lack of success with riding it out. Giving up riding it out also means giving up a coping resource: the sense of personal worth that is derived from the belief, "I am tough enough to tough this out."

4. For many people riding it out is part of a concept of self-reliance that also includes "Take action to solve your problems." To sustain this inconsistency requires a certain mental blindness, and the blindness permits the part that demands action to semi-consciously berate the part that rides it out.

5. Riding it out means remaining in pain. Chronic pain may cause the victim to withdraw from others, and the others to withdraw from him. This diminishes social resources.

6. Riding it out is not the same as denial, but it usually leads to denial on many components of suicidal pain: *This* (embarrassing problem) doesn't bother me. Denial on pain is a leading cause of depression. Denial on bad feelings often comes out in other ways: alcohol, drugs, reckless behavior, violence, stress induced physical disorders. Denial prevents the constructive discharge of painful feelings.

7. Riding it out usually involves the concealment of one's real condition. This leads to less than honest relationships; often times others sense that something is being concealed and keep a wary distance.

8. Holding off on doing anything until you get desperate means waiting until you are least able to make informed and sensible decisions about recovery programs. It means continuing to be in a condition in which you are less able to recognize and respond to the needs of loved ones.

9. The next point can best be made by means of an example. I once spoke in the classroom of a teacher who told us how her husband had suffered a painful physical condition that left him bedridden and unemployed. He eventually became very suicidal. For many months he had little contact with his male friends, while his wife frequently discussed their problems at school with other female teachers and staff members. People who are prone to use the ride-it-out strategy usually have, as friends, people who are also prone to use the ride-it-out strategy. And they not only use it on their own problems, they use it on other people's problems as well. "Anything I do will be useless or make it worse," can be used on others as well as the self.

Organizations and social groups transmit strong ride-it-out messages. "Don't talk about it, you might give people ideas," and "Once they're going do it, they're going do it and you can't stop them," imply "Say nothing," and "Do nothing." The mythology of suicide has an unstated corollary: Active measures to prevent suicide will either be wasted effort or make things worse. A major cause of suicide is the universal fear, "If I try to help someone and they commit suicide anyway, I am going to feel terrible." This fear causes people to act on the rule "Don't get involved," and thereby deprives the suicidal of coping resources. The fear is passed on from generation to generation and from groups to individuals. The primary reason why the suicidal use the ride-it-out strategy is personal interest; they want to avoid more pain for themselves. The social ride-it-out messages are not motivated solely by the desire to help keep the individual alive. The non-suicidal want you to ride it out because they (both individually and in collective group resources) do not want the discomfort and inconvenience that helping you may require, and they believe that helping you will cause other suicidal people to present themselves for assistance. They also believe that helping you with your pain may put the idea of suicide in someone else's mind, and cause that person to commit suicide. Society wants you to ride out your pain not so much because it believes that riding it out is good for you, but because it believes that your riding it out is good for society and for other potentially suicidal people.

For someone already burdened with suicidal pain, this situation leads to a difficult assessment. The victim must evaluate to what extent his belief that he should ride it out actually accords with what is in his best interest, and to what extent the belief simply results from cultural conditioning and enjoins him to act in a way that is not in his interest. Even if he determines if the latter is the case, he is still burdened with a further problem. It appears that "Take no action to reduce suicidal pain, either for yourself or for another person," is as much a norm of our culture as "Don't steal," and "Honor the flag." Obedience to these other social norms, even when it runs contrary to personal interest, is part of the social contract. Should we not also be obedient to the norm that says, "Ride it out"? The answer is no. The norms have exceptions. If you need to steal a loaf of bread to keep someone alive, or tear a strip of cloth to make a tourniquet, no one will feel that you have done something wrong. And strong cases can be made for the general social norms that these actions violate. Without them it would be difficult for society to exist. No case at all can be made for "Ride it out;" it is supported by nothing but ignorance and prejudice.

Recovering All By Yourself

Riding it out means hoping things will get better if you do nothing. A second recovery strategy does not advocate doing nothing, it encourages active measures on the side of life as long as they do not involve appeals to others for assistance. Like riding it out, to use only one's own resources for recovery avoids the social prejudice against the suicidal. It surely has had successes as well as failures. To attempt recovery without the aid of others, however, also has some disadvantages.

1. If it is to have the best chance to succeed, a recovery program that relies entirely upon the self requires that you be fully knowledgeable in every area in which you have suffered pain or been deprived of resources: child psychology, family psychology, depression, bereavement, sleeping disorders, etc. As people find out when they get

into recovery programs, simply suffering these pains does not mean that you know all there is to know about what caused them, and what can be done to treat them. There probably is no single person anywhere who knows all there is to know about every pain you have. There are also the problems of self-objectivity and overcoming denial while you are disabled by suicidal pain. I have never known anyone with suicidal pain whose self-perceptions were undistorted. To try to recover entirely on your own deprives you of resources for understanding your pain.

2. You are following a model that you do not use in other healthcare areas. You rely on other people to help you with heart problems and dental problems, and to help protect you from occupational hazards, automobile accidents, and criminal assault.

3. People in support groups have something valuable that you lack: experience with recovery.

4. Part of recovery means learning how to have better relations with other people. Many suicidal people fear they will be rejected for being suicidal, for particular parts of their pain, or simply in a vague and shamebound way for being who they are. If your recovery program does not involve other people, then you are not likely to make much progress on this fear.

5. "I'm a self-reliant person," is a part of your self-image that you feel is positive, and is something that helps you cope with your pain. To give up this resource can be a frightening thought. It is likely that you are, or were, a member of a group of people who each have similar concepts of self-reliance, and who admire each other for being self-reliant. You may feel that being less self-reliant threatens group disaffiliation, or threatens the possibility of rejoining if you are separated from the group. Perhaps you had a parent who admired self-reliance. These fears are natural, but they should be weighed against the consideration that depression, failure to recover from depression, and suicide also cause disapproval and group disaffiliation.

6. "I'm not a weak incompetent. I don't need other people to help me recover," is grandiosity. It copes with pain by saying "I'm better." This negative coping mechanism is part of depression, and a part that will remain unexamined in a self-only recovery program.

7. Doing it all on your own usually requires dishonesty with other people. In your social relationships you will have to pretend to be something you are not — i.e., not suicidal. This is a strain on you, and to not find anyone else who can honestly give you some acceptance will make it very hard to develop self-acceptance. If you see a doctor for a medical examination, you are unlikely to tell him that you want to find out if organic factors are contributing to your depression and suicidal feelings. If others do not know what your real situation is, they are unlikely to be optimally effective as resources.

8. Feelings of self-responsibility for recovery are apt to inaccurately color your efforts to understand your past, present, and future. You may fail to recognize that large parts of your pain are things for which you are not responsible. You may also believe that depression and suicidal feelings occur only to people who are weak and lack will power, and you may berate yourself if your recovery does not proceed smoothly. Besides having difficulties with accurately understanding your condition, you are also likely to have problems with perfectionism and impatience. Without the input of others, you are unlikely to appreciate that nearly everyone has problems, setbacks, and makes mistakes in recovery. When we are in a lot of pain, we want it to end quickly, yet impatience can undermine recovery from emotional problems just as it can cause setbacks for recovery from physical problems. Without people who are patient with you, you will have a tough time being patient with yourself.

The loneliness of some suicidal people has parallels with the severe loneliness of crossdressers. I once heard a member of a support group for transvestites and transsexuals speak about her condition. (She defined a transvestite as someone who thinks about himself as a man and a transsexual as someone who thinks about herself as a woman.) Despite considerable psychotherapy, she said that she had no explanation for the ultimate origins of her compulsive thinking and behavior. She thought that the disposition to crossdress might be inborn, and she mentioned crossdressing incidents from her childhood that she regarded as a form of child abuse. In any event, as an adult, she believed that she and the other members of her support group were people who no longer had a choice. She said that crossdressers find themselves with lives that have a great deal of fear and pain.

Inwardly they are tormented by the awareness that their feelings and behavior are at odds with the concept of masculinity that their culture has educated them to have. They experience tremendous conflicts in trying to deal with family, friends, employers, and the outside world. If they are open and honest about their situation, they are subject to physical, verbal, and emotional abuse. If they are secretive, they suffer loneliness, isolation, and despair over not being able to have honest relations with others. They live with chronic fear of physical harm and personal exposure. The speaker had tried to hang herself when she was a teenager. No studies have been done on this risk group, but anecdotal evidence suggests that crossdressers have higher than average rates for suicidal ideation and behavior.

CHAPTER EIGHT

GROUNDWORK FOR RECOVERY:

PART II

Evidence that Recovery Happens

Evidence that recovery is possible, a pain-coping resource, is not something to which the suicidal have much access.

1. For many problems there are self-help groups and programs that contain members who are in every stage of recovery. These stages are marked by reductions in pain and increases in coping resources. Joining such a program is a powerful experience for someone who believes his condition is hopeless. Unfortunately, there is no "Suicidals Anonymous". Many suicidal people do not believe that their pain matches up with any available program; they may practice denial on a problem; they may not know about available programs; they may not be fully aware of the relationship between a traumatic situation in their past and their current pain; or their pain may include considerable fear of contact with others, and the lack of knowledge that virtually all self-help programs are undemanding of newcomers.

2. A character that does not exist in television and popular fiction is someone who has recovered from a suicidal condition. The suicidal require courage and determination to stay alive in a world that treats them badly, but their story has not been told.

3. There is very little publicly available self-help literature by or about recovered suicidal people. This is especially true for older males, the group that has the highest rate of completed suicide. Academic literature on suicidal people focuses on their lives prior to treatment. Post-recovery material that would inspire hope is almost non-existent.

4. In the United States today there are at least 10 million suicide attempters, and several times that many serious considerers, who are now no longer suicidal. Evidence that these people exist and have recovered is unavailable to people who are, or will be, suicidal. This lack of information is a major gap in our suicide prevention resources; it is caused by stigma and prejudice. The formerly suicidal fear that they will suffer pain if their prior condition becomes known. This fear is legitimate: job and social discrimination are real; rumor and gossip are real; taunts and innuendoes are real; stigma and shame for the family are real. Evidence for hope is a resource that prevents suicide; the suicidal are deprived of this evidence by social prejudice.

5. Existing theories of suicide make it difficult for the suicidal to recognize common features of their condition. "I feel hopeless and my condition is unique," is a more despairing pair of beliefs than "I feel hopeless and millions of people with a similar condition have recovered." Many suicidal people fail to see themselves in accounts of suicide that emphasize anger turned inward, developmental deficits, a search for reunion, or a desire for revenge. "More pain than I can cope with," is a concept with which any suicidal person may identify. While no two suicidal people have identical aggregates of pains and resource deficiencies, the condition of each shares both a common structure and many component problems with millions of people who have recovered. Recognizing that each of the formerly suicidal were able to recover by reducing some of their pain, and increasing some of their resources, is a reasonable basis for hope.

The Wages of Recovery

A suicidal person is deterred from seeking help by the knowledge that if he recovers, he will subsequently carry the fear that someone will toss "ex-mental patient" or "suicide attempter" in his face. He will forever be someone who is tainted. He may lead an exemplary life before, during, and after his crisis, yet those who learn he was once hospitalized, or saw a therapist, have a social license for suspicion and distrust. This fear of future pain adds to current pain.

There is a sense in which this taint is real. Though it may cause the victim real suffering, it does not exist in the person who supposedly has it. The taint exists in the minds of the people who carry the license to be suspicious of the character of anyone who was once suicidal. As with other forms of prejudice, holders of the view "Once suicidal, forever untrustworthy," do not do so on the basis of evidence. Studies on the moral behavior of the post-suicidal do not exist. The prejudice is held because it helps the non-suicidal feel better about themselves. They are the mental and moral superiors of the post-suicidal individual. They have not engaged in his immoral thinking and behavior, and he, not they, has a life-long structural defect.

This variety of prejudice is probably no more eradicable from the human community than other types of longstanding bias. We can however, hope to make progress against it. We can directly fight stigma, we can conduct studies on the moral behavior of the post-suicidal, and we can work toward the recognition that the post-suicidal compose a very substantial percentage of the general population.

Post-Suicidal Attitudes Toward Suicidal Conditions

After a period of acute suicidal pain has passed, considerers, low-lethal attempters, and those around them often express the attitude that "I guess I wasn't really suicidal," or "He wasn't really suicidal." The victim is under pressure from the family and the larger community to practice denial and minimization. "If he's not ready to jump, he's not serious," has the post-critical stage analogue of "If he didn't make a serious attempt, he wasn't serious about it." The voluntarist position supports this attitude. If the important factors are choice, intention, and motive, and these things never came into existence, then there is no reason to suppose that the person was really suicidal. The aggregate pain model believes that the condition of having strong suicidal feelings is serious; more pain, or the withdrawal of resources, can result in suicide. In the immediate aftermath of a crisis the victim's condition is usually only slightly less precarious, and denial on the seriousness of the condition can discourage continuation with a recovery program.

In the longer term, however, it may be felt that this form of denial is harmless. As far as the initial victim is concerned, it often is. People recovering from the disease of substance abuse have to keep their guard up; one drink or drug can quickly return them to their former nightmare. A great many former substance abusers regard a fresh consciousness of how bad it was back then to be an essential coping resource. This does not seem to be the case among the formerly suicidal — people who say they had suicidal feelings when they were in high school or college, were getting a divorce, or were grieving the death of a loved one. Though it may take time to reach this stage, once they are recovered many of the formerly suicidal are able to endure disappointments without a resumption of their suicidal condition. On the aggregate pain model this is to be expected; the recovered suicidal are average people with average amounts of pain and pain-coping resources. The aggregate pain theory does not claim that being suicidal implies having a life-long disease or structural defect. Consequently, as far as the initial victim is concerned, to have a memory of the suicidal condition that reduces current pain may be more benign than to practice a similar form of denial on other types of conditions. When recovering alcoholics slip into denial, they take a drink and quickly reconvince themselves, and their acquaintances, of the seriousness of their prior condition. Denial on the seriousness of a previous suicidal condition need not lead to significant increases in pain or decreases in resources, and need not have analogous consequences.

At interpersonal and social levels, however, this self-deception of the post-suicidal is not harmless. If recovered considerers and low-lethal attempters generally practice denial on the seriousness of their former condition, they cannot help but reinforce the myth of "Not serious. Just wants attention." To the currently suicidal, people whose conditions are serious, the post-suicidal are unavailable as sources of hope.

Pats on the Back

Recovery from suicidal conditions is usually treated as something that does not warrant expressions of approval. One reason is that "Don't talk about it," applies to recovery, as it does to every other situation involving suicide. A second reason is denial that there is anything to be recovered from. A third and more painful reason why significant others withhold praise, congratulations, and even expressions of support is that doing so enables them to inflict punishment on the victim. Punishment is not limited to the overt infliction of pain or deprivation; it can also take the form of withholding earned benefits. Withholding praise for successful recovery is punitive, especially for the depressed, since a common precipitating factor in depression is the investment of great effort in something for which one has gotten little reward. The feeling that the punishment is justifiable has two causes. The first is the judgment that the victim deserves to be punished for having gotten himself into the stigmatized condition in the first place. The second is that relatives of recovered sufferers regard themselves as having been made to suffer unfairly, and as being permanently stigmatized themselves. To refuse to acknowledge the achievement of recovery is a way to justifiably punish the cause of the pain. Withholding praise is a form of punishment that does not discharge the resentment; since the anger remains, the non-approval is self-perpetuating.

Many suicidal people come from family, work, school, and social situations where "You are not good enough," was a recurrent message, no matter what they did or did not accomplish. Within these situations, "Your recovery is not enough," can be an anticipated response. "I'm not enough," was internalized long before the suicidal condition developed and can continue afterward with the supplements of "My recovery is not fast enough," and "My level of recovery is not enough."

A Double Bind

One part of the mythology of suicide holds that considerers and attempters never were in a condition that required recovery. The road back to normal life should be short, achieved in the time it takes to snap one's fingers. It is nothing for which one should be congratulated. Another part of the mythology holds that anyone who was ever suicidal is inherently defective in mind and morals, and should never again be trusted. Both myths have a common denominator: they deny recovery ever happens. Suicidal people, struggling to recover, are repeatedly battered by combinations of these two myths.

The Rights of the Suicidal

The expression "rights of the suicidal" is usually taken to refer to the alleged rights to complete confidentiality, to refuse treatment, to reject involuntary institutionalization, and to commit suicide. The underlying conception of rights in this context is the traditional one of non-interference. In these areas other persons, or society in general, should not interfere with the decisions or expressed wishes of suicidal people. In the non-interference conception it is generally held that a person does not have the right if at least one of three conditions is satisfied: the exercise of the right harms others, the person is either not an adult or not of sound mind, or there is overriding social need. An example of the latter condition is when a government interferes with someone's liberty by inducting him into the army. In suicide it is rare to find cases in which we can be certain that both of the first two conditions are not met. Most suicides cause harm to others. Soundness of mind, in suicide prevention work, should be a broader concept than absence of insanity or intoxication. It must include full knowledge of one's self, one's situation, and one's alternatives. This is rarely, if ever, had by anyone, and certainly not by people whose great pain has disabled their cognitive capacities. More directly, the overwhelming majority of the utterances of "I want to die," have "I want to live," as their real meaning. There is no known criterion by which the suicidal person, or his acquaintances, can distinguish genuine presentations of the rationality of suicide from cries for help.

Debate about the rights of the individual are, in mirror image fashion, debates about the behavioral guidelines that other people or society in general should follow with respect to that individual. Our views about *his* rights are also views about *our* right to take or not take certain actions that affect his liberty. These debates, which we, not they, conduct, are adversely affected by the same unconscious needs that generate and sustain our abusive and self-interested mythology of suicide. The debate about his needs and his interests is deeply affected by the unacknowledged needs of the non-suicidal to cope with their fears of blame, guilt, responsibility, and vulnerability. The non-suicidal do need to cope with their emotional turmoil. But rather than argue about rights, a better way to cope is to adopt the no-fault view of suicide, and the guideline, "Always take extra steps for the side of life."

At a social level, debate about the non-interference rights of the suicidal is a red herring that deflects public attention from the real issues. The irrelevancy of the debate can be seen by comparing the right to commit suicide to the right to have a fatal heart attack. Perhaps people do have a right to have a heart attack, but should "the right to have a heart attack" be the leading issue in public policy discussions about heart disease?

A more progressive framework for discussions of the rights of the suicidal is the modern view that statements of rights are statements of needs: a right to education, to medical care, to equal opportunity. Many contemporary recovery programs have "Bills of Rights" as part of their literature. (A number of items on the list below have been borrowed or adapted from the handouts of various support groups.) These handouts, most of which employ the need concept of rights, clearly serve useful purposes. Unfortunately, the study of how and why they are helpful is a neglected topic in academic literature. These statements of rights develop senses of self-worth, help people to manage new post-crisis senses of identity, and function as manifestoes of how the victims want to change the nature of their interaction with the rest of the world. They sanction changes in personal behavior, and insist on changes in social behavior. Statements of rights help undo the effects of having internalized social attitudes that negatively judge victims of the condition under treatment. These ends are obviously desirable for people trying to recover from suicidal pain, and could not help but have an effect on the social ideology that causes such statements of rights to be necessary. For the suicidal, at least, aggressive assertion of need is better than defensive resistance to interference. The suicidal commonly believe that they are worthless, that they do not deserve assistance and respect, and that discrimination, prejudice, and abuse are the just deserts of anyone in a suicidal condition. We need to empower the suicidal with permission to resist the harm that is unwittingly inflicted upon them. They need verbal and cognitive tools to resist social sources of suicidal pain; they need to regain the feeling that they have some measure of power to affect what happens to them.

Rights of the Suicidal

Suicidal people have a right to treatment for alcoholism, drug dependency, eating disorders, compulsive sexual behavior, sleeping disorders, phobias, anxiety attacks, stress, homelessness, sexual dysfunction, emotional problems, and conditions in physical ill-health. Young people have the right to receive treatment regardless of age or family consent.

A right to an equal share in the allocation of healthcare educational and research resources.

A right to have counselors who are trained and supported in their work with the suicidal.

A right to not be suspended from school or job. A prior suicidal condition is not a legitimate basis for discrimination.

A right to have police officers, counselors, and administrators be educated about the legal rights of suicidal people.

A right to better protection against detainment and restraint without sufficient cause.

A right to not be manipulated for the benefit of the non-suicidal.

Denial, hostility, prejudice, discrimination, rejection, minimization, and belittlement are violations of the rights of the suicidal.

A right to not be a scapegoat.

A right to reject abusive treatment.

A right to put an end to conversations with people who seek to demean, abuse, and humiliate the suicidal.

A right to reject demands to justify one's condition, feelings, or beliefs.

A right to reject the judgmental labels of others.

A right to not be blamed for being suicidal.

A right to not be interrupted, corrected, or informed when trying to express or reach an understanding of one's condition.

A right to serious attention at all stages of a suicidal condition.

A right to a plurality of recovery programs.

A right to non-judgmental and supportive counseling for each condition that is a source of pain.

A right to ask for what is needed for recovery.

A right to not have to suffer to get what one needs.

A right to as much time as needed to find and pursue a path to recovery.

A right to have one's self and one's problems seen as part of life, not as alien entities. A right to acceptance within the human race.

A right to be treated as a person in pain, not as a moral outcast. A right to not be approached with a presumption of distrust and suspicion.

A right to not be seen as permanently damaged or unreliable.

A right to not be blamed if the honest expression of suicidal feelings causes others to feel uncomfortable. A right to not be seen as the cause of those uncomfortable feelings.

A right to one's feelings and beliefs, and to express them in one's own way.

A right to be what one is.

A right to reject demands to apologize for being oneself.

A right to be with people who are supportive, rather than abusive.

A right to reject demands to be perfect.

A right to become a new self, rather than an expectation to return to an old self.

A right to set limits.

A right to not be held responsible for another person's problems.

A right to say no, without shame, to demands to do things that one is not yet ready to do.

A right to change one's mind and elect different courses of action.

A right to make mistakes.

A right to be seen as someone who can be helpful to others who are in pain, and to share what one has learned with others.

Recovery from Shame

Prior to the development of their condition, suicidal people spend their lives uncritically accepting the belief that it is shameful to be suicidal. As they try to recover, their acquaintances and their community continue to believe that it is shameful both to be and to have been suicidal. From a personal standpoint, the belief that these negative attitudes are warranted can be reduced by intellectually accepting a view, such as involuntarism or the biochemical theory of depression, that regards the suicidal condition as non-moral. But this kind of belief can only be partially effective against the combined forces of prior social conditioning and the ongoing prejudices of one's acquaintances and community. The suicidal are still left with residual feelings of personal shamefulness, and with the belief that they remain shameful in the eyes of others.

Agnes Heller, although she does not apply her views to recovery from suicidal pain, has located the source of this problem in her essay on shame:

> External authority not only prescribes proper behaviour but also offers modes of conduct for persons who have failed to act according to the requirements set by the authority. Repentance means putting things right and everyone knows how they can be put right. Shame is a tormenting feeling. It needs outlets, and meticulous prescriptions for proper 'repayment' serve as such. The mode of 'repayment' can be very painful, but if it is carried out properly the crumbled person regains his or her posture, the disgraced person his or her honour. (1985, p. 20)

Shame, whether or not it is deserved, leaves its sufferers with the feeling of indebtedness. Victims feel that they should do something to set things right with whomever — family, organization, social class, profession, community — they believe has been offended or harmed by the shameful behavior, and who continue to look upon them as being shameful people. This aspect of shame is not part of any psychiatric program for recovery for depression, but it is dealt with directly in the Twelve-Step Anonymous groups. These groups operate under the view that addictive behavior is not a moral issue, but a disease. But they also have a principle that members make amends to anyone their behavior has harmed, and members serve the larger community by making their program available to anyone who actively suffers from the addictive condition. Many members find these activities to be adequate outlets for feelings of shame indebtedness.

A suicidal person, however, can find "modes of conduct" that tell him how to put right his feeling of shame indebtedness in neither the norms of his community nor in any available program of recovery. As Heller's remark about the mode of repayment indicates, the shamed person is supposed to suffer pain, or at least not enjoy life, until the debt is repaid. If there are no socially recognized modes of repayment, then the shamed person has no alternative but to suffer indefinitely. Not only does he never lose the feeling of shame indebtedness, but anyone who knows of his condition may continue to regard him as shameful. The non-suicidal also have no awareness of modes of conduct that repay the shame indebtedness of having been suicidal, and they have no basis from which to cease their negative attitudes. Even if as individuals they accept a non-moral view of suicide, they are still influenced by their prior conditioning and the force of social opinion. How can a suicidal person ever gain a sense of social acceptance of recovery, as long as a belief in his indebtedness is still felt by others? This can be excruciating for people whose problem essentially is that they have more pain than they can cope with, and it is a significant source of hopelessness in the suicidal. The absence of social norms for the repayment of shame indebtedness for having been suicidal is itself a cause of suicide. (The volunteers on a suicide hotline I worked on included a few people who had once been suicidal and had made substantial progress in recovery. Some of these people seemed to have a semi-conscious sense of shame indebtedness as one of the motives for their volunteer service. These particular individuals, perhaps because of the personality traits of shamebound people, were excellent phone workers.)

Understanding

Suicidal people frequently say, "No one understands." Sometimes this means that no one at all understands, sometimes that no one besides the speaker understands. What it is that no one understands may be the suicidal feelings, the entirety of the painful condition, the fact that the speaker feels hopeless, or the fact that he feels powerless to improve his situation. A lack of understanding is painful, whether it is in oneself or others. To have the desire for understanding frustrated is additionally painful. When understanding is provided, as it may be by a friend, counselor, or self-help group, the pain is reduced.

Understanding something involves knowing what the causal sequence is that led to the situation in question. If I know the cause of something, I understand why it happened. Since the causal background of human emotion and behavior is extraordinarily complex, it follows that understanding is nearly always something that is only partially accomplished. Our partial understanding of something is achieved in bits and pieces. Sometimes, of course, we do feel that we have immediately gotten full understanding. For example, in the evening I may find myself being inappropriately angry at someone at home, and then recollect that during the day I repressed an angry feeling toward someone at work. When I assume the earlier incident caused the latter I may have a feeling of full understanding, but this is illusory. The significant increase in understanding has been mistaken for full understanding. I may not know why I am the sort of person who would take offense at the situation at work, why I repress my feelings in that sort of situation, or why I am the sort of person who would ventilate his anger in a subsequent situation. My understanding of the evening's episode has increased, but it is still only partial. (At a theoretical level, this mistake is made by approaches to suicide that consider only parts of the victim's pain. Psychoanalysis uses its techniques on material from the unconscious to gain knowledge about part of the causal history of someone's pain, and assumes that this partial understanding is full understanding. Similarly, cognitive psychology is able to provide insight into a part of the causal framework of suicidal pain, and claims that the distorted thinking process is the entirety of the problem of suicide in people who suffer depression.)

The pain exceeds pain-bearing capacity theory is a non-technical causal model; it is designed to help all of us understand suicide. The limitations of other approaches to suicide leave more than 90 percent of all suicidal people, their friends and counselors, and the survivors of a suicide victim without useful models for understanding suicide. Engineers have a better understanding of why bridges collapse than ordinary citizens, but ordinary citizens can readily grasp the idea that bridges will collapse if their frameworks are weakened, or they suffer too much weight and stress. Moreover, if suicide is not voluntary, then we are not faced with the burden of trying to explain and understand something that is, by definition, outside the causal sequence of natural events.

Suicidal people, and those who would help them, can gain understanding of their situation by identifying the sources of pain and the absences of coping resources. The understanding is unlikely to ever be complete, and it is unlikely that it can be wholly generated by the suicidal person or a single counselor. A person might gain understanding about pill dependency from a support group, understanding about a social problem from a friend, and understanding about grief after death from a religious counselor.

The business of suicide prevention can be more effectively conducted if we have realistic expectations about understanding. Suicide has no single cause, so not finding that single cause need not be a chronic source of pain and frustration. Small achievements in understanding the causes of one's pain, for example, recognizing repressed envy toward a sibling, are solid steps toward recovery. As with any large scale project, small achievements on a daily basis often do not result in an immediate feeling that progress is being made. The progress is real, even if it requires time for insights to accumulate and sink in. And, increased understanding is only one way to reduce pain and increase resources. Improvements in physical well-being, habits, environment, and relations with others may also be necessary.

Patience

A step toward reduced pain and increased resources is the cultivation of the quality of patience. This is an activity that itself requires a great deal of patience.

Patience is an unpopular concept in American culture. Faced with a bad situation, the person who adopts a "Let's change things now," attitude is most likely to win social approval. In almost any field of endeavor, we admire those who get results quickly. We see impatience produce success both in large scale public affairs, and in the business of our personal lives. Even though we may not like to be on the receiving end of other people's impatience, we generally admire it as a personal quality. The patient, on the other hand, are thought to be lacking in healthy self-interest. Get there quicker. Get it done sooner. These values bring success in so many areas that we inevitably try to apply them everywhere. It is not difficult to see that some people sometimes go too far. Chronic impatience with others can provoke considerable resentment. Chronic impatience with oneself risks chronic unhappiness.

In suicide prevention we look for healthy ways to reduce pain in both the short- and long-term. Patience is better than impatience. Patience does not mean do nothing, or ride it out. Patience means accepting that certain processes in the natural world take time. Problems in both physical and emotional health rarely heal overnight. Impatience in situations that will not yield to impatience only produces more pain. In these situations, patience is the fastest way to recover.

Recovery from suicidal conditions is one of the most poorly understood human processes. We spend millions upon millions to study the process by which soy beans develop; the process by which someone goes from being suicidal to normal life receives virtually nothing. The bereaved have stages of grief to give themselves, and their counselors, some idea of their status. Recovery programs for substance abusers have anniversaries of sobriety and other criteria by which progress may be recognized. Our unwillingness to look at the aftermath of non-fatal suicidal crises gives us an absence of stages of recovery criteria that people in pain could use as goals or markers. The suicidal believe that there is a vast gulf between being suicidal and the enjoyment of ordinary life. In reality there are interim periods of time during which recovery work must be completed. There is no evidence that this recovery work is something that happens in an instant. Whatever the process is, it takes time to complete and patience to endure.

Patience from other people may be harder to get for recovery from suicidal conditions than it is in any other area of emotional health. The cardinal rule is that other people's impatience says nothing about you, but only about the discomfort that your condition has aroused in them. They will indicate that failure to achieve instant recovery means that you are a willful malingerer. This is false, but unfortunately the impatience of others is like self-impatience, it retards recovery.

"Why aren't you farther along?" is the knee-jerk question of modern America. It can always be asked of anyone about any endeavor. Why aren't you farther along with your career, your education, your home redecorating project, your diet, etc., etc., etc. "Why wasn't more done sooner?" often seems to be the theme of 75 percent of the nightly news. It is such a deeply ingrained part of our thinking process, that it seems like heresy to suggest that sometimes we do it too much. It puts the victim of the question in a defensive position of having to discuss his presumed shortcomings. It gives the questioner a comfortable structure for his own behavior and feelings. While it masquerades as encouragement, it is often nothing more than abuse.

This is especially unfair in the case of the suicidal. No one knows how long recovery is supposed to take. The literature on recovery, being non-existent, contains no timetables that say that for suicidal people of types x, y, and z, recovery usually takes time periods t1, t2, and t3. There are no studies that show that telling suicidal people "Hurry up and get better," succeeds in speeding up recovery. Impatience helps the non-suicidal cope with their feelings, and makes the suicidal feel worse.

Problems with both patience and acceptance inevitably follow from the fact that the self and others can only hope for partial understanding. If we have full understanding, we can be fully patient and often fully accepting. Since we lack full understanding, we cannot help but have difficulties with patience and acceptance.

Acceptance

A large part of the thinking of suicidal people can be articulated as, "Life with these things in it is unacceptable." These things can be anything that causes human pain: poverty, loneliness, the loss of a loved one, mental illness, a disabling injury or accident, impotence, lack of approval from family or a social group, feelings of hopelessness and powerlessness. Some people have identities that are focused on a single talent, skill, or attribute; the loss or threatened loss of that quality may cause overwhelming despair. A small step toward relief for the frozen nature of these pains is to gain an increased appreciation of the roles played in them by envy, shame, self-pity, and grandiosity. A second step is to gain increased acceptance of the fact that the pains exist and will not go away quickly. Acceptance can reduce the phenomenon of pain on pain, and help interrupt pain-increasing vicious circles. Our cultural prejudices cause people in pain to automatically suffer four additional pains: both externally and internally they are negatively judged for being in pain, and for not immediately getting themselves out of pain. Acceptance of pain can be increased by recognizing that these judgments are unfair. In nearly every case, the causal history of the suicidal condition extends to factors that are far beyond reasonable limits of individual responsibility. It is rare that the pain from these causes can be remedied overnight.

The same kind of acceptance can be developed toward not only particular sources of unhappiness, but also to the suicidal ideation and feelings that one has in addition to one's particular problems. Victims of suicidal conditions suffer from social rejection and from their internalization of social rejection. To the self and others, to be in pain is to be unacceptable, and to be suicidal is also to be unacceptable. Acceptance, the antidote to this rejection, begins with the recognition that there is no badness in the suicidal person. The conceptions of the badness of suicidal people stem entirely from the ignorance and prejudice of the larger community. A part of the pain of the acutely suicidal person is the feeling of estrangement from the rest of humanity. This pain is partly caused by his internalization of our culture's alienating mythology, and it is aggravated because a part of him subscribes to the social norms of the non-estranged, and negatively judges the part that feels estranged. The recognition that there are no basic differences between the suicidal and the non-suicidal can relieve this pain and contribute to greater self-acceptance. Giving up the "blame the victim" position, giving up the doctrine of mental and moral inferiority, and giving up the view that "He's different," are major steps toward a relief from self-hatred. Our ideas about what is negative about ourselves, and what is positive about ourselves, largely come from external sources. These external sources, particularly the moral climate of our childhood, tend to inculcate ideas in us that are in the interest of the external sources, not in our own interest, and among these ideas is an exaggerated conception of self-responsibility. In depression and suicide some of these ideas can cause us a great deal of unnecessary additional pain. Learning something about the causal history of these ideas can help relieve that pain, and move us away from self-rejection and toward self-acceptance. A further important step toward self-acceptance is to receive some acceptance from other people. In contemporary America, support groups are often a more reliable resource for acceptance than family, friends, and healthcare professionals. Fellow strugglers for understanding, patience, and acceptance can provide types of assistance you are unlikely to find anywhere else.

CHAPTER NINE

THE SURVIVORS
OF SUICIDE VICTIMS

The "survivors" are the relatives, friends, acquaintances, and caregivers of a suicide victim. Nearly all societies have mourning rituals. After a death, survivors need to go through a grief-work process before they can return to normal functioning. When the deceased is a suicide victim, this process is much more difficult to complete. The grief reaction to death by illness or accident includes denial, shock, guilt, anger, and depression. Death by suicide intensifies all these, and may also include feelings of shame, failure, and rejection. There are many additional burdens for the mourners of a suicide victim:

1. Stigma — For centuries suicides, suicide attempters, and their families were badly treated by civil and religious authorities and by the general public. They were denied last rites, subjected to criminal penalties, and were the objects of social contempt of every sort. Some developments in modern science have added a fourth source of stigma: various psychological theories have held that suicide is caused by problems in parent/child relationships. Although the degree of stigma attached to suicides by these sources has diminished, it is still very real.

2. Pain and Anger — Unexpected deaths usually produce the initial defense mechanisms of shock, numbness, and denial. All these are increased when the death is a suicide. As they recede, reality sinks in.

This reality is more painful than other forms of grief. Survivors may experience great anger — at other people, at the victim, at God, at themselves.

3. Saying Goodbye — When someone dies by terminal illness, survivors often have a chance to say goodbye. This can be of considerable value in the grief-work process. Suicide survivors regret not having had this opportunity. What makes this especially difficult is that the suicide victim, without their knowing it, may have said goodbye to them. It is not uncommon for the suicide to tell a survivor, "I love you," within hours of his death.

4. Health — Health problems, such as diabetes and high blood pressure, may get markedly worse after the suicide of a relative or friend. Survivors may have lengthy periods of heightened anxiety over the welfare of themselves and other survivors.

5. Anniversaries — Holidays and the anniversaries of the birth and death of the victim can be very difficult.

6. Less Support — Historically, society denied the rituals of a funeral and a mourning period to the survivors of a suicide. Although this is no longer the case, the amount, quality, and duration of social support that they receive is still much less than normal. Some of the lack of support is due to uncertainty, fear, and aversion to pain: "I don't know what to do"; "I'm afraid I might say the wrong thing and make it worse"; and, in an unarticulated way, "I feel uncomfortable being around people in pain. My discomfort will be painful for me and, since I don't think I can hide my discomfort, it will add to their pain."

7. Limited Assistance — The special problems of the survivors of suicide receive little attention in the training of therapists and counselors. There is little publicly available literature. Because suicide is not talked about, counselors for every population underestimate the extent to which their caseloads include survivors.

8. Trauma to the Family — The family system of which the suicide was a member suffers a tremendous shock. Seventy percent of the parents of teen suicides eventually divorce. The nature of the death increases the difficulty of resolving estate, insurance, and child custody issues. Families frequently move after a suicide. They are angry at the social stigma that has unfairly been placed upon them.

9. The Mystery of Suicide — In cases of death by accident, illness, old age, alcoholism, and homicide, the survivors know what killed the deceased. They have something specific on which to focus their feelings of guilt and anger. Survivors of suicide, however, often become preoccupied with wondering how the suicide could have happened. Only about 10 percent to 15 percent of all suicides leave notes, and these are usually unsatisfactory as explanations. Existing theories of suicide do not provide answers that survivors can assimilate, and the feeling that the cause of the suicide remains a mystery causes the mourning process to be more difficult and to last longer.

10. Assault on Values — The survivors usually come from the same social, economic, and educational background as the victim. They shared the same values and attitudes. The survivor may think to himself, "This person thought life is not worth living, and he was a lot like me, so what should I think?"

11. Loss of faith and trust in oneself and others — Survivors may lose self-esteem and worry about suicidal feelings in themselves and others. Child and adolescent survivors may feel, "You made me suicidal."

12. Friendships become weakened or lost, and survivors have difficulty making new ones. Each encounter with someone new may be approached with dread and anxiety. Will this new person innocently ask, "How many children do you have?" and how should I respond?

13. Delayed Grief — It is not uncommon for the mourning process to be arrested for an indefinite period — sometimes decades — and then resume forcefully. This may be occasioned by some other crisis in the survivor's life, and can be extremely distressing. "Waves of grief" are common for immediate survivors during the first year or longer.

Survivors are often burdened with deep and complex feelings of guilt:

14. The most basic feeling of guilt is due to the facts that we are not perfect and that we make choices in how we deal with others. After suicide it is normal to have exaggerated feelings about one's ability to influence the life of another. The survivor may brood obsessively about things he wishes he could have done differently.

15. Guilt may help keep feelings of anger toward the deceased repressed, and keep conscious thoughts of anger from being expressed to

others. The repression of anger is supported by an adage that it is wrong to think or speak ill of the dead. Not getting these feelings out may make the grieving process more difficult.

16. Sooner or later the survivors will have a few moments or hours in which they forget about the death and enjoy life as they previously did. When this interlude ends — with a jolt — they may have a surge of guilt.

17. Feelings of guilt often lead to self-punishment and denial. Survivors may refuse to participate in activities that normally bring them pleasure. They may fear that feeling pleasure may cause them to feel more guilt.

18. If the deceased was a burden to the family, they may have a feeling of relief. They may then feel guilty for feeling relieved.

19. Survivors may have disturbing dreams about the deceased. Some may express ideas that cause the dreamer to feel guilty.

20. It is common for survivors to idealize both the victim and the relationship they had to him. This factor may increase the guilt feelings.

21. Feelings of guilt can be very persistent. They do not seem to fade and lose strength in the same way that other emotions do.

Talking About It

Writers on suicide bereavement are unanimous in saying that it is essential for the survivors to talk about it. They say that the word "suicide" should be used, and encourage the survivors to talk about the death with each other. They feel that it is desirable for the conversations to take place in the home, that they begin as soon as possible, that they include children, and that each person share feelings and thoughts with as many other survivors as possible.

The growing number of self-help support groups for the survivors of suicide victims have much to teach the world about coping with pain. Members simply share their experiences and provide mutual support. A small group in Brooklyn that I have attended is facilitated by two women who lost a friend to suicide. Neither is a professional counselor;

both are employed in the business world. Group members simply share experiences and provide support for each other. They sometimes talk on the phone between the once a month meetings and actively support an annual regional conference on survivor issues. Attendance at just a single meeting of this type of group can help relieve the feeling of being alone with the tragedy, the feeling that no one understands, and the feeling that there is no process to suicide bereavement. The support groups help circulate literature, much of which is written by the survivors themselves. One handout contained

> I wish you would not be afraid to speak my child's name. My child lived and was important and I need to hear his name.
>
> If I cry or get emotional if we talk about my child, I wish you knew that it isn't because you have hurt me; the fact that my child died has caused my tears. You have allowed me to cry and I thank you. Crying and emotional outbursts are healing.
>
> I wish you wouldn't expect my grief to be over in six months. The first few years are going to be exceedingly traumatic for us. As with alcoholics, I will never be "cured" or a "former bereaved parent", but will forevermore be a "recovering bereaved parent".
>
> I wish you understood that grief changes people. I am not the same person I was before my child died and I never will be that way again. If you keep waiting for me to "get back to my old self", you will stay frustrated. I am a new creature with new thoughts, dreams, aspirations, values and beliefs. Please try to get to know the new me -- maybe you'll like me still.[1]

Unfortunately, talking about it is not easy. For centuries suicide was one of those things that should not be talked about. Even today many suicides are kept secret from family members as well as outsiders. People are afraid to talk because they are afraid of how the other person may react — and of how they may react. Simply by offering to listen we can do a great deal to help a survivor cope with the stigma and taboo, and to come to terms with his grief.

The "leave it to the professionals" myth is a strong isolating factor in survivor situations. A police officer told me about the suicide four years earlier of his cousin-in-law and fishing partner. The victim had been under treatment for a drug problem. His father had committed suicide twenty years earlier by a different method. I asked the officer if he had ever spoken with his cousin or her two adolescent children about the death. He quickly responded, "They went for counseling." This lack of communication is sad; as the case histories at the end of this chapter indicate, the children need positive adult figures in their lives.

Secrecy

Those who work with survivors feel that there are very few situations where secrecy about suicide is a good policy. Children, for example, will nearly always find out anyway, and often under less than desirable circumstances. Secrecy, partial secrecy, and delays in providing information usually create resentment and distrust. Resentments and distrust damage relationships among survivors, and survivors especially need strong and supportive relationships. Children are profoundly affected by a suicide in the family. They very often, on their own, reach the conclusion that they are somehow to blame for the death. To not include them in bereavement activities and discussions does nothing to discourage this idea. The people who keep the secret usually say they are doing so for the protection of others. Any benefits of secrecy for those being protected are unproven, and the secret-keepers are spared an unpleasant task and have bolstered their own feelings by saying that others cannot cope. To inform people in a timely and supportive manner is less bad than having them find out in other ways.

Duration of Grief

The mourning process is greatly extended when death is by suicide. Unfortunately, we live in a culture in which faster is better, much better. The social stigma attached to this type of mourning means that both the survivors and the people around them will feel social pressure to have the mourning period come to an end. Survivors who do not perform or pretend to perform the impossible task of "snap out of it and get on with your life," will suffer further stigma and isolation. The fact that this type of mourning takes a long time, makes it take an even longer time. Survivors need all the patience that we can give them.

An effect of the stigma is that the survivors of a suicide victim are reluctant to reach out for fear of rejection and negative judgment. A strong sense of personal privacy may be good in many situations, but in our relationships with people in pain it often contributes to isolation and a weakening of support systems. We need to be willing to take an extra step to assure them of our concern.

Something not often appreciated is that bereavement — after death by any means — may interact with other problems in a way that has one similarity with substance abuse. Denial on the pain of a loved one's death, or being frozen in a painful stage of grief, are often factors that block recovery in other areas. After substance abuse, bereavement deserves priority in any recovery program. To bide one's time and hope for spontaneous remission is not often the best policy after a profound loss.

Caregivers as Suicide Survivors

Healthcare workers, mental health professionals, counselors for at risk populations, and many others are likely to know and care about someone who dies by suicide. They experience versions of many of the emotional reactions that happen to immediate survivors. Unlike family and friends, caregivers have the grim advantage of knowing that they are at risk to suffer this kind of loss. As with survivors of someone who dies by terminal illness, caregivers can to some extent prepare themselves for the grief-work process.

A first step in this process is to put suicide postvention policies and training in place before it becomes necessary to use them. As with planning for other types of unhoped for crises, this practice will help reduce the likelihood that there will be need to use the procedures.

A second step is to recognize that perfectionistic standards among suicide prevention workers will do more harm than good. Many suicides are preventable, but the prevention of all suicides is an impossible goal. Suicide will happen, and it will happen in organizations that have the best available programs and procedures. If the caregivers were doing what they could in the circumstances, they cannot be faulted.

During the latter stages of the grief-work process it is helpful for caregivers to remember that their relationship with the deceased had its positive aspects. A caregiver can make up a list of the things he brought to your life, and you brought to his life. The support given to the person may have reduced his loneliness, and lengthened his lifespan and improved its quality. Even in the cases where what we have to give is not enough, what we do is still worthwhile. In *On Death and Dying*, Elisabeth Kubler-Ross describes what it is like to befriend the terminally ill. She says that these people are glad to be interviewed by her seminar because of "...the need of the dying person to leave something behind, to give a little gift, to create an illusion of immortality perhaps." Without knowing it, the people we lose do this; they come to occupy special places in our memories. To accept these memories shows our care and concern, and it changes us as individuals. If taken properly, these changes can be positive.

Involuntarism, Aggregate Pain, and Survivng a Suicide

A primary aim for the involuntarist conception of suicide is that it be a useful tool for survivors to have in trying to cope with their own pain. Our culture views suicide as an act that is chosen, and for which the agent is morally responsible. Though there are some people who regard some suicides as morally good acts, most people, and society in general, regard at least most suicides as morally wrong. Given the enormity of the action, some go on to the characterize the suicide as a morally bad person. The idea that a loved one and his actions are bad is very painful. It contributes to the internal sense of contamination that many survivors feel, and it contributes to the great anger they often feel toward the deceased. Moral condemnation of suicide is deeply ingrained in our culture; it is difficult to conceive of an alternative.

The involuntarist theory says that the suicide no more chooses his death than the heart attack patient his coronary, or the cancer patient his tumor. Sometimes pain becomes literally unbearable; this causes suicide. Events that we are powerless over are not events we choose; they are not events for which we are morally responsible. Since we are not responsible for these events, they are not morally good or bad and should not be used to assess the goodness or badness of the deceased. There is no basis in morality for blame or condemnation of the suicide. He is a victim, not a perpetrator.

Many survivors brood obsessively about "the cause" of their loved one's death. The aggregate pain theory provides a plausible explanation of why the event of suicide happens. Suicide does not have a single cause; there are thousands of causally significant factors. We can no more get a full understanding of a suicidal condition after a person is dead than we can while he is alive. The familiar complaint of survivors, "I don't think I'll ever know why it happened," a complaint that frequently annoys their acquaintances, is entirely legitimate. What it would take to understand fully someone's suicide is not something we are going to get in our lifetimes. We can continuously develop a partial understanding of his death by learning what we can about the causal history of his pain and his coping resources. We can gain information, learn more about conditions that affected the person, and improve our theoretical understanding of the causes of suicide. In reaching an improved understanding, immediate survivors have an additional burden. The emotional impact of the loss can make it difficult for them to think about the event at all, let alone think about it as clearly as they would other matters in their lives. As they work at coming to terms with their grief, they will be in a better position to develop an improved understanding of why the suicide happened.

A second reason why it is legitimate for survivors to say, "I don't understand," is that this is an accurate statement about their own pain. Not having any understanding of a major trauma in one's life is itself an agonizing pain on top of the original pain. The statement is a request for help in reducing this pain. It is usually made to people who are less emotionally burdened, and may be in a somewhat better position to help survivors understand the event. Unfortunately, the standard response that survivors get to this request is "Stop dwelling on it; put it behind you and get on with your life." This helps its speaker cope with his own discomfort, but adds — a lot — to the pain of survivors. The desire for understanding is a desire to reduce turmoil and confusion, and to increase coping resources. It is also part of a quest for a measure of acceptance. Involuntarism hopes to move suicide from the morally unacceptable to the morally neutral. Since suicide is an event in the natural world, we can hope to develop an understanding of it that approaches our understanding of death by other natural causes. The

measure of acceptance that we do reach for death by other means is
something that we can work toward in responding to suicide. The need
for acceptance is why some survivors develop attitudes of moral
approval about some suicides. Their need for acceptance is legitimate,
but a moral approval approach for suicide postvention makes it
difficult to formulate an adequate approach for suicide prevention.

The aggregate pain view of depression may be of some assistance to
survivors as they seek to deal with their own pain. Freud developed
the psychoanalytic theory of depression by comparing it to mourning in
ordinary life. Mourning in ordinary life, however, does not receive the
social disapproval that depression does. It may be more helpful to
compare depression to grief after a stigmatized death. Both the
depressed and the survivors of a suicide victim suffer increased pain
and decreased resources because of social prejudice. They suffer from
external sources, and they suffer because they have internalized these
prejudices. Freud argued that anger was the major component of
depression; later analysts added guilt as a significant factor. Many
approaches to grief emphasize these emotions, and neglect envy,
shame, and self-pity. These latter emotions are often major parts of
grief after suicide, and it can be helpful to reduce some of the pain they
cause.

The role of volition in our mythology of suicide leads us to apply
supererogatory standards to victims of suicidal pain. "Supererogatory"
is a term in moral philosophy that means above and beyond the call of
duty. In suicide we expect people to endure, no matter how intense their
pain or how long it lasts. This is an unfair standard; it demands the
impossible. Survivors often apply supererogatory standards to
themselves. "I should have done more. I should have seen. I should
have known." These standards are unfair. In most cases the survivors
were doing what most people in our culture would do if they were in
similar situations, and in many cases the survivors were already doing
much more. What they recognized and knew about the situation, prior
to the suicide, is what most people would have recognized or known. It
is normal to be uncertain about what to do and what to believe about
someone else's suicidal pain. To be worn out and frustrated, and to have
limits to fatigue and frustration, are completely normal. I have
listened to many survivors review the few days prior to a suicide, and I
have rarely heard anything for which someone should feel guilty.

Survivors are themselves at higher risk for suicidal feelings. This may lead to feelings of blame toward the deceased: "You made me suicidal," "You made our daughter suicidal," "You left me with a permanent fear that there will be other suicides in our family." As with death by other means, suicide can result in many forms of hardship for the family, and these also may be blamed on the victim.

The causal sequence of these events is undeniable. Suicide causes great pain for the survivors, and also diminishes their personal and social pain-coping resources. Since not all survivors become suicidal, it is not the only causal factor in their suicidal feelings, but it surely has major importance. Is it fair, though, to say that the suicide is morally culpable for causing his survivors to suffer these hardships? If his suicide was involuntary, then he is not personally responsible for its consequences. Two analogies may help us gain perspective. If there is a high incidence of heart disease among my older relatives, then my risk is increased, and their premature illnesses and deaths cause me pain and diminish the quality of my life. If I read this information in Heart Association literature, I experience feelings of concern, but I do not blame my relatives for putting me at risk and causing me harm. Relatives of alcoholics are often angry at the alcoholic, and at the problems alcoholism has caused them. They may even feel resentment for the greater risk of alcoholism for themselves and other relatives. Their blame and anger begin to subside when they come to accept the disease concept of alcoholism. It is a normal part of the grieving process to feel blame and anger toward the suicide. If the process is to be a process, we need to try to move beyond these feelings.

Let's Reject the View that Suicide is an Act of Rejection

"He rejected us," is a statement frequently made about completed suicides. The suicide is said to be someone who must have hated his family and friends. The judgment draws support from the anger-turned-inward theory of depression and suicide. Sometimes it is supported by the victim's behavior shortly before his death.[2] The view that suicide is always or frequently an act of rejection is endorsed throughout the literature. It is repeatedly asserted by the most recent book on survivors:

> For most survivors, after the shock and helplessness, the strongest feeling is the recognition that they have been rejected in a profound and personal way. The suicide survivor knows he has been left behind by someone who chose to do it.
>
> The survivor is rejected by someone who did not consider him important enough to remain living for; abandoned by someone he loved; and accused as if the dead person were pointing a finger and saying "You did not do enough for me."
>
> Suicide is the ultimate rejection, ...[3]

The aggregate pain theory rejects the view that suicides hate their families and intend to cause them pain and social harm. It believes that we should regard suicide as an event that involuntarily happens when pain exceeds coping resources. Chapter 2 argued that suicide is not an intentional action, has no motive, makes no statement. As with death by other means, the event of suicide says nothing at all about whether the victim loved or hated his family. Suicide causes pain and harm to the survivors; it may cause more pain and more harm than any other type of death. But the view that the pain and harm are intentionally caused by a malevolent agent is an unproven and unjustified prejudice. It is a doctrine that causes survivors immense pain; its rejection may be one of the most useful measures we can take in the postvention of suicide.

A step toward breaking the grip that this part of the mythology of suicide has upon us is to consider what the suicide was like before the onset of the painful conditions that led to his death. Suicides I have known were normal people. My ex-roommate in college loved each member of his family. In his relations with others he had above average friendliness. A professor in graduate school, who committed suicide while suffering from cancer, was markedly more pleasant and considerate to his students than were many other professors. An AIDS patient whose death was hastened by self-starvation was angry at another patient who had stolen money from him. He had been using his small income to supplement the dreary and unappealing hospital food. But, prior to his last two months of life, he had been quietly helpful to other patients, and during his last few weeks expressed love for his family and care for others. Listen to accounts given in survivor groups and you will hear the stories of people, who during the course of their lives, were not rejecting, abandoning, uncaring, or inconsiderate. No studies exist that show that the life histories of suicides contain higher than average incidences of these patterns of behavior. If someone has a lifelong pattern of being a family hater, a rejecter, or an abandoner, then it might be reasonable to appeal to these as explanatory concepts. But there just is no evidence that suicides are people whose lives are characterized by these kinds of behavior.

A second step is to recognize that the presence of negative feelings toward others in people who die by suicide is not sufficient to prove that they wish to reject or abandon. All of us, all of our lives, have negative feelings toward loved ones. They are mixed in with positive feelings, and their existence says nothing about our overall attitudes and affections toward others. When I was on a suicide hotline I would sometimes ask callers if they had thought about the effect that their suicide would have upon their families and friends. The responses I got, listed in order of frequency, with the most common first, were:

1. immediate change of subject.

2. It'll hurt, but they will get over it.

3. They don't care, they won't miss me.

4. I don't care, I'm angry at them.

5. I hate them, I want to hurt them.

As I developed the aggregate pain theory, I began to realize that each of these responses is an effort to reduce or minimize pain. Each response, as with all of the behavior of suicidal people, is part of the effort to stay alive. Subjects that cause pain are avoided. Pain that might happen to loved ones is minimized. 3. contains elements of 1. and 2.: avoidance, denial, minimization; elements of 4. and 5.: the discharge of anger; and informs the listener of the emotional need of the speaker. I learned that it was usually surprisingly easy to listen to people who gave responses of types 4. and 5. After they had vented their anger, sometimes at length, their positive feelings for others would often emerge and the suicidal agitation would dissipate. Their anger co-existed with their love. In ordinary life, the existence of mixed feelings means that we cannot make automatic inferences about the overall state of mind of the person; why should we apply a different standard to the suicidal?

Most survivors of suicide, who are said by theory to be rejected and hated, are in fact normal people who have done nothing that would merit abnormally negative behavior from the victim. If you had asked the victims, before they developed their suicidal conditions, if their relatives deserved hatred, rejection, and abandonment, they would nearly all have said no. The situation is similar to the man who yells at his children because of problems on the job. "He hates his children," is not an adequate explanation for his behavior. It is not even true, and would not even be a part of a fuller and more adequate explanation. "He must have hated us," is not true of the suicide, and we have no reason to assume it would have any part in a full explanation of suicidal behavior. We have no reason to suppose that when suicides die that their love for others is not still with them, and has not helped them withstand their pain for as long as possible. Unfortunately, their love for others and their other coping resources are sometimes not enough to stave off the aggregate effect of all the things that cause them pain.

What is unmentioned in discussions about the rejection theory of suicide is that many victims die by means, such as single car accidents, that avoid the "suicide" label. Fear of bringing shame upon the family deeply influences the behavior of the suicidal. It both deters them from dying by suicide and is a resource on the side of life, and deters them from seeking help and deprives them of resources. It is also a fear that influences the means of suicide. The fear of bringing shame upon the family may cause the suicidal to have less aversion to death in an auto accident than they have for suicide by other means. If their pain becomes great enough, and the means are available, they will become unrecorded suicides. Although suicides, official or otherwise, cause horrible pain to the family, not all of them show no evidence of concern for the family's welfare. Behavior that supports the rejecter stereotype exists, but it is likely that it characterizes a small percentage of the total suicide population.

Suicidal people are burdened with a tremendous problem in pain management. Since their great pain is disabling, they are likely to be even less rational — much less rational — in coping with it than the man who gets angry at his children. When human beings are in great pain, they can get angry at anything and everything in their immediate environment. The difficult, unpleasant, disorderly, and provoking behavior that sometimes occurs in the few days prior to an attempt is not voluntary, it is caused by great pain. The behavior is a desperate and irrational effort to stay alive, to discharge pain, to grasp at improbable solutions for reducing pain, to attract the attention of people who might find some way to help them. It is unrealistic to expect all people who are in this much pain to become saints, and stop being human beings. Were they not in great pain, the negative behavior would not exist.

A venerable tradition in Western literature holds that crisis reveals the true self. The evidence that this leads to excitement and enjoyment in fiction is so overwhelming that it seems like heresy to suggest that it might not be true of reality. But in terminal conditions of every sort, it is very dubious. This is especially true in suicide. "Not the person I knew," is how many survivors characterize their loved one during the period of time just before he became a suicide. This profound personality change, which is concurrent with massive pain, is behavior that he did not have earlier in life. Acute and prolonged physical and emotional pain erode and destroy personality and character. Theories that judge, and do so on the basis of behavior in these circumstances, are unfair to the victim and unfair to his family.

Mental Illness, Suicide, and Surviving a Suicide

Survivors need clearer hypotheses about the relationships of mental illness to both suicide and to the mourning process after suicide. "Did my loved one commit suicide because he was crazy?" and "I'm in horrible pain. Am I going crazy?" are questions that survivors can ruminate about for years. The turmoil is prolonged by not having specific ideas to use to help sort out the confusion.

It would be very desirable if the expression "mental illness" lost its stigma and its power to evoke prejudice and discrimination. The aggregate pain view of depression is designed to help reach this goal. It de-emphasizes hostility and inherent deficiencies, places the pains of depression on a continuum with those of ordinary life, and recognizes the social contribution to the pain of depression. Unfortunately, the stigma of "mental illness" will not disappear in the near future, so we need to determine if we can reduce the extent to which casual use of the label adds to the pain of the suicide survivor. A first step is to develop a less stigmatizing view of the role of mental illness in the death of the loved one. The second step is to argue that suicide bereavement is not itself a form of mental illness.

The aggregate pain theory believes that suicide happens when a person's resources are overwhelmed by the combined force of all the things that cause him pain. The direct causes of suicide include many things that are not classified as mental illnesses: substance abuse, bereavement, physical illness and disability, stresses of adolescence, mid-life, and aging, social prejudice against the suicidal, losses of status, security, or important relationships, and countless other painful conditions. Though not all suicides have diagnosable mental illnesses, many do, and this is a major source of their pain. Most suicides suffer from depression; smaller numbers suffer from manic-depression, schizophrenia, paranoia, or agoraphobia. It is rarely, if ever, the case that the mental illness was the only source of pain in the person's life, or the only reason he was deprived of coping resources. Consequently, the statement "The cause of his suicide was mental illness," is rarely true. Suicide does not have any single cause.

To my knowledge there are no studies that correlate suicide survivorship with recognized mental illnesses. Perhaps a study in the future will find that survivors have a higher incidence of depression, but this will only show that the depressed survivors are burdened by two painful conditions, not that suicide bereavement is itself a mental illness.

Bereavement is such a universal fact of human life that it cannot be considered a special problem in psychiatry. Grievers of children, auto accident victims, homicide victims, and AIDS victims usually suffer more because the deaths are especially tragic, or are unexpected, violent, or stigmatized. Combinations of such additional factors introduce complexities and increase isolation and suffering. Death by causes other than illness in old age is also a universal fact of life, and the additional pain and problems in coping with grief in these situations do not mean that the mourners suffer from a mental illness. Suicide bereavement is on a continuum with bereavement after other types of death, and the other mourning conditions are not regarded as mental illnesses.

The prejudices about pain discussed earlier single out greater than average sufferers as having something wrong with them. This is a source of social disapproval both for suicide survivors as a group, and for those among them who suffer more than others. The injustice of this social practice needs to be articulated and rejected: to suffer more than others is not proof of mental illness or moral inferiority. The implication that suffering more means "Something is wrong with you," unfairly adds to pain. Most survivors, both those who continue to be in pain and those who have found ways to reduce substantially their suffering, are simply average people who are, or were, in a lot of pain. The existence of this pain has no negative implications for their mental health status.

"It Must Be Something in the Family"

Several decades ago there was a popular view that mental illness is caused by bad parenting. (For a clear and vigorous denunciation of this position, see Walsh, 1986.) This view is now less widely held in professional circles. Many researchers believe that mental illness is caused by biochemical, nutritional, or genetic imbalances. We are also moving toward a view of many types of family problems that regards many parents as themselves victims of social and personal forces beyond their control. Though its effects are still present, the role of the bad parent theory on social and professional opinion is declining.

Unfortunately, the view that "It must be something in the family," is still alive and well in popular thinking about suicide. This is a single cause approach to suicide, which is rejected by the aggregate pain model. The circumstances of family life, when we are children and when we are adults, are major factors in how much pain we suffer, and in the strength of our resources for coping with pain. There is no justification, however, for assuming that family life or bad parenting is the sole determining factor of suicidal conditions. Some suicides had deprived or traumatic personal histories; other people had similarly disadvantaged childhoods and did not become suicides. Some suicides came from loving families that were not seriously dysfunctional, while other children of those families did not become suicides. The quality of family life does not enable us to predict suicidal behavior; it cannot be used as a single cause. We do not have to appeal to volition to explain the difference in these cases. Just as some siblings may be born with greater or lesser physical strength, they may be born with greater or lesser capacities to endure pain. Over the course of our lives each of us suffers different amounts of pain from the world outside the family, and socially acquires different coping resources. The family is not responsible for pain and coping resource problems that come from factors outside family relationships. Since family members are themselves partly at the mercy of forces beyond their control, they are not morally responsible for at least some of the pain that happens within the family.

One of the most common factors for strong and persistent suicidal feelings in a young person is a death or terminal illness in the family. This is a family problem, but it is not something for which the family can be blamed. Families do get blamed for things that are often parts of the causal history of the pain of suicidal young people: physical, sexual, or emotional abuse; alcoholism, drug addiction, mental illness, or criminal behavior in the family; requiring that the child be the parent for younger siblings; neglect, abandonment, and homelessness; separation from siblings in foster care programs. These situations happen; to approach them with a theoretical commitment to the position that the child's suicidal behavior is volitional is neither enlightening nor useful. The immediate cause of many of these children's pains and resource deficiencies are the problems in the family, though in many cases the family is itself a victim of larger social forces. We need to recognize that family dysfunctionality — the extent to which it does not meet the physical and emotional needs of its members — is a matter of degree. Few families are untouched by any of the problems above, or by problems now destigmatized, such as divorce and remarriage, that a generation ago would have been included in the above list. It is probable that children from families with many of these problems are more likely to become suicidal, as children or as adults, than are children from families with few of these problems. The latter group, which has a lower rate, is a large population. A low rate in a large population is a lot of people; one cannot assume that being suicidal implies having suffered a deprived or traumatic childhood. And even in cases where childhood has been exceptionally painful, the problems invariably included events such as death, physical illness, family relocation and other factors that are beyond the control of any family member. Inadequate parenting is sometimes a major cause of suicidal pain; it is rarely, if ever, the sole cause. In many other cases of suicidal pain the behavior of the parents was indistinguishable from that of millions of parents whose children were not suicidal.

The continuation of the blame-the-family prejudice is abetted by our cultural preoccupation with teen suicide. Only seven percent of all suicides happen to people under the age of twenty. Even in this group, to attribute suicide to problems in the family is narrow minded. It ignores social forces that adversely affect family life, such as the rise in the availability of drugs, and the decline in availability of such extended family members as grandparents, aunts, uncles, and cousins. Older males have the highest incidence rate for completed suicide. Major factors in this group — stresses of retirement, death of a spouse, physical illness — have little or nothing to do with shortcomings in the family. Yet relatives of suicides in this age group also suffer from the pervasiveness of the blame-the-family myth.

Besides being mistaken, family blaming is extremely impractical for the purposes of suicide prevention. Fear of shame keeps both the suicidal individual, and his family, from seeking and continuing with help. Within the family it creates a system of denial that deters communication among relatives and encourages family members to cast blame on each other. For the victim it adds to his negative self-image: If I'm suicidal, I must be from a bad family. The myth has an exceptionally strong self-perpetuating dynamic. The family is itself a powerful educator of social prejudices about the family. The myth that suicidal conditions are a family shame is perpetuated from one generation to the next, whether or not there has been a suicidal condition in the family. The idea that the family of a suicide is shamed is something we have all grown up with; survivors feel the brunt of this internal negative judgment and assume that others negatively judge them as well. This is a major source of lasting pain.

Child Survivors

Survivors who lost a parent when they were children have been given less than adequate representation in the suicide survivor literature and at conferences for survivors. Survivors who lost a parent when they were adults are represented as much as those with other survivor relationships, such as spouses or parents who lost a child, but there are virtually no publicly or privately available first-hand accounts by child survivors. (The one published child survivor account is Christopher Lukas' last chapter in *Silent Grief*. Two professional papers on child survivors are Cain, 1972, and Dunne-Maxim, 1987.) There are hundreds of thousands of child survivors in the United States. As the table in Chapter 11, page 283 makes clear, the average suicide is neither a teenager nor a senior citizen, but a person in his early forties. A large number of suicides die at an age when their offspring would be children. The children's suffering, on average, is greater than that of other suicide survivors. There is no justification for the lack of attention to their needs. We can begin to make progress by articulating three factors for this neglect.

1. Their pain is great and lasting; increased suffering means increased estrangement from non-sufferers. The pain of child survivors is more difficult for non-sufferers to accept and to respond to simply because it is greater.

2. Child survivors are prone to suicidal feelings themselves and often want to talk about these feelings. This is unwelcome to the non-suicidal.

3. The basic reason for neglect of the needs of child survivors is the greater pain and horror others experience when we try to comprehend their plight. Even to think about what the child of a suicide victim must suffer causes us to gasp. This special pain we experience at witnessing the pain of child survivors exists because each of us has a primal fear of childhood abandonment. This fear, and efforts to repress it, are basic parts of human nature. As we grow older we want to believe our parents are good, we want to not have the painful feelings that accompany the fear of abandonment, and our parents want us to have positive thoughts and feelings about them. Though we are not consciously aware of it, the fear of abandonment is always there. This fear of abandonment is why learning about the circumstances of children in foster care programs arouses such strong feelings of pity and anxiety. It is why we also have the reaction of sharp anger toward the children's parents. The situation of child survivors of suicide strongly raises the fear of abandonment, and just as strongly demands that we repress consciousness of that fear. "Don't talk about it. Don't think about it," is a rule that people in ordinary life apply to the entire topic of suicide. Certain parts of the subject, such as geriatric suicide or the

problems of survivors in general, are talked about or thought about less than others. The problems of child survivors may receive more social avoidance than any other major issue in suicide. Child survivors, through no fault of their own, arouse in other people a strong fear of being abandoned by their own parents. This deprives the child survivors of social resources for coping with their pain. Instead of neglect, we need to make additional efforts to develop a positive social response.

While child survivors receive less than adequate attention, the special problems of geriatric survivors have received no acknowledgement at all. Older people who lose a loved one to suicide are liable to suffer more pain because they have more years of bonding to the victim. Their dependency needs are increasing; the victim may have been someone they had counted upon to help meet those needs. Not only can their pain be greater than that of younger adult survivors in these respects, but they have increasingly fewer resources to cope with the death because of the general loss and dispersal of resources that accompany aging. These factors — fewer friends, fewer nearby relatives, less money, less physical mobility, less ability for self-protection from crime, cultural denial on the needs of the elderly — add to isolation and make bereavement hurt more and last longer.

The Quest for Information About the Suicide

Survivors of suicide victims, both those for whom the loss is recent and those for whom it is not, often have a strong desire to learn more about the circumstances that surrounded the death. This desire is natural and normal. The circumstances before and after most suicides cause survivors to have much less information than is had by those who survive other types of death. Death by suicide is more painful, and the greater pain provokes a greater desire to learn about the cause of death. Suicide is itself one of the most poorly understood causes of death. "How could this happen?" is experienced much more strongly by suicide survivors, and a more strongly felt question gives rise to a stronger desire to find answers.

One of the most appalling attitudes of mental health professionals is that many consistently downgrade and belittle the importance and

validity of this desire for more information. This attitude is not based
on the evidence. There are no studies that show that obtaining more
information is harmful to survivors, or otherwise retards the
bereavement process. The attitude ignores the fact that this is a desire
to ground the pain in reality, not in emptiness and speculation. This
attitude does not respect the right of suicide survivors to have as much
information about their loss as do the survivors of other types of death.
The belief that you may not have all the information causes a lasting
sense of insecurity, a permanent feeling of waiting for the other shoe to
drop. The belittlement of the need for information is sometimes
supported by the charges that the survivor is trying to deny or to escape
from reality. This is the opposite of what the survivor is doing; the
charges themselves deny the reality and validity of his needs.
Negative coping mechanisms are booze, drugs, social isolation, and
silence. The attempt to get more information is none of these; it is a
positive coping effort. Some survivors succeed in getting more
information, and feel that the information has resolved some of their
concerns. Even those who try and do not succeed at least answer the
question, "Can I learn something more by going to source x?" Negative
attitudes toward the desire for more information simply repeat in the
same form — "This is for your own good," — the self-serving abusive
secrecy that surrounded the original trauma.

"He Gave Me Permission"

It is not unusual for a younger relative of a suicide to develop the idea
that the deceased has given him permission to commit suicide. The
whole of the psychological origins of this idea is unclear, but a few
contributing factors may be noted. The structure of this belief — *He
gave me* permission — and its personal quality (permission has not
necessarily been given to others) are partly due to the fact that a
suicide survivor often develops the feeling that he had a special
relationship or bond with the deceased. A second consideration is to
recognize that many societies are, or have been, divided according to
social castes; members of these castes may have distinct sets of rights
and responsibilities; and the possession of these rights and
responsibilities are usually transmitted genealogically from one
generation to the next. Though it seems offensive to our democratic

ideals, we cannot hold that it is unusual for someone to believe that he has a right not had by others in his community, and that he has that right because of some distinctive feature of one of his ancestors. At a personal level, it is probably normal for a person to believe that it is particularly acceptable for *him* to engage in at least some types of behavior that characterized his older relatives.

To help break the hold that this idea may have upon a survivor, it may be useful to examine "He gave me permission to commit suicide," from a conceptual standpoint. *Perhaps* there are situations where one person could give another person permission to commit suicide. Military or espionage cases might be examples. Religious martyrdom, where the death of one martyr is held by advocates of the religion to be an ideal for others to emulate, might be claimed to be a situation in which someone is given permission to commit suicide. These contexts, however, are not similar to those of most suicides. In ordinary suicide, it is simply mistake to believe that one person can give another person permission to commit suicide.

First, let us assume, as some people do, that suicide is morally permissible. On this hypothesis, "He gave me permission," is similar to one average citizen telling another average citizen, "You have my permission to breathe, vote, and own property." Since the second person already has these rights, it is a mistake for him to believe that his permission to do these things was given to him by the first person. On a second hypothesis — suicide is not morally permissible — it is also a mistake to believe "He gave me permission." It is no more reasonable to claim that suicide is permissible because a relative has died by suicide than it is reasonable to claim that someone has a right to murder or steal because he had a relative who murdered or stole. The third possibility is to consider the kinds of situations in ordinary life where one person can grant another person permission to do something. I can give someone permission to use my car, or, if I am an instructor, permission to take a make-up examination. But it is not within the sphere of my authority to give someone permission to use a car I do not own, or to take a make-up examination in a course I do not teach. Suicide falls into this latter group; with the possible exception of the extra-ordinary cases mentioned above, it is not within the sphere of anyone's authority to give another person permission to commit suicide. The event of one person's suicide says nothing about the permissibility of someone else's suicide. This is the conclusion we should expect from the involuntarist position. Since suicide is not an act of any sort, it is not an act in which the victim confers upon his survivors a right that they previously did not have.

Suicide Causing Survivor Suicide

There have been few studies on possible causal relationships of suicides among relatives and acquaintances. On the whole, the conclusions of these studies are uncertain. Some studies found no correlation, others found a limited amount of evidence that suggested that survivors have increased risk. (A list of references is in Lester, 1986.) The only other available body of evidence is the personal observations of suicide prevention workers and participants in survivor support groups. In these contexts it is not uncommon to encounter situations in which a suicide is an important part of a survivor's suicidal pain. In the case histories at the end of this chapter, the death of the parent was apparently not preceded by another suicide in the family. At least one child in each family subsequently attempted suicide. Relatives of suicides seem to have a somewhat higher risk for completed and attempted suicide, and are much more likely to have strong suicidal feelings and ideation. The survivors' apparent increased rate for completed suicide needs to be put into perspective. Among members of the general population, 98 percent to 99 percent will not have their official cause of death listed as suicide. The rate for family members of a suicide victim is probably in the range of 97 percent to 98 percent.

Various hypotheses have been proposed to account for the survivors' increased risk: innate factors of genetics or biochemistry; acquired biochemical changes due to the traumatic effects of the suicide; patterns of child rearing or family dynamics. All of these hypotheses locate the entirety of the problem within the family, and assume social factors make no contribution to the causal relationship between one suicide and another. Given our present state of knowledge, all of these hypotheses are difficult to evaluate, and difficult to implement into suicide prevention work. We do not know how to identify the allegedly significant biochemical or genetic factors. The psychological dynamics of the families of many suicides are apparently indistinguishable from patterns found in millions of families where suicide did not occur. The aggregate pain model deserves consideration as an alternative to these hypotheses. Suicide causes family members massive, complex, and lasting pain. Suicide profoundly diminishes their pain-coping resources. The aggregate pain model enables us to identify accurately many of the factors that cause survivors to have increased risk of suicide. It provides us with a specific strategy to help relieve their suffering. It enables us to recognize and reduce the social forces outside the family that increase the risk of subsequent suicide.

Other Survivor Situations

A subject that needs an academic study is the comparison of survivorship issues after death by suicide, homicide, AIDS, drug overdose by a drug abuser, and other stigmatized fatalities. (such as the driver in drunk driving fatalities, and deaths that occur within the context of criminal activity) Survivors of these deaths must deal with problems of stigma, shame, denial, isolation, anger, secrecy, prolonged grieving, fears for other survivors, lack of trained counselors for their type of grief, and the lack of publicly available literature. Having spoken with survivors of these deaths, I recognize that this will not be a popular proposal. Survivors of each type of fatality often say, "Our pain is different. No one suffers the way we do." In suicide *prevention* activities there is a tendency of the people involved in one stigmatized area to resist the association of their work with another stigmatized area. This resistance is *much* more pronounced in postvention activities. Yet what we need is not just progress in individual areas of stigma and prejudice, but also progress against stigma and prejudice themselves.

THREE SURVIVOR CASE HISTORIES

The women interviewed for these case histories lost parents to suicide and suffered periods of suicidal pain themselves. These survivor accounts, and the one in Chapter 10, are brief sketches of events that have enormously complicated and multi-generational causal histories. Each account contains elements that both indicate the need for theories with special strengths, such as psychoanalysis and cognitive psychology, and that also disconfirm the claims of these theories to be complete and accurate explanations for suicide. Miss C.'s suicidal crisis, for example, involves problems with a lack of nurturing from parental figures, but the antecedent traumas occurred in adolescence, not early childhood. Some of her thinking patterns have cognitive distortions, but she has these beliefs even when she is not suicidal. Other aspects of her crisis can best be viewed through the lens of the involuntarist position. Her behavior concerning shooting, jumping, and ingesting pills follows the pattern of the least fear theory of the means. Her suicidal feelings moved from anger to hopelessness, and then, during a siege of physical illness, to powerlessness. Aside from these theoretical concerns, the three women articulate many of the practical needs of child survivors.

Miss A.

Miss A.'s mother committed suicide when she was 43 and Miss A. was 12. Although Miss A.'s family is ethnically Jewish, her mother's father practiced a Protestant religion. Miss A. says that when her mother was a teenager, she was criticized by the grandfather for having physical features that were "too Jewish". Miss A.'s mother left the first college she attended in her freshman year for emotional problems of an unknown nature. Miss A. suspects that this included a suicide attempt, and believes that her mother made another attempt when Miss A. was six. Miss A. has an essay her mother wrote as a graduate student in social work. It describes an episode of severe depersonalization. After marrying a professional man, the mother had four children in less than five years: a daughter, Miss A., a son, and a third daughter. Miss A. remembers her childhood as being full of arguments and discord. Even as infants the care for the children's emotional and physical needs was erratic, they were often simply left alone without supervision or food. Her mother on occasion suffered physical abuse. Her father claimed the abuse was self-inflicted; her mother and her mother's parents claimed it was inflicted by the father. There were many three-way legal battles (each parent and the mother's parents) over separation, child custody, violations of child custody agreements, restraining orders, police calls to the home, and divorce. "In the custody battles we weren't children, we were pawns." Miss A. remembers her mother being thin, sleeping a great deal, and possibly having a pill dependency. As far as she remembers, her mother did not suffer a major bereavement or physical health problem in the years prior to her death. When Miss A. was nine or ten, her mother missed an appointment with a psychiatrist, locked herself in her bedroom (which had a Yale lock), and took an overdose. The eldest daughter called the police, who broke down the door and took her to a hospital. She was in a coma for two weeks. Miss A. visited her in the hospital and made her promise never to do it again. Miss A. says that, as a child, "I had no friends. I would run home right after school to make sure my mother was still alive." Miss A.'s parents divorced and the father won custody of the children. In the few weeks prior to her death, Miss A.'s mother, living with her parents in another state, secretly made out a new will and used forged prescription slips to obtain a large number of sedatives. When the grandparents left town for an overnight visit, Miss A.'s mother took an overdose, vomited, and choked to death.

Evidence that the death was a suicide was destroyed. A physician who was a friend and business associate of the grandparents certified that the death was simple choking, not suicide. The body was cremated before the children were notified that their mother had died. Though other relatives confirm that the death was by self-poisoning, the grandparents continue to deny it, and this is one of several factors that have created rifts among family members. To this day, seventeen years later, the grandparents refuse to tell the grandchildren the location of their mother's remains. All of Miss A.'s older relatives, even those who privately admitted that the death was a suicide, were generally unwilling to discuss the death with other family members or with outsiders. Miss A. was the exception. She says that since her mother's death, whenever she met someone she would introduce herself as, "I'm

Miss A. My mother killed herself." These opposite types of behavior are a major part of the rift between Miss A. and other family members.

Miss A. recalls swallowing a bottle of aspirin and vomiting when she was seven. She does not recall what events or circumstances led up to the attempt. After her mother's suicide, her father expected her "to be the responsible one" among the siblings. She took her mother's seat at the dinner table. Her father, however, "did not like to come home," and a maid served as a mother figure. Miss A. had earlier been embarrassed when her mother walked around the house naked. While she was an adolescent her father often made lewd remarks to Miss A. about herself and about other women. Though she was her father's favorite, and was disparagingly referred to as her "father's child" by her mother's parents, she has never had an emotionally supportive relationship with him. For a period of time she idealized her mother, "I thought she was this saint that the world had killed," and suffered feelings of guilt, "At one point, I felt that my neediness killed my mother." After her mother's death she became more extroverted and involved with sex and drugs. She often left home for brief periods. During one such episode, at age 14, she was seduced by the father of a friend of her sister's. On many occasions she went to mental health clinics for treatment for depression and emotional problems. In each case she was refused treatment because she was a minor who did not have, and would not seek, her father's consent. Though Miss A. also sought help from school and legal sources, adults uniformly refused to believe her descriptions of her unbearable home life. She maintained superior grades — her father insisted that "School is your job," — but her hopes that she would thereby win his approval and improve conditions in the home were in vain. "I did this, and I did this, and I did this — and it didn't work." When she was 15 she collected a large number and variety of pills from friends at school. She told one teacher — "the one I knew wouldn't do anything," — that she was going to commit suicide. On the evening of the third anniversary of her mother's death — "I didn't want reunion. I just wanted to be dramatic," — she ingested the pills and drank a quantity of alcohol. When she woke the next morning, "I was surprised I wasn't dead, and not real happy about it, either." That evening she cut her arms and was hospitalized. Despite the father's remarriage when Miss A. was 16, conditions in the home did not improve. Two months after the marriage, Miss A.'s younger sister, then 13, ran away from home and was a missing person for four months. The father regarded his stepchildren as "good" models for his own "bad" children. "I was constantly criticized. He would come in my room in the middle of the night, and wake me up just so he could yell at me." Every adult in Miss A.'s life held the view that her pain and her problems were her own fault.

Miss A. attempted suicide again in her early twenties. She had been "feeling really depressed for a really long period of time," and had saved up many different pills that had been left at her house by other people. She ingested the pills and a quantity of alcohol at the beginning of a long weekend when she knew that she would be alone: "I wanted it to either work or be one that people would not know about. ... It is humiliating to be in that position after an attempt has not worked." She was unconscious for three days, during which she vomited. When she awoke she cancelled an appointment with her therapist, and for several days was frightened because she was physically unable to hold up her head. There was a further less serious attempt a few years later. "This was after I finally — for the first time in my life — experienced not being depressed. It felt different. A part of me wasn't sure I wanted to die. ... The whole time growing up I could never remember not wishing I were dead. It was such an amazing experience when it was not there." She describes the predominant feeling prior to each attempt: "... the sense of being in overwhelming pain, and being really tired. That it's just so much work, it's so much work to be alive. ... It's never been a situation of where something happened and I decided to kill myself. ... With all the suicide attempts its always been something that I worked up to; it's never been something where somebody did something, or something bad happened that day." As an adolescent she sought help, as an adult she felt that it was pointless to turn to others. Whenever suicidal feelings increased, she withdrew and stayed alone. Miss A.'s struggle with depression has been made worse by the fact that since childhood she has suffered from a poorly understood connective tissue problem that causes her almost chronic pain and fatigue. On the means of suicide she says that she is afraid of heights, and has no access either to a gun or to a car and garage. "Anything that I would feel might not work and would possibly mutilate me I wouldn't do. Or anything that would cause me too much pain."

Miss A. not only wants to learn more about the circumstances of her mother's death, but, like many child survivors, she has a strong desire simply to find out what kind of person her mother was. She has been rebuffed in many attempts to learn more. "If I were an adopted child, and I wanted to find out about my birth parents, that's now acceptable. If my mother died of some natural cause while I was an infant, it would be acceptable for me to want to find out about her. But because she killed herself, my desire to find out about her is pathological. ... There's a kind of sense of 'Oh, well, why don't you let it go? Why are you doing this?' ... Partly it's because anybody who knew us, anybody who knew her, deserted us. I mean, they left us there. So now, when I go back, it brings up their guilt. And their stuff. And so the easiest way to view it is, somehow, 'Oh no, we're going to have to deal with this woman's crazy daughter.'"

For the last two years Miss A. has been intermittently helped by anti-depressant medications. She attends survivor meetings because they provide acceptance, "Whether it's two years later or sixteen years later, nobody says, 'Why are you still crying?'" She does clerical work and hopes to resume painting and sculpture. Her chief preventive measure for suicidal feelings is "... to get rest, to have time alone, time to organize things, time to play." She can accumulate a great deal of fatigue, and it takes her a longer-than-average amount of time to recover. She now regards work with others as something of a quick fix: "If I'm feeling bad and someone calls me up with a crisis, I snap out of it right away, but it only lasts as long as *their* crisis lasts. ... One of the things when you are not taken care of, that you do to get taken care of, is to take care of everyone else. ... Over the years I used to collect crazy people and nurture them. And I'm slowly stopping it." She has been in a nurturing relationship with her boyfriend of several years, and, "I'm angry at him, because I don't know if its going to change." She says that she has learned that "More people will be with me if I do not appear needy," and "I have to be self-sufficient or I can't live." She continues, "Even now, I could really use a parent. ... I'm supposed to have gotten something together because I'm 29, and I'm not a kid. And I get that from my father. But I didn't get to do all the other stuff. How am I supposed to arrive here? For me, the suicide is not about my mother. It's everything that happened. I'm not grieving my mother. I'm grieving me." For many years Miss A. has been tormented by the question of having children herself. "How can I choose something if I don't know if tomorrow I'm going to kill myself. How do I know that I'm not going to just fall into the abyss. I don't know that." Although she feels her own risk of suicide has lessened, her three siblings also suffer from depression and suicidal thoughts, and she fears that any child she has would be fated to suffer from the same illness.

Miss B.

Miss B.'s father committed suicide when he was 54 and she was 15. Eight years later Miss B.'s stepfather, aged 54 and married to her mother for only three months, also committed suicide. Miss B.'s parents were from mulatto communities in the South and came north to earn graduate degrees. Miss B.'s father, the youngest of 11 children, was raised by his eldest sister and her husband. Three of Miss B.'s father's elder brothers passed as white, left the family, and were never heard from again. His brother-in-law/surrogate father helped Miss B.'s father establish a dental practice. Ten years later her father was drafted during the Korean War to practice dentistry on black soldiers. After his discharge he had to start over, and never quite regained what he had lost. Miss B.'s mother's mother, the only grandparent she ever knew, "... had that air of superiority. Everybody was beneath her. She kept talking about her white father, and she constantly put down her black mother. ... It was all this 'high yellow' mentality." The grandmother felt that neither the father nor, many years later, the stepfather, were good enough for her daughter. When Miss B. was a child, the family's ethnic and social situation was not talked about in the home. The family was socially isolated, "We never felt we were part of anywhere." The parents non-verbally maintained the beliefs, "The rest of the world is the enemy. The family nucleus is it. Don't trust anybody. Never let anyone know what you think or what you feel." Miss B. says, "Early on, I didn't really develop friends. ... I'd just come right home from school. And kids would say, 'What are you?' Because I looked so different. And they'd say, 'Are you Jewish? Are you Italian?' And they'd also say, 'Mira, mira,' and they'd think I was Spanish. I'd come home crying cause I couldn't figure out, no one would explain to me, what I was. So my father would just say, 'Go tell them you're a Kickapoo Indian.' ... So I would use that, and I started very early in my life fooling people. ... My whole game in life was to fool everybody, to not really be real. ... So this sense of identity, I never really had. It's just 'You're different. But you're better.'" Miss B.'s father suffered adult onset diabetes and, six years prior to his death, had a slight heart attack. He did not comply with prescribed dietary restrictions. Alcoholism and pill dependency steadily increased. During the last three years of his life Miss B.'s father frequently stayed home from work and drank. On occasion his wife suffered physical abuse. Miss B.'s brother, who was two years older and adopted the role of the more "responsible" child, often stayed home from school to protect his mother. Miss B. remembers two episodes that may have involved attempted suicide; after one of these her father was hospitalized and restrained in a psychiatric ward. Three years before his death he was deeply affected by "... the assassination of Martin Luther King. And I really think that's what put him over the edge. Because I remember he changed when Martin Luther King was killed. I think his hope for the world or whatever, and himself, sort of went up in smoke. ... That's when he really started to crack, to go off." For reasons unknown to Miss B., her father had earlier broken off relations with his oldest brother-in-law, the man who had raised him. This man died a year before Miss B.'s father died, and the father was hurt that they had never reconciled. Miss B. says that she was not emotionally nurtured by her mother, "She was an enabler. Her way of loving is to provide food, and money if you need it." As to her father, Miss B. describes herself as a covert incest survivor, "I was his little princess, the closest person to him. His need for love, he got a lot of it from me."

At 15 Miss B. would avoid coming home from school until six o'clock, when her mother got home from work. The one exception was Tuesday, when she had to come home early for a music lesson. Her brother was away at his first year at college. One Tuesday, her father "waited until I got home," and consumed more than a liter of liquor in front of her. He "acted crazy," and threatened to kill her cat and smash her violin. He chased her around the house, alternately crying and being angry. Miss B. remembers cowering in the basement, wishing, as she often had over the previous three years, that he were dead. Her father swallowed 250 seconal tablets in her presence. He went upstairs and slammed the door. Some time later, after a period in which she heard no noise, Miss B. crept upstairs and found her father unconscious. She attempted to administer mouth-to-mouth resuscitation, but vomit came out of his nose and mouth in spasms. He had choked to death. Miss B.'s mother and then her grandmother arrived at the house shortly afterwards. They called the father's best friend, a physician. He signed the death certificate as a heart attack so the family could collect the life insurance. "I was told by the same family friend, when my brother was coming in on the bus, that night, 'I don't want you to tell your brother anything, ... I don't want you to tell him how he died,' and ... woooo ... [I thought,] 'I'm bad. I did it. I was bad. Suicide was bad.' And, ... he didn't want it to get out, because, here he was signing off on a death certificate." Miss B.'s mother maintained to everyone, including Miss B., that the death was by heart attack. But the mother did not know the details of the father's last hours alive, and Miss B. was afraid that if she related these and expressed her belief that she should have been able to stop it, then her mother would hate her. Miss B.'s grandmother, who angrily cursed the father "for what he had done to us," was the one person with whom she thought she could discuss the death. But Miss B. was afraid to talk to her grandmother, who berated her father's character, and what had been a close relationship grew distant. Nearly a decade would pass before Miss B. would be able to begin talking about her father's death with other people. For the next fifteen years, Miss B. suffered feelings of guilt, "... because I did not stop him and I had wished him dead."

Miss B. had never thought about suicide before her father's death, afterwards she thought about it constantly. On the first anniversary of his death her cat died, and she made suicidal gestures. Miss B. then went to college and became rebellious. She used drugs, became involved with Eastern philosophies, and "I got attached to the sickest, craziest people." She began to study both social history and her family's history. Her education was twice interrupted by leaves of absence of more than a year. She says, "My mother would behave as if there were one reality. And inside I knew there was a completely different reality. So I thought something was wrong with me because I wasn't buying my mother's reality. ... So I started to think I was crazy." Six years after her father's death she attempted suicide by cutting her wrists. Soon afterwards she told her brother that her father had committed suicide. Once said, it was never mentioned again until several more years had passed.

During Miss B.'s last year at college, her mother met and married a man she had known thirty years earlier when she was in college. He was also a dentist, had been divorced for 16 years, and had a daughter two years older than Miss B. Miss B. and her stepfather hit it off so well that "Once again I had the feeling that I was the surrogate wife."

Besides a special emotional bond, Miss B. believes that the two had a special sense of mutual understanding: he admitted that he was bisexual and she was beginning to acknowledge her own bisexuality. Her mother was aware of her second husband's bisexuality, but "pretended that it was not real." Miss B. believes that her stepfather may have had a pill dependency. Two months after the wedding her stepfather did not attend her graduation, as he had promised. Three weeks later the stepfather phoned his male lover from a hotel room and asked him to come and get him. The male lover mistakenly went to the wrong hotel, and the stepfather committed suicide with a shotgun. Miss B. was devastated by the news of his death. While this suicide did not cause her guilt, she did feel, "I'm next. My turn. It's OK now. It's like a sign I needed to be with them."

Miss B.'s next five years were full of turmoil and pain. She had many short-term jobs and unstable relationships. One relationship was with a man in his early fifties. "When he hit 54, I was crazy the whole year." One therapy program gave her a deep awareness of her emotional suffering, but left her with no program or direction for recovery. She found help, and found that it was helpful to help others, in a self-help organization for issues of sexual identity. Using her father as an example of someone who was isolated and would not talk, Miss B. believes that suicide involves massive anger that cannot be expressed outward. "They involve everyone around them in the pain of it. ... It's like, 'See. So there.' It's like their last gasp. 'See, you didn't help me. See how bad I felt. See. See. See.' *That*, I've learned, is what I need to get angry at." She has great fear of abandonment, and became very suicidal when a female lover broke off a relationship. "I wanted to get even with her. I was feeling suicidal. But why did I have to make sure she knew it? And she did. She came looking for me. She drove by my house. Rang the doorbell. The phone ringing. Not answering it. Listening to the messages — I had my machine on. I set it up. Because I was really going to do it. But I set it up to let her know 'You did it, you should of ...' I didn't have to do that. If I wanted to just kill myself, why do I have to go the point of making sure she had the guilt attached to it? That's a very real thing that happens when the person is just so angry and ready to do it. They want the other person to suffer too."

Miss B. would not want to attempt suicide with drugs and alcohol. "I thought my father felt himself die, ... that he was aware that he was choking on his vomit and could do nothing about it because his body was anesthetized by the drugs. ... I would never use that way." She says that she cannot stand guns and would not know where to get one, hanging is too slow, and she would not want to try cutting again. She believes her first preference would be carbon monoxide asphyxiation, because it is painless and does not mutilate the body. Because "I love flying," her second preference would be to get high and drunk and then jump. During suicidal crises Miss B. can go back and forth between awareness of extreme pain and reunion fantasies: "... the pain would get so strong and then I would slip into these fantasies that Daddy would be there and would help me, and so that would take the pain away." She says, "To this day, to this moment, I still think he was the perfect father. ... I need to hold on to the fact that he was my great Daddy. ... I can hold on to thinking of him as a victim, but then I don't really heal because I need to direct my anger at somebody. I went through a period of blaming society, but that prevented me from looking at my mother's role in the dysfunctional family system."

Approximately five years ago Miss B. reached her bottom and began to make progress toward recovery. During this period she has seen a Gestalt oriented therapist "to heal my lack of nurturing as a child." She participates in a number of 12-step groups and in suicide survivor groups. For two years she has taken a dietary supplement to help manage manic-depressive tendencies. Within the last year she has gradually lost the feeling, "I'm next." Though she became financially able to do otherwise, Miss B. lived for years in a poor and dangerous neighborhood. Like many chronically suicidal people, she has had difficulty overcoming the thought pattern "Why bother making an investment in x? I may be dead soon." She is currently moving to a safer neighborhood. She has a productive and stable occupation, and, by choice, has had no romantic involvements for the last year.

Miss C.

Miss C.'s father committed suicide when he was 42 and she was 15. Miss C. was the eldest of six children. She says that she was her father's favorite, and that, of her two parents, he was her favorite. In his work he had reached a prominent position in his community. She describes her father as quiet, particularly after the onset of his depression, and as having a strong sense of responsibility. Miss C.'s father was a rescuer; at one point he put all of his time off from his own job into rescuing his own father's small business from bankruptcy. He took his children to church when he was not ill, was not socially isolated, and had no serious problems in physical health that she remembers. On a few occasions he expressed the wish that his wife would convert to Catholicism. Three months before his death, Miss C.'s parents purchased a larger house for their family. For the last three years of his life, Miss C.'s father suffered from depression, missed periods of work, and was treated with medications and shock therapy. He slashed his wrists a week prior to his death. Miss C. believes that there may have been two previous attempts, one by self-poisoning. His suicidal episodes and periods of depression were not talked about directly; the family referred to these situations as, "Daddy's sick again."

One morning the grandfather accompanied Miss C.'s father to an appointment with his psychiatrist. When they got to the office building, Miss C.'s father said, "I don't want to go to this man. I want to go the V.A. hospital." The grandfather said OK, but as they walked back toward the car, Miss C.'s father suddenly ran in front of a truck and was killed. The suicide, with an inch-high headline and vivid eyewitness accounts, was reported on the front page of the next day's newspaper. (Miss C. has the clipping and read it aloud during the interview. It includes an obituary account of the major events of her father's life and lists Miss C. and the other survivors.) Miss C. struggles to describe the silence after her father's death: "There wasn't any way to hide it from anybody. But all that we did later on was just never talk about it. It wasn't a question of people didn't know. The whole damn city knew. I mean I had to go back to school. Kids from my class were at the funeral and at the wake. Even then, I didn't talk to them about it. It was like [affected tone], 'Hi, how are you?' But I mean, we just couldn't, ... you know, ... I mean, ... It was just un- ... What could you say, you know? As a kid? I mean my mother was upset. I think adults talked more. But adults didn't talk to us. ... I didn't talk about it until a couple years ago in the survivor group. I mean, except to my few shrinks."

Miss C.'s mother, who she remembers as being cold and unemotional and who "carried the ball for three years while my father was sick," suffered a breakdown in the months following her husband's death. She was diagnosed as schizophrenic and hospitalized for several months. As a teenager, Miss C. had to take her mother to the state hospital on a number of occasions. In terms of agitation and eccentricity, Miss C. says that her mother was much sicker than her father ever was. She attempted suicide once with pills and Miss C. worried, with some reason, that her mother would also run in front of a motor vehicle. Currently her mother is in a nursing home, diagnosed as manic-depressive.

During the mother's initial hospitalization, Miss C.'s three brothers were placed in an orphanage and a sister was cared for by another family. For a month or two a housekeeper cared for Miss C. and the other sister, but this woman left after breaking an appliance. Miss C. says, "After my mother had her breakdown, I carried the ball. For years I was the only responsible adult in the house." She and her siblings currently disagree over who was hurt the most by her father's suicide and her mother's subsequent breakdown. She has suffered because she had a special relationship with her father and because of the responsibilities she had to shoulder. The younger children say they were traumatized by the several months in the orphanage: conditions were poor and "We didn't know if we were coming back."

Miss C. is now 39, a healthcare professional, and lives alone. She has had problems with indebtedness for years. She attends suicide survivor support groups; only recently has she been able to talk to close friends about her father's death. Approximately a year ago, a male therapist on whom she had become dependent terminated their relationship. She became enraged and fought for months to re-establish the relationship. At the survivor group she would sobbingly compare her abandonment by her therapist to her abandonment by her father. After six months she gave up hope that she could resume therapy with this counselor, and her depression took a different turn: "I moved from angry suicidal feelings to hopeless suicidal feelings." A month after this transition she developed a severe intestinal disorder that caused her to lose 20 pounds in a few weeks. She was hospitalized for a week. Her weight loss problem stabilized, but the ailment was never specifically diagnosed and continued to cause her discomfort and extreme fatigue. She was terrified of losing her health: "Who will take care of me? ... No one has taken care of me since I was 15. Either I take care of myself or I will die. There is no in between in my life." During this period she gave someone money to obtain a gun for her, but the person simply disappeared. She thought of jumping: "I really didn't have the nerve.

I'd go up on the roof [of the apartment building] and I just couldn't jump off. I couldn't even put my leg over. I don't know how people do it." She took an overdose of anti-depressant medication and was hospitalized a second time. This was her first and only suicide attempt. She now has a stable relationship with a therapist, calls hotlines, and attends support groups for codependency problems — "It's very easy to hide your own needs when you're meeting someone else's." Her depression and suicidal feelings have abated over the last six months, but "I still feel that the only person who can make me feel better is my father."

CHAPTER TEN

COUNSELORS

This chapter provides counselors and friends with guidelines for the management of the initial interview with a suicidal person. It includes many suggestions that are standard parts of existing suicide prevention programs. Partly because I "worked backwards" in an effort to understand why these techniques were effective, I was led to a general theory of suicide that supports these guidelines, rather than to the mental and moral model with which they are incompatible. Hopefully, the effectiveness of these techniques and our understanding of them can be improved if we pursue our work within a framework that is non-stigmatizing and non-prejudicial.

Preparation for the Initial Encounter

Be willing to give help sooner

The mythology of suicide holds that its prevention should be a last minute activity. Until then the victim is not serious, just wants attention, and is unworthy of assistance. This view has only to be stated to be seen to be absurd. Early assistance reduces the duration of suffering, keeps problems of mental health and substance abuse from becoming more deeply entrenched, keeps the person from developing additional problems, reduces suffering for the victim's relatives, and reduces risk of attempted and completed suicide. Programs to provide earlier assistance have been successful in other areas of public health; there is no reason why we cannot do the same in suicide.

An organization that does not practice this policy is the New York City Police Department. Suicide prevention posters were put up in each precinct house following a year in which there were 10 officer suicides, including the suicide discussed on page 219 in this chapter. An officer from the same precinct house was suffering from depression because, he said, his ex-wife would not let him see their children. A supervisor noticed his unhappiness and talked to him about it. The officer readily followed the supervisor's suggestion that he go downtown to the department's Psychological Services. After he talked about his depression, the psychologist asked him if he was suicidal, or if there was any reason his gun should be taken from him. When the officer answered no to both questions, he was simply told to go home, and given no recommendations for further treatment. Officers who answer yes to these questions have their guns taken from them and are placed on restricted duties. They suffer a stigma that does not go away; their careers are permanently harmed. This pattern — judge the person as not suicidal and provide no assistance, or judge the person as on the verge of death and provide a last-minute crisis level of response — makes effective early presentations impossible. Try to imagine what it is like to face a world that says, "We will help you only if you are on the brink, and, while we are helping you, we will inflict more pain on you."

Be Yourself

Nearly all suicidal people suffer from loneliness in some form or another. Simple contact with another human being can provide relief for their pain. In much of your work it may be comfortable and efficient, for both you and the people you see, if you maintain the role of physician or guidance counselor. For the suicidal, however, these roles reinforce rather than relieve their sense of estrangement from others. Friends of the suicidal do not have to be more than they are. "I'm not enough to deal with his situation," is an attitude that often causes the suicidal to suffer increased isolation. Most of us experience pain and frustration if we are in situations for which we cannot find solutions. But if you simply supply the suicidal person with average human companionship, you are doing a lot more for him than if you avoid him.

Cry For Help

All suicidal behavior short of a fully lethal attempt is part of the effort to stay alive. The real meaning of "I want to kill myself," is "I want to stay alive, but my pain is threatening to exceed my coping resources." It is not his fault and it is not your fault that suicidal presentations for help are often made in ways that are indirect, difficult, or unpleasant. The communication of suicidal feelings is a positive sign, no matter how negative it appears to be on the surface. Tell the person that he has done the right thing by seeking help.

Positive attitude toward you

If a suicidal person turns to you, it is likely that he believes that you — more than any other person he knows — are more caring, understanding, accepting, willing to give your time, informed about coping with misfortune, or willing to protect him from pain causing breaches of confidentiality. Counselors often have an opposite initial reaction: Why is this person doing this bad thing to me? This reaction is natural: the person may have a hostile demeanor; the counselor has heard all his life that suicide is a hostile act, and that the suicidal are manipulators; defensiveness is a normal response to anxiety. You need to remind yourself that he has singled you out as a good bet to provide him with help.

The positive opinion of you as a help provider is probably justified. Suicidal people often believe, "I'm good and the rest of the world is bad," or, "It's because I'm good that I suffer so much." As I argued earlier, these beliefs are used to cope with pain; suicidal people, as a group, are morally neither better nor worse than average. Though no studies have been done on this subject, my impression is that the people to whom presentations get made *are* people who are better than average. This is true not just of those school counselors who see a lot of suicidal students, but also foster parents. Foster parents have a negative image in the popular imagination, but in workshops for child care programs I have learned that many are caring and open-hearted people. Besides their foster children, and their own children or grandchildren, some of the foster parents have time for many other children in their neighborhoods who need someone to talk to. Because they are good people, they are more likely to be presented to by someone in suicidal pain.

Fear

In the encounter between the suicidal person and his potential helper, there are two people who are afraid. The fears of suicidal people were listed in Chapter 4; a response to the fears of friends and counselors is one of the most neglected and urgent projects in the prevention of suicide. We must begin by recognizing that it is normal for friends and counselors to have these fears. The fears are partly due to human nature, and partly due to the prejudices of our culture. We do not choose to have them, and to hope that work with the suicidal will ever become free of fear is an impossible goal. With education and experience, however, our degree of fearfulness can be reduced.

1. "If I try to help him, and he later commits suicide, then I am going to feel terrible." Constructive involvement on the side of life reduces the risk of suicide. If an attempt occurs, you will at least know that you did what you could. To have an awareness of the situation and not get involved will not insulate you from bad feelings if a suicide happens. A key to the reduction of fear is to reject from the outset the idea that "I" am responsible for the prevention of someone's suicide. In the causal history and current circumstances of a suicide attempt there are a thousand deficiencies of pain-coping resources; your presence or absence is only a single factor. The anxiety generated by this fear is significantly reduced when you cooperate with others to help reduce the risk of suicide. In this context your role will often be secondary and limited to a few specific actions.

2. Fear of manipulation. It is infuriating, embarrassing, and humiliating to discover that our money, time, or energy have been deliberately "taken". We are angry at ourselves, angry at the perpetrator, and angry that others may regard us as a "sucker". Since the suicidal are said to be manipulative, we are understandably averse to the idea of spending time with someone who is suicidal.

This kind of manipulation, which may be comparatively common in business or social situations, is extremely rare in connection with suicide. People in pain usually do not have several of the capabilities or qualities that are required for manipulative behavior: foresight, planning, and practical experience. Suicidal people simply want to have their pain reduced. If you talk with them, you will find out that people using the word "suicide" have genuine problems in living with which they are unable to cope. "Manipulative" is a concept that the non-suicidal use to cope with their own feelings. They are frightened, and if they conceptualize this as the fear of being manipulated, then they have made some sense of their anxiety, done so in a way that does not reflect badly upon themselves, and given themselves license to feel and express anger at the source of their discomfort. As it is used in normal life, "I got manipulated by so-and-so into doing ... ," is rarely true in work with the suicidal. The residual bitter feeling of having been used is not often experienced after you have spent time helping someone who was suicidal. (To be sure, however, negative feelings that are common in the aftermath of other helping situations, such as disappointment over a lack of gratitude and appreciation, are unfortunately also common in work with the suicidal.)

Something similar to manipulation, that is practiced by some suicidal people, is exaggeration of pain. Suicide hotlines often advertise themselves as being willing to accept calls from anyone who wishes to discuss any type of problem, yet have policies of giving more time to callers who say they are having thoughts of suicide. Some regular callers, people who are lonely and depressed, figure this out, and always say that they are suicidal. This situation — the exaggeration of the complaint to get better or quicker attention — is common in all areas of health care and in all of life. This exaggeration of neediness is not done by all suicidal people, and no studies have been done to show that the suicidal are more prone to this type of exaggeration than the non-suicidal. It is likely that the percentage of the suicidal who exaggerate their risk is less than the percentage who either understate the seriousness of their risk, or are unwilling to disclose the full extent of their pain. Exaggeration is not "just wants attention"; these people need relief from pain, and have conditions that are better to respond to sooner rather than later. Who can blame them? Resources for the depressed and the suicidal are in short supply; people who do not vigorously pursue self-advocacy often do not get minimally adequate levels of attention for their needs. Healthcare workers may become irritated by patients who are pushy, but it is not the fault of the client, or of the healthcare worker, that the available social resources are inadequate. Since this form of exaggeration is so common, we do not feel that responding to it is the same as being manipulated, being taken, or being duped.

While exaggeration is less than manipulation, coercion is something that is more. In the course of several hundred talks to social workers and educators, I have been told of one or two cases in which someone said to a social worker, "Unless you write a report recommending that I be given custody of my children, I'm going to kill myself." Although coercive situations are rare, the idea of being "taken hostage" is so frightening that it affects our reactions to everyone who is suicidal. Unfortunately, a search of the literature has turned up no studies on this issue. The direct effort to coerce others is distinct from the cry for help: "If I lose custody of my children, I'll kill myself." Since it can be difficult to tell the two cases apart, the initial response should be to treat the behavior as a cry for help. If it goes beyond that, it should be treated as extortion. I have suggested to counselors that they get a witness and call the police if they believe that the presentation is coercion. Extortion in ordinary life is usually some version of "Give me your money or I will commit an act of violence against you." Extortion in suicide is "Give me what I want or I will commit an act of violence against myself." Police are often called unnecessarily by counselors for the suicidal. These are cases in which the person is not at immediate risk of an attempt, but the counselor feels inadequate to deal with someone who expresses suicidal thoughts, and wishes to be relieved of what he incorrectly regards as his responsibility for someone's suicide. In the coercion case the police are not called because the person is suicidal, but because he is coercive. To respond to this type of behavior is not within the province of healthcare workers. [1]

What are we to do about the person who says "I want all of someone's time or I commit suicide,"? This behavior characterizes a minority of suicidal people, but is so memorable that it colors our view of the entire population. Whether the situation is marital, boyfriend/girlfriend, or a gay or lesbian relationship, the person is in extreme pain. The loss of the loved person is simultaneously a source of pain and a loss of a principal resource for coping with pain. The suicidal person is full of fear for the future. Suicide happens in these situations, and these people should be responded to by reducing pain and supplying resources. To be involved in these situations, as the other person, or as a friend or counselor, is one of life's less pleasant experiences. It is understandable that we should be loath to become involved, but the suicide risk period does not last indefinitely. People do get helped through these crises all the time, and the people who help them are not worse for having done so. This behavior does not deserve to be called manipulation; it is not voluntary, and does not have the kind of foresight and planning that go into the manipulative behavior of ordinary life.

3. Fear of dependency. The suicidal are emotionally needy, and there is a fear that if you help someone through a crisis, he will make heavy demands on your concern for an indefinite period of time. There are emotionally needy people, suicidal and non-suicidal, who want to come back repeatedly to people who once offered them some comfort and assistance. It can be very unpleasant to be on the receiving end of this behavior, and it is understandable that we should fear involvement in this situation. No studies have been done on the extent to which this behavior characterizes the suicidal. Chronic dependency should be distinguished from two similar types of situations. The first is suicidal pain that is precipitated by a major trauma. Many victims of a major trauma want to talk about it again and again for a period of weeks or months. Eventually they come to terms with their loss and cease to place demands on friends and relatives. The second situation involves children. Counselors in the school system, who help a child through a suicidal crisis, often find that the child wants to check in with them once or twice a week for the rest of the school term. Often these children do not receive enough parenting at home. The relationship with the counselor helps to meet their real need. Both situations are common in work with the suicidal. Though they may try your patience, they are bearable and manageable. What the chronically dependent want, however, is beyond what others can reasonably be expected to provide. This again is a situation where a small percentage of the suicidal has a behavior pattern that discourages others from being involved with anyone who is suicidal, and fosters the false belief that all suicidal people are prone to permanent excessive dependence on others. With experience it is not difficult to recognize the chronically dependent, and to make the limits of what you are able to provide clear from the outset. Underlying chronic dependency are usually chronic problems in physical or mental health, or addictive behaviors. The chronically dependent person, or his intimates, may benefit from involvement in support groups that explore codependency issues.

The aggregate pain theory does not have specific proposals to make about the difficult problem of chronically and excessively dependent patients and clients. Some of its general proposals may modestly reduce

the size of the problem: provide help at an earlier stage, improve the
help offered, provide more support for primary caregivers, employ
weaker conceptions of confidentiality, improve our understanding of the
self-prevention of suicide, assault the malevolent social conditions
that make suicidal pain hurt more and last longer, reject the view that
it is desirable for a suicidal person to develop a heavy dependency on a
single therapist (as, for example, is advocated as being generally
advantageous in the psychoanalytic treatment of mental health
conditions) reject the single cause and single cure approaches to suicide,
strike down policies that deny the suicidal access to recovery programs,
improve access to treatment for physical health, improve our
acceptance of vicious circle problems, and improve our attitudes about
recovery from suicidal pain.

4. "If I help one, more will follow." This is a common fear among school
counselors. Individual counselors fear that they will be swamped by
students who claim to be suicidal; administrators fear that giving
attention to suicidal students rewards suicidal behavior. In one sense
the fear is legitimate. If programs are made available for stigmatized
conditions, conditions for which only a few of the people who need help
currently seek it, then a greater number of people are likely to present
themselves. This places greater demands on the service providers, but
the end result, better assistance for those who would otherwise have
died or suffered longer, is not something to be feared. Counselors who
begin seeing more suicidal students do get more burdensome workloads;
they do not get a large number of students who have no serious problems.
Though they become more skilled at dealing with more difficult
situations, they need more support from co-workers and administrators.
Two other factors behind this fear are not legitimate. The first is that
non-suicidal students will use "suicide" as an attention getting ploy. As
far as I know, there is no research or anecdotal evidence that this
happens when organizations develop suicide prevention programs. The
second factor is the belief that suicidal behavior is being rewarded.
Ask yourself what behavior is rewarded by the development of a rape
crisis program. The provision of improved services rewards help-
seeking behavior by those already in pain; it does not reward the crime
that caused the pain. Suicide prevention programs reward help-
seeking behavior, they do not reward becoming suicidal. The
development of a program means that more people will receive

treatment for the condition, not that more people will get the condition that needs treatment.

5. Fear that the presentation is a prank. This does not happen often in work with the suicidal. I have never heard of a face-to-face presentation in which a person who said he was suicidal had no problems that needed assistance. "Pseudo-suicides" happen sometimes on hotlines, and apparently sometimes in other situations. I once took a call from someone who said he had overdosed, and who then gradually became non-responsive. When I reviewed the call with other phone workers I found out that two calls with the same identifying details had been made in previous months. These events happen. But just as false alarms do not mean that the fire department should not respond to real fires, pseudo-suicides do not mean that we should do less than our best for people who are genuinely suicidal. Unfortunately, these cases, which are much rarer than false fire alarms, have the same effect: they deprive people in need of life-saving resources.

The partial decomposition of the fears of potential helpers of the suicidal is not a pleasant task, particularly for someone who wants to argue that the suicidal are not bad people. Though our fears of these situations contain inaccuracies and distortions, it cannot be denied that work with the suicidal may involve being in unpleasant situations, and having uncomfortable emotions. Our fears, rational or otherwise, are real. There is no magic bullet that will make them disappear. Work with the suicidal necessarily involves overcoming personal fears, and the fear of suffering prejudice from third parties. These are people who will say that you are a sucker to feel sorry for people who just want attention, or are angry administrators who believe that the organization would have no suicidal members, if no one were willing to offer to help to the suicidal. With time and experience, much of the discomfort caused by these fears subsides. In ordinary life we sometimes apply the terms "courage" or "cowardice" to voluntary behavior in fearful situations. Some people believe that suicides had the guts to overcome the fear of death; others believe that suicide is a gutless way to avoid facing up to problems. The aggregate pain theory does not believe that suicide is voluntary, and consequently does not believe that these terms are appropriate. The behavior of people not in overwhelming pain, however, is voluntary, and when they act despite their fears, or fail to act because of their fears, these terms are appropriate.

Make a prior decision to take it seriously

After listing the bad things that could happen to suicidal people if they sought help, I went ahead and told them that they should try to seek help anyway. Now I need to do the same with potential caregivers. Just as trying to get help is better than riding it out, trying to provide help is better than aversion and avoidance. At least 90 percent of the people who present themselves as suicidal will not become suicides, become chronically dependent on the caregiver, try to coerce the caregiver, or try to play a prank. They simply want relief from overwhelming pain.

You should make a prior decision to take each presentation seriously. You will be able to focus all of your attention on the situation, and you will not have to continually or intermittently wonder if the person's sincerity is questionable. You will have less anxiety and greater objectivity during and after the encounter. Your prior decision determines your behavior; you are not being manipulated or controlled by the other person. You will not afterwards wonder, "Maybe I should have taken it more seriously." "Take it seriously," is the right course of action in nearly every case, and during the initial encounter you are never in a position to be certain if this is one of the few cases in which the person is not in genuine need of assistance.

When I discuss the warning signs I usually illustrate them with examples that demonstrate the necessity — and difficulty — of taking each presentation seriously. Under "imaginary loss of health" I mention that I was told by several sources about a Bronx police detective who became increasingly convinced that he was suffering from terminal cancer. This conviction was not altered by several medical examinations that turned up no evidence of the disease. His efforts to discuss his health with others were rebuffed. "What? How can you think you've got cancer if the doctors can't find anything?" Isolation increased, he went into Van Cortland Park, sat down on a bench, and killed himself with his revolver. A second example concerns a 17-year old private high school student who had a talent for drawing caricatures of teachers and fellow students. A few days after he jumped to his death, I discussed his suicide with several people who knew the boy and his family. They were in a state of deep shock, and their shock was compounded by the fact that the only warning-sign factor of which they were aware was that two days before his death he had told some other students that he was thinking about suicide. Because of his reputation as a humorist, these other students thought he was joking, and told no one about his remark.

The aggregate pain approach does not believe that the other police officers or the other students can be faulted for their responses. They behaved as most people would behave in similar situations. These two cases — and many, many others — demonstrate the need to work toward social conditions in which suicidal people can more easily ask for help, and the non-suicidal can more easily give help.

First reactions

For many reasons, the initial encounter between a suicidal person and his acquaintance or counselor may not go well, or be too brief. He is full of fear and pain; you have been caught off guard. Since suicidal presentations are infrequent, it is normal to be caught off guard. Though you may be dissatisfied with your initial reaction, self-criticism or criticism by others is not justified. Social prejudice, stigma, and especially fear do not vanish overnight, and cannot help but affect your response, even if you have extensive education in suicide prevention. If you are unhappy with the outcome of your initial encounter, it is advisable to seek the person out for a second meeting. Counselors who have had such second meetings report that they usually have much more constructive results.

Initial Response

Listen

Simple listening is the best initial course of action with anyone who is suicidal, has attempted suicide, is the relative of a considerer, attempter, or completer, or is a friend or co-worker who has just spent time with a suicidal person. Sympathetically acknowledge what they say, ask for details, and be willing to listen to the most painful aspects of their situation.

1. If a despairing person is allowed to unburden his troubles to a sympathetic listener, he nearly always feels better by the end of the conversation. This sounds like an empty truism that cannot be of much value. Since anyone can listen, people with special training should be able to do more. But if you experience it a few times, you will find that listening has unique value in work with the suicidal. It provides acceptance, patience, understanding, and relief from anxiety and anger. It has no substitute, and there is nothing better that you can do.

You are bound to feel anxious and uncomfortable if someone talks to you about a situation related to suicide. We have a natural aversion to listening to a suicidal person because it means remaining in a situation that is painful for us. We need to remember that the kinds of discomfort we experience at different stages of the interview do not last forever and do not cause us harm. We should model patience with pain, both our own and that of the suicidal person. Besides aversion, many people respond to personal discomfort by immediately taking some other form of action to reduce their anxiety. Counselors who work with some types of problems, perhaps drugs or truancy, often feel that aggressive, "take charge" behavior is the best way to conduct the interview. In the initial interview with a suicidal person, however, it is better to simply listen, to be passive rather than active.

2. If someone has an opportunity to ventilate hostile feelings toward himself or others, then he is less likely to discharge his feelings in physical behavior. The content of his ideation may not change much during the conversation, but the energy and anxiety behind the rage can be dissipated. Listening is especially important with young people and recovering substance abusers; it helps them learn new ways to cope with their pain.

A case illustrating both the need to be listened to and the need to ventilate occurred to an officer in Manhattan's 17th Precinct. He was sent to investigate a report of a man with a gun. When he arrived at the apartment, the door was part way open. He went inside and saw a man with a gun pointed to his head. This man had driven to another state, purchased a pistol, returned to New York, phoned his estranged girl friend, and told her that he was going to kill himself. She called the police. The officer told me, "I started talking to him. I thought that what you were supposed to do is talk people out of suicide. He turned the gun on me and told me to shut up. He had some things he wanted to say. He got them off his chest, and then he gave up the gun."

3. The listening technique of reflection, developed by the psychotherapist Carl Rogers, is very effective during the early part of the conversation with a suicidal person. At the simplest level, this involves reflecting back the factual or emotional content of what the person has said to you. "My lawyer cheated me!" can be reflected as "You're angry at your lawyer?" This technique may seem overly simple, but it definitely works, and, in a stressful situation, simplicity is a blessing. The person may be sobbing, hysterical, disoriented, have a strong accent, or otherwise be difficult to understand. Simple reflection nearly always gets a positive response, a gasp of "Oh, yes!" The person usually knows that he is difficult to understand, and the fear that that he may not succeed in making himself understood adds to his anxiety. He will be glad that someone cares, listens, and tries to understand. After a few minutes his agitation usually begins to subside, and you will become accustomed to his voice patterns.

4. Passive listening is especially important if you are with someone from a different cultural background. As cultures and subcultures from around the world interact with American life, there are thousands of variables in pain-causing events and coping resource deficiencies. Suicidal people are usually able and willing to explain cultural differences of which you are unaware. If you simply accept what the person says and do not attempt to impose your interpretation on his situation, then your understanding will be improved and his sense of alienation will be reduced.

Language

Much of the popular terminology for suicide is adversely affected by cultural mythology. These expressions make effective counseling more difficult. Cries for help are not threats; interviews are not confrontations; suicide attempts, no more than heart attacks, are not successes or failures; suicidal people have infantile or dependent personalities only if they behave in those ways when they are not full of pain; suicide is not a solution, escape, or option; there is nothing dramatic about being suicidal. These expressions estrange the suicidal from the non-suicidal, and cause counselors to have false conceptual models for the suicidal condition.

His point of view

The suicidal person may express ideas that you feel are inaccurate. Remember that during the initial interview your primary goal is to reduce pain, not correct false beliefs. Arguments with suicidal people never get anywhere; the effort to accept his way of looking at things can do a lot to help develop rapport and understanding.

A danger in being sympathetic is going too far. "I know just how you feel," is often belittling and is rarely true. We bring our entire life history to each event in our lives; since you both have had different lives, you are unlikely to have had identical emotional reactions to similar events in your personal lives. "I know just how you feel," stops conversations; it says "I don't want to hear about it anymore."

Interruptions

Interruptions are often a poor move in counseling the suicidal, as well as in many other situations. Whatever the surface content of the interruption, underneath there is frequently denial, fear, invalidation, rejection, and belittlement. Interruptions are often attempts to control the situation in ways that benefit the interrupter. Interruptions are a red flag for emotional abuse in many family and social situations. If you have the urge to interrupt, you might first consider whose needs are served by the interruption. Interruptions should be avoided not only if they are negative, but also if they are bright ideas, penetrating insights, or factual input. Try to imagine what you would want if you were full of pain and wanted to pour out your story. Would you want a counselor who squelched whatever you wanted to say, a counselor who felt it was important to prove to you and to himself that he was a good counselor?

Acceptance

Suicidal people suffer massive rejection from themselves, their acquaintances, and their society. Fear of more rejection is an omnipresent part of their lives. During the initial interview it is important to avoid rejection and to provide acceptance.

1. The suicidal express values and ideas — "My life is not worth living. My future is hopeless." — that are directly at odds with the beliefs of the people who try to help them. "Your ideas are wrong," helps the counselor discharge his own feelings, but is of no benefit to the suicidal. It only increases their feelings of alienation from others. Their negative ideas and feelings are involuntary; to be told to alter them immediately is an impossible request, and increases their feelings of powerlessness.

2. A second common type of rejection is to deny the severity of the person's situation. The short antidote to this problem is to remind yourself that the reaction to many completed suicides is "Those problems were not enough to commit suicide over." It is invalid to project your own feelings about what makes life worth living onto another person. You do not know how much pain his problems cause him, or how strong his coping resources are.

An example of this is the recent suicide of a young police officer. He had three warning signs associated with police suicide: alcohol abuse, trouble on the job, and marital or relationship problems. His relationship problem was that he had two girlfriends: one to whom he was engaged and another with whom he was also in love. This was one of the circumstances that made his death puzzling to fellow officers. As a counselor who has seen ten lonely people in a row, you might have difficulty taking a presentation by this person seriously. "Come on. Two people are in love with you. Problems, sure, but suicidal?" (And you might also have some unconscious moral disapproval or envy.) As with other types of rejection, denial and belittlement do not make someone feel better. They increase feelings of isolation; they increase the feeling that no one understands; they demean the person's ability to assess accurately his own condition. A rejection of his estimate of the severity of his pain is a poor basis for a program of recovery.

3. A suicidal person is likely to feel that he is at fault and a bad person simply for being in pain. He is also apt to have those attitudes toward whatever specific types of pain he suffers: bereavement, assault, physical or mental illness, substance abuse. He may have heard, "It's your fault you are in this mess," dozens of times, and he may have had

that thought thousands of times. The rejection of blame from others and from the self is an essential step toward acceptance and recovery.

4. It is often helpful to both make it clear that you are on the side of life, and yet still convey the idea that he is an OK human being whether or not his crisis ends in suicide. This is difficult for voluntarists. If they believe that suicide is undesirable, they cannot help but negatively judge the person they believe chooses it. If they have the romantic view of suicide, they lack a basis for concerted action to prevent death. The involuntarist position enables us to provide unconditional acceptance of the person and his pain, and enjoins us to take direct action to provide him with a wide range of resources.

5. Acceptance is something that comes in degrees; there are occasions when you will find aspects of someone's physical or verbal behavior unacceptable. He may, for example, explicitly discuss causing harm to others. In these situations you can simply listen, let the person ventilate, and look for aspects of his fear, frustration, or anger for which you can express sympathy.

6. The suicidal have been told that their minds are morally inferior, structurally defective, cognitively distorted, and biochemically deficient. They fear that they are losing their capacity to understand themselves and the outside world. They may have specific fears about insanity or AIDS related dementia. You should validate the usually considerable extent to which they accurately perceive reality.

7. Some school counselors claim that if you let people talk about their problems, you have reinforced both their having the problem and their having the bad feelings caused by the problem. The policy of these counselors is to permit students to talk only about positive things in a positive way. The self-serving nature of this position is evident from the fact that these same counselors usually indicate that listening to people talk about their pain causes them considerable discomfort: "Personally, I can't stand listening to people talk about depression." These counselors usually cite behaviorism as a justification for their position, but it is questionable if behaviorism does justify this policy, particularly for the initial interview. Is it "Be positive," that is rewarded, or is the reward really being given to "Don't talk about your problems," "Repress painful emotions," "Be insincere," and "No matter how bad you feel, adapt your behavior to the emotional demands of

others,"? Virtually all suicidal children in New York City have serious and legitimate problems in their lives; many come from dysfunctional homes where they are expected to obey "Don't talk about it." To accept all of the bad feelings relieves part of the stress, reinforces honesty and help-seeking behavior, and provides a more accurate basis from which to develop a program of recovery.

8. The victim is often afraid to reveal particular components of suicidal pain: "If I tell others about these things, they will reject me and then I will be in more pain." These can include all the things that are regarded as stigmatizing or embarrassing in our culture, or the victim's culture of origin, as well as his specific feelings of being suicidal, depressed, afraid, hopeless, powerless. Besides a willingness to accept all of these problems, counselors must also recognize that suicidal pain may include things that do not usually or apparently cause others much unhappiness. "That's nothing to get upset about," is belittlement that makes the pain worse, not better. Sometimes people, particularly men, are unwilling to reveal to themselves how much pain an event in their lives has caused them. They may have an image of themselves as being invulnerable to certain types of pain, and practice denial on an event that threatens to embarrass that image. Coercion is not likely to be productive, but you need to give suicidal people opportunities to talk about everything that may be bothering them. How can they have a feeling of acceptance and understanding unless they have been able to disclose everything they want to talk about?

Vicious circles

Suicidal people usually have problems that feed off each other. Individual variations are endless, but a simple example is someone who cannot get a job because of poor health, cannot get health treatment because he lacks money, and lacks money because he cannot get a job. Even if the suicidal find people who are willing to discuss individual difficulties, they rarely have opportunities to discuss the interaction of their problems. Vicious circle problems make others feel uncomfortable; many counselors either deny that they exist or claim that listening to this type of problem is unproductively dwelling on the negative, and may increase the victim's feelings of powerlessness and hopelessness.

Vicious circle problems are real; avoiding them will not make them go away. Suicidal people are often grateful for the opportunity to unload these frustrations, and it significantly increases feelings of understanding and acceptance. A willingness to explore these aspects of the person's situation will leave you with a more accurate and cooperative basis on which to proceed. Suicidal people often reject themselves, and are rejected by others, simply because they are in pain. This causes them to feel yet worse. Acceptance during the initial interview provides relief for this and for many of their other vicious circle problems.

Look for strengths

After the suicidal person has told you about his problems is the time when you should respond with comments about things that you sincerely believe are of value. If you do this earlier, he will wonder if he will still be acceptable when you find out the rest of his story. It is better to say, "I feel you deserve credit for x, y, and z," or, "I see someone who is a good person because of x, y, and z," than, "You ought to feel better about yourself because of x, y, and z." The latter sentence tells him that he should start feeling better right now, which may not be possible. It may even be perceived as containing a conditional threat: Start feeling better about yourself or I am going to disapprove of you. Statements of the first type may not immediately change his emotional condition, but they at least alter his cognitive state: Someone I respect thinks I'm OK because of x, y, and z.

To be phony in the plus department is a minus: your statements have to be accurate and sincere. It is normal for a victim of depression to compulsively discount praise. His suspicion of inaccuracy or insincerity is likely to cause him to have at least one of several reactions. The first is that you think he is stupid or easy to manipulate. The second is "I don't have those qualities. [Or, those qualities are not worth much.] Therefore, there is nothing good about me." The third is "He's stupid. He has no understanding of my situation. He won't be able to help me." The best way to respond to discounting is not by argument, but with simplicity, directness, accuracy, and sincerity.

Impatience

Many components of suicidal pain are made worse by impatience. Impatience leads to an unwillingness to try longer roads to recovery, the premature abandonment of courses of action that do not bring immediate relief, and more acute disappointment with setbacks. It will be difficult for counselors to respond to the impatience that the suicidal have with their conditions, unless counselors first recognize their own difficulties with impatience.

Caregivers have greater pride, pleasure and enthusiasm when they work with people whose problems are easily solved. They frequently receive positive reinforcement from their clients, their peers, their supervisors, and their inner senses of personal satisfaction. The converse consequence of this situation is that people with more difficult problems are avoided, or contact with them is terminated as quickly as possible.

Caregivers have ample cause to be impatient with suicidal situations. They fear blame if the client dies by suicide; it is not pleasant to be with someone who is in a lot of pain; responding to suicidal people is rarely part of their job description; and their relationship with the suicidal person is usually a source of discomfort and impatience for their supervisor. However, there is no evidence that an attitude of "Hurry up and get better," is conducive to recovery. This attitude causes the suicidal to have two additional pains: "I am a nuisance," and "Something must really be wrong with me, I'm not getting better as fast as I should." This form of impatience is a response to the needs of the caregiver, not the victim. There are no timetables for recovery from suicidal pain. Each person's pain and coping resource situation is individual. No one knows in advance how much time and effort will be required to reach a lasting recovery. It is not helpful to adopt a blame-the-victim position if your treatment program does not achieve positive results within its usual span of time, nor is it helpful to blame the counselor. When impatience does not work, it leads to frustration and anger. This happens not just over the course of longer treatment programs, but also during the initial interview. If the suicidal person does not start to feel better after thirty minutes, the counselor often starts to feel worse. The counselor wants reassurance that he has done some good, and sometimes the client's pain is such that he shows no outward change. The way to deal with this anxiety is to recognize that you can do the best you can with what you have — and no more. Beyond the fulfillment of your basic responsibilities, you are powerless over his emotional condition. Even if he does not experience a positive mood change in thirty minutes, or thirty days, you are still doing all that you can to help him stay alive. Your fear — "If he does not start feeling better right now, he will soon kill himself," — is not valid. Suicidal people can continuously feel bad for long periods of time. Over that period of time, your calm patience will be a better resource than anxious panic. It will enable both of you to have more honest and accurate attitudes about suicidal pain. A great many problems in work with the suicidal may be traced to impatience:

1. Quick Referrals. The quick referral is a common response to the suicidal. Many social service organizations have the quick referral as their primary suicide prevention policy. The rationale is "We're not equipped to handle that." Any staff member who spends more than a few minutes with a suicidal person will be criticized on the grounds that "You're not qualified to handle that." This is common in school situations, even when the suicidal child has been unable to establish an on-going relationship with an outside service provider. With or without the de facto policy of quick referrals, work with the suicidal produces anxiety, and the temptation to give the person a list of phone numbers or addresses can become quite strong.

It is essential to provide suicidal people with a large number of resources for recovery. They often need support to initiate and continue with recovery programs. But when referrals are made out of fear and defensiveness, their effectiveness is likely to be minimal. Quick referrals are always perceived as rejection. The cognitive distortions of depression will generalize "This person or organization does not want to see me," to "No one wants to see me," and, "I don't matter to them," to "I don't matter to anyone." The suicidal person turned to you because he thought you were his best bet for care and concern, for understanding, for relief from loneliness. A quick referral does not decrease these pains, it adds to them. Studies in other areas of health care have shown that the likelihood that the patient will follow advice for further treatment is increased if two conditions are met during the initial interview: the patient felt that the healthcare worker had a genuine interest in his welfare, and felt that he had been given an opportunity to disclose fully the nature of his problems.

In any referral situation you should encourage the person to check back with you, and make an effort to arrange a follow up consultation with the other organization.

2. Arguments. All workers in suicide prevention have learned that arguments, rational or otherwise, get nowhere. "Suicide is morally wrong," and "Your problems don't justify suicide," reject, belittle, and alienate. They do nothing to decrease pain or increase resources. "That's foolish," and "Don't be stupid," are common responses to presentations of suicidal feelings. These statements help their speakers cope with their own emotional disequilibrium, but they add to the pain of the victim. They imply intellectual and moral inferiority, and insinuate that the victim is a superficial person with superficial problems. Arguments misread the presentation as a statement of intention, instead of seeing it as a cry for help. Just as chest pains in the apparently healthy are sufficient reason to seek medical care, suicidal pain, in whomever it occurs, is a legitimate reason to ask for help. Consider an analogy from another area of public health: each August a dozen or so young men die from the stress of pre-season football practice. Nothing is morally wrong with them; they were born with congenital abnormalities of which their families, coaches, and medical examiners were unaware. Suicide is similar: levels of pain that many can endure may be intolerable to a few. To belittle the suicidal for having insufficient pain or inadequate reasons is to be like the coach who belittles the athlete for having dizzy spells during wind sprints.

3. The Challenge. Audience members at suicide prevention talks sometimes ask, "Shouldn't you just say to the person, 'Go ahead and do it,'?" All police officers have heard a story about a veteran cop who said this to someone perched on a window ledge, and, in the story, the person comes back inside the building. Several teachers have told me that they responded to in-class presentations by throwing open a window, and challenging the child to jump. In these accounts the child did not jump, but in two other situations, related to me in confidence by district administrators, the child did go out the window. One was from the fourth floor, the other from the second floor, and neither leap resulted in death.

This suicide prevention procedure is based upon the assumption that the people who talk about it are not serious. The assumption is not true; most completed suicides tell others about their pain shortly before their deaths. This procedure, when done in public situations such as a classroom or group meeting, is also based upon the view that the cry for help is an illegitimate request for attention that intends to frighten and manipulate others. Morally improper behavior deserves the punishment of public humiliation. The humiliation is not only retributive punishment, it also deters others from similar misdeeds.

The challenge to go ahead and do it is simply a crude version of something that happens in all situations involving suicide: the non-suicidal take action to reduce their own anxiety. The challenge discharges hostility and serves as a form of social control to minimize help-seeking behavior. People who are accustomed to being in control of situations are especially prone to "Dare them to do it," thinking and behavior. But the challenge has real benefits for no one, and only adds to the pain of the victim.

4. Problem Solving. You can do a lot to help someone during the initial interview, but it is unlikely that you can solve his problems. The attempt to problem solve invariably involves both an overestimation of your own capabilities, and an underestimation of the depth of the suicidal person's difficulties. It presupposes an inequality — you are better than he — and does so in an insulting way: if you can solve his problems in just a few minutes of your time, he must be stupid if he cannot solve his problems on his own. It belittles his pain by the supposition that it is small, or easy to fix. A common trait of problem solving is the suggestion of coping strategies that are viable options only for the non-suicidal. Short stints of physical exercise, or efforts to meet new people, are effective ways for the non-despairing to get out of mildly unhappy periods of ordinary life. As coping resources for the suicidal they are insufficient, and end up further alienating the person from the rest of humanity. "I tried that and it didn't work. Something must really be wrong with me."

Problem solving does not work in actual practice. You will make ten suggestions, and the suicidal person will tell you why each of them did not work in the past, or will not work in the future. When you run out of ideas the conversation is in a negative place: the situation seems hopeless. You have growing frustration, and this leads to hostility and defensiveness. When the suicidal seek help, their primary aim is the reduction of pain, not the solution of problems. The things you can provide during the initial interview — acceptance, patience, understanding, relief from pain-on-pain vicious circles, evidence of care, relief from being alone with the problem, a reduction in fear and anxiety, the first steps toward programs of recovery — do not solve problems of romance, finance, child custody issues, or disabling injuries. But what you provide does relieve pain and increase resources, even if it does not do so in identifiable and discrete ways. Problem solving entails denial on the severity of suicidal pain, and, as with all forms of denial, it is part of the problem, not part of the solution.

The aggregate pain theory does not require that counselors be more than they are. They do not have to solve problems, and they do not have to be beacons of hope. The "reasons for living" approach to suicide prevention can be seen as a special type of problem solving, and as a response to impatience with the suicidal. As discussed earlier, the myth of the inner light is based upon a false model of the suicidal condition, and puts too much of a burden on the counselors and friends of the suicidal. The idea of being asked to produce reasons for someone to stay alive is intimidating, the task of providing modest measures to relieve pain is not.

5. Snap out of it. The "it" includes not just suicidal feelings and ideation, but also all forms and any combination of mental illness, substance abuse, bereavement, eating and sleeping disorders, and despair due to losses of health, home, personal security, job, and companionship. "Snap out of it," insinuates that the victim is a malingerer, tells him that he is a nuisance, and adds extra measures of pain and pressure to those he already has. He is morally inferior: if he remains in his condition it is because of weakness of the will. "Snap out of it," assumes that he has problems that can be snapped out of, that they have quick solutions, that they are not serious, and that he remains in his situation because of voluntary choice.

"Snap out of it," is abusive. It kicks people when they are down. It makes people in pain feel more hopeless, more powerless, more frustrated, more estranged from humanity. It says, "I don't want to be bothered with your pain any longer." For people not in great pain, "Snap out of it," may be helpful advice if they have trouble getting going in the morning. For the despairing, however, it has no positive and many negative consequences. *None* of the conditions associated with suicide can be snapped out of. Schizophrenia does not get lifted in a moment's notice by an act of will. No one goes from addiction to happy sobriety in a single day.

"Snap out of it," provides immediate emotional relief for its speakers. Not only is the condition of the person he is with not serious, its improvement requires no assistance from anyone else. "Snap out of it," absolves its speakers from the suggestion that they might have done anything to cause or to prolong the painful condition. "Snap out of it," carries the presumption of superiority: "If I were in your situation, I would, by an act of will, not be in any pain at all; and I would not make a pest out of myself." Adults who use "Snap out of it," in their work with young people model an abusive strategy for dealing with other people's pain: paper it over with a remark that ignores the depth and difficulty of the problem. A somewhat less abusive alternative to "Snap out of it," is "You'll feel better tomorrow," a sentence whose main purpose is to help its speaker feel better today.

6. Self-esteem programs. Problems with self-esteem are often significant parts of a suicidal person's condition. Schools and other organizations that already use self-esteem programs to deal with drug abuse, teen pregnancy, and dropout prevention sometimes want to incorporate suicide prevention activities under the self-esteem program umbrella. For people who are not yet suicidal, these activities may well be beneficial. But for those who are in acute pain, the "Let's feel better about ourselves right now!" approach can be counterproductive. On a number of occasions I have co-presented a workshop for students with a counselor from the school. During the first part several students may share quite painful experiences. Then the counselor leads a self-esteem exercise and roughly 85 percent of the group discharge their feelings by enthusiastic participation. For the other 15 percent, however, estrangement from "normal" is written all over their faces. The same phenomenon occurs in individual counseling. A girl tearfully talks about her mother's recent suicide attempt, and within a few minutes the advocate of self-esteem tries to change her feelings. Self-esteem programs may have a place in the primary prevention task of keeping people from becoming suicidal in the first place, but in crisis intervention contexts they are sometimes misused in an effort to take a shortcut to recovery. A focus on self-esteem fails to provide opportunities for ventilation, and for the articulation and treatment of other components of suicidal pain. Neglect and denial of major parts of

the person's pain often repeat in another form some of the initial causes of the low self-esteem.

Understanding

Most suicidal people believe "No one understands." *What* it is that no one understands is their suicidal pain. The non-suicidal do not suffer this kind of pain, and consequently do not have the additional pain of believing that no one understands. "No one understands," is often used to express several other painful feelings:

a. No one cares. No one is concerned enough to look into my situation and give it the attention and support it needs. I am alone with my pain.

b. Everyone misunderstands. Someone with no opinions about the causal history of the suicidal pain does not understand; someone with mistaken opinions both misunderstands and fails to understand. Misunderstandings of suicidal pain are usually partly due to the mythology of suicide: it's his fault he is in this condition; he just wants attention; he is trying to get back at us.

c. fear and hopelessness. If no one understands, how can anyone take action to make things better?

For people in great pain, being understood is a need. If the need gets some satisfaction, the suffering will get some relief; if the need is frustrated, the pain will get worse. Relief for a. and b. can be provided by someone who is willing to listen with sympathy and acceptance. Implementation of the aggregate pain model is intended to provide some relief for c. Suicidal pain has no single cause and no single cure. Each person brings to his crisis a history of thousands of pains and thousands of deficiencies of pain-coping resources. Complete understanding is impossible, but a level of partial understanding is available immediately and can be improved upon indefinitely. Large components of suicidal pain can be understood, and much of the pain that is understood can eventually be reduced in programs of recovery. As pain is reduced, and resources are increased, the suicidal feelings will eventually subside, and the person will regain the enjoyment of ordinary life.

A special problem for counselors occurs when they have listened to someone unload all of his troubles, and they then find themselves with the feeling, "He says he is in suicidal pain, but his problems don't seem that bad." This can be a very natural reaction. You may have recently spent time with someone who has suffered a long series of horrible misfortunes and not committed suicide, and now this person, with much smaller problems, says he is suicidal. This cognitive dissonance — the problems do not add up to suicidal pain — causes counselors to believe they have not understood the person's condition. This lack of understanding is uncomfortable, and can produce the familiar reactions of "He hasn't told us everything. There must be something more," or, "He's not really suicidal. He just wants attention." The first reaction is always true in the sense that no one is ever fully aware of all of the causes of his suicidal pain, but not always true in the sense of that the person has withheld a shameful secret. Even when there are things that he is afraid to reveal, his fear is not his fault. And even if he confides more fully, you may still feel that it does not add up to suicide. The best way to cope with this problem is to remember that, after many suicides, everyone who knew the victim said that they could not understand how the suicide could have happened. *This* cognitive dissonance — their understanding of the person's condition, and the fact of his suicide — is extremely painful and long lasting. If you accept from the outset that we never do fully understand why someone is suicidal, then it is easier to accept counseling situations where the problems do not seem to add up to suicide. To sincerely accept that people are in as much pain as they say they are in, and to respond accordingly, can save you from a much more profound sense of not understanding later on.

ASSESS RISK

Ask the Question

It is normal for us to feel ambivalent about revealing painful or embarrassing problems. We want assistance, want to ventilate, want relief from feeling alone, and want validation for our assessment of the situation. But we are also afraid of being judged and rejected, of being subjected to social stigma, and of frightening and being a burden to others. A common way to cope with this dilemma is to engage someone in conversation about related but more socially acceptable topics, and hope that the listener will provide an opportunity in which the more painful subject may be discussed. Training programs for counselors often encourage them to "Ask the next question."

In suicide prevention the next question is "Are you having thoughts of suicide?" If you are with someone and the idea "suicide risk" has crossed your mind, there is a good chance that the person has done something to cause you to have that thought. That something is a cry for help; you should respond any time your instincts have been aroused.

A number of hospitals in New York City admit more than 200 young people each year for attempted suicide. A study at one hospital in the Bronx found that 50 percent of the adolescent females had seen some type of healthcare provider within two weeks prior to the attempt. In these initial contacts the young women rarely said that they were suicidal. They complained of headaches, abdominal pains, sleep disorders, stress at school or home. A study of geriatric suicide reports

> ... in the months preceding their deaths, a very large percentage of older suicidal men are under a physician's care. It has also been shown that although older patients will apprise their physicians of their depressed feelings, very few, if any, will voluntarily tell their doctors of their suicidal ideas. The patient's reticence may result mainly from the physician's failure to ask direct questions about the possibility of suicide. Most patients will readily discuss their suicidal feelings when asked. (M. Miller, 1979, p. 19)

"Are you having thoughts of suicide?", said non-judgmentally, is a difficult question to ask. It violates one of the major taboos of suicide: Don't talk about it, you might give someone the idea. When you are actually in the situation, it seems especially dangerous to talk about suicide with someone who is already making complaints associated with suicide. Moreover, the taboo says that if you talk about it, it is *you* who gives him the idea. The idea of suicide, however, is constantly in the newspapers and on television programs; it already is in everyone's mind. If you ask this question to someone who has communicated the cry for help, you are doing several good things for him: showing that you care, that you take him seriously, and that you are willing to let him share his pain with you. These are things that he wants and is not getting from other people in his life.

If he is not suicidal, he will simply tell you so. If he is suicidal, he may answer "Oh, yes," with a gasp of relief. The discussion of suicidal feelings in a non-judgmental atmosphere can significantly reduce pain and suicide risk. You may wish to mention that most people have thoughts of suicide at some point in their lives. The thoughts are caused by pain and fear; they do not mean that the victim is a bad person.

In workshops for counselors of high risk populations, I have an exercise in which I go around the room and ask each counselor to ask me if I am having thoughts of suicide. The assumption of the exercise is that they have spent some time listening to someone talk about his problems, they have warning sign evidence for depression and suicide risk, and then the person makes one of the statements below. Each of these was actually said shortly before a completed or attempted suicide, or by someone who was acutely suicidal.

I'm so depressed, I just can't go on.

I want to go to sleep and never wake up.

Sometimes I wish I were dead.

None of you are going to have to worry about me anymore.

I'm going away for a real long time.

I think death is someplace peaceful.

I'm going to join my mother by Mother's Day.

[shake hands]: I'm going away now. I just wanted to say goodbye and tell you that our friendship has meant a lot.

Do you think suicide is sinful?

Is there a euthanasia society for the emotionally disabled?

This world is an evil place. I don't want to live in it and I don't want my baby to live in it.

I found some rope in the back yard. The FBI left it there. They want me to use it.

I'm a good person in a bad world. I tried to find some happiness for myself, but it didn't work out.

Sometimes I think everybody would be a lot better off with me not around here.

I got all my prescriptions refilled yesterday.

Yesterday when I was at my uncle's I went looking around. I found out where he keeps his revolver.

I'm afraid something bad is going to happen. I don't want it to happen, but I'm afraid it's going to happen.

Does God punish people who hurt themselves?

I know what I have to do.

Two people in my family have done it. My mother tried it six weeks ago.

Voices have been telling me to do things.

My therapist has a policy of terminating contact with suicidal clients.

I'm having shameful thoughts. I can't bring myself to say the word out loud.

Do you think if people talk about it, they are likely to do it?

I want to thank all you people at _____. It's not your fault nothing worked out.

I used to think everybody had a purpose and you shouldn't go until God called you.

   Most counselors are able to ask the question, or something similar, such as, "Are you thinking about hurting yourself?" Some of these counselors say that they doubt that they could do it in a real life situation; a few others are unable to ask even in the exercise context. Unfortunately, few suicidal people know that they may be with someone who is a good counselor, and *is* able to help them with part of their pain, but is himself unable to raise the issue. The taboos and fears are strong; an exercise such as the above is only a single small step toward helping counselors feel more comfortable with the topic of suicide. A second step is to think about how the suicidal person will feel if he senses that you are unable or unwilling to discuss his condition: I'm frightening to others; A part of me is bad; I am unacceptable; Others don't care if I live or die; I don't matter; My problem is not something that should be talked about; I'll have to deal with this on my own. Depressed people are always prone to interpret others' reactions to them in ways that reflect negatively on themselves; your reluctance to respond to their suicidal condition will be no exception.

Assess Risk

If you get a yes answer to the question about suicidal thoughts, you should find out how far along his ideation has progressed. Does he have a plan; has he acquired the means; has a time been set for the attempt? Many suicidal people simply have the thoughts, and have not focused on a means, such as jumping or self-poisoning. To have a plan in mind is not the same as having acquired or specifically selected the means. Some people have the means readily available, but have not thought about when they would do it, or they specify a date that is several weeks in the future. The same objections that are raised about the use of the word "suicide" are also raised about asking these questions: they give the person ideas and abet the progress of his ideation. This objection is not supported by the evidence. These questions have been asked tens of thousands of times in assessments of suicide risk in clinical situations and on hotlines. They did not push people closer to suicide. When your "next question" gets a negative answer, as it does at some point in more than 95 percent of all risk assessments, it can be a relief for both of you. His anxiety over his suicidal condition can drop when he realizes, "I haven't really thought it out that far, I must not be that bad off." When you give the person an opportunity to talk about the extent of his ideation, you learn more about his specific risk and his general situation, you establish a closer and more accepting relationship, and you permit him to unload feelings he has not shared with anyone else. When he gets his ideas out in public space they will look and sound a little different. This disparity creates a doubt, "Is this what I want?"

Suicide risk assessment is one part of the interview where you may wish to introduce types of factual information that may help keep the person alive. Whether it is advisable to do this in every risk assessment is doubtful, but there are many cases in which something like one of the following may be appropriate: When death does occur from medication overdose it is usually not a pretty sight. Often the victim drowns or chokes in his own vomit. ... Some people who attempt using that method neither die nor completely recover from the injury; they end up with permanent disabilities. ... I spoke with a police officer who has seen two people jump to their deaths. Both started screaming in terror as their bodies neared the pavement.

Counselors ask about the problem of client sincerity in these assessments, and the possibility of mood swings shortly after the interview. They may have had experience with someone who denied that he was suicidal, when they had strong independent evidence that he was. (The person may have written a note or told a friend.) There are cases of people who seemed fine one day, and attempted or completed suicide the next. These are both very real problems, but they do not invalidate the usefulness of asking about suicide ideation. Most suicidal people will honestly disclose the extent of their pain. People who are afraid that accurate answers will bring them more pain, as well as people who may soon suffer increased risk, will at least know that in the future it is OK to seek help. To ask for a full disclosure of their condition shows that you are on the side of life, no matter what the response.

SPECIFIC ACTIONS

Remove the means — Detoxify the home — Do not leave him alone

"If they can't do in one way, they'll find another way," is a basic part of the mythology of suicide. In both individual situations, and at the level of social policy, it supports the belief that action to reduce access to the means is a waste of time. The myth is false. Spend time listening to acutely suicidal people and you will discover that most have very specific feelings and ideas about the means of suicide. Amount and duration of pain, disfigurement of the corpse, probability of disablement, and many other factors influence their thinking and behavior concerning the means of suicide. The risk of suicide may be modestly reduced by a reduction in the availability of the means. More importantly, it directly shows the suicidal person that you want him to stay alive. It is a stronger way to say "I care," than to simply say "I care." Suicidal people discount expressions of support from others; physical action on the side of life is the hardest form of behavior to discount. Your knowledge of the availability of the means, and your inaction to remove them, will very likely be interpreted as lack of care, and as tacit permission to commit suicide.

When acquaintances consider taking action about the means, they are often concerned with issues of trust. They reason that leaving the means available shows trust; removing the means shows distrust. Distrust is painful, and they worry that the additional pain of distrust may push the person closer to suicide. One premise in this argument is correct: additional pain does push suicidal people closer to death. The flaw with the argument is that for suicidal people, "Do people trust me with the means?" is a much smaller concern than "Do people care if I live or die?" Acquaintances take their care for the victim for granted, the victim does not. When I talked with people after suicide attempts they often said, "I told them about the pills. And nobody did anything!" Inaction about the means is always interpreted as lack of care; it is not interpreted as a sign of trust. The desire to be cared about is a much more fundamental part of human psychology. Things that are perceived as insults to caring are not quickly forgotten; after the suicidal condition has passed you will have many opportunities to show trust.

Most suicides occur when the person is alone. As with access to the means, being left alone can be interpreted as lack of care and as tacit approval of the suicide. Members of support groups for the survivors of a suicide victim sometimes say, "But you can't watch someone twenty-four hours a day." This is true, of course, and its speakers are usually people who made extraordinary efforts on the victim's behalf. The problem is to avoid the same kind of black-and-white thinking that characterizes the thought processes of suicidal people: we can't do everything, so there is no use trying to do anything. Companionship is a resource. It comes in degrees, and the more someone has, the less likely he is to commit suicide. In other areas of health care we do not have magic bullets, but we do successfully implement intermediate measures that reduce suffering and prevent death.

Get Help for Yourself

There is a type of pride that says, "I should be able to solve my own problems. I should not admit to others that I cannot manage my own affairs." This is not the best attitude for a suicidal person to have, or for someone who works with suicidal people. Suicide prevention should not be regarded as a Lone Ranger activity. The distribution of anxieties and responsibilities makes it easier and much more effective. Consultations with others will provide relief from stress, objective insights, and additional information. Failure to review the situation with others deprives the suicidal person of resources for his pain.

There is something basically stressful about listening to someone talk about suicidal feelings and ideation. Again and again, I have noticed in myself, in people with little experience in suicide, and in people with considerable experience, that there is a tendency to respond to this stress with one of two types of distortion of the seriousness of suicide risk. The first type of distortion is belittlement and denial on the severity of the person's problems. The second is to be deeply moved by the severity of his problems, and to reach an inaccurately low prognosis for recovery. A review of the situation with a sympathetic listener invariably helps correct both types of distortion.

You should try to network with a number of different people. If you work with survivors, and listen to their accounts of the last days of the victim's life, you cannot help but be struck by an awareness that at least some of these suicides might not have happened, if the different people who knew different aspects of the person had shared information. The suicidal, like most of us, live in different social worlds: the family, different sets of friends, the girlfriend, the neighbors, the people at work, the people at school, the healthcare providers. The more people you contact, the more information you gain and the more resources you can develop. Two people care is stronger than one person cares, and two people care together is a third positive force. I am not acquainted with completed suicides in which there was an excess of supportive communication.

In all aspects of work with the suicidal person it is natural and normal to suffer from doubt, uncertainty, and indecisiveness. A simple and efficient way to resolve these dilemmas is to always take an extra step for the side of life.

When you reach out to others, the chances that you will get a bad response are excellent. "Why bother me with this? I can't do anything," "It's not serious. He just wants attention," "It's his decision. Don't get involved," "We can't do anything without the parent's written permission." (The latter statement is a common response from some hospitals and mental health clinics in New York City. It is not true; New York State law permits treatment for children in life-threatening situations, even if parental consent is unavailable. The official, as opposed to de facto, policy of the city hospital system is that no child in need may be refused treatment.) After non-cooperation, the second most common bad response is criticism for the messenger. Your communication causes discomfort to the people you contact; they may respond by ventilating hostility at you. These bad responses do not mean that anything is wrong with you, or that you have taken a wrong course of action. You have done the right thing; sometimes, unfortunately, you have to be persistent.

Method B

Many counselors are employed by organizations that are unwilling or unable to provide them with adequate support in their work with suicidal students or clients. The organization may be unwilling to put a suicide prevention program in place before it is needed, or even after need has been demonstrated; or the program may exist only on paper and not in reality. Other staff members may be unwilling or unable to respond to impromptu requests for assistance. There may be an unwritten organizational rule that different groups or individuals are to function independently in their normal activities, and counselors may wonder if a suicidal situation justifies breaking the rule. "I'm on the third floor in the West Wing, and the other counselors are on the first floor in the East Wing," "I haven't talked to my Principal in two years," turf issues, and a thousand other familiar problems inhibit supportive communication in work with the suicidal.

A first step toward improved communication is to recognize that the current situation is usually not the fault of the people presently employed by the organization. Patterns of non-communication may have been established by people no longer employed by the organization, and unwittingly accepted as normal by their successors. Intra-organizational communication about the problems of suicidal students and clients is strongly affected by the myths, taboos, prejudices and stigma of suicide. Organizational problems are often created or made worse by outside social forces not directly related to suicide, or by the policies of parent organizations. A second step is to realize that presentations by suicidal students or clients are excellent icebreakers. You can use the situation to open up on-going lines of communication with hitherto inaccessible individuals and groups. Single presentations are usually not enough to move unresponsive organizations toward the development of suicide prevention policies and education programs for staff members. Several presentations within a short period of time, however, can help generate some momentum toward this goal. If one counselor presents the situation of his suicidal student or client to the organization, then perhaps a second and third will also.

My work brings me into contact with dedicated individuals or small groups who try to assist suicidal students or clients in environments that are profoundly unsupportive. The most common time for students to present seems to be Friday afternoon. In some of these situations the parents were previously unresponsive, and the counselor has already learned the hard way that the local mental health facility will not see adolescent considerers without written parental consent. Counselors in these situations use Method B: they develop an ad hoc suicide prevention team for each suicidal individual. The team includes available staff members, teachers, relatives, clergy, outside service providers, neighbors, friends, or acquaintances. Virtually any responsible person who is willing to lend any level of support, including simply "being there", may be asked to participate. (The recruitment of neighbors, fellow patients, or members of the student body as suicide prevention aides is usually not mentioned in the regulations of governing organizations, and may be of questionable legality. Method B is used by counselors whose only alternative is to leave the person with no assistance at all.) The counselor secures the permission of the suicidal person to enlist the support of each member of the team. Team members need to be informed about basic suicide prevention measures: take it seriously, listen supportively, get rid of the means, do not leave the person alone, no secrets. Provisions should to be made for communication among team members. Team members are often used in subsequent crises, either with the same person or someone else. Though they lack professional skills, these informal support networks often function well for short-term periods. The fear that suicide considerers will become excessively dependent on any one person is distributed. The ad hoc support teams have an informal and democratic atmosphere; hierarchical support systems are usually more impersonal and less flexible. The disadvantages of ad hoc teams are the lack of support for the team leader, and their less than optimal access to longer-term recovery programs. Ad hoc suicide prevention support systems are likely to be with us for some time to come; it is unfortunate that they remain unstudied by academic and professional research programs.

The support group approach is often opposed by guidance counselors or administrators who believe that no students or teachers should be allowed to talk with the suicidal student. A policy of "This matter should be dealt with by professionals only," leaves its victim stigmatized and isolated. His loneliness is made worse. If he suffers from depression, he is likely to interpret the loss of support as further evidence for lack of care. Since no one talks to him, he is unable to correct his false beliefs about himself and his world. The usual causes for the loss of support, however, are a desire to pass on the alleged responsibility for the potential suicide to an outside service provider, or desires by in-house counselors to protect their territory and to send a "We're better," message to teachers and other staff members. This behavior has harmful consequences in the longer run. In school settings, it teaches students one of the basic fears and myths of suicide: If I get involved, I might say the wrong thing and cause someone to die. The policy deprives victims of what they need to stay alive, and sets others on a lifetime path of aversion toward the suicidal.

No Secrets

Secrets in situations involving suicide have a different underlying psychology than secrets in ordinary life. When people become friends they normally exchange confidences that they do not share with people outside their relationship. This is how they show and receive trust and acceptance, how they identify themselves to each other as friends. This is simply part of normal life. The dynamics of fatal secrets are not normal. It is the part of the person that is afraid of more pain that says, "Keep this a secret." It is the part that wants help that indicates that the "this" is suicidal ideation and feelings. The fatal secret dynamic is highly transitive. During a suicide prevention workshop at a methadone clinic the staff psychiatrist shared this experience:

> His teenage son had a friend who told the son that he was suicidal. The son told the father and the two of them discussed the situation for a good part of an evening. The psychiatrist knew the other boy's parents, and twice had his hand on the phone to call them. Each time his son talked him out of it. Two days later the boy jumped from a sixth floor window. He survived, but suffered major injuries.

Both boys issued cries for help with their own situations, and both were afraid of what would happen if help was gotten. The psychiatrist wanted to call the family, but was afraid of the consequences of the call: "I wanted to show my son that I could trust his ability and judgment to handle the situation." Just as the real meaning of "I'm suicidal," is "Please, help me," the real meaning of "Keep it a secret," is "Please, no more pain." Do both: try to get help and try to do it in ways that do not cause the victim more pain.

This example shows that the guidelines that counselors follow on the job have to followed off the job as well. Another example of the fatal secret dynamic came from a principal who spoke about a telephone call she took from a parent: "My daughter won't be in school for a week. She attempted suicide. Please don't tell anyone." You may be caught off guard by such a request, and agree without thinking it through. It is the part of the parent that wants help that accurately reports the situation, and the part that is afraid of more pain for the child, and for the family, that asks that the information be kept secret. Board of Education guidelines specify that a student's suicidal condition is not to be kept secret from the parents, but say nothing about whether a parent's request for confidentiality is to be honored. Yet the principal needs to review the situation with the child's counselor, and, if possible, network with outside service providers. Breaking such secrets and mobilizing support for the person is not incompatible with doing it in ways that do not make the person's pain worse. It is done all the time, and done successfully.

It does not feel good to break a secret. But when the secret is suicide, it does not feel good to keep it either. Keeping the secret has a small selfish pleasure: "I'm special. This person trusted me with something important." Fear and anxiety outweigh this pleasure, and the pleasure will vanish if the suicide occurs. Secret bearers, often through no choice of their own, have been placed in a situation where the emotional turmoil makes it difficult for them to sort out the relevant issues. Consciously, they may wonder if it is best for the suicidal person if they seek help. Under the surface, however, questions of self-interest may become factors. Secret keeping affects our self-image: Am I someone who can be trusted with a secret? A sense of personal integrity is important, but keeping secrets about suicide — as with the secrets involved in sexual and physical abuse — does not improve one's integrity and emotional development. To break these types of secrets does not mean that the person cannot be trusted with the kinds of secrets that ought to be kept. Imagine that a loved one of yours attempted or completed suicide, and you discovered that someone knew the attempt was likely, and kept the secret. Would your estimation of that person's integrity increase? After a suicide, relatives and friends sometimes mention that someone did know an attempt was imminent, and did not tell anyone. They are *not* happy that the secret was kept; they usually feel anger and disbelief. Breaking the secret leads to a different type of "What happens next?" anxiety, but it also brings relief from stress, and from being alone with the knowledge of the suicidal person's condition.

Friends and counselors sometimes question the no-secrets rule by arguing that their relationship to the potential victim is a supportive resource, and, if they break the secret, the person may end the relationship. Sometimes the person ends up being glad that the secret was broken, and sometimes he becomes very resentful. The first point to note is that he can get angry with you, even if you *do* keep the secret. "If he had really cared, he would have done something," is sometimes said after a suicide attempt. Inaction, even when it has been promised, can be interpreted as not caring. Suicidal people, as with some people in non-suicidal situations, sometimes put others in situations where they are damned if they do and damned if they don't. Suicidal people are in horrible turmoil; no matter what course of action you take, you may find yourself on the receiving end of involuntarily expressed anger. Even aside from the risk of completed suicide, keeping the secret does not guarantee that the relationship will continue. Breaking the secret does not insure that the relationship will also be broken. It is unfair and unpleasant to be placed in this dilemma; the way to deal with it is to get help both for yourself and for the suicidal person.

Confidentiality

Confidentiality in suicide prevention is such a difficult and complex subject that an entire book ought to be written about it. As a tip-of-the-iceberg example of some of the issues, consider the following:

1. The Chancellor's regulations for the New York City public school system state, "It is the responsibility of every staff member to report knowledge of any potential suicide victim to the designated school authorities whether or not the student has requested that the information be kept confidential. The person designated ... must report such activity to the parent or guardian."

2. The Department of Health employs counselors who work in the public schools, and who have more flexible guidelines on parent notification: "Ensure that parent, legal guardian or other responsible adult is informed."

3. Some counselors in the public school system use a policy held by many mental health professionals: "Share information only with other professionals."

4. Most teachers, and many counselors and administrators, do not know what the regulations are on confidentiality in suicide prevention, or even that the regulations exist.

5. Some schools attempt to follow 1. to the letter. 1. is legally necessary; if you were the parent, you would want to know; and in most cases notifying the parent is the best course of action. Unfortunately, some children live in abusive homes, and the regulations require notification even if a prior notification has simply caused the child to suffer more pain. I have attended conferences where senior administrators have told staff members, "There are times when you just have to throw away the book."

6. In some schools different counselors follow different policies.

7. Some schools, out of ignorance or non-compliance, have, in a de facto sense, no guidelines at all. To have no guidelines at all is not a good

policy in suicide prevention. These schools are more likely to have the gross examples of the mistreatment of the suicidal that are mentioned elsewhere. Without answers to the question, "What am I to do next? What happens next?" staff members are afraid to have any involvement with suicidal children. Their individual and collective non-verbal discouragement of presentations for help for oneself, or for another child, are strong and effective.

8. As is apparent from 1.-7., the city school system has de facto anarchy on the single specific confidentiality issue of who should be contacted. This example is extreme, and partly due to the size of a system that serves 940,000 students, but these kinds of problems are repeated in many other organizations. Policies on confidentiality, knowledge of the policies, and compliance with the policies vary considerably from individual to individual and organization to organization. A further complication is that different organizations or parts of organizations fill different social roles, and serve different populations; no single policy of the type mentioned in 1.-3. is likely to be suitable for all purposes.

The formulation and implementation of policies on confidentiality must recognize a basic psychological principle: people are more likely to present themselves for help if they believe their confidences will be protected. The difficulty, of course, is that increased confidentiality means decreased ability to gain access to pain-coping resources. Counselors who speak to no one can get no additional help; professionals who speak only to professionals cannot contact the family.

A suicidal person may ask for his "right to complete confidentiality." Complete confidentiality means that the listener shares information with no one. In actual practice, I know of no healthcare organization that believes that this right exists. Many organizations claim that information will be shared only within the organization, or only with other professionals. Most require that a supervisor or co-worker be notified, and none forbid the counselor from reviewing the situation with someone else. Discussions of the justification of rights to confidentiality are usually based on utilitarian grounds, not on claims about the innate rights of man. The policy about sharing information only with fellow professionals, for example, is said to benefit both counselor and client, and to not discourage presentations for help in the way that a policy about parental notification does. Moreover, what suicidal people really want is not "my rights", but relief from pain. The request for confidentiality is, at bottom, an expression of fear that breaches of confidentiality may cause more pain, and for the suicidal, more pain may cause death. They fear that even if they do recover, the quality of their future life will suffer if they have to bear the stigma of having once been suicidal.

A certain degree of confidentiality is necessary, but complete confidentiality is ill-advised on practical grounds. I believe that a good guide through the many problems of confidentiality is the policy:

Share information in ways that reduce pain, not aggravate it.

This principle enables us to gain maximum access to resources. Suicidal situations are individual, and in some cases the inflexible principles, "Inform the parents," and, 'Share information only with other professionals," plainly give the wrong guidance. It might be objected that the lack of specificity in this principle, coupled with imperfect judgment and knowledge by the counselor, may lead to more problems than are currently had with the less flexible principles. The risk of these problems may be reduced by requiring consultations with co-workers before the matter is taken further. A second objection is that this principle, like other weak conceptions of confidentiality, will discourage presentations. This issue may be dealt with by providing students and clients with specific examples of how the organization works to avoid the aggravation of pain. For example, when I give talks with Department of Health employees, I mention that their regulations state that the students' medical records " ... may be coded for 'Risk-taking behavior' or other appropriate entry; 'suicide risk' should not be written." Policies such as these alleviate specific fears, assure suicidal people or their friends that you are sensitive to their needs, and encourage presentations for help. It needs to be mentioned, of course, that breaking confidentiality about risk for suicide does not mean that confidences about the details of the person's problems should not be respected.

A final objection to the principle is that it deprives suicidal people of venues where they can have assurances of complete confidentiality, and that this is a distinct and important resource. In practice the principle does not do this. "Share information in ways that reduce pain," is intended to be a guide for friends and counselors who are in situations where they cannot, and should not, maintain complete confidentiality. It is designed to help these people cut through the welter of conflicting, overlapping, incomplete, and imperfect conceptions of limited confidentiality. The principle makes explicit the rationale behind other conceptions of confidentiality, and simplifies decision-making procedures. Complete confidentiality is still available; there are many hotlines that accept anonymous telephone calls. Some hotlines do not trace, others trace only when an attempt is imminent or in progress.

Policies that permit or require the counselor to access a broad range of resources are difficult to manage during the initial interview. The best approach is to try to enlist the cooperation of the student or client: 'My policies require that I not keep this to myself. I need to get some support for you and for myself. Who do you feel we should contact about this?"

The Demoralizing Incident

The demoralizing incident occurs when

a. A counselor, relative, or friend makes considerable effort to get assistance from a healthcare facility for a suicide attempter or for an acutely suicidal person,

and

b. The facility either refuses to provide treatment or gives a level of assistance that is grossly inadequate for the severity of the situation.

This is very disheartening. During talks with school personnel, social workers, and police officers it is almost the norm that one or two members of the audience will express frustrations and disappointments over such experiences.

In our efforts to cope with these experiences we need to realize that no organization or individual will act in a perfectly appropriate manner in all situations involving suicide. Each of us has an understanding of suicide that is very inadequate, and each of us and our organizations are affected by the myths, stigmas, prejudices and taboos that surround the subject. Given the number of people affected by completed and attempted suicides, and by the anguish of suicidal feelings and ideation, it is clear that American society gives a disproportionately low share of public resources to suicide prevention education, research and treatment. Unenlightened attitudes about suicide, and great fear and defensiveness, are unfortunately quite normal obstacles in work with the suicidal.

It does not help matters to lapse into cynicism. We need to see difficult experiences as opportunities for improvement. A good strategy to use when problems arise is to have your supervisor or principal talk with the supervisor at the other facility. These difficulties do not occur because the counselor is inadequate for his job; they occur because of problems that are out of his power to manage. The development of higher level lines of communication is a good way to channel frustration in a positive direction.

Success in the management of an initial interview is frequently defined as the placement of the person into an on-going program of recovery. In work with the suicidal this is often not achieved. In these cases, however, the counselors do not fail. It is not their fault if the larger community — and parts of their own organization — are less than cooperative. These counselors successfully supply two basic needs of the suicidal: evidence of care and evidence of hope. It is worse to suffer pain alone. Friends and counselors who are merely willing to be there are resources that reduce pain and prevent suicide. They negate the pain of feeling "I'm so bad that people do not want to be with me." In work with the suicidal it is natural to want to look away. It is positive to simply stay in the situation, even if, at the time, it seems that no progress is being made.

Demoralizing incidents sometimes end with worse consequences than reduced morale. The following survivor case history is presented in detail because it bears upon many issues discussed in this book, and because we need to remember that demoralizing incidents are not the sole cause of suicide.

A Case History

Ellen's boyfriend Jim committed suicide 15 months ago in her home. Jim was 42 and originally from a small town in Scotland. His Catholic mother periodically suffered from a disabling medical condition; his

Protestant father was a physically abusive alcoholic. Years ago in his family history, one of Jim's uncles committed suicide. The family lived in extreme poverty. Jim, the oldest of eight children, was sometimes sent out to steal food. At 12 he was arrested and sent to a juvenile home for a year. During his detention he did not see or hear from anyone in his family. He left home for good when he was 13 and a half. He later spent many years in the merchant marine, sending money home to his mother. His body became covered with tattoos. An accident aboard ship broke his back and both legs. Though he was hospitalized for a year and suffered recurrent pain throughout his life, he recovered and walked without limping. At age 21 Jim and a cousin in England had a daughter, but neither Jim nor anyone else in his immediate family ever formally acknowledged that the daughter was his. Jim eventually settled in the United States, developed a small construction business, married, and had a son who was nine at the time of his father's death. Jim joined Alcoholics Anonymous eight years before his death. Two years later, his marital relations poor, he met Ellen and eventually divorced his wife. Ellen and her husband, to whom she is still legally married despite their having been separated for many years, have two adolescent children. Ellen's husband is also a member of A.A. Two years before his death, Jim became disenchanted with other members of A.A. and stopped attending meetings. During this period he got a call that his father was dying of conditions caused by alcoholism. At first Jim said that he would not return to Scotland. He had told Ellen that he hated his father. Three days later he changed his mind, but the father died when Jim was in transit. He was hurt that he had never made peace with his father. Jim began to drink in secret in the year before his death. He lost his business and had to work for other people. After his death Ellen discovered that he had secretly accumulated thousands of dollars in debts. He injured his back a few months before his death, and then, while drunk, broke his arm in an auto accident. Jim wanted to marry Ellen, but she told him she would not do so until he stopped drinking. Jim had the Scottish personality trait of being very private and reserved; he rarely volunteered information about himself, his problems, or his feelings.

Ellen knows of two prior suicidal incidents in Jim's life. The first was nine years earlier and occurred while Jim was drunk and in the presence of his wife. The second occurred three years before his death and when he was sober. Jim was possessive; during an episode of jealous anger toward Ellen he jumped off a shallow cliff and said that he wished it was much higher. Five days before his death, after an extended binge, Jim slashed his wrists in Ellen's home. She called the police and paramedics; he was taken to a large urban hospital. His cuts were stitched after a long wait, and there was a further wait before he saw a hospital psychiatrist. Five minutes before the interview, he told a police officer that he would like to have the officer's pistol so he could "blow my head off." The officer and Jim both told the psychiatrist about this request. Jim was interviewed by the psychiatrist for a few minutes and told to "go home and stop drinking." He was given no referral or recommendation for a treatment program. Ellen and the police officer were dumbfounded, but the psychiatrist left that area of the building and the hospital staff refused Ellen's request that she be allowed to talk to him or to any other staff member. The next day Ellen took Jim to another large hospital where the program director was more sympathetic to Jim's situation. He agreed with Jim and Ellen that Jim needed a long-term alcohol rehabilitation program, but said that his hospital's program would not accept anyone unless they first went through a short-term alcohol detoxification program. The director contacted several detox facilities, but they had waiting lists of up to three and a half months. He finally advised that Jim go to a third, more remote hospital, and lie about the location of his residence. This third hospital had no beds available in its detox unit, but, after hours of waiting, finally admitted Jim to the psychiatric unit. Ellen says, "That was really awful. Locked doors. Really crazy, crazy people. ... The staff knew nothing about alcoholism." Jim was afraid of violence from other patients, did not want to take required sedatives, and believed he did not belong there. The staff told him he could be discharged only if he showed signs of feeling better. On the second day he played ping pong and made crafts, and on the third day he was released. When Ellen got home from work, he was at her house, drunk and unconscious. She called more detox facilities. None had beds available. She called two members of A.A. who had been close to Jim and had seen him recently. Both claimed that A.A. policy required that they not come to her home unless Jim called for help himself. She called a younger sister of Jim's, who lived in the same city and was also an alcoholic. The sister said that members of Alanon had advised her "to detach." Ellen took her children to her parent's home and returned to her own home at midnight. Jim was still unconscious. He awoke at 3

A.M.; quiet, apologetic, and shaky. As they spoke, Jim said that he wanted to talk to his father. He also said, "I'm in terrific pain," and "There is no sense in talking. Jim is gone." Jim was proud that over his whole life he had overcome tremendous pain and hardship. "Use will power," was his personal motto. Two days after he broke his arm, he took off the cast and went back to work. In the last year he was extremely critical of himself for being unable to control his drinking on his own, or to reverse his worsening condition. Ellen says, "I thought he was the strongest man in the world in every sense of the word. ... But, he was like a little boy at the end. Not this big strong man at all. He was very childlike.' She says that she still believed that Jim would get through this crisis, because he had gotten through so much.

Jim was asleep when Ellen left for work that morning. He called her at 10:30, very depressed. Though he did not specifically mention suicide, "He said to me, with an edge in his voice, 'You'll be strewing roses on my grave.'" She called her therapist, who told her that he would try to get Jim into a hospital, but not to worry because Jim definitely would not kill himself. She called Jim's sister and found that Jim had already called her. Jim had told his sister that he was building a scaffold to hang himself. The sister told him to stop fooling around and upsetting her. Jim had also called a friend he worked with, and told him also that he was building a scaffold to hang himself. The friend called the sister, and she told the friend that she did not think Jim meant it. At the end of the day, Ellen arranged for a friend to accompany her home. The friend went in the house first, and found Jim's body hanging from an electrical cord.

As the police normally do with suicides by hanging in Ellen's city, they refused to take down the body until the medical examiner's truck arrived. This was not for more than 12 hours, long after photographs had been taken and any evidence collected. This policy added to Ellen's horror, as it does for other survivors of suicide by hanging. Ellen later received a letter that Jim had written to her the day before he died. It contained a poem, said that he was in a lot of pain, and expressed his love for her. "He said he didn't want to die, but he didn't want to live." He said that life "is very hard." Jim also wrote a suicide note that was addressed to her. As is sometimes done with suicide notes in this city, particularly if the addressed person and the deceased are not legally related, the police have refused her many efforts to see the note. She has been told that she has no right to it, and that it was in her best interest that she not see it. Ellen says, "But who were they to know what is in my best interest? And I felt, and my therapist felt, that I should have it. For a kind of closure, or healing. No matter what it said. Even if it said I did it, or whatever. They were his last thoughts, and I felt they should be validated. Someone who cared about him should look at them. And they still have not given it to me, or a copy of the note either."

Later, at different times, Ellen met with Jim's ex-wife, his sister, and his daughter. Jim's ex-wife was very angry with Jim, as she had been for many years. Ellen learned that Jim, while drunk, had visited and called his ex-wife several times in the last months. Ellen and the ex-wife parted on good terms. Ellen has a mixed relationship with the sister, since the sister believes that the suicide would not have happened if Ellen and Jim had married, or if Ellen had "noticed the signs" earlier. Intellectually, Ellen does not agree with the sister's viewpoint. Emotionally she regrets not being aware of the extent of his drinking or of his risk for suicide, and she wonders about what she might have done differently. Because of the problems in the family, the daughter did not learn of her father's death until five months after it happened. She traveled to this country, made considerable effort to meet people who knew her father, and talked at length with Ellen. Jim's ex-wife has told Jim's son that the death was by heart attack. Because the suicide occurred in her home, Ellen gave the same cause of death when she informed her children. "I didn't want them to be frightened in their house." Ellen learned from the sister about an incident that took place back in Scotland one month after the death. Jim's youngest brother came home from military service to find that his wife had left him for another man. He got drunk and tried to hang himself, but someone found him in time to stop the attempt. As far as Ellen knows, no one at the three hospitals that Jim went to in the last week knows that he committed suicide.

Ellen is not angry with Jim; she still feels close to him. She believes she was "off-base" with him because she did not think he would commit suicide, and because he kept secret his debts, his visits to his ex-wife, and the extent of his drinking. She is left with a type of self-doubt that is common among surviving spouses and lovers: she worries about being similarly "off-base" in the future, about being generally unable to perceive other people accurately. She has had no relationships since his death. Ellen has not felt suicidal, even though she has had periods of depression so bad that she "could understand wanting to die." Because she has two children, "I can't allow myself the luxury of being depressed for too long." Ellen has continued in therapy and attended a few survivor meetings. She is preoccupied with her busy and stressful job, from which she has taken no vacations.

WARNING SIGNS AND RATING SYSTEMS

The warning signs are a popular concept in suicide prevention. It is felt that if caregivers and acquaintances learn the behaviors, emotional changes, life-event histories, and demographic factors associated with suicide, then they will be able to recognize people at risk and take appropriate action. As far as I know, no studies have been done to determine how many suicidal people are actually brought to the attention of caregivers as the result of someone's having noticed the warning signs. If attempts and statements about suicide ideation were deleted from the warning sign list, I suspect that the percentage would be quite low. For reasons given below, it is very difficult to use the warning sign list for the purpose for which it is apparently intended. "Warning Signs" are something of a myth; they imply that suicide prevention can be simpler, easier, neater, less painful, and more efficient than it really is. As the case history above indicates, this myth about the warning signs can add to the pain of the survivors.

The view that we should limit our public suicide prevention activities to education about the warning signs is a position that does not disturb much of the mythology of suicide. It says that all we need to do is communicate information; there is no need for us to change our moral attitudes, no need to change our repertoire of emotional responses. People with information can spot the warning signs and respond; we can pretend that the many completed suicides who had few warning signs did not exist. The suicidal person himself remains beyond the pale of human nature; attempts to use education to affect his cognitive and emotional condition, and his help-seeking behavior, are hopeless. If we avoid the issue of trying to get the suicidal person to reach out before his condition manifests itself in observable deterioration, and we avoid the issue of why he cannot be as direct and persistent in seeking help for his suicidal condition as he is about non-stigmatized physical illness, then we can avoid looking at the cultural context that makes these positive changes impossible.

Although warning signs are not very useful for their intended purpose, or sufficient by themselves to bring about social progress, they do have important roles in suicide prevention. They are an adequate introduction to the nature of suicidal pain, and help people emotionally adjust to the idea of personal contact with a suicidal person. While the mythology of suicide says, "Don't think about it," the warning sign approach gives acquaintances permission to review and try to assess the seriousness of the person's condition. Warning-sign education helps people move away from social aversion, and toward constructive involvement. The handout I use contains the following:

WARNING SIGNS

A. Conditions associated with increased risk of suicide

1. Death or terminal illness of relative or friend.

2. Divorce, separation, broken relationship, stress on family.

3. Loss of health (real or imaginary).

4. Loss of job, home, money, status, self-esteem, personal security.

5. Alcohol or drug abuse.

6. Depression. In the young, depression may be masked by hyperactivity or acting-out behavior. In the elderly, it may be incorrectly attributed to the natural effects of aging, or it may be due to side effects of medications taken for other conditions. Depression that seems to disappear quickly for no apparent reason is cause for concern. The early stages of recovery from depression can be a high risk period. An increased incidence of suicidal behavior has been found among persons suffering from anxiety disorders or panic attacks.

B. Emotional and behavioral changes associated with suicide

1. Overwhelming Pain: pain that threatens to exceed the person's pain-coping capacities. Suicidal feelings are often the result of longstanding problems that have been exacerbated by recent precipitating events.

Precipitating factors may be new pain, or the loss of pain-coping resources.

2. Hopelessness: the feeling that the pain will continue or get worse; things will never get better.

3. Powerlessness: the feeling that one's resources for reducing pain are exhausted.

4. Feelings of worthlessness, shame, guilt, self-hatred, "no one cares". Fears of losing control, harming self or others.

5. Personality becomes sad, withdrawn, tired, apathetic, anxious, irritable, or prone to angry outbursts.

6. Declining performance in school, work, or other activities. (Occasionally the reverse: someone who volunteers for extra duties because he needs to fill up his time.)

7. Social isolation, or association with a group that has different moral standards than those of the family.

8. Declining interest in sex, friends, or activities previously enjoyed.

9. Neglect of personal welfare, deteriorating physical appearance.

10. Alterations, in either direction, in sleeping or eating habits.

11. (Particularly in the elderly) Self-starvation, dietary mis-management, disobeying medical instructions.

12. Difficult times: holidays, anniversaries, the first week after discharge from a hospital; just before and after diagnosis of a major illness; just before and during disciplinary proceedings. Undocumented immigration status adds to the stress of a crisis, and decreases access to resources.

C. Suicidal Behavior

1. Previous suicide attempts, "mini-attempts".

2. Explicit statements of suicidal ideation or feelings.

3. Development of suicidal plan, acquiring the means, "rehearsal" behavior, setting a time for the attempt.

4. Self-inflicted injuries, such as cuts, burns, or head banging.

5. Reckless behavior. (Besides suicide, other leading causes of death among young people in New York City are homicide, accidents, drug overdose, and AIDS.) Unexplained accidents, particularly among children and the elderly.

6. Making out a will, or giving away favorite possessions.

7. Inappropriately saying goodbye.

8. Verbal behavior that is ambiguous or indirect: "I'm going away on a real long trip," "You won't have to worry about me anymore," "I want to go to sleep and never wake up," "I'm so depressed, I just can't go on," "Does God punish suicides?" "Voices are telling me to do bad things," requests for euthanasia information, inappropriate joking, stories or essays on morbid themes.

If I spend an hour reviewing these conditions, half the time will normally be taken up by questions, or the sharing of personal experiences by audience members. This hour is emotionally engaging, somewhat draining, and has a positive effect on the willingness of audience members to talk with each other about suicide, and to respond to people in need.

Many suicide prevention programs attempt to use the warning signs as a system that will rate suicide risk. Some systems include demographic information about groups with higher than average incidences of completed suicide: older white males, younger black males, adolescent Native Americans, peacetime military personnel, medical doctors, psychiatrists. Other systems may include stress scale ratings for painful life events: divorce, job loss, enrollment in a new school. The rating systems use point totals or some other method to formulate a lethality scoring table. The table usually divides its subjects into high, medium, or low risk for completed suicide. Counselors are advised to pursue different courses of action depending on the ranking assigned to the subject. The many drawbacks and necessary qualifications render this approach useless in actual practice:

1. It is statistically true that people with many of the warning signs are at higher risk than people with few of these conditions. But a low rate in a large population is still a lot of people; many completed

suicides were individuals who would have been classified as medium or low risk. As a practical matter, any suggestion of a suicidal condition has to be taken seriously.

"It's the ones you would never suspect," is part of the mythology of suicide. "The ones who do it, don't talk about it," is a corollary to "The ones who talk about it, just want attention." "The ones you would never suspect," is part of the fatalistic do-nothing attitude about suicide prevention. It ignores the fact that if the stigma did not exist, it would be easier for people to seek help. Suicide does happen to people you would never expect, people who score low on the rating systems. My friend in college was one of them. But suicide also happens to people who told others they were suicidal and had many of the conditions listed above. Suicide happens both to people who score high, and people who score low.

2. The scoring systems I have seen are biased against the prevention of *attempted* suicide. Subpopulations in the United States can vary widely in their ratio of attempted to completed suicide. Adolescent Hispanic females in New York City have a high rate for attempted suicide and a low rate for completed suicide. The ratio in this group may be greater than 500-to-1. The scoring systems are usually measures only for completed suicide; someone who gets a low mark for risk of completed suicide may still be someone at high risk for attempted suicide. The fact that the systems assess only risk for completed suicide is simply a continuation of the prejudice that denies serious attention to the needs of attempters and considerers.

3. Scoring systems are useless with populations that are already at high risk, and have the problem of false positives. Each time I have given a talk at a psychiatric halfway house, a counselor has remarked, "Our clients already have all of these." A great many people can have many bad things happen to them, and, because of their resources, not become suicidal.

4. Rating systems encourage the prejudice of evaluating whether the person's problems "justify" suicide.

5. One stress scale rating system used in adolescent suicide prevention programs in New Jersey communities assigns 98 points for the death of a parent, 80 for the loss of a pet, and 31 to starting a new job. ("The Adolescent Life Change Event Scale" by Nina Rogan and Maria

Hussey. It is modeled on "The Social Readjustment Rating Scale" [for adults] by Thomas H. Holmes.) Presumably, an adolescent who has lost a parent is under less stress than one who has lost a pet and started a new job. The scale omits mention of crime victims, sexual assaults, homelessness, and runaways. It does not distinguish between the death or terminal illness of a parent in a two-parent family and a death or terminal illness of a parent in a single-parent family. It does not recognize that the impact of an event can vary according to the person's cultural and ethnic background. It is not easy to see how some obvious flaws with scoring systems can be patched up. How can such a system avoid the patently false assumption that even within a cultural group, the same event can effect different people differently? Rating systems institutionalize the prejudice against greater than average sufferers. The suicidal include not just people to whom a greater number of bad things have happened, but also people who have suffered more from their individual misfortunes

Stress inventories, like warning signs, can be useful for purposes other than the assessment of suicide risk:

a. They avoid the fallacy of the single cause of suicide.

b. They prompt both counselor and client to consider important factors that might otherwise be overlooked. This is particularly true of stresses that affect the entire family system.

c. The enumeration of all the things that cause the person pain usually reduces the pain of feeling "It's all my fault."

d. Programs using stress inventories usually recognize that improvement is made on an incremental basis, and reject the view that recovery is an all-or-nothing process.

The aggregate pain approach obviously regards properly done inventories as useful in suicide prevention. But because of the large extent to which we are ignorant of suicidal pain and pain-coping resources, we are not in a position to use the inventories to formulate an adequate suicide risk scoring system.

SPECIAL GROUPS

Adolescents

There are several good reasons to give special attention to suicidal behavior among young people:

1. The official rate for completed suicide for people under the age of 25 has increased significantly over the last several decades.

2. Young people have a higher than average rate for attempted suicide.

3. There is evidence of an increase in suicidal behavior among pre-adolescents.

4. Society has a special obligation to concern itself with the welfare of the young.

5. Schools and child care agencies are appropriate places to disseminate information about critical issues in public health.

We should recognize that teenagers, the 13-to-19 age group, have an incidence rate for completed suicide that is no greater than that for the general population. The 19-and-under age group accounted for 7 percent of all suicides in the United States in 1986. While many areas of suicide prevention are neglected, teenage suicide commands most of the interest and attention of the general public. The reasons for this discrepancy are discussed in Chapter 11.

There are a number of special stress factors for this age group:

1. In a short period of time adolescents must cope with major physical, emotional, sexual, social and educational changes. Pressure from parents and peers, often conflicting, adds to the stress. The highest rates for completed teenage suicide are among older males of all ethnic groups. They are at the stage when the pressure of the major developmental task of adolescence — independence from the family — is at its peak.

2. Young people are liable to suffer at least as much pain as adults. They can become victims of trauma and loss of every sort. A general

problem in suicide prevention, denial of the severity of the situation, is particularly common in work with young people. You cannot assume that other people suffer painful events in the same way that you suffered them (or imagine that you would suffer them). Situations as diverse as a death in the family or non-acceptance by one's peers normally affect young people more strongly than they do adults. As with members of every age group, teenage expressions of suicidal ideation need to be taken seriously.

3. Young people have fewer resources with which to cope with life's difficulties:

a. They do not have a life history in which they have experienced misfortune, lived through it, found ways to cope, and moved on.

b. They have limited experience in coping with issues of sexuality and sexual identity.

c. They have little or no freedom to change family arrangements, residences, schools, or to obtain private counseling.

d. They are inexperienced in using their own efforts and the assistance of others to improve painful situations.

e. They have poorer vocabularies with which to articulate their problems to themselves and others.

f. They live in a society where instant gratification is the norm; they do not know that many problems take time to resolve.

4. Teenagers, like many adults, do not have realistic conceptions of death. They may fantasize about being present at their own funerals, about being at peace, or about being reunited with a loved one. Their stronger level of denial about their own mortality manifests itself in greater willingness to engage in reckless behavior.

5. Counselors who deal with children under the age of 15 frequently mention two factors in discussing suicide attempts and expressions of suicidal ideation. The first is physical, sexual or emotional abuse in the home. The second is severe family loss or dislocation due to death, terminal illness, divorce, separation, remarriage, substance abuse, mental illness, or institutionalization.

6. Teenagers with disabilities have additional hardships in the effort to reach adolescent developmental goals. They have difficulties in learning to deal with social, sexual, and family issues. Young people with learning disabilities have a higher than average incidence of depression.

7. A high risk period for suicidal behavior is during a disciplinary crisis, or shortly before a disciplinary crisis is expected.

The Elderly

The elderly have the highest suicide rate of any age group; have a lower ratio of attempts to completions; tend to use more lethal means in attempting suicide; and have greater risk for completed suicide if they have had a previous attempt. The warning signs that were listed earlier must be taken seriously. Those that are particularly significant for this age group are:

1. death of a loved one, especially a spouse.

2. problems with physical or mental health.

3. losses of economic status, social status, sense of self-esteem.

4. threat of relocation, loss of mobility, loss of personal security.

5. declining capacity for coping with problems.

6. feelings of loneliness, of being a burden, of being unwanted.

7. neglect of personal health.

Alcohol and drug abuse are serious problems among the elderly. One, or the other, or both, are involved in at least half of all suicides among older Americans. An older person may have discovered that mixing a small amount of alcohol with a small amount of prescription medication will produce a stronger effect than larger quantities of either substance taken alone. This may cost less money, and require fewer trips to liquor stores and medication providers. This behavior is medically very dangerous and needs to be strongly discouraged.

There is some evidence that physicians for the elderly are less inclined to suggest and encourage medical procedures that will prolong life and improve its quality. Advocacy for recovery programs in physical and mental health, by the self and by relatives and friends, is particularly important for this age group.

An issue in the prevention of geriatric suicide, which recurs in different forms in every area of suicide prevention, is that counselors and friends give themselves reasons for backing off. "This person is an adult; I should respect his right to privacy; I should respect his right to do what he likes." In many cases the real motive for backing off is fear. The counselor or friend misinterprets his own behavior as "I'm acting out of respect". The elderly person also misinterprets the behavior, but instead perceives it as "I'm not worth bothering about". Here, as elsewhere, the side of life requires that that you take a step beyond normal expressions of care and concern.

In *Suicide After Sixty*, Miller writes

> In order to ameliorate this problem, there must first be drastic changes in how society views and treats its oldest members. Until we are able to effect some of these basic changes, we should expect to see older people continuing to kill themselves in large numbers. (P. 22)

The elderly deserve better treatment, but this statement is also true if we replace "its oldest members" and "older people" with "suicidal people".

Emotionally Disturbed People

Some counselors are asked to spend time with people who have delusional beliefs about reality. Often emotionally disturbed people do not respond to your presence and the things you say with the types of verbal and non-verbal feedback that non-delusional people do. They may rave uncontrollably about things that make little sense. You may be left feeling inadequate and frustrated, because you did not achieve a normal level of conversational interaction.

The majority of people with schizophrenia and paranoia, as well as depression, manic depression and agoraphobia, are not suicidal. But they are nearly always extraordinarily lonely human beings. They suffer from the social stigmas associated both with mental illness in general and with their particular type of illness. Their illness causes them to become alienated, to withdraw from others, and become more lonely. And, because of the growing estrangement and loneliness, their disorder gets worse. To be in this Catch-22 situation for months or years produces a horrible loneliness that is beyond the imaginations of people who have never suffered from mental illness.

You do something positive for emotionally disturbed people simply by being with them in a way that is calm, patient, sympathetic, and non-judgmental. They are afraid of "going crazy", of losing control, and of losing their capacities for being understood by others. If you listen you will find aspects of their story — concerns for personal health or safety — that are connected to reality and to which you can sincerely respond. "All the psychiatrists are poisoning the water supply," can be reflected as "You're worried about people's health?" In many cases, if you are patient and persistent with this approach, you will be able to develop a more normal conversation. It is unfortunately a part of their illness that they may do little to indicate that they recognize and appreciate your attention. But in some sense they do know that another person is there and is listening to them.

It is stressful to be with emotionally disturbed people. You may not feel that this is the most effective use of your time on the job. But at the level of one human being to another, you are doing something positive. While you are with them, their loneliness is less terrible.

Third Parties

Third parties are persons who are concerned about someone they know who may be suicidal.

If a third party turns to you, your first reaction should be to respond to his needs. Listen, sympathize with his stressful situation, and reassure him that he has done the right thing by taking the situation seriously and seeking out help. By listening you help the third party calm down and review the situation objectively. Many third parties are responsible individuals, with support they will help develop constructive courses of action. Though it does not happen often, you may suspect that the third party is really the person at risk. Sympathetic listening will give you an opportunity to turn the conversation toward his own problems. The question — "Are you having thoughts of suicide?" — can be asked of the third party: "Have you ever been in a situation where you have had thoughts of suicide?".

You and the third party can review the basic suicide prevention procedures: the warning signs as an inventory of suicidal person's pains and resources, listening to the suicidal person, assessing risk, removing means, not leaving the person alone, seeking professional help, and getting further help for yourselves.

Programs for Organizations

Suicidal people may present their condition to anyone in their environment: relatives, friends, fellow students or patients, secretaries, security personnel, coaches, dormitory resident assistants, co-workers, teachers, and counselors and healthcare workers in any area and at any level. The basic goals of an organization's program should be to create conditions that enable any student, client, patient, or staff member who is at risk of suicide to present at the earliest possible time, to improve the management of these presentations, and to improve their outcomes by effectively reducing pain and increasing resources. The development of a committee of about eight people — for an average-size school — is a good way to increase the number of presentations. This provides your population and staff members eight choices of people to turn to for help for themselves or others. It is a manageable size for the distribution of responsibilities, mutual support, the collection of information about the person's condition and available resources, and the protection of confidentiality. Committee members should have diverse skills and experiences, and reflect the diversity of the organization. Organizations that use a broad-based and collegial committee structure avoid problems that arise over turf issues. Guidance counselors, health counselors, drug counselors, school psychologists, special education counselors, dropout prevention workers, school nurses, and other staff members can be highly opinionated about which counselors should be seen for which type of problem. As this general attitude affects suicide, it usually has one of two consequences. The first is that different counselors or groups of counselors each see suicidal students or clients, and do not support or communicate with each other. The second response is that duties and responsibilities are restricted to the counselors' designated areas of expertise, and none or few of the counselors are receptive to presentations by suicidal students.

The committee, which may either be new or be the enhancement of an existing committee, should have the word "suicide" as part of its title, or as an explicit part of its description. "Suicide" has a uniquely powerful effect on giving first and third parties permission to present. It conveys acceptance, understanding, information. If committee members bear the label "suicide", the people they see will be more willing to disclose their problems candidly and fully. Some organizations use a title such as "Children/Clients in Crisis" since it empowers the committee to respond to a range of problems. If committee members are able to calmly and supportively discuss taboo subjects such as suicide, child abuse, or sexual assault among each other, then that will have a positive ripple effect throughout the organization. (A fear of dealing with various issues among key staff members will have a negative ripple effect.) Committee members need to reach a consensus about the interpretation of policies and procedures.

Committee members should help educate each member of the organization in each of the following:

a. the fears, myths, and stigmas of suicide,

b. warning signs,

c. basic suicide prevention procedures,

d. specific procedures and policies of the organization,

e. the names of the committee members.

Individuals involved in any type of formal or informal counseling should have a workshop in listening skills, assessing suicide risk, and enlisting the cooperation of the suicidal person. The committee may arrange for inservice training programs on the conditions associated with suicide: bereavement, substance abuse, mental illness, eating disorders, domestic violence, and other issues appropriate for your population. Crisis intervention is a painful subject, and on painful subjects people have short memories. An ongoing program that keeps knowledge of basic procedures fresh is a critical aspect of your organization's response to suicide. It should be stressed that none of these problems affect just patients or clients, and that basic guidelines should be followed off the job as well as on. Ideally, organization members will have a favorable attitude toward the policies, procedures and personnel involved in suicide prevention. They should believe that following procedures will benefit the person at risk, and will not result in criticism of their own actions. Praise for the way in which specific situations are handled is an excellent practice, but rarely happens because of the myths "Don't talk about it," and "Wasn't serious, just wanted attention." Policies and procedures need to be subject to ongoing review and revision.

Finally, the committee may become involved in one of the genuine frontiers in suicide prevention: educating up. Senior administrators, board members, government officials and legislators usually have the same beliefs and attitudes about suicide as the man on the street. Their fears and aversion about responding to the problem of suicide are usually greater than average. Progress in this area is as difficult as it is necessary.

CHAPTER ELEVEN

POSITIVE STEPS IN SOCIAL POLICY

Social Action

Our federal, state, and city governments take very active roles in the prevention of death by homicide, transportation accidents, occupational hazards, cancer, heart disease, and AIDS. They take a less active role in the prevention of death by suicide. This inactivity is due solely to fears and false beliefs that shroud the topic of suicide. Social action could prevent death and suffering, improve the general quality of life, and need not have large financial cost. During the last decade we have become accustomed to news reports such as the following:

> The number of traffic deaths and accidents attributable to drunken drivers has dropped steadily over the last five years in New York and New Jersey, state statistics indicate. ... The reductions, according to safety officials, follow police crackdowns on drunken driving, public information campaigns and the raising of the drinking age ... (*The New York Times*, August 27, 1986.)

There is no shame to requests that government take steps to protect us from other threats to life and health; there should be no shame in doing the same for suicide. There is no basis to suppositions that concerted effort to reduce the losses due to suicide cannot be effective. First, we need to examine a key element in the mythology of suicide.

"Once They Decide, They Can't Be Stopped"

"Once they're going to do it, they're going to do it, and there's nothing you can do to stop them," is a belief often expressed about suicide. At some time prior to the fatal act, the suicide makes up his mind, and is thereafter unstoppable. From the claim that the suicidal person is unstoppable, the mythology of suicide infers that suicide cannot be prevented, and then, in turn, infers that no one but the victim is to blame for his death. Although "once they decide" is a myth that is profoundly harmful to the suicidal, most of the harm is indirect. Unlike "lacks will power" or "manipulative", this myth does not directly add pain on pain. The myth is most strongly believed by people who are at a considerable distance from the suicidal person: the general public, administrators, and social policy makers. The sequence of thoughts — Nothing can be done, Suicide cannot be prevented, There is no point in trying to prevent suicide — is the great rationalization for social inaction. A second way in which the myth deprives the suicidal of resources is that it is part of the basis for individual third parties to decide not to become involved in efforts to assist in suicidal situations. A third function of the myth, of course, is to support denial on social complicity in the causation of suicide.

This part of the mythology of suicide makes three mistakes. It contains an invalid intermediate inference, it is based upon a false view of the mind of the suicidal person, and it espouses false values concerning the relief of human suffering. The premises of the argument say only that the person is unstoppable *after* he allegedly decides, nothing about his stoppability prior to the decision. Even if we accept all the premises in this model — suicide is voluntary, and once a person decides he becomes ruthlessly determined — we could still seek to reduce suicide by positively influencing people prior to the decision. There is no reason to assume that he might not make the decision if he were reached by a program for mental illness or drug abuse, provided with relief from physical pain, or given information about the effects of suicide on survivors. The inference from "Nothing can be done after he decides," to "Nothing can be done," is fallacious. People are susceptible to influence prior to decisions of every sort; even if suicide is voluntary, there is no reason to suppose that it should be an exception.

In our evaluation of the myth as a model for the mind of the suicide, we need to give consideration to the time of the alleged decision.

Review your experiences with major decisions in people's lives: enlistment in military service, termination of pregnancy, marriage. Does the decision occur when the person considers the option, initially consents, makes the plans, sets the date, or travels to the location where the event is scheduled? Since people can change their minds at any point in this process, we must say that the decision, in an irreversible sense, does not occur until the event occurs. Suicide, even if it is voluntary, is no different. Suicidal people come in off the ledges of tall buildings, and counselors often hear stories that include "I had the gun in my hand," "The pills were on the table," "I got dressed and went down to the subway station."

Sometimes, in ordinary life, we meet people who have a bullheaded determination about the achievement of their goals. If one means does not succeed, they will try another. If success does not come easily, they persist long after others would have given up. Some of us are like this occasionally, a few of us are like this a lot. There are no studies that show that suicides tend to be people with greater than average levels of determination. The myth is supported by a few anecdotal accounts of people who made a series of highly lethal attempts during a single siege of suicidal feelings, but there is no evidence that this behavior characterizes more than a small percentage of the highly suicidal. The actual behavior of most suicidal people is the opposite of the myth of determination; they probably have more vacillation than people facing any other major life event. Many people who experience a mental event of "I'm going to commit suicide at some future time," do not become suicides. Rather than resolutely marching to death, a more accurate image is that of someone who feels helplessly passive as he tries to endure waves of pain, someone who tries to cling to life by his fingernails. The final days of many suicides contain combinations of events that are inconsistent with determination to do any one thing. Within a single day, a person may refill all his prescriptions, make efforts to carry on normal life, and issue cries for help. Retrospectively, nearly all suicides can be seen as people whose final days, weeks, or months included behavior that was designed to reduce their pain, and improve their lives.

A further objection to the ruthless determination model is to consider what happens when the ruthlessly determined achieve their goal. Sometimes they do develop second thoughts about the advisability of their quest, but it is rare for them to get these second thoughts immediately. In suicide immediate second thoughts are not rare. A man who survived a leap from the Manhattan Bridge was later interviewed on television. He said that after he left the bridge, the first thought that crossed his mind was "This is a mistake." Hendin writes

> Over the past thirty years I have seen four people who survived six-story suicide jumps. Two wished to survive as soon as they had jumped, two said they did not, but one of the latter two who professed to be furious at having survived made no subsequent attempts. (1982, p. 210)

I have spoken with police officers who have seen people jump to their deaths. They said that some of these people started to scream in terror when their bodies neared the pavement. A 20 year-old man in Queens swallowed a hundred anti-depressants, and then later called for an ambulance. When he arrived at the hospital he told the doctor that he wanted to live. His heart stopped, and he died before the effects of the poison could be reversed.

"Once they decide, they become ruthlessly determined," is not an accurate model for suicide. Anecdotal evidence indicates that the suicidal have *less* determination than people faced with other major life events. There is no justification for the argument, "Nothing can be done about suicide because the victims unstoppably pursue their goal." Suicide is not only not a choice or a goal, it is not one that is ruthlessly pursued. The model provides no justification for social inaction in the prevention of suicide.

The false premise of the myth is "If they are going to commit suicide (and nothing can stop them), then there is no point in getting involved." A less explicit part of the myth is "And, if they are not going to commit suicide, then there is also no point in getting involved." Are these guides to our behavior morally acceptable? Contrary to everything that is known about suicide, suppose that we can be certain, at least in some cases, that someone will become a suicide. It is still false to claim that we should not get involved. People with terminal conditions have a right to social support to improve the quality and quantity of time they have left. Why should the suicidal be treated differently? Secondly, again contrary to what we know, let us assume that we can definitively ascertain that someone in suicidal pain will never attempt or commit suicide. Here too it is false that there is no point to getting involved. Our support can reduce the duration and intensity of his suffering, and he has as much right to our aid as any other person in pain. Social policy makers often assert that they want to put their resources where they can make a difference. But the "difference" in suicide is not just between living and dying, but also in the quality of life for those who survive and those who do not.

Legislation to End Discrimination: Admissions

People who express thoughts of suicide are routinely refused services by service providers of every sort. Though the problem is most acute with alcohol and drug facilities, it is normal in other areas of public health. Dual diagnosis complaints among city social workers are common: "The AIDS program won't take him because he is has a mental health condition, and the mental health program won't take him because he has an AIDS diagnosis." In one referral situation I learned that phobia clinics are afraid to see phobic people who have suicidal feelings. Suicidal insomniacs are not welcome at sleep disorder clinics. New York City's Gay and Lesbian Switchboard has an index file of private psychotherapists to whom they make referrals. Ninety percent of the cards have a notation that indicates that the therapist does not accept clients who have thoughts of suicide. The common response of providers of both mental and non-mental health care is "We're not equipped to handle that." The only alternative is the psychiatric facilities of city hospitals. City hospitals are often at 100 percent occupancy for their inpatient facilities, and have long waiting lists for their outpatient programs. They can provide immediate assistance only if the person is on the verge of death, or has already injured himself. Even with greater funding, improved hospital emergency services are not going to reach people sooner rather than later, or make a substantial contribution toward a reduction of prejudice and stigma.

The written and unwritten policies of "No suicidals here," should be struck down. It is a violation of basic human rights to deny people access to treatment programs. It prolongs pain. It withholds coping resources. The actual rejections themselves add to suicidal pain. It is morally disgusting to make the suicidal suffer inferior access to healthcare services.

The "No suicidals here," policies are without rational foundation. No comparative studies have ever been done on this subject. Assuming that they have suicide prevention and postvention policies, and appropriate staff training, will healthcare organizations that admit people with suicidal thoughts and feelings have more completed and attempted suicides than those that do not? For entire communities, are there fewer suicides when all organizations, save psychiatric hospitals, practice the "No suicidals here," policy? Do organizations, such as substance abuse facilities, do a better or worse job in their primary function if they refuse to respond to suicidal members of their target populations? No scientific evidence exists on these questions, one way or the other. The people who endorse and enforce the policy of "No suicidals here," claim allegiance to science, yet the policy is based on ignorance, prejudice, and fear.

Aversion to the suicidal exists at both higher and lower levels than organizational admissions policies. A senior administrator of a government drug treatment program told me that he needs to do everything he can to combat the myth of the inherent self-destructiveness of drug abusers. Since the myth of self-destructiveness causes a sceptical public, and their legislators, to believe that drug abuse programs are an ineffective waste of resources, he believed that the best way to win support for his program was to minimize any association between drug abuse and suicide. At an individual level, many counselors believe, "I'm here to deal with alcohol, teen pregnancy, dropout prevention, the homeless, the disabled; I'm not here to deal with suicide." This attitude is tinged with inconsistency; people in each of these groups have a greater than average tendency to have suicidal feelings. Though no studies have been done on this issue, my impression is that counselors in these areas who have an understanding and acceptance for suicidal people, and have institutional suicide prevention support, are much better at their primary functions than counselors who lack these assets.

The aversion, avoidance, and discriminatory policies of caregivers both discourages presentations and cannot help but adversely affect general social attitudes toward the suicidal. Who can blame the average citizen for wondering, "If professional counselors are afraid of the suicidal, what should I think? Why should I get involved?" When the suicidal seek assistance and receive aversion, it can only increase their feelings of hopelessness and worthlessness. Their sense of estrangement from the rest of humanity increases.

The current system encourages lying. Counselors often coach their clients to not divulge their suicidal feelings so that they may gain entry to treatment programs at other facilities. Dishonesty and distrust are a poor basis for recovery.

A few suicidal people may need special medications, 24-hour watches, or even restraints. But most suicidal people are not on the verge of death, and their risk management problems can be handled with the existing resources of most social service programs.

Terminations

Legislation to prohibit discrimination against the suicidal means not only not denying them admission, but also not terminating treatment if they become suicidal. An occasional call at the suicide hotline began, "I told my therapist I was suicidal. He terminated me." (A variant was "I'm afraid to tell my therapist that I'm suicidal. He has a policy of terminating suicidal clients.") When I ask psychiatrists and psychologists about this problem, three things happen:

1. They become visibly upset.

2. They say either that it does not happen; it rarely happens; or, it should not happen.

and 3. They change the subject.

The suicide literature contains no material on this problem, but it is a dark little secret that has enormous power over the entire profession of psychiatry and psychotherapy. It is one of the reasons why this profession has less public respect than do professions in other areas of health care.

Legislation that required professional counselors to have support systems for suicide prevention and postvention would be a major step forward. Each of us is finite, fallible, imperfect, limited. For any number of reasons, a therapist may by unwilling or unable to continue treatment with a suicidal client. But why is there no system to provide back-up support for both of these people? Why do the suicidal have to be put out in the cold? On a few occasions I have talked with counselors who have been on the other side of this sorry situation. They suffer feelings of anguish, guilt, and inadequacy. They and their profession, like many of the suicidal, are trapped in self-defeating conceptions of shame and secrecy, pride and self-reliance.

Legislation on the Means

Alvarez reports that the poet, Robert Lowell,

> ... once remarked that if there were some little switch in the arm which one could press in order to die immediately and without pain, then everyone would sooner or later commit suicide. (p. 135)

Measures that limit access to firearms, drugs, poisons, or heights will help reduce the incidence of suicide. We need improved ways for society to tell its members that it is on the side of life, and legislation on the means can be a good vehicle for this purpose. Difficult-to-open caps on medicine containers are a nuisance, but they unmistakably say that we care about child safety.

Though we can and should seek to reduce the availability of many of the means of completed and attempted suicide, our first priority must be firearms. In 1986, 58.7 percent of all suicides in the United States were by gunshot. (*Statistical Abstract*, 1989) A study reported in *The New England Journal of Medicine* (Kellerman, 1986) reviewed all gunshot deaths that occurred over a six-year period in King County (Seattle), Washington. The total number of suicides by any means during the six years was 1,049. Four hundred and sixty nine, or 45 percent, were by firearms. There were a total of 398 gunshot deaths of all types that involved a firearm kept in the home. Three hundred and thirty three of these deaths, 83.7 percent, were suicides. Three percent of the firearm deaths in the home were accidents, 12.6 percent were homicides, and two deaths involved the justifiable homicide of an intruder. The authors concluded, "The advisability of keeping firearms in the home for protection must be questioned."

It is unfortunate that a bill mandating a seven day waiting period for purchasers of handguns has yet to be enacted by Congress. A desirable clause in future legislation would require that prospective purchasers be given a pamphlet that explained the health risks of firearms in the home. Such a pamphlet might include the account of a suicide of a young man in Brooklyn. The means was an unlicensed revolver that belonged to a relative: "None of us had any idea he knew where the gun was kept."

The Mixed Blessings of Social Progress

In earlier periods of history society used barbaric methods to communicate its disapproval of suicide. The body would be burned at the crossroads, the estate seized from the survivors. Fortunately, these things are no longer done. Barbaric practices, however, had a certain utility: the idea that suicide ought not happen was unmistakably expressed. In modern society, the conception that suicide is a terrible tragedy is watered down by assimilating it to views about euthanasia, personal rights, and romantic crises of personal meaning. We need to seek new methods to communicate a clear social message about the undesirability of the event of suicide.

I have asked police officers and government officials about New York State law on suicide, and have been given four different answers:

1. suicide and attempted suicide are both legal

2. suicide and attempted suicide are both illegal

3. suicide is legal and attempted suicide is illegal

4. suicide is illegal and attempted suicide is legal.

No one seems to know. As far as the general public is concerned, the de jure status of suicide is obscure. Except for a required autopsy, no action is taken against a completed suicide, his estate, or his relatives. Police officers frequently handcuff people they believe to be suicidal, and do not receive reprimands. Some suicide attempters are briefly detained in hospitals; they are usually released when there is some improvement in the physical harm caused by the attempt. Hence, some version of 3. appears to be the de facto policy. Compared to barbaric social statements, or to our unambiguous legal and social rejection of homicide, this is not a strong statement against suicide. Besides legal judgments about harm to life, government has other ways to express social opinion, such as the war on cancer. Nothing similar exists for suicide.

Our social policy — do little to prevent suicide — is something of which the suicidal are aware. The belief, "My community is indifferent as to whether people with my problem live or die," is not a resource on the side of life. Indifference is not as punitive as barbarism, but it is still painful. Inactivity is a stage on the road to progress, but let us hope it is a stage that we will soon move beyond. Once we reject the view that suicide, attempted suicide, and suicide ideation are voluntary behaviors, we can abandon the view that suicide is a legal or moral issue. If we view it as a problem in public health, then we can make the same kind of social statement about its desirability that we do about disease and fatal accidents.

Advocacy

American democracy is sometimes viewed as a system in which various interest groups non-violently compete for their share of public services. Organizations that represent business, labor, senior citizens, women and ethnic groups work with varying degrees of success to promote and protect the welfare of their constituents. Some political theorists believe that group competition is the essence both of what democracy is, and what it ought to be. In both description and prescription this political theory has its merits. It is true that groups that clamor for attention improve their chances of getting it. This seems to be a good; none of us wants to live in a community that is unresponsive to the wishes of its members. The problem is that groups with equal needs may be unequal in their abilities to compete for attention. The suicidal are prevented from forming a group that can effectively lobby for their needs by stigma, prejudice, and the isolating and impermanent nature of their condition. In a political system where public health policies are driven by demand, rather than need, people who make no demands will be shortchanged in the satisfaction of their needs. Is it conceivable that the suicidal could respond to advice such as this:

> The handicapped themselves must come out of hiding
> and become a visible, articulate and organized group

capable of effectively presenting their needs and asserting their rights. They must graduate from a concern with individual problems to the larger issues common to the greater number. (New York City Commission on Human Rights, 1972)

Social prejudice deters people from publicly identifying themselves as being suicidal, or as having been suicidal. The suicidal have no discernible tendency toward group affiliation. The result is that the public and its legislators are poorly informed about the facts, values and needs of treatment, education, and research in the prevention of suicide. Since public health policies are based upon demand, suicide receives a disproportionately low share of the public dollar.

Minorities

In his study of gay and lesbian suicide, Eric Rofes argues that

While lesbian and gay male activists have understandably remained aloof from the basic issue of suicide in the gay population, properly fearing that anti-gay forces would use the statistics as ammunition for their "gay-is-sick" campaigns (as they have done), ... lesbians and gay men need to arrive at a broader understanding of the issues concerning suicide in the gay population. (1983, p. 24)

A similar aversion to suicide is prevalent among advocates for other minority groups. The keynote speaker of a conference given by the Black Alumni Association of the City College of New York decried the fact that so many of the workshops were on such negative subjects as suicide, drug abuse, teen pregnancy, AIDS, dropout prevention, and literacy, and so few were on positive subjects. "Promote the positive," is surely a legitimate means to reach worthy goals. Group leaders want their members to develop positive self-images, and want to develop more positive images in the minds of people outside the group. But "Avoid the negative," reinforces the stigma of suicide. Suicidal members of minority groups receive the message "You are unacceptable," from both their general culture and their smaller community.

There is a virtual absence of non-English language suicide prevention information in the United States. An unfortunate consequence of the strength of monolingualism is the view that non-English public education materials should exist only in areas that directly affect the well-being of the larger community. Non-English materials are readily made available on public health subjects that are believed to meet this condition — AIDS, reproductive health, substance abuse — and are unavailable in areas such as suicide, or mental health, that are not believed to affect general welfare. Efforts to distribute bilingual materials to counselors for New York City's one million Hispanic residents have been met with the comment, made by those acquainted with suicide statistics, "But Hispanics have low rates." This point of view commits a familiar fallacy: it does not recognize that a low rate in a large population is still a lot of people. It also ignores greater than average risk among subpopulations: attempted suicide among adolescent females and, many corrections officers believe, completed suicide among younger male inmates. A third type of resistance comes from administrators who say, "We don't need that here. Our counselors are bilingual." "We don't need that here," is denial on the problems of bilingual counseling. These counselors are more likely to initially read material in their first language, and have greater need for material in their second language. Many bilingual counselors are in job situations where they are not supposed to have a weaker language, and this deters them from making requests for bilingual training materials. Counselors are usually pleased to receive the information in both languages. This is especially true in suicide. In using their second language with suicidal people, counselors who may be quite fluent find they have feelings of insecurity and inadequacy that they do not have in discussing other subjects.

Me and Mine

Vast sums are spent on research to protect us from death by heart disease, cancer, diabetes, and auto accidents. We gladly support research and prevention measures in these and other areas, partly because there is no stigma to saying, "It could happen to me or mine." A sizable portion of public monies spent on police, judicial, and correctional services is dedicated to protecting us from homicide. It is a little tough to say, "I'm afraid of being murdered," but not difficult to express fear of being mugged, of being caught in the cross fire of a drug shootout, or of being on an airplane targeted by terrorists. Who among us will say he is unacquainted with a fear of AIDS?

Public sentiment to dedicate more resources to research and prevention activities in suicide is nil, largely because no one will acknowledge the fear that suicide may happen to himself or to a loved one. This level of public sentiment is not in accord with the reality of social need. In 1986, out of 2,105,400 deaths from all causes, 30,904 were suicides, 21,731 were homicides, and 47,865 were motor vehicle accident fatalities. (*Statistical Abstract*, 1989. 1986 is the latest year for which national statistics are available. A bibliography and technical discussion of the issues in the accuracy of suicide statistics is in O'Carroll, 1989.)[1] Many suicides are unrecorded; a small number of these suicides are victim precipitated homicides, or are listed as highway accident fatalities. The real number of suicides may be nearly double the real number of homicides, and approach the real number of highway accident fatalities.

There is a double impracticality to not providing suicide prevention education and research with a fair share of public support. Can it be denied that there are important and as yet undiscovered connections between suicide and the full range of other self-destructive behaviors? Self-destructive behaviors often have significant roles in the causal histories of virtually every leading cause of death: the three conditions mentioned above, heart disease, cancer, and diabetes, as well as hepatitis, emphysema, ulcers, infant mortality, and all types of accidents. It is irrational to try to increase understanding in other areas of public health, and to shun suicide.

It is not difficult to discredit the belief that "Suicide is not going to happen to me or mine." One and four-tenths percent of all deaths are recorded as suicides; the real figure may approximate 2 percent. Let us assume that the average person has 24 close relatives: 4 grandparents, 2 parents, 2 siblings, 1 spouse, 2 children, 2 grandchildren, 2 steprelatives, 2 aunts, 2 uncles, 3 cousins, 1 niece, 1 nephew. The chances that you will become a suicide are 1 in 50. The odds that you or one of your relatives will die by suicide are 1 in 2. Of the 50 people you know best, 1 will become a suicide. During your lifetime you are likely to come to know well at least 500 people. Ten will be suicides. These are the figures for completed suicide. Multiply by at least 5 for attempted suicide. If your immediate family has five people, the odds are 1 in 2 that one is, or will become, an attempted suicide. Suicide, either completed, attempted, or considered, does happen to you and yours. The number of families untouched are a minority.

Denial on suicide risk is similar to denial on substance abuse. "X will never happen to me," is falsely believed by tens of millions of people: I smoke, but I won't get cancer or emphysema; I drug, but I won't become addicted; I drink, but I won't become an alcoholic. Few people, with some children of suicides being an exception, grow up believing they will become suicidal. Yet many do. Similar denial occurs for risk within the family. Each year several hundred thousand people sadly discover that they falsely believed, "Suicide is not going to happen to one of us."

In other areas of public health people normally believe "It is not going to happen to me," and still have rational behavior patterns. The odds of death in an auto or boating accident are on a par with the odds for death by suicide, yet millions of car and boat owners routinely comply with laws on seat belts and life preservers. They know that the odds are small that they will need these safety measures, yet they regard safety as a serious problem, and respond accordingly. They perceive no cognitive dissonance between "small odds" and "serious problem". Suicide is the same: "small odds" and "serious problem" are both true.

Absolute numbers may be a more effective way to present the public health problem of suicide than percentages. It does not seem very substantial to say that officially 1.4 percent of all deaths are suicides or that the real rate may be 2 percent. A different way to present the information is to use the 2 percent estimate on the 250 million population estimate for the United States. Five million people now alive will die by suicide. Twenty-five million more are, or will become, suicide attempters. Suicide has been, or will be, seriously considered by more than 50 million people. It is difficult to practice denial and minimization on numbers such as these.

Recovery Rates

Professionals and the news media readily provide us with information about the probabilities of recovery from serious conditions in many areas of public health. We are accustomed to receiving information in the form "Type x cancer has a recovery rate of yy percent if it is detected in time." Information that stresses recovery rates is positive, and is aimed at victims or those who worry that they may become victims. It encourages early prevention measures, and says, "Let's put our energy into recovery." Public information about suicide follows a different pattern; we are provided only with *non*-recovery rates. We may be told that 10 percent of all suicide attempters eventually become completers; or that 10 percent of the population will suffer major depression at some point in their lives, and that 10 percent of these people will become suicides. The kind of information conveyed is the same, but the manner of presentation does not emphasize positive action, or a positive outcome. This is unfair, the suicidal need hope, and they need to take and be encouraged to take steps to bring about recovery. Also missing from the non-recovery message is the implicit general message: let's try to improve the recovery rate. Non-recovery rates put the focus on fatalities and their prevention. Recovery rates put the focus on a condition that may or may not lead to death. The view that what is important in suicide are the fatalities, and that what is important in other areas are life-endangering conditions, is nothing more than the prejudice that considerers and low-lethal attempters are "not serious, just want attention." "Let's stop fatalities," is a very different message from "Let's provide care for considerers and low-lethal attempters." Cancer prevention is the effort to prevent the existence of cancers, not just fatalities. Highway safety tries to prevent all accidents. Law enforcement tries to prevent all assaults. No analogous concern exists for suicide.

The Material Costs of Suicide

Campaigns for other areas of public health have been supported by studies that document financial cost. This has never been done for suicide. The costs are larger and broader than we might expect.

1. Many suicide attempters are taken by ambulance to hospitals and treated in their emergency rooms. Some are kept overnight, and others are voluntarily or involuntarily kept for periods of several days or weeks. The cost of a hospital bed is in the neighborhood of $500 per day. These funds must come from somewhere — the suicidal person, his family, a private insurer, or the city, state, or federal governments. Paramedic fees vary according to distances and services provided. No statistics are kept for attempted suicide, but a number of city hospitals report admitting 200 adolescent attempters each year.

2. Eighteen thousand times a year the New York City Police Department takes an emotionally disturbed person into custody and transports him to a healthcare facility. A significant but uncounted percentage of these people are suicidal. Officers do not like to get this call because it is often difficult and it "blows the whole shift." Officers must stay with the person in the waiting room until he is admitted to the hospital (or denied admission), and then must file a report. This adds up to a lot of man-hours, and, as with other social services, these are man-hours that could be spent in other areas.

3. Probable suicides must be given autopsies. The New York City Medical Examiner's office is budgeted at $1,000 per autopsy. If the suicide occurred in a private residence, a police officer is required to stay with the body until it is picked up. This assignment is often given to junior officers who either remain alone with the corpse or are present when relatives suffer the initial stages of shock and grief. Officers in New York City are given no training for this duty.

4. Healthcare workers, police officers, paramedic personnel, subway motormen, and others are sometimes profoundly disturbed by suicides. This contributes to demoralization and job turnover.

5. After suicide many families suffer divorce or relocation of the home. Suicide complicates the resolution of estate and child custody issues. Relatives often suffer increased emotional and physical hardship.

6. Attempted and completed suicide, and suicidal depression, have costs in terms of disability compensation, lost earnings, lost time at school, lost tax revenue.

7. While many members of the general public believe that suicide is largely a teenage problem, in the literature on suicide one often sees an

inference of the form, "The elderly have the highest rate, therefore most suicides are among the elderly." This inference is not valid. Although younger adults have a lower rate for completed suicide than older adults, there are a great many more younger people than there are older people. The age breakdown (from the National Center for Health Statistics, United States Department of Health and Human Services) for suicide in the United States in 1986 is:

5-9	5
10-14	250
15-19	1896
20-24	3224
25-29	3429
30-34	3282
35-39	2852
40-44	2161
45-49	1895
50-54	1841
55-59	1916
60-64	1866
65-69	1707
70-74	1707
75-79	1433
80-84	850
85+	578
age not given	12
total	30,904

In terms of absolute size, the greater part of the problem of suicide receives the least attention. The average suicide occurs to a person in his early forties, and costs him approximately 25 years of life. If we distributed this loss of life equally throughout the population, and two people out of each 100 die by suicide, then the average person loses six months of life to suicide.

Material benefits of suicide prevention

"How can we do suicide prevention to minimize attempted and completed suicide?" is not the best question. It may be better to ask, "How can we do suicide prevention to maximize social benefit?" Suicidal young people in urban communities usually have multiple problems and come from families with multiple problems. Because the children may be more Americanized, speak better English, and be better connected to social services, New York has a long tradition of children being points of contact and intermediaries in family healthcare problems. A presentation by a suicidal child (or for the child by a friend or young relative) is an opportunity for healthcare and social workers to respond to someone who is at risk of becoming pregnant, a school dropout, involved in substance abuse, or involved in crime. It is an opportunity for intervention in circumstances that may lead to venereal disease or AIDS; it is an opportunity for earlier diagnosis and treatment for problems in physical health, including vision, hearing, and learning disabilities. The child's home may be affected by domestic violence, child abuse, elder abuse, immigration problems. One model for suicide prevention says that suicide's sole cause is a mental defect in the victim, and the potential victim should be sent directly to a psychiatrist. In New York City, at least, this model does not work. Many providers of mental health care are too expensive for most city residents. Public programs are overburdened and have long waiting lists. Elmhurst General Hospital in Queens, the largest service provider in the largest borough, will not treat suicidal children unless they have already suffered a physical self-injury, or they have written parental consent for treatment. This consent is frequently not forthcoming. Adult suicidal New Yorkers are often shut out of treatment programs by some variant of the dual diagnosis problem. The report "Outpatient Mental Health Services", prepared by the New York State Commission on Quality of Care for the Mentally Disabled at the request of the state legislature, found that

> With few exceptions, state and non-state providers, alike, complained that local coordination of mental health outpatient service provision is poor. As a result, programs often compete for referrals of "desirable" individuals, while other people, often with more

complex needs and multiple disabilities, are deemed inappropriate for all available programs. These criticisms are particularly voiced by freestanding mental health outpatient providers who feel that they are unfairly disadvantaged by hospital based and state psychiatric center providers who can easily "cream" referrals for their own outpatient programs from their inpatient services. (p. 20)

The aggregate pain model holds that all personal and family problems contribute directly to suicidal conditions and that no one should be denied access to programs for any of these problems. As a public health policy, this means that any problem had by a suicidal person, particularly problems in areas other than mental health, will be more likely to receive earlier treatment. A good suicide prevention program results in not just fewer suicides, but also earlier treatment for physical health problems, earlier intervention in abusive family conditions, and fewer dropouts, runaways, unwanted pregnancies, and substance abusers. The potential material benefits are large.

Public Debate

Smoking. AIDS. Air Pollution. Birth Control. Safety on the job, in the home, on the highway, in the air. We engage in public social policy discussions in nearly all areas of public health. Most of us have mixed feelings about the process. We are brought up to recognize the virtues of the free exchange of ideas, yet privately we often feel that many of the participants are ill-informed, self-serving, exploitative, backward, and boring. As wearisome as these debates can be, they do help educate and mobilize public opinion in positive directions.

Public discussions of suicide occur in one context: the immediate aftermath of a sensational tragedy. The public's conception of suicide is partly formed by those suicides that help sell newspapers and get television ratings. The most influential parts of the news media are located in cities; urban areas are their primary audience. The focus on teen suicides in affluent white suburban communities neatly fits the anxieties and psychological needs of the urban community. It ventilates the malicious side of envy and enables city dwellers to continue to believe falsely that "(Teen) suicide doesn't happen here." Since suicide is not covered in the news media in between sensational deaths, many people believe that the issue is "just a fad" or "just a media thing." This belief — a strategy to minimize the problem — is entirely false. Suicide statistics have amazingly little variation from one year to the next. The pattern set by news media coverage — for a few days after the tragedy it is OK to talk about the suicide, and then silence — is unfortunately repeated in treatment given to survivors of a non-sensational suicide. For a short while after the death many people who know the family will express sympathy. Then there is nothing. Family members still reel with pain, and their acquaintances would prefer not to think or talk about it any longer. If we can conduct a public discussion of suicide issues in between sensational deaths, then citizens will be able to have more frequent and more informed private discussions about suicide, in the same way they do about other public health concerns. This climate will make it easier for suicidal people to ask for and be given assistance in coping with their pain.

Blame and Perfectionism

Every aspect of suicide is befogged by an atmosphere of blame. The victim is blamed for getting into his condition, for not getting out of his condition, for being a moral inferior, for being a nuisance, for being a threat to the well-being of others. Blame for the victim was abetted by a trend in psychotherapy in the 1960s and 1970s toward exaggerated conceptions of personal responsibility: you are responsible for everything that has ever happened to you. The trend shifted to a different slogan in the 1980s: you may not have chosen the bad thing that has happened to you, but you can choose how you respond to it. A major part of the pain of "blame the victim" is the extent to which the victim has internalized these values and attitudes, and applied them to himself as he has developed his suicidal condition. "Blame the victim" helps non-victims cope with the unpleasant experience of someone else's pain, but it makes the victim feel worse. "Blame the victim" deters people from seeking and continuing with assistance and treatment. "Blame the victim" causes suicide, and this part of the fog is not going to lift until we abandon the view that suicide is voluntary.

"Blame the family" is not an improvement. Like "blame the victim", it ignores the social contribution to suicidal pain. It causes more pain to both the suicidal person and his loved ones. It estranges the family from the community. The moral histories of many suicidal people, and of many of their families, are indistinguishable from the moral histories of many of the non-suicidal and their families.

A subgroup that is particularly victimized by the blame drenched environment of self-destructive behaviors is that composed of children whose parents have attempted or completed suicide. Children in these situations inevitably think, "What did I do to cause this? What should I have done to prevent it? What was wrong with me that caused this to happen?" This ideation and emotion causes lasting harm. Some of it may be inevitable, but surely some of it is due to the blaming social atmosphere that surrounds suicidal behavior. If we can diminish the atmosphere of blame, we can reduce the harm caused to child survivors.

It is neither warranted, nor helpful, to blame the caregivers, blame the friends, blame the news media, or blame the people in physical proximity to the suicide or suicide attempt. Behind each suicide is the entire history of the individual's pain and his coping resource deficiencies. No individual, or group of acquaintances, is responsible for this pain aggregate. The attitudes, values, and behavior that relatives, friends, and caregivers have toward suicide are functions, not of choice, but of hundreds of years of ignorance and stigma. Fear of blame operates strongly on friends and caregivers. Fear of blame — "If I try to help and he committs suicide anyway, I will feel terrible," — deprives the suicidal of pain coping resources, and is a major cause of prolonged misery and death.

The people involved in suicidal situations did not originate the fears and false beliefs that make those situations worse. It is not their fault that suicide receives an unequal share of social investment in education and research. "Blame society" may seem to be a logical alternative in a quest to find a target for blame, but this is a futile gesture of doubtful legitimacy. Societies, or at least their governments, sometimes do appear to make decisions for which they ought to be held morally accountable. In suicide, however, this type of specific decision has never been made. The social policy, or rather non-policy, of "Do nothing," has been the rule for more than a hundred years. The barbaric customs and laws of earlier centuries have been replaced by social passivity and indecisiveness. All of the other leading causes of death have massive campaigns waged against them; the problem of suicide has been allotted little or nothing. Ordinary citizens, legislators, and academic professionals are paralyzed by that contradictory morass that constitutes received opinion about suicide. Society cannot be blamed for not making a better choice, until it is able to conceptualize alternative and more enlightened policies and practices. Fear of awareness of social complicity in suicide amounts to fear of blame, and the best way to reduce that fear is to develop a blame-free view of suicide. We must begin with the recognition that we are all victims of the false mythology of suicide.

Perfectionism

It is an obvious truth that no organization or individual will respond in a perfectly appropriate way in every situation that involves a suicidal person, yet staff members everywhere pretend that it is false. Fear of blame causes defensiveness; extreme fear causes extreme defensiveness. Through no fault of his own, a suicidal person evokes the knee-jerk response of the pretense of perfectionism. People around him walk on eggshells. No one wants the blame for how he got to where he is, and no wants the blame should his suicide occur. Perfectionism — denial on mistakes and shortcomings that inevitably occur to all of us in efforts to help during suicidal crises — often coexists with denial on the existence of the crises themselves. Organizations that do not have suicide education and prevention programs will maintain that they do a flawless job of dealing with suicidal clients. Then they invariably add something to the effect that "We rarely get them." On many occasions a school administrator has told me, prior to my talk, "It's not much of a problem here." Later, during the workshop, his jaw drops as staff member after staff member brings up cases involving suicidal children.

Most short-term and all long-term suicidal patients and clients have been caused pain, and denied resources, by inadequately trained and supported counselors and organizations. Two common mistakes stem directly from perfectionism itself:

> Our program is perfect. If you are suicidal, or still suicidal,
> then something is wrong with you.

Our program is perfect. There is no need to do anything,
such as develop a referral system, to try to improve it.

When beaten-down people are victimized by these forms of
perfectionism they do not always respond graciously. The ensuing
mutual exasperation and hostility make progress toward recovery
difficult. Sometimes perfectionism does not lead to antagonism, but has
an opposite effect. Many suicidal people expect too much of themselves,
and quickly adapt to perfectionist standards that are part of the
organization's self-image. An on-going part of the patient's pain then
remains untreated. Organizations and counselors need to take the lead
in acknowledging and accepting limitations in themselves.

Part of the problem in perfectionism is the comparative rarity of
suicidal situations. Counselors in areas such as substance abuse, or
dropout prevention, often begin their careers with idealistic
expectations. After they have worked with a number of cases they
eventually develop more realistic expectations about what they can
and cannot accomplish. The recognition and acceptance of their
limitations enables them to give up perfectionist expectations for
themselves, and for their clients, and to become more effective in their
work. But since they work with the suicidal only occasionally, they do
not have an opportunity to go through this adjustment process, and
their perfectionist attitudes remain unchanged.

Sole Reliance on the Mental Health Profession

Many suicidal people have belief systems that can be summed up as
"Society's answer to suicide is psychiatry; psychiatry is not working for
me; therefore I have no alternatives." Both premises of this argument
deserve a response. We can work toward improved treatments for the
mental illnesses associated with suicide and for the improved
availability of these treatments for people in need. In the future,
hopefully, psychiatry can work for greater numbers of people. In the
present, however, we can abandon the view that the mental health
profession should be the sole responder to suicidal pain.

There is no single cause for suicide. The aggregate of suicidal pain
includes many things that are not mental illnesses. Depression itself,
when decomposed, includes many components that are utterly ordinary.

The answers to a great deal of suicidal pain can be found outside psychiatry. We can make practical changes in social policy that will reduce the risk of suicide. We can reduce the prejudice and stigma of suicide. We can improve access to treatment programs for problems other than mental illness. A support system that depends solely on mental health professionals cannot hope to be as strong as a system that includes both healthcare workers from other areas and informed non-professionals. In the urban community in which I live, at least, the mental health profession does not have the resources to respond adequately to the number of suicidal people who seek treatment. This situation will not improve if we move to an "earlier rather than later" suicide prevention program, and expect to maintain our present high level of dependence on psychiatry.

Taboo Topic in Training

No training in suicide prevention is provided for most of the people who become one of the following: medical doctor, nurse, other type of healthcare worker, counselor or administrator, teacher, police officer, religious counselor, and counselors in the areas of substance abuse, domestic violence, child abuse, sexual abuse and assault, sexual dysfunction, reproductive health, sexual identity, disabilities, and geriatrics. Their instructors modeled the behavior of don't talk about it. Instructors who do talk about suicide often provide nothing more than a short survey of theory, statistics, teen suicide, and the warning signs. This models the behaviors of talk about it briefly; avoid the issues of fear, social prejudice and suicide postvention; and don't talk about suicide prevention among your peers. People in all these fields have their entire careers controlled by unacknowledged, unexpressed, and unexamined fears and misconceptions about suicide. They will avoid contact with suicide as much as they can, and, when they do encounter a suicidal person, they are likely to respond with prejudice, hostility, abuse, fear, and ignorance. As generations of caregivers before them have done, they will inculcate the same attitudes and beliefs in their successors. A number of professional groups have rates for suicide that are higher than average. They do not deal with suicide in themselves, or with their peers, any better than they do with their patients or clients. Mandatory training is a necessity; it must be training that recognizes that suicide can happen to a member of any group.

A common objection to proposals for training in suicide prevention and postvention is that "If we give time to suicide, we take time away from something else." The first response is to suggest that if the job deals with more problems than can be covered in a given period of time, then the training period should be longer. Americans complain about many things, but that their healthcare workers are overtrained is not one of them. The second reply is that the skills necessary to give an improved response to suicidal people will improve caregivers' skills in their primary duties.

Education About Survivor Issues

An unexplored area in suicide prevention is the education of the general public about the pain suffered by surviving relatives and friends. "I could never do that. It would hurt my family too much," is sometimes said both by people who are suicidal, and people who are not. Though I do not believe that suicidal people should be forced to discuss this topic, it is sometimes helpful to raise the issue in crisis counseling, most often with parents of young children. I am unaware of any studies on the subject, but it is reasonable to suppose that fear of bringing shame upon the family is a resource that helps people endure suicidal pain. Suicidal people, as with all of us, have very inadequate ideas about the effect of suicide on their families. Is it unrealistic to suggest that an education program for the general public about the problems of survivors would not only motivate suicidal people to seek help sooner, but also move the non-suicidal to a greater level of acceptance and support for help-seeking behavior?

An objection that might be raised is that the survivors themselves are well-educated about the effects of suicide, and they have a higher than average suicide rate. They know how much suicide hurts others, and that knowledge does not seem to help them. The reply to this objection is that knowledge of the consequences of suicide is a relatively modest coping resource, and to experience the consequences is horribly painful. The pain of a loved one's suicide outweighs any positive learning experiences that such an event might cause.

What happens after a suicide and what happens before a suicide are not causally independent. The fears, stigmas, prejudices, myths (something more, nothing can be done, blame the victim, don't talk about it, he wants to hurt others, snap out of it), aversion, silence, and unconscious self-interests that permeate both situations have much in common. The attitudes and beliefs that people develop after a suicide — largely by watching how other people react — are carried with them for the rest of their lives, and communicated to many other people. They bring these attitudes into suicide prevention situations, and, for the most part, these attitudes add to the pain and decrease the resources of the potential suicide. We cannot make progress in prevention until we make progress in postvention, and vice versa.

One place to consider interrupting the self-perpetuating cycle of stigma and taboo is with our social tolerance for the deliberate falsification of death certificates. Two instances of this are described at the end of Chapter 9. Who can deny that thousands of similar cases have occurred each year, year after year, decade after decade? The physicians who sign these certificates are reacting to pre-existing prejudice and stigma; they are in a situation of shock and turmoil; they want to protect surviving relatives from further pain and hardship. Yet once the certificate is falsified, these physicians have a strong professional interest: the facts about the victim's death must be kept secret for the remainder of their careers, indeed, for the remainder of their lives. At some level, they cannot help but follow and support the "don't talk about it" social norm that applies to the entire topic of suicide. Their social attitudes influence their profession; the attitudes of their profession influence the attitudes of society as a whole.

Ordinary Language Theories

Progress in the prevention of suicide can be achieved if we improve the belief systems and communication abilities of the following:

1. suicidal people

2. their relatives, friends, and acquaintances

3. the general public

4. healthcare workers

These improvements will be most easily realized if we develop a general theory about suicide that uses only the resources of ordinary language. Nothing can do more to reduce the actual and perceived estrangement between the suicidal and the rest of the human community. An ordinary language theory will give the suicidal, and those around them, the ability and the willingness to take action to reduce pain and increase resources. It can be a powerful tool to reduce social oppression and bring about positive change. The more esoteric a doctrine is, the more it deprives the suicidal of pain-coping resources. It reduces the number of people who are willing to help, and it discourages self-help. Suicidal people struggle to understand their pain; esoteric doctrines cause them to suffer increased feelings of inferiority and inadequacy. These doctrines leave the unrecovered with the permanent feeling that a solution to their problems exists, but is out of their reach because of lack of access to the esoteric resources.

The aggregate pain approach, and the material on envy, shame, self-pity, grandiosity, prejudice, fear, the mythology of suicide, and the vicious circles of suicidal pain, are intended to show that we have barely scratched the surface of our capacities to use ordinary language to come to an understanding of suicide.

Referral Systems

It seems obvious that any worthwhile social service organization would maintain a comprehensive, up to date, and easily accessible list of outside agencies that provide services needed by clients or students. Obvious or not, most organizations do not do this. At several city health clinics, for example, I was shown photocopies of a single page of phone numbers that was prepared at least 15 years ago. The numbers not only did not have the 212 and 718 prefixes, they began with the alphabetic exchanges: MU-0-0000. Most of the agencies on the list no longer existed. This example is extreme, but 95 percent of the organizations I have worked with fall far short of having a minimally adequate referral system. This negligence has several causes:

1. The belief that the development of a referral system is work appropriate only for uncreative drones.

2. At staff meetings it is announced that everyone will contribute. In private conversations it is said that someone ought to do it. No specific individual is assigned the responsibility; the job never gets done.

3. It is permanently on lists of things to do, and permanently at the bottom.

4. Denial. Staff members of organizations with bad referral systems will maintain to outsiders, to clients, and to each other at meetings that their system is perfectly adequate. Everyone is aware of the problem, and everyone obeys the rule, "Don't talk about it." Bad attitudes about the development and maintenance of referral systems are taught from one generation of employees to the next.

5. "Develop referral system" is not included as a line item in the budget.

6. The organization has negative biases about the abilities of other organizations to respond to the needs of their students or clients.

7. Many organizations have excessively narrow referral policies. Counselors for children, for example, may be permitted to give referrals only for problems had by the child, not for problems had by older family members. Administrators argue that restrictive referral policies enable counselors to remain focused in their work. These policies, however, interface poorly with reality. Problems in the individual are affected by problems in the family, and the family may be affected by social ills of every sort. Counselors in these organizations are usually frustrated and unhappy. They are unable to make connections, and the agony of their students and clients is prolonged unnecessarily.

One school counselor, whose desk had been inspected to make sure that she had referral information only for children, told me about a case in which she had invited a parent in for a conference to discuss the child's problems in school. The mother had a cut lip and black eye, and confided to the counselor that she had been beaten by the man in her home. The policies of the counselor's supervisor forbade giving the mother a referral to programs for battered women. A few months later, in another borough, I attended a youth conference at which a 15-year old boy described the conditions in his family that were factors in his two suicide attempts. These factors included physical abuse his mother suffered from her common-law husband, who was a drug addict.

8. The myth that "If they need it, they'll find it." To find it, the suicidal need to get the referral from somewhere. If each agency they turn to has this attitude, they will never find it. After hearing, "I don't know where you go to get that," from several social workers, they are likely to conclude that what they need is not available, and stop seeking it. Worse yet is that many organizations even have this absurd belief about their own services: "If they need us, they usually find us." As with all myths, these ideas exist solely because of the self-interested needs of the people who believe them. For their ostensible subjects, these ideas cause prolonged pain and death. Many conditions that need referrals do not get better with time; their treatment becomes more difficult and less likely to succeed.

Bad referral systems both cause and are caused by staff turnover. Good referral systems increase morale, confidence, job satisfaction and productivity. Good referral systems are not tacked on or supplementary services: they are essential parts of healthy organizations.

Teen Suicide

The 19 and under age group accounts for 7 percent of the suicides in the United States, and the rate for completed suicide in this age group is no greater than that for the general population, yet popular consciousness about the problem of suicide is preoccupied with its incidence among young people. A major underlying reason for this is that adults find teen suicide less uncomfortable to talk about than adult or geriatric suicide. Adults are not teenagers, and not going to become teenagers; the focus on the problem in another population deflects attention from the problem as it affects themselves. The attention to teen suicide is a coping strategy for adults; it reduces their fear of their own suicides. The behavior we model for children,

> It is OK to talk about suicidal behavior in another
> group; it not OK to talk about it in your own group,

is a classic instance of adult hypocrisy. It teaches children that the way to cope with anxiety is to displace the fear onto other people. In the 1950s it was common to hear the view that suicide was a serious problem in Scandinavian countries. The contemporary version of this pattern has a difference: it exploits our own children. The exploitation of children to satisfy adult needs has a name: child abuse. There are healthier ways for adults to cope with their fear of suicide among themselves.

This hypocrisy is nearly always a part of suicide prevention programs for organizations that work with young people. The organization will have policies, procedures, and programs to respond to suicidal behavior among students or clients, but none for responding to suicidal behavior among staff members. Our programs need to reflect the fact that both young people and adults may encounter suicidal people of any age. Our prescription for teenage suicide should be similar to a basic concept of family therapy: we are unlikely to make much progress with young people until adults recognize and begin to deal with the problem in themselves. Programs for suicide prevention need to employ the non-hypocritical patterns used for health education in smoking, cardio-pulmonary resuscitation, and dietary management.

Suicide Prevention for the Terminally Ill

We should have the same suicide prevention policies, procedures, and behavior toward the terminally ill that we have toward anyone else. The terminally ill are not immune to suffering suicide because their pain exceeds their coping resources. Doubtlessly, they have greater than average risk. Though many suicides among the terminally ill are involuntary, perhaps some are voluntary, and fall into the much discussed category of rational suicide. From the standpoint of suicide prevention, however, I do not believe that we have any method to distinguish between genuine and apparent cases of potential rational suicides.

Suicidal people, terminally ill and otherwise, often present their condition with rational argumentation: I have nothing to live for, the present is full of pain, the future will be full of pain, I am a burden to others, I should put myself out of my misery. Most of these people sincerely report their pain, and may be quite persuasive in communicating their feelings of hopelessness. Yet I have observed many such cases, including those involving terminal illness, in which the suicidal feelings passed when pain was reduced, and additional resources were provided. The overwhelming majority of these presentations, at least, are cries for help. Consciously, the person believes, "I want to end it all;" unconsciously, he wants to live, and the desire for life causes him to tell others about his suicidal feelings. There is no way for the others — and very likely no way for the victim himself — to distinguish the cry for help presentation from a genuine case of contemplated rational suicide.

The appropriate response to "Can you get me the pills to do it with?" is to sympathetically let the person pour out the whole story of his pain, and then follow normal suicide prevention procedures. These include reducing access to the means and enlisting the support of others. AIDS patients in the latter stages of their disease suffer physically, emotionally, socially, and nutritionally. There are *always* obvious steps that can be taken to reduce their suffering. The suicidal AIDS patients I spoke with usually developed these feelings during a period when their physical health worsened and they suffered an emotional loss. If the two causes of increased suffering were reduced by a modest amount, the suicidal feelings passed. Since there are so many opportunities to provide relief from suffering, it is not difficult to do effective suicide prevention work with the terminally ill. Modest improvements in their situations can bring substantial changes in emotional outlook. The terminally ill have just as much right to suicide prevention efforts as anyone else. The presence of the serious illness does not negate this right, any more than it negates their right to be protected from death or injury by any other means.

Anecdotal and personal experience suggests that there are four situations that present increased risk for suicidal behavior among those affected by AIDS. The first is the initial diagnosis of the presence of the antibody to the HIV virus. These people may be free of secondary illnesses, and able to lead comparatively normal lives, yet the diagnosis and the issues of loss and separation bring a tremendous increase in pain. They fear, often accurately, that many of their previous resources will soon become unavailable. The second situation involves an emotional loss such as the death of a friend or fellow patient, or a major rupture with friends or family. One AIDS patient told me on several occasions that although he was comparatively healthy, he did not leave the hospital on passes because he was afraid he would use drugs. Use of drugs in the recent past had caused him to suffer physical relapses. He also said that he still enjoyed getting high, and often wondered why he bothered to try to stay healthy. He expressed the view that since he was going to die, he might as well get high and stay high. After being in this emotional condition for several months, there was a confrontation with his family. Several other family members had just been diagnosed as HIV-positive, and since he was the first to be diagnosed, they blamed him for introducing the disease into the family. The patient went on a drug binge and died of pneumonia within several days. The third situation, mentioned above, is the simultaneous increase of physical and emotional suffering. The fourth situation, which is associated with the "giving out" transition (what voluntarists call "giving up"), is when increased physical suffering is accompanied by difficulties in communication due to general weakness, pneumonia, thrush, mouth and gum cancer, deafness, blindness, or physical immobility. There is a lack of attention to the communication problems of the terminally ill. This is an area in which it should be possible to improve the quality and longevity of their lives.

In the development of our views on suicide prevention work with the terminally ill, we should consider how much of the "right to die" debate is really due to the emotional needs of those who are not terminally ill. We want guidelines to help manage our emotional discomfort, and discussions of the rights of the terminally ill are often little more than disguised quests for rules for our own behavior. Secondly, the overly generous assumptions we make about the capacities of the terminally ill for rational deliberation are usually based not upon the evidence, but upon our own emotional needs. We fear being in conditions where volitional capacity and control are diminished; consequently we practice denial on the obvious cognitive and volitional constraints that are caused by physical and emotional suffering. Here, as elsewhere, it is a fallacy to regard this situation as one that produces an opportunity for a noble choice. We imagine or exaggerate good aspects of basically bad situations so that we can cope with our fear of being in that situation, our fear of being envied by someone in that situation, or our pain at seeing a loved one suffer.

People who are asked to either

a. not intervene in the development of a suicidal condition, or

b. assist with the means of suicide.

wonder, "Should I respect his rights?" People asked to do a. should consider how much of their feeling is due to a personal need to maintain an emotional distance from the person and his situation. People asked to do b. should consider whether this course of action — sometimes simply because it is an action — is one that is less painful for them personally than the alternatives of non-involvement or involvement on the side of life. On a few occasions I have talked with people who had done either a. or b. prior to the completed suicide of someone who was terminally ill. The non-interveners and assisters were caring and sincere, but they had no special powers to discern the entirety of the contents of the minds of their acquaintances or themselves. We are often mistaken about understanding the causes of our own behavior, and the behavior of other people. We may believe that requests for a. or b. are motivated by rationality, when in fact they are caused by the desire to stay alive. We may believe that our motives for an action are solely to promote the best interests of another, and later realize that our actions had self-interested causes of which we were unaware. The circumstances of terminal illness, for both the victim and his acquaintances, are not conducive to clear thinking. The best course of action is to simply do our best to reduce pain and increase resources. The willingness to provide suicide prevention assistance to *anyone* does not require a special philosophical decision. It is no different from the willingness to give medical aid to someone with a broken leg, or the willingness to give food to someone who is hungry.

Barriers In Between

The problem of suicide, which on superficial inspection seems impossible, has a different appearance when it is decomposed into many smaller elements. A useful model for the prevention of suicide is to see it not just as an issue of pain and resources for coping with pain, but also as an issue of the barriers in between. Each item listed below is an area in which we can make progress. Though many entries in the pain category are beyond the scope of the suicide prevention worker, all of the items in the next two categories are areas in which we can take immediate steps toward a better tomorrow. These improvements do not require magical changes in human nature, and they do not require the vast resources that are now devoted to other areas of public health.

Major Components of Suicidal Pain

physical pain
psychological pain
death or terminal illness in family
mental illness
alcohol and/or drug abuse
sexual assault or abuse
crime victimization
physical abuse
emotional abuse
eating or sleeping disorders
disruption or dysfunction in family
loss of esteem, security, health, talent, status,
    job, money, relationship, home,
loss of physical or mental capacity
social isolation and loneliness
feelings of hopelessness and powerlessness
stress
confusion
anxiety
vicious circle problems
prejudice and stigma for suicidal pain
other forms of prejudice and stigma
loss of any resource for coping with pain.

Barriers In Between

fear
stigma and prejudice
ignorance
silence
denial, minimization, belittlement
negative moral attitudes, blame for the victim
verbal and emotional abuse of the suicidal
hostility
the non-suicidal's uses of the suicidal for their own purposes

Myths: just wants attention, manipulative
        motives of revenge and escape
        suicide is rational, a solution
        blame the family
        suicide prevention is a last minute activity
        suicide is romantic and dramatic
        being suicidal is good for you
        attempts get it out of your system
        it must have been something more
        suicide is voluntary
        they can't be stopped
        the suicidal need an inner light
        suicidal pain is psychological pain
service providers who will not provide or continue with services
inadequate referral systems
quick referrals
confidentiality problems
        too little: breaches that cause more pain
        too much: secrecy, limitations on access to resources
being trusted with possession of the means
pressure to hurry up and get better
interruptions
inappropriate language: "threat", "confrontation", "success", "failure"
ignorance and false beliefs about the effect of suicide on survivors
false conceptions of themselves and each other that are had by
    both the suicidal and their counselors
lack of information and education for both the general public
    and professionals
lack of public and private support for education and research
theories of suicide and depression that ignore much of the pain
esoteric theories of suicide and depression
single cause theories of suicide
caregivers' perfectionism and fear of blame
false conceptions of self-reliance, ride it out strategies
no words for one's pain
no role models for recovery
denial on the existence of recovery

Coping Resources

patience
acceptance
understanding
tolerance
compassion
no-fault theory of suicide
comprehensive examinations for physiological causes of suicidal pain
improved models for what suicide is
improved theories and treatments for depression
ordinary language theories
decomposition of suicidal pain
new conceptions of the rights and worth of suicidal people
studies on suicide self-prevention
role models for recovery
hope appropriate for a condition with a high recovery rate
recognition for recovery
efforts to help others with their pain
willingness to give and get help sooner rather than later
support groups
professional treatment
improved support for survivors
education about suicide's effects on survivors
reduced stigma, prejudice, ignorance, and denial for suicide
     and the components of suicidal pain
improved treatment for the components of suicidal pain
improved policies, support, and referral systems for caregivers
legislation on discrimination against the suicidal, and on
     access to the means
education for the public and caregivers about suicide
increased support for research

Hope for the Suicidal

A starting point for an improved response to the problem of suicide lies with the development of a new appreciation for suicide considerers. People who suffer suicidal feelings and ideation, and never attempt, constitute the large majority of the suicidal. They suffer untold millions of man-years of agonizing pain. It is from this group that attempters and completers come. Considerers occupy the bulk of counseling efforts in schools and social service agencies. No other group is co-extensive with the group of people who comprise suicide considerers: for each condition or finite list of conditions one can name — depression, schizophrenia, substance abuse, bereavement, disabling illness or injury, loss of important relationship — there are considerers who do not fit the description, and non-considerers who do fit. Considerers, as a group, are independently worthy of concern in research and education. Their condition is worth responding to simply in itself, because it leads to other serious conditions — such as substance abuse as a negative pain-coping device — and because it can lead to attempted suicide and death. Instead of the denigration "not serious", we should approach considerers with a positive attitude: they have successfully prevented their own suicides. Yet unlike attempters and completers, considerers are not recognized as a distinct group in ordinary life and language, and are only occasionally referred to in academic discussions by an artificial term such as "considerers" or "ideators". As a distinct group, considerers are given virtually no attention in research on suicide. The focus of research and crisis management programs — and the only programs we have are for crisis management — is on "weeding out" considerers from those who are considered to be at imminent risk of a highly lethal attempt. This narrowness is an attempt to minimize the problem of suicide. The acutely suicidal need our attention, but to ignore the non-acutely suicidal is completely counterproductive. If we recognize that the problem of suicide directly affects ten to twenty million people a year, then we cannot help but turn our attention to broader concerns of social policies and attitudes. Hope for the suicidal can be increased if we give proper attention to *all* people who suffer from suicidal feelings.

Prior approaches to suicide — psychoanalysis, the cognitive theory of depression, the effort to develop anti-depressant medications, the myth of the inner light — have had the common denominator that they hoped to reduce the incidence of suicide without requiring changes in social policies, attitudes, or values. These approaches believed that the solution to suicide was to make changes in the people who were the cause of the problem. All of these approaches practice denial on the social causes of suicidal pain. Social forces prevent victims from receiving help sooner, and they make the process of recovery needlessly difficult. The quest for a magic bullet — a cure for suicide that leaves unchanged the ideology of the social oppression of the suicidal — is a pipe dream. The search for the magic bullet causes us to ignore dozens upon dozens of modest steps toward progress and enlightenment. An improved social environment would be dedicated to incremental social change, and this path is the true hope for the suicidal. Once we recognize that suicide is not a matter of choice, will power, or moral rectitude, but a situation in which aggregate pain exceeds aggregate resources, we will be able to recognize the need and the opportunity to make the necessary transition to a more compassionate future.

Our social behavior about the prevention of suicide is currently wholly determined by the blind forces of the historical development of our species. Some aspects of our behavior — willful ignorance related to the means of suicide — should be regarded as positive. Other aspects — the taboo on public discussions of suicide — have mixed benefits at best. Many aspects — the social oppression of the suicidal — are wholly negative. As we have in many, many areas of public health, we can begin to implement rational means to modify social behavior so that we can alleviate human suffering. At both individual and social levels we can learn to act with understanding and foreknowledge, and gain greater freedom over the forces of nature. Acceptance of the involuntary nature of suicide will ultimately provide us with greater freedom, not less.

CHAPTER TWELVE

APPENDIX

This chapter addresses technical issues in theory about depression and suicide. It is intended to provide further support for the general theses of this book and to continue the analysis of the social oppression of the suicidal. The first section argues that we do not need the concept of intention to explain the role of suicide notes, or to distinguish between suicide and accidental death. The second section provides more detail for the aggregate pain critique of the psychoanalytic theory of suicide. The third section critically assesses Aaron Beck's cognitive theory of depression and suicide. The fourth section argues that the aggregate pain theory can provide an adequate basis for understanding both the role of contagion in suicide and the strong public interest in suicide by contagion.

SECTION ONE

INTENTION AND SUICIDE NOTES

At the end of *Clues to Suicide* Shneidman and Farberow provide the texts of 33 notes written by completed suicides.[1] If you have access to this book, read the notes and ask yourself if these suicides happened because the victims were pushed to their deaths by horrible pain, or if they happened because the authors were choosing to realize a desired goal. In nine notes the writers characterize themselves as having no choice. (1-A, 4-B, 7-B, 9-B, 11-A, 12-A, 17-B, 29-B, 32-B. An example, from note 4-B, "I don't want to go but there is nothing else to do.") In six notes the writers say they have only one choice. (5-B, 14-A, 22-B, 24-B, 26-A, 30-B. From note 26-A: "Everything is kind of mixed up with me and what I am doing is the only way out I guess I can think of no other ... ") Since choice requires alternatives, "one choice" is no choice. In these 15 notes the writers believe they are going to die, but see death as something they have no choice about. Is it fair or accurate to say they want death? Fourteen other notes do not give clear indications as to whether the victim wants his death. (2-A, 6-A, 10-B, 13-A, 15-A, 16-A, 19-B, 20-B, 23-A, 25-B, 27-B, 28-A, 31-A, 33-B. The entirety of 13-A: "Dear Mary. Im sorry for all the trouble Ive caused you. I guess I can't say anymore. I love you forever and give Tim my love. I guess I've disgraced myself and John I hope it doesn't reflect on you.") In 29 of 33 notes there is no clear evidence that the writer wants to die. The remaining four notes, three of which indicate they were written by men with terminal illnesses, characterize the death as the "best" alternative. (3-A, 8-A, 18-B, 21-A. From 3-A: " ... I have been feeling bad for 2 years, with my heart. I knew that if I went to a doctor I would lose my job. I think this is best for all concerned.") Believing that one's death is best for all concerned is still not conclusive evidence of intent. This belief, my death is best for all concerned, might be had by a *non-suicidal* person who wants and intends to live, but has a terminal condition that is a great burden on his family. Believing that one's death is the best option, as just four of the note writers indicate, is strong evidence but does not prove intent. In the other 29 notes there is no strong evidence of intent. What is evident, on reading all of the notes, is that the writers were brought to their conditions by great pain.

What do suicide notes reveal? Notes, as expressions of anger, sorrow, and anxiety, do what non-suicidal expressions of emotion do: they are attempts to discharge and cope with the feelings that are being experienced at that moment. In some cases people write notes and then do not commit or attempt suicide. In these situations writing the note may have helped prevent the death. In the notes collected by Shneidman and Farberow it was sadly not enough. What we need to realize is that the writing of the note is evidence that the person is still struggling to cope with the pain. Suicide notes, if kept private, are not cries for help. But that does not mean that they are not manifestations of the desire to stay alive.

INTENTION AND ACCIDENTAL DEATH

Litman (1984, 1987) reviews the use of the psychological autopsy within the legal system and argues that the concept of intention enables us to distinguish between suicide and accidental death. In accidental death a person falls from a tall building and dies because his foot slipped. In suicide a person falls from a tall building and dies because he wanted to die. The first person did not intend his death; the second did.

I believe that we can make this distinction without ascribing to the suicide the intent to die, the desire to die, or any other mental quality that is allegedly peculiar to suicide. The second person above died because his pain exceeded his pain-coping resources; the death of the first person had different causes. In the practical activity of trying to distinguish between suicide and accidents both intentionalism and involuntarism would work in similar ways. Both would look for evidence that the victim "had suicide in mind." The intentionalist sees the statement, "I don't want to live anymore," as evidence of intention; the involuntarist sees it as evidence that pain threatens to exceed pain-coping resources. In the necessary activity of determining the cause of death the two approaches would not substantially differ. Involuntarism can work just as well as intentionalism, and not require that we make stigmatizing assumptions about the victim.[2]

When applied to situations other than accidents, involuntarism and intentionalism may classify some cases differently. Intentionalists regard what the person has in mind as crucial:

> We would not certify as suicides, however, the deaths of persons who, because of mental disorders, committed acts that they themselves felt would not result in death. An example is the case of the man who climbed into the lion's area of a zoo under the delusion that he was a Biblical prophet with lion-taming powers, but the lion killed him. (Litman, 1987, p. 88.)

On the involuntarist theory this is not so clear; we would have to know more about the causal history of the delusion. If it was directly caused by a religious experience or a psychoactive drug, then the death would not be a suicide. But if the delusion were caused by massive pain, and many delusional people suffer from terrifying fears, then it would be a suicide.

SECTION TWO

PSYCHOANALYTIC DOCTRINES ON SUICIDE

This section reviews two psychoanalytic approaches to suicide. The first position argues that suicide is committed by individuals who lack adequate self-regulatory interior structures; the second claims that suicidal behavior results from a failure of adaptation. The extended quotations below are presented as further documentation for the claims that psychoanalysis has an inadequate conception of suicidal pain and an excessively negative view of the suicidal person.

MENTAL INFERIORITY

> Those unfortunate people who reach adulthood without having developed sufficiently stable self-regulatory structures remain vulnerable to crises of aloneness, self-contempt, and fury that may bring about suicide, or dangerous suicide attempts. In order to minimize emotional distress they must rely on such resources as they can find outside themselves, since they lack anything inside adequate to accomplish the task. (Maltsberger, 1986, p. 17)

This is an example of what Allport termed "the inferior brain." Psychoanalysis believes that suicidal people are mentally inferior, and that this inferiority is caused by a developmental failure during the first five years of life. If you are suicidal, it is because you always had this deficiency. Barring full scale psychoanalysis you always will have it. For all of your life, if you are to stay alive, you will be excessively dependent on external resources. The cause of suicide, suicidal behavior, and suicidal thoughts is entirely within the victim.

Is this accurate? Some people have a bad time of it during the first five years of life and then have normal lives later on. Other people have apparently normal early childhoods and yet become depressed when they are middle-aged or older. Many people have a suicidal crisis and, without the assistance of psychoanalysis, regain the enjoyment of ordinary life. To be sure, analysts have responses to this criticism. Maltsberger argues, "Outwardly manifest adaptation does not necessarily betray the structural deficiency that makes a patient reliant on external sustaining resources." (1986, p. 59) Like popular mythology, psychoanalysis believes that crisis reveals the true self. This claim lends itself to a thought experiment, one that would be practically possible were it not morally repugnant. If psychoanalysis is correct, we could distinguish between apparent and genuine adaptation in a group of apparently normal people by stripping them of all external resources. Permanently deprive them of family, friends, health, work, companionship, recreation. (To model reality, we would have to do more. We would continuously remind them that others have the good things of life, be angry at them for not also having these good things, and repeatedly tell them that the only reason they have impoverished lives is that they have failed to use their will power.) The members of this group who became suicidal would be the structurally defective, and those who endured their losses gracefully would be deemed sound of mind. This is a ridiculous consequence, but this is the state of the art in American psychiatry: no matter what happens to you, if you become suicidal it is because you have a defective mind. You reached " ... adulthood without having developed sufficiently stable self-regulatory structures."

It will be helpful to consider a case study provided by Maltsberger and to observe which factors psychoanalysis regards as important in the causal history of a suicide attempt:

> *Case 19.* Mr. G., a 63-year-old retired office worker, was transferred to a psychiatric inpatient unit after surviving an almost lethal overdose of digitalis. A former alcoholic, the patient had overcome his difficulties and become well known for his volunteer

work. A stroke left him with a thalamic infarction. He experienced great difficulty in urinating. Frequent catheterization became necessary and his leg brace was commonly wet with urine. The stroke left him subject to severe attacks of pain in which his hand, arm and leg felt as though they were being crushed in a vise or pierced with sharp needles — the worst experiences of pain in his entire life. Further, his ailments forced him out of the home he had shared for some years with friends. What he ostensibly found intolerable was physical decay and the suffering for which he could find no relief. He had hoarded digitalis, planning to commit suicide for years, promising himself "escape" when the suffering became too much. But careful examination showed that in fact what made it intolerable was the loss of his pet dog "Fidel."

When asked what he imagined it would be like to be dead, Mr. G. began to cry, and confided that he hoped Fidel would be there "on the other side" waiting for him. He was careful to point out that he had no sense of certainty, but a strong hope, about life beyond the grave. The patient told the examiner about Fidel eagerly, in great detail, weeping all the while as he explained how inseparable they had been. Fidel accompanied him to banquets, appeared on the platform with him, had attracted the notice of celebrities. For years Mr. G. had secretly smuggled Fidel into movies. His intelligence had been noted by everyone; the patient and his pet had enjoyed a complete mutual capacity to understand each others' thoughts and feelings. They were the closest of friends.

When Fidel was 13 years old "he developed diabetes and required insulin injections"; urinary incontinence followed. On the advice of the veterinarian the dog was given "euthanasia." After cremation his ashes were dispersed on a beach where "by coincidence" those of a friend's wife had been scattered before. Mr. G. liked to imagine that she and Fidel were keeping each other company.

Before this hospitalization the patient had not seen the connection between Fidel's illness and "euthanasia" and his own incontinence and suicide attempt.

Mr. G.'s mother had been physically and emotionally abusive; he had relied on his father and brother to raise him. From the age of 14 he was never without a dog and earlier would leave for school a half hour early in order to "have conversations with four dogs who lived in the neighborhood." When asked if he would have attempted suicide had Fidel remained at his side Mr. G. exclaimed indignantly, "What? Leave Fidel? Never!"

Maltsberger comments

In this case it is obvious that the patient had a life-long reliance on dogs as sustaining resources, not having developed interior structures to help ward off the affects of despair. Having lost his dog, the patient actually believed that his equilibrium might be restored by recovering his pet through suicide.

and concludes

Suicidal crises can be expected to appear in those patients who lack the necessary structure to protect themselves from the intolerable affects of suicide (aloneness, self contempt, murderous hate) and who must rely on sustaining resources outside themselves to maintain equilibrium. A crisis will develop when the sustaining resource fails. (1986, pp. 46-48)

We can agree that the loss of his pet was the factor that precipitated Mr. G.'s suicide attempt, but why should it be singled out for special significance? Most of Mr. G.'s pain has nothing to do with the pain involved in his relationship with his mother, the alleged inferiority of his "interior structures," or the death of his pet. He had survived the loss of many other pets without attempting suicide. Why is the death of the pet more significant than the factors that precipitated his becoming a suicide considerer long before the attempt occurred? Mr. G.'s deficiencies are the resources of ordinary life: health, home, work, volunteer work, friends, companionship, entertainment, social appreciation. His physical illness and disability cause him horrible physical, emotional and social pain. Omitted by Maltsberger is the pain of being someone who was suicidal. Did Mr. G. try to talk about his suicidal ideation with others prior to the attempt? If so, did the others respond supportively, or did they respond with avoidance and aversion? If he did not talk about his feelings, then this further feeling — "There is a part of me I cannot share with others," — contributed to his isolation from other people. Because Maltsberger focuses on the points he wishes to make about fantasies and external structures, he does not tell us much about Mr. G.'s emotional condition. One suspects that an analyst would have to go through contortions to try to fit Mr. G.'s pain into the anger-turned-inward theory of suicide. Mr. G. is a man burdened with self-pity, shame, envy, and fear.

Maltsberger treats the reunion fantasy as a key element in the suicide attempt. As he mentions in another passage, it is not unusual for suicidal people to manifest an abnormal attachment to a pet. This is especially true in elderly people who have lost many of the resources of ordinary life. In Mr. G.'s case the attachment evolves into the reunion fantasy. But his behavior does not go beyond the range of normal until he suffers all of his other problems. The death fantasy is an involuntary response to great pain; it is not an original cause of suicidal behavior. If the "bad thought" is a key to Mr. G.'s condition, should our treatment priorities focus on his fantasy, and give lesser consideration to his other needs? At a social level, the psychoanalytical view of Mr. G.'s condition allows us to continue to deny that social mistreatment of the elderly, the disabled, and the pained has any role in the causation of suicide. The psychoanalytic approach cannot help but deter people from seeking help. To avoid the stigma of "mental defective" you must ride out every siege of pain without asking for external support. This view holds that the suicidal person's problem is his excessive need to rely on us, not our deficient support of him. Requests for help are evidence of mental inferiority, the healthy person should not have need for external assistance. Since suicide is a problem in self-regulation, it is by definition, not a social problem. Social pains are not factors, social resources are not factors.

FAILURE OF ADAPTATION

An outline of the psychoanalytic approach to suicide may be drawn from the paper "Psychoanalytic Theories of Suicide" by Robert Litman and Norman Tabachnick. (Litman, 1968)

> Some of the more important unconscious fantasy systems which contribute to every suicide take the form of wishes as follows:
>
> (1) A tired wish for escape, surcease, sleep, "death."...
> (2) A guilty wish for punishment, atonement, sacrifice, to make restitution. ...
> (3) A hostile wish for revenge, for power and control, to punish and to murder. ...
> (4) An erotic wish for passionate masochistic surrender, the greatest ecstasy, for reunion with the loved dead. ...
> (5) A hopeful wish for rescue, rebirth, rehabilitation, a new start, and a new life. ... (p. 74)

> From a clinical point of view, there are a great number of predisposing conditions that more or less favor suicide, although they are not the precipitating mechanisms. These include (1) disorganized or disharmonious ego structure which splits up under relatively low conditions of stress; (2) a tendency of the unconscious sexual drives to be fixated at infantile attitudes, especially strong tendencies toward sadism and masochism; (3) deformities of the superego due to cruel parents, dead parents, parents who hated the child, or possibly due to some constitutional inherited trait of exceptional destructiveness in the superego; (4) strong attachments to dead loved ones, the idea of death, and the fantasy of being dead; (5) chronic self-destructive living patterns expressed, for example, in homosexuality, drug addiction, or compulsive

gambling; and (6) extremely dependent or "symbiotic" love relationships characterized by preverbal communication patterns, an inability to distinguish the self from the other, and an inability to survive separation.

SUICIDE AS ACTION

One of the great unsolved problems is how to predict which potentially suicidal patient will actually act out suicidal fantasies. Psychoanalysts have noted that individual suicides involve certain specific suicide mechanisms. All of these mechanisms involve a breaking down of ego defenses and the release of previously inhibited destructive instinctual energy. Examples are: (1) the loss of love objects, especially when the union has been symbiotic; (2) narcissistic injury of the ego, symbolically through failure or by direct physiological damage due to fatigue or toxic substances; (3) direct damage to the ego's defensive and integrative functions and processes by many drugs, but especially by alcohol and barbiturates; (4) overwhelming affect due to rage, guilt, anxiety, or combinations, especially when carried to ego exhaustion; (5) extreme splitting of the ego with the setting of one sub-self against the rest; and (6) a special suicidal attitude and plan often based on identification with someone in the past who was suicidal. (p. 77)

Litman and Tabachnick suggest that the problems of the suicidal may be viewed as problems in adaptation:

In general, it could be stated that suicidal phenomena often represent a failure of adaptation and, simultaneously, an attempt to achieve a new and better adaptation. (p. 78)

How helpful is this as a theory for suicide prevention? "What can I do?" remains unanswered for the suicidal individual, his friends and relatives, his counselors at school or church, his medical doctor, his general community. Not only will all these potential sources of help not know what to do, they will be thoroughly intimidated from wanting to get involved on the side of life. The theory uses the fantasies to stigmatize the victim with motives, goals and desires that are contrary to life. On the aggregate pain model, the actual role of death fantasies is small, and it is on the side of life, not death. The first three predisposing conditions stigmatize the victim with an inferior brain, and are regarded as conditions for which there is little hope of recovery. The problem of being homosexual and leading a happy life is seen as a problem in the individual, not as a problem between the individual and the larger community. The pain of longer and deeper mourning, after suicide and after death by other means, is a problem of identification and attachment; society makes no contribution. The list of emotions that contribute to suicidal pain does not include envy, shame, or self-pity. There is not a word on physical pain or physical illness; nothing in this theory suggests that relieving physical pain should be a priority in suicide prevention.

The general principle about adaptation is intended to apply both to completers and to attempters and considerers. It says that completed suicide occurs because the victim failed to adapt to life and sought (by escape, restitution, revenge, reunion, or rebirth) a better adaptation in death. Presentations by attempters and considerers occur because of the failure of adaptation and the desire to get help. (" ... suicidal individuals who by assuming the helpless role, declare they are out of the running and must be treated as needy individuals who are to be given time and instruction on how to live." p. 80) Involuntarism accepts only the latter aspect of this principle: presentations by attempters and considerers are cries for help. Completers do not wish for death, and it is neither fair nor accurate to say that their problem (or that of attempters or considerers) is a failure of adaptation. The failure of adaptation theory puts the problem entirely in the victim; none of the problem is in us. But we add to the pain of people who have suicidal feelings, and if they are members of other stigmatized groups, we add more pain. Consider further the problems of aging. Are they due to a failure of the elderly to adapt, or to a failure of society to provide its older members with meaningful social roles? "Look for the failures of adaptation," is a theory that prejudges and blames the victim; it tells us to ignore much of the cause of suicidal pain.

SECTION THREE

THE COGNITIVE THEORY
OF DEPRESSION AND SUICIDE

A basic principle of cognitive psychology is that our emotional reaction to an event is determined by the cognitive interpretation we place upon the event. As Beck explains, an event happens, we interpret its meaning, and we react emotionally:

> Consider the following example of how a specific external event evokes meaning for different people. A teacher remarked to her class that Tony, a bright student, received a low grade on a test. One student was pleased — he thought, "This shows I'm smarter than Tony." Tony's best friend felt sad (as did Tony): He shared Tony's loss. Another student was frightened: "If Tony did poorly, I may have done poorly also." Still another student became incensed at the teacher: "She probably marked unfairly if she gave Tony a low grade." By being "unfair" to one student, she had violated a cardinal rule and, therefore, she could be unfair to any student. Finally, a visiting student had no emotional response at all: Tony's grade had no special meaning for him.
>
> This example demonstrates an essential relation: The specific content of the interpretation of an event leads to a specific emotional response. Further, based upon an examination of numerous similar examples, we can generalize that, depending on the kind of

> interpretation a person makes, he will feel glad, sad,
> scared, or angry — or he may have no particular
> emotional reaction at all. (1977, p. 51)

If we have distorted cognitions, we will have distorted emotional
responses:

> A person who attaches an unrealistic or extravagant
> meaning to an event is likely to experience an
> inappropriate or excessive emotional response. A man
> lying in bed who imagines that each noise is a burglar
> breaking into his house will feel excessive anxiety. (p.
> 52)

Beck argues that if we interpret an event as meaning the loss of
something of value, we will experience sadness. If our cognitions related
to loss are distorted in certain ways, we will suffer depression. "The
depressed patient shows specific distortions. He has a negative view of
his world, a negative concept of himself, and a negative appraisal of
his future: the *cognitive triad*." (p. 105) Some of the attitudes and rules
that predispose people to depression are

1. In order to be happy, I have to be successful in
whatever I undertake.

2. To be happy, I must be accepted (liked, admired) by
all people at all times.

3. If I'm not on top, I'm a flop.

4. It's wonderful to be popular, famous, wealthy; it's
terrible to be unpopular, mediocre.

5. If I make a mistake, it means I'm inept.

6. My value as a person depends on what others think of
me.

7. I can't live without love. If my spouse (sweetheart,
parent, child) doesn't love me, I'm worthless.

8. If somebody disagrees with me, it means he doesn't
like me.

9. If I don't take advantage of every opportunity to advance myself, I will regret it later.

and

1. I should be the utmost of generosity, considerateness, dignity, courage, unselfishness.

2. I should be the perfect lover, friend, parent, teacher, student, spouse.

3. I should be able to endure any hardship with equanimity.

4. I should be able to find a quick solution to every problem.

5. I should never feel hurt; I should always be happy and serene.

6. I should know, understand, and foresee everything.

7. I should always be spontaneous; I should always control my feelings.

8. I should assert myself; I should never hurt anybody else.

9. I should never be tired or get sick.

10. I should always be at peak efficiency.
(pp. 255 & 257)

Negative expectations about the future, hopelessness, is what causes depressed people to become suicidal:

... the suicidal behavior of the depressed patient is derived from specific cognitive distortions: the patient systematically misconstrues his experiences in a negative way and without objective basis, anticipates a negative outcome to any attempts to attain his major goals or objectives. (Beck, 1975, p. 1147)

Cognitive psychologists believe that the reason why depressed and suicidal people suffer so much pain is that they have false and distorted ways of thinking about reality. Their method of therapy is guided by the principle " ... rectify the false belief and you alleviate the symptom." (1977, p. 212)

Cognitive psychology believes that depression is directly caused by distorted thinking; physical pain, emotional pain, and factors outside the victim do not cause depression. Physical pain and external events must be interpreted or given a meaning for there to be an emotional reaction. If our interpretations with respect to loss are distorted, we will feel sadness when we ought not feel it, or for longer than we ought to feel it, or more intensely than we ought to feel it. This excessive sadness is depression.

Cognitivists are correct in their claim that depressed and suicidal people have faulty thinking patterns. The identification and description of these patterns is a significant contribution. This is a theory that is good for part of the problem of depression and suicide; it errs in trying to be a complete explanation. Since cognitivism locates the entirety of the cause of suicide within the mind of the victim, it contains the stigmatizing characteristics that are common to mentalist approaches to suicide. It uses the language of intent, desire, and volition:

> Suicidal intent was conceptualized in terms of the relative weight of the patient's wish to live and his wish to die, his psychological deterrents against yielding to suicidal wishes, and the degree to which he has transformed his suicidal wishes into a concrete plan or actual act oriented toward death. (1975, p. 1147)

> *Intent* is defined as the seriousness of the wish of a patient to terminate his life. (Beck, 1974a, p.45)

> The choice of suicide as a means of escape is often based on an unrealistically negative appraisal of the prognosis for other forms of escape (for example, medication, hospitalization, vacation, temporary leave of absence). (1977, p. 292)

Fortunately the sense of mental inferiority one gets from other theories is less in cognitive psychology. The skewed thinking patterns are on a continuum with patterns of ordinary cognition and are regarded as comparatively temporary. Someone with depression is not presumed to be "damaged goods" for the entirety of his life. A second improvement is that cognitive psychology has a less frightening view of the suicidal person than does psychoanalysis. If the suicidal are filled with murderous rage, and Thanatos is on the verge of overpowering Eros, then it would be reasonable for us to recoil at the prospect of social contact with such creatures. But if they are merely victims of distorted thinking about themselves and their future, then there is no cause to regard them with fear and aversion.

A problem with cognitive psychology is that there is not enough in it to explain why suicide happens. A great many people have the ideation expressed by "It is all hopeless. Things will never get better," and yet few attempt suicide, and still fewer complete. The psychoanalytic concept of murderous rage turned inward has sufficient power to explain why people die. Suicide is a special type of murder. The aggregate pain theory claims that suicide happens when pain overwhelms. But many people have very distorted pessimistic thinking and do not die. As the cognitive psychologists have shown, the same thoughts, rules, and attitudes recur in many depressed people. Why do some attempt or commit suicide, and others do not? Beck argues that depressive ideation is made worse by cycles of negative feedback and that these vicious cycles increase feelings of sadness. (1977, p. 130) But these negative patterns are found in many people who do not attempt or complete. "Pathogenic" ideation is not sufficient to explain why suicide happens.

A second problem with the cognitive theory is that its limited view of the cause of suicide among the depressed — cognitive distortions — leads to a limited approach to suicide prevention: correct false beliefs and attitudes. This addresses only a small part of the pain of suicidal people. How should we respond to depressed and suicidal people in the physical and social circumstances of Mr. G.? Putting aside the issue of death fantasies, it hard to see why our primary method of treatment should be the correction of the ways in which they distort the hopelessness of their situations. These people have many of the cognitive distortions Beck describes, but this is not all or even most of the cause of their pain. Suicide prevention with people with conditions as bad or worse than Mr. G.'s can be very effective — sometimes amazingly so — but the necessary response involves attending to basic human needs for relief from pain, companionship, social support, meaningful activity, and time to adjust to loss and transition. It might be replied that these measures are so obvious that anyone would know this. But a theory of suicide should have these measures, obvious or not, as one of its consequences. Theories that place limits on the causes of depression invariably place limits on our response to depression. Like psychoanalysis, cognitive therapy addresses only a small part of the overall causes of suicidal pain, and not even the most accessible parts of the pain. Pessimistic ideation in the suicidal is largely caused by physical and emotional suffering, rather than vice versa. Loneliness is painful, and the pain may vary with the rationality of our ideas about our loneliness (i.e., "It will always be like this.") The pain can be relieved by improving our thinking processes, but it can also be relieved by reducing isolation.

Because of its focus on cognition, cognitive psychology provides a very incomplete account of the emotional pain of depression and suicide. In *Cognitive Therapy and the Emotional Disorders*, Beck presents analyses of just three emotions: sadness, anger, and anxiety. Sadness results from preoccupation with loss; when cognitively distorted, it leads to depression. Anger results from preoccupation with an unjust attack or infringement upon one's boundaries; distortions lead to paranoia. Anxiety is caused by preoccupation with danger; cognitively distorted anxiety results in phobias. Beck believes that each mental illness is due to cognitive distortions that relate to a single emotion. Basic aspects of the way in which fear and anger, two of the emotions he does discuss, contribute to suicide are simply ignored. Neither his account of depression, nor his account of anxiety, contain a single word about the massive level of social fear of depressed and suicidal people. For Beck these fears have no role in the cause of suicide. The fears that are listed in Chapter 4 are as worthy of scientific inquiry as any other fears that negatively affect public health. They are usually ignored because the blame-the-victim prejudice of theory and culture demand ignorance and denial. Cognitive psychology would seem to have a special problem in this area. Since it is committed to the view that depression and suicide are caused by distorted thinking, it would have to argue that these fears are irrational; the people who have them are like the man who believes that every noise is caused by a burglar breaking into his house. But these fears are not irrational, they have a legitimate basis.

Before turning to paranoia, Beck provides an analysis of anger in ordinary life. His examples include being upset with someone's behavior at a party and being inconvenienced on the highway by someone who disregards an accepted rule of driving. He concludes

> The conditions that *accentuate anger* after an offense has occurred may be summarized as follows: (1) offense perceived as intentional; (2) offense perceived as malicious; (3) offense perceived as unjustified, unfair, unreasonable; (4) offender perceived as undesirable person; (5) possibility of blaming or disqualifying offender. (1977, p. 73)

What Beck fails to observe is that this is a good description of society's accentuated — and distorted — anger toward the suicidal. The idea that *our* cognitively distorted anger toward the suicidal may have a causal role in suicide is not present in cognitive psychology.

Does depression involve only sadness? Look at the rules listed earlier: the cognitive distortions of depression essentially involve envy, self-pity, and shame. I ask the reader to reflect upon depression as he has experienced it in himself or other people. Is it simply sadness plus faulty beliefs, or is it not more often a lusher and riper entity? Depression is not only more than sadness, it is sometimes less. Beck briefly mentions the emotional deadness that characterizes some depressed people; he attempts to explain it with the concept of apathy.

> While the usual consequence of loss is sadness, the passive resignation shown by some depressives may lead to a different emotional state. When the depressed patient regards himself as totally defeated and consequently gives up on his goals, he is apt to feel apathetic. Since apathy often is experienced as an absence of feeling, the patient may interpret this state as a sign that he is incapable of emotion, that he is "dead inside." (1977, p. 120)

This is inaccurate. The horrible condition to which Beck refers is a very far cry from cognitively distorted apathy. Apathy, torpor, lethargy, and sluggishness are conditions sometimes had by the non-depressed. In ordinary life we can often apply some of the "oomph" that is called will power, and get out of these conditions. Depressed people often suffer from these conditions in stronger and more profound ways. As a method of getting out of these more severe conditions, will power is less successful, but people with depression and apathy are sometimes able to get themselves moving for short periods. Emptiness, deadness, the feeling that there is nothing inside, and the feeling that one is a robot are conditions that are very different from apathy. The experience of apathy, and the experience of the absence of feeling, are two different things. The absence of emotion had by the severely depressed is not experientially similar to the experiences of ordinary life. Being asked to stop being apathetic is like being asked to lift a very heavy weight. Even if you cannot do it, you can at least try and experience a feeling of struggle and resistance. Asking the profoundly depersonalized to feel their feelings is like asking them to make two and two equal three. I had this condition a lot during the first year of my depression. Though it is often briefly mentioned in the literature, I have never seen it accurately described. In my case it was not correlated with equally profound senses of hopelessness and apathy; I had more of those later on. People with extreme torpor and apathy cannot get much done; depressed people with no awareness of emotion can often adequately walk through the routines of life. Beck's position is a theoretical analogue to a common prejudice of counselors: instead of accepting as sincere and experientially accurate the report, "On the inside I experience no emotion, only cognition," the position claims that the victim is misreporting or misinterpreting emotions he does have. The confusion of depersonalization with apathy occurs in theory, not in the cognitive distortions of the depressed.

The depressed often report a profound sense of fatigue. To observers, and to the depressed themselves, it frequently seems that this fatigue, as well as apathy and inertia, coexists with an intense but below the surface struggle. Psychoanalysis argues that this is due to a number of unconscious psychic factors, including the effort to repress anger and guilt, and to a battle between the life instinct and the death instinct. The aggregate pain theory in this respect follows the structure of analysis: it believes that the struggle is a matter of intense denial on a host of painful emotions, and a battle between pain and the pre-cognitive desire for life. These struggles, which are not consciously cognitive, produce genuine fatigue. Since cognitive psychology is limited to conscious cognitions, it is unable to provide an adequate explanation for this aspect of depression. Beck claims, "His easy fatigability results from his continuous expectations of negative outcomes from whatever he undertakes." (1977, p. 130) The expectation of negative outcomes may explain why someone might easily lose interest in continuing or completing a task, but easily losing interest and easily getting tired are different things, and chronic suffering from an omnipresent sense of exhaustion is a third thing. Loss of interest may be partly caused by negative cognitions, but fatigue is caused by hard labor. Very sick people may experience exhaustion even though they are inactive; the body — "with a mind of its own" — is fighting the illness. Inactivity and fatigue are not signs that the suicidal have negative cognitions, much less wishes to be inactive; they are signs of a struggle on the side of life. Whether it is waged by a person who is suicidal or non-suicidal, whether it is cognitively experienced or not, a sustained battle to stay alive will wear the person down and cause fatigue.

It is similarly hard to see how the "stimulus — cognition — emotion" approach can explain the "shock" phenomena of ordinary life. In my own reaction to learning of the death of someone I know, it is often a day or two before the information sinks in. The interval between believing the person is alive and having a fuller emotional reaction to the death is similar (but not identical) to my emotional condition prior to the death. How is a theory that believes that our emotions are purely determined by conscious cognitions to explain the roles of shock and denial in our emotional responses? Human experience, ordinary and extraordinary, contains a variety of "non-feeling" conditions. Involuntarism regards these as pre-cognitive — and involuntary — coping mechanisms. Not feeling is better than being overwhelmed by horrible feelings. Beck is committed to the view that all reactions are cognitively determined, and he describes the causal force of the cognitions related to apathy in a way that is eerily similar to Freud's description (quoted in Chapter 2) of the death instinct: " ... he is drawn toward a state of inactivity. He even seeks to withdraw from life completely via suicide." and " ... the patient's powerful desire to seek a passive state ... "(1977, pp. 121 & 123) Beck regards deadness and apathy as evidence of negative desire. I believe that the evidence is equally good for the view that fatigue, inactivity, numbness, and emotional emptiness result from the struggle to stay alive.

To recognize part of the prejudicial attitude that cognitive psychology has toward the suicidal we need to look at Beck's views on the mechanisms of sadness and depression.

> Freud and many more recent writers have attributed the sadness to a transformation of anger turned inwards. By a kind of "alchemy," retroflexed anger is supposedly converted into depressed feelings. A simpler explanation is that the sadness is the result of the self-instigated lowering of self-esteem. Suppose I inform a student that his performance is inferior and that he accepts the assessment as fair. Even though I communicate my evaluation without anger and may, in fact, express regret or empathy, he is likely to feel sad. The lowering of his self-esteem suffices to make him sad. Similarly, if the student makes a negative evaluation of himself, he feels sad. The depressed patient is like the self-devaluing student; he feels sad because he lowers his sense of worth by negative evaluations. (1977, pp. 115-6.) [3]

This devaluation of self-esteem is *self*-instigated? Even in this example, much less as a general theory, this is a stretch for the concept of self-instigation. Beck believes that cognitions determine emotions. A student with different cognitions — the assessment is not fair, the assessor is not competent — would respond with a different emotion. A student with distorted cognitions — If I'm not on top, I'm a flop — would respond with sadness even if his evaluation was above average but not the best. Each of these reactions Beck regards as self-instigated. This is a sophisticated version of the popular slogan:

> You are not responsible for what happens to you, but you are responsible for how you react to it.

Consider a child who has been repeatedly told that if he is not on top, he is a flop. If the child's scores at school or play are less than others, he will feel miserable. Is this bad feeling self-instigated?

Beck's view on the sources of the cognitive distortions is that:

> These incorrect conceptions originated in defective learning during the person's cognitive development.
>
> His problems are derived from certain distortions of reality based on erroneous premises and misconceptions. These distortions originated in defective learning during his development. The formula for treatment may be stated in simple terms: The therapist helps the patient to identify his warped thinking and to learn more realistic ways to formulate his experiences. (1977, pp. 3 & 20)

Though it may not seem like much, there is a vast difference between characterizing the problem as defective learning, and characterizing it as defective teaching. Defective learning is the inferior brain, as are the deformed superego, the innate biochemical deficiency, the genetic flaw. All of these say the problem is in him, not in us. At the end of his book Beck says

> It is not necessary to get at ultimate causes of his misinterpretation of reality — either in terms of their historical antecedents or present "unconscious" roots. The therapist focuses more on *how* the patient misinterprets reality rather than *why*. (1977, p. 319)

This is the stone wall of denial on the social causes of suicidal pain. A suicidal person is socially exposed to "his" warped thinking from cradle to grave. The distortions allegedly peculiar to the warped thinker are everywhere. The rules and attitudes listed earlier are had by parents, teachers, and peers. It is reasonable to suggest that the propensity to think in these ways is largely derived from the outside world, rather than originating from within the victim. Negative thinking patterns contribute to suicidal pain, but their causes are as least as much social as personal. Some of the distorted ideas include those concerning suicide itself: selfish, manipulative, his problem, lacks will power, etc., etc., etc. If, after decades of faulty teaching, we become suicidal, we will apply these ideas to ourselves and they will make us feel worse. Is this extra pain self-instigated?

An objector to the position that defective teaching causes the cognitive distortions might agree that the distorted rules are prevalent in our society, and then ask why they affect some people rather than others. The propensity to depression and suicide must be in the people who suffer the illness — they must be inherently defective in cognitive developmental capacity. The response is that the rules are noxious in the same way as air pollution. Pollution adversely affects the health of some people more than others, but we do not blame them for auto-immune pollution deficiency. The elderly, children under 13, asthmatics, people with lung and heart disease, and pregnant women are more likely to be harmed by by air pollution, but the additional suffering is not due to a deficiency in them; it is due to external social problems.

The problems that the depressed have with cognitive distortions have a second cause that cognitive psychology does not consider: massive pain. Beck believes that excessive suffering is caused by distorted cognitions, but he ignores the possibility that suffering, distorted or undistorted, can contribute directly to distorted cognitions. When people are in considerable pain, their cognitions are less rational than when they are in less pain. When their suffering is relieved by techniques other than cognitive therapy — by reducing physical or emotional suffering — the distortions subside as well. Cognitive psychologists are correct in claiming that faulty cognitions add to suicidal pain (not only the ones they list, but also those that are part of the mythology of suicide), but these cognitions are not the sole source of suicidal pain. Suicidal pain results from an interactive mixture of social, cognitive, emotional, and physical components. Responses in any of these areas can reduce pain and suicide risk.

Hopelessness is the key concept for the cognitivists' theory of suicide. They have a theory about why people are depressed: distorted thinking. However, some depressed people are suicidal and some are not. Cognitivists believe that the level of hopelessness explains the difference. Cognitivists recognize that this is not sufficient to be a complete theory of suicide; although most suicidal people may be depressed, there doubtlessly are some suicides who do not suffer from depression. An example might be someone with a terminal illness who " ... may have a relatively undistorted negative view of the future."

(1974a, p. 53) Cognitivists believe that the common denominator of all suicidal people, depressed or not depressed, is hopelessness. In the article in *The Journal of the American Medical Association*, Beck writes:

> ... hopelessness was conceptualized in terms of a system
> of cognitive schemata that share the common element
> of negative expectations. (1975, p. 1147)

Cognitivists believe that hopelessness is purely a matter of cognitions, distorted or undistorted, and has nothing to do with physical and emotional suffering. This is a very incomplete account of how people develop hopelessness. It may be true of a few people: they read a pessimistic book and develop a pessimistic frame of mind. Many people, however, can read such a book, or have the distorted thinking patterns listed earlier, and not become pessimistic about the future. For most of the latter group to experience hopelessness, they would have to have the additional impetus of personal suffering. The cognitivists' hypothesis, "believing bad" is a necessary and sufficient condition for "feeling bad," is a formula that oversimplifies human experience. Hopelessness is not simply a cognitive entity; it is an emotional condition as well. It is common for someone with a terminal illness to express, verbally or non-verbally, a sentiment such as:

> Intellectually, I know it's hopeless, but something in me
> keeps trying, keeps hoping.

People with suicidal depression often make statements that express:

> Intellectually, I know things may get better. But I am
> just so beaten down that I feel it's all hopeless.

The first person has a system of negative beliefs, and yet still has hope at a non-cognitive level. Members of the second group have belief systems that are not completely negative, yet they are full of despair. Hopelessness has both cognitive and emotional elements; they are distinct and sometimes at odds with each other. We are frequently aware of this in ordinary life when we sense a dissonance between our emotional expectations and our cognitive expectations.[4]

It might be argued that we should still give hopelessness a central role in the causation of suicide. Someone might accept the above objection to cognitivism, and suggest that hopelessness — cognitive and emotional, distorted or undistorted — is the common denominator in suicide, and hence its cause. The aggregate pain view agrees that feelings and beliefs of hopelessness are common among the suicidal, but this is still not enough to explain suicide. If you spend time with the suicidal, you will spend time with people who suffer profoundly from both emotional and cognitive hopelessness. Yet many still do not attempt suicide. The main reason they do not attempt is that the life instinct is still in them. All living things are born with it. It is perhaps the most basic aspect of our natures. We share it with creatures that have little or no cognitive or emotional development. These creatures do not stay alive because of cognitions or emotions, they stay alive because the desire for life stems from factors that are developmentally prior to beliefs and feelings. Even when hope is gone, this primitive desire keeps people alive. And even when overwhelming pain causes suicide, there is no reason to suppose it is still not there until the moment of physical death. We do not have sufficient reason to deny that the desire for life is not still present the moment the trigger is pulled or the leap is made. Many attempters express the desire to live immediately after the attempt is initiated. This happens even in situations where the means are highly lethal.

One of Beck's descriptions of depression concludes "Finally, the desire to live is switched off and replaced by the wish to die." (1977, p. 104) This is a natural position to hold if you have a cognitively oriented view of human nature. People stay alive because they have pro-life cognitions; suicide occurs when they have anti-life cognitions. If you believe emotions are determined by cognitions, then you need not consider the possibility that emotions and cognitions can be discordant in life-threatening situations. And you can pretend that millions of years of biological programming have no effect on the causation of suicide. Our genes, however, are non-cognitively and non-emotionally programmed to keep us alive. This is why suicide does not happen to the overwhelming majority of people who have the cognitions and emotions of hopelessness. In their most basic natures, these people do not wish to die, they want to stay alive. It is a mistake to characterize the cognitions and emotions of despair as negative or as wishes for death. These thoughts and feelings are involuntary responses to massive pain, and they are desperate measures on the side of life, not death.

The feeling of powerlessness — "Nothing I can do will improve my situation," — is an important part of the suicidal condition. In this respect cognitivism contains a special case of theory on suicide being out of joint with practice. The cognitivists' therapeutic techniques for depression deal extensively with powerlessness, but the concept is unmentioned in their theory. One reason for this neglect is that the theory of cognitivism includes the concepts of volition and intention that are part of our culture's general denial on our powerlessness over suicidal pain. A more specific reason is that, from a purely conceptual standpoint, powerlessness seems to be simply a part of hopelessness: "Nothing can improve my situation," seems to include or entail "Nothing I can do can improve my situation." If our cognitions follow this logical relationship, then our cognitions related to powerlessness are simply a part of our cognitions related to hopelessness. Then, *if* the cognitivist hypothesis that cognitions determine emotions is true, the feelings of powerlessness should be part of the feelings of hopelessness. Emotions, however, have a logic of their own. The cluster of feelings involved in "Things will never get better," is simply different than the cluster of feelings involved in "I'm no longer able to do anything to make things better." Hopelessness is bleak, cold, and tired; powerlessness involves frustration, bitterness, and disconsolation. They are different emotions, just as anger and envy are different emotions, and they make independent contributions to the aggregate of suicidal pain. (That different emotions can give rise to similar cognitions is a contradiction only if one accepts the cognitivist principle that cognitions determine emotions, or its opposite. If emotions and cognitions are causally independent, then there is no reason to suppose that relationships that hold between cognitions must also hold between the corresponding emotions.) Suicidal hopelessness says that the present is miserable, and the future will contain nothing but more misery. As bad as this is, there is at least something in it that reaches out to the future. Suicidal powerlessness more intensely involves the present: "I've lost my ability to cope with life." On the aggregate pain model, it is not difficult to understand the importance of powerlessness. Suicide is largely self-prevented by the utilization (consciously or unconsciously) of available pain-coping resources. (A sense of hope may be one of these resources.) To feel — and, to a lesser extent, to believe —

that one is losing one's ability to resist pain that threatens to overwhelm is a terrifying experience. Negative expectations about the future may make someone miserable, but an escalating sense of personal powerlessness says, "I'm in trouble now." The cognitivists' research program emphasizes that hopelessness is a predictor for suicide attempts. It would be interesting to see the results of similar studies on powerlessness.

Attention to the feeling of powerlessness can give us an improved understanding for one of the phenomena associated with suicide: the alleged planning for the event. Hoarding pills, as Mr. G. did, is regarded by the volitionists as evidence for the intention to die. On the aggregate pain view, this type of activity is something that the suicidal person does to cope with current feelings of powerlessness. At an unconscious level, it is action on the side of life, not death. In Mr. G.'s case the activity may have delayed the suicide attempt. In a case with which I am acquainted, a similar activity helped to prevent the attempt from occurring. This middle-aged man became acutely suicidal when, within a short period of time, he twice tested positive for the presence of the HIV antibody, he developed symptoms of the early onset of AIDS, and he became too weak to continue with a physically demanding job. It has often been noted in passing that suicide seems to happen to people for whom control over their lives is an important concern, and this man's personality was of this type. His situation included a number of unpromising factors in addition to ill-health, financial problems, and lack of employment. He told several people that he planned to commit suicide within a few weeks by self-poisoning. At this point he went shopping for his own funeral, and eventually made arrangements with a firm that agreed to provide the services he wanted at what he felt was a reasonable price. The purchase of the funeral helped him cope with his feelings of powerlessness, and, like the cries for help, helped him survive his siege of suicidal pain.

SECTION FOUR

CONTAGION

Contagion is a part of the problem of suicide that commands considerable public attention. The Centers for Disease Control recently supported a research project on the epidemiology of suicide.[5] The study applied sophisticated mathematical techniques on United States mortality data from 1978 to 1984 to assess suicide clustering: the extent to which a greater than average number of suicides occurred closely together in a given geographic region during a given time period. Clustering and contagion are different concepts. Contagion means, at least, that a subsequent suicide was causally influenced by a prior suicide. Clustered suicides may have been caused by contagion; or there may have been a greater than average number of individual suicides for individual and unconnected reasons; or there may have been a greater than average number of suicides for a common reason — for example, an economic downturn in the community — that was not the event of a prior suicide. And not all cases in which one suicide influences another may be clustered. A suicide in New York may have some role in another suicide twenty years later in Los Angeles. Suicide contagion, in the popular imagination and in the CDC study, is a short-term phenomenon, but on the epidemiological model, at least, there are no a priori grounds for this temporal limitation.

While clustering may be given a definition that stipulates regions of geography and periods of time, contagion in suicide is a very obscure concept. The development of adequate criteria for contagion is not likely to be achieved easily. "The suicide of A had a causal role in the suicide of B" is clearly inadequate. The death of A may have had financial repercussions that facilitated the death of B, even if B had no knowledge of the death of A. Gould's description of contagion is designed to avoid this problem:

> Suicide "contagion" is the process by which one suicide facilitates the occurrence of a second suicide. Contagion assumes either direct or indirect awareness of the prior suicide. Various suicide contagion pathways may exist: direct contact or friendship with a victim, word-of-mouth knowledge, and indirect transmission through the media. (1989, p. 17)

These criteria still fall short, as the following counterexample indicates. Let suicide A be the highly publicized death of Donald Manes, the Queens Borough President, and assume that suicide B is the subsequent death of some other resident of Queens. Hypothetically, assume that Manes had opposed certain zoning changes that were put in place by succeeding political forces, and that B had read of Manes' suicide but paid no special attention to it. The zoning changes eventually lead to events that threaten B with eviction from his apartment and imminent homelessness, and this crisis precipitates B's suicide. This satisfies Gould's criteria, but is not what we would regard as a case of suicide by contagion. Contagion in suicide requires more than causal role plus awareness, but what that more might be is very unclear. It is also not clear that we should uncritically assume that awareness is even a necessary condition. (This assumption is also made in Centers for Disease Control, 1988, p. 10: " ... the vehicle for such contagion is information, ... ") Consider a situation in which a suicide is kept secret, the suicide and its consequences affect the behavior of the secret bearers, and this altered behavior is a factor in the suicide of someone from whom the secret was kept. If we are to use the epidemiological model to help understand suicide, then we must recognize that there is no a priori basis in this model that requires us to include awareness as a mode or partial mode of transmission. (Something analogous to this has become an accepted part of the family therapy approach to the disease of alcoholism. While in treatment an alcoholic may first learn that a grandparent he never knew was also an alcoholic. Family therapists believe that in many such cases that unarticulated rules concerning denial and shame are transmitted from one generation to the next, and the alcoholism of the grandson can be causally influenced by the alcoholism of the grandparent.)

I do not have a criterion to distinguish cases in which causal influence is akin to contagion, and situations, such as the Donald Manes example, where it is not. From a practical standpoint, this is unnecessary, as long as we articulate and reject the way that prejudice and mythology distort and exaggerate our view of the role of contagion in suicide, recognize that there are ways to account for the phenomenon of contagion that do not use prejudicial concepts, and recognize that in practical work we should continue to apply the same basic principle: reduce pain and increase resources.

In the popular imagination, a major part of the problem of suicide are sequences of "copycat" suicides that are clustered together and are somehow linked. The CDC study looked for clusters of any sort — linked or unlinked — and found no evidence of clustered suicides among adults. Gould reports that " ... cluster suicides account for approximately 1-5% of all teenage suicides." (1989, p. 25) The 1986 *Statistical Abstract* reported 2,146 suicides in the 10 to 19 age group; 3 percent of this figure is 64. It is not clear from the preliminary reports of this study if the *initial* suicide in the cluster — one that presumably is not causally influenced by a prior suicide — is included in the 1-5% figure. A cluster of four consecutive suicides includes at most three that are causally linked to a prior suicide. In either case, clustered suicides, in which there may be a causal link to a prior suicide, account for approximately two-tenths of 1 percent of the 31,000 suicides that occur each year.

A number of studies have investigated the effect that either prominent news media coverage of suicide or television dramas of fictional suicides have had on the suicide rate. In both areas there is disagreement in research findings: some studies indicate a slight rise in suicide; others indicate no change. Some researchers, including Gould, join the general public in believing that contagion is a significant factor in suicide. However, the CDC and media effect studies have nothing in them that indicate that these forms of clustering — let alone contagion — account for more than a tiny percentage of the 31,000 annual suicides.[6]

Most people who work in suicide believe that in some sense contagion can be a factor, though their actual reasons for believing so have little to do with statistical surveys. The real evidence is anecdotal:

acquaintance with an infrequent case in which the factor just seems to be present. I have listened to more than a hundred survivors discuss the suicide of a relative and *one* case involved an apparent contagion factor. This was a young woman who had recently suffered several emotional and physical disappointments, and who shot herself a half hour after watching an afterschool movie about suicide.

Over the last decade there has been substantial media attention to two clusters of five or six suicides each in Westchester, New York, and Plano, Texas, and the simultaneous multiple suicide of four people in Bergenfield, New Jersey. The actual incidence of suicide by contagion, however, is much less than what the public believes it to be. Why does this disproportionate interest exist, when so many other factors are present in so many more suicides? We need to consider what the contagion view says about the causation of suicide: one particular suicide is caused by a previous suicide. If suicide is caused by suicide, then the non-suicidal are not to be blamed. Contagion, like the rest of the mythology of suicide, helps us practice denial on social complicity in the causation of suicide. It replaces blame the victim with blame a previous victim. The emphasis on contagion in suicide says that the suicidal are contagious creatures, dangerous to others. This belief is a license for defensiveness and aversion. The suicidal are themselves aware of the social fear of contagion; this adds to their pain and further estranges them from the non-suicidal. If a condition is contagious, then those close to the victim are themselves likely to be contaminated. A sense of contamination is often had by survivors, and the contagion theory is a large part of the reason why the survivors of a suicide victim suffer from isolation and stigma. Life in the age of a genuine epidemic makes clear a third factor for the interest in contagion: we are afraid that the condition will spread to ourselves. Talk about the transmissibility of suicidal feelings among teenagers (i.e., the mechanism is teen-to-teen, not teen-to-adult or adult-to-teen) is a way to discharge fear that the feelings are transmissible to or by ourselves. The self-centered aspect of the contagion theory of suicide is an important part of the taboo and stigma that surround the entire subject of suicide. The average person wants to avoid all contact — mental, emotional, and physical — with the suicidal. From a personal interest standpoint, given what we know about evolution, it is hardly surprising that humans should react strongly to suggestions of contagion. It *is* reasonable for the non-suicidal to fear dying by suicide, and it is reasonable for them to hold beliefs and take actions that help them cope with this fear. But when the fear is exaggerated, unacknowledged, and part of a network of false and misleading beliefs, it becomes expressed in forces that lead to prejudice, injustice and increased suffering for undeserving victims. The fear is exaggerated. Nearly all of us, if we read newspapers or watch television, are exposed to suicide for most of our lives. Yet 98 percent of us do not become suicides, and contagion is a discernible factor in only a tiny percentage of the remaining 2 percent. The fear that "It might be contagious to me," is part of the cause of "Don't talk about it," "The good man sucks it up," and aversion to the suicidal and their survivors. A better way to cope with our fear of our own suicide is to develop and implement rational policies that will reduce completed suicide, and reduce the suffering of attempters, considerers, and survivors of suicide victims.

Sequential suicides in which there seem to be causal links may be used as the basis for objections to the involuntarist and aggregate pain positions. These positions are committed to the view that causal links between suicides must be explained purely in terms of increased pain and decreased pain-coping resources. The aggregate pain explanation, which is plausible for suicide among surviving relatives, seems less convincing when applied to situations where the victims were not personally acquainted. These are situations where a second suicide is apparently precipitated by the suicide of a celebrity, fictional character, or fellow resident of a community. These subsequent suicides are sometimes said to be imitative, either in the mere fact of being suicides, or because of common traits, such as similarity of means. Imitation ordinarily implies volition and the intent to copy or mimic. Writers on contagion in suicide freely use the mentalist terminology discussed in Chapter 2, sometimes suggesting that a desire for notoriety is the motive for the suicide. Two replies can be made to this objection. The first is that the initial suicide may have caused added pain for the subsequent victims, even though the individuals may have been unacquainted. A suicide may cause people who are already suicidal to have increased feelings that it is hopeless to expect recovery from suicidal pain, or that the world is an uncaring place. The first suicide may cause non-suicidal acquaintances of the second victim to ventilate abusive prejudice about the subject of suicide. Highly publicized suicides come to the attention of many suicidal people, and the increase in pain may precipitate an attempt in people whose pain and coping resources are precariously balanced. The second reply is to question whether we need the concepts of intention, motive and purpose to explain the causal connection between sequential suicides. Simple principles of association may be adequate to account for the phenomena that are referred to as imitative. New York City police officers strongly associate the concept of suicide with the expression "eat the gun." Residents of the San Francisco area strongly associate suicide with the event of jumping from the Golden Gate Bridge. People do not choose to associate these concepts; the association is derived from their environment. If prior experiences with suicide have caused a victim to strongly associate suicide with a certain means, and that means is involved in his death, then it is likely that there is a causal connection. But this connection is not imitation, at least not in the sense of volition, intention, and motive. The victim is in enough pain to have thoughts of suicide, and simply by association he also has thoughts of a particular means or location. Involuntarism believes that the means of suicide is a function of fear and accessibility. Accessibility has both physical and psychological components. Psychological accessibility includes such things as knowing the physical location of the means, knowing how to use the means, and the strength of association of suicide with that particular means. If someone vividly associates suicide with a certain means, and the suicide is by that means, then the causal connection can be explained without the more complex and ultimately prejudicial concepts of imitation, motive, and purpose.

Imitation is a concept that disguises social complicity in suicide. It explains the death of B by saying that B, on his own initiative, imitated the suicide of A. But social forces often determine what particular concepts an individual associates with suicide, and these can determine the extent to which particular means may be psychologically accessible. For the purposes of suicide prevention, we should note a consequence of the associationist explanation: the weak or non-existent association of suicide with a particular means is a resource that helps one endure suicidal pain without dying.

Simultaneous suicides pose further objections to the involuntarist thesis. The simultaneous suicides of four people by carbon monoxide poisoning in a parked car does not seem to be the same kind of event as the simultaneous fatal heart attacks of four strangers while riding in the same elevator. The latter event would be an extraordinarily rare coincidence. The former event, also rare, appears to be coordinated, and coordination seems to require volition and intention. Suicide is a rare event. It occurs to one person in fifty and only once during that person's life span. Though rare, simultaneous suicides of people who know and are with each other happen with greater frequency than chance would predict. How could this be, unless the parties choose to be suicides? The first point to note, as some writers have, is that some cases of apparent simultaneous suicide involve elements of homicide. Only one of these deaths is a suicide, and if the individual suicide is involuntary, both deaths are involuntary. The second point is that some apparently simultaneous suicides are actually sequential. In pairs of potential victims, the first suicide causally affects the second person. Sometimes he also becomes a suicide, and sometimes he finds "he cannot go through with it." Explanations of these events need not include volition and intention any more than an account of an individual suicide. Next we should recognize that while double suicide is an extremely rare event, anecdotal evidence suggests that one of its more common forms is that of an elderly couple where at least one person has a disabling or terminal illness. Is it implausible to suggest that for both people pain has simultaneously exceeded coping resources? The individual causal histories of pain and resource deficiencies in multiple suicides usually have many common elements. The parties are in pain and at a loss for ways to cope with their pain. The simultaneity of their suicides may be due to two types of factors that do not involve volition. The first is that interactive forces among the individuals may further increase pain and decrease resources. A communicates feelings of hopelessness and powerlessness to B, B's despair worsens, and B's reaction in turn causes A to feel yet worse. If C becomes convinced he will become a suicide, and communicates this to D, D may become so deeply affected that he also becomes convinced he will become a suicide. The second factor is that people sometimes do things in groups that they would not do as individuals. In other situations, group participation causes a reduction in fear among group members, and this reduction in fear is a non-voluntary consequence of group membership. If behavior in groups is *less* volitional than individual behavior, then the existence of simultaneous suicides is not necessarily evidence against the involuntarist position.

NOTES

CHAPTER ONE

1. (*p.* 2) This appears to be the position of Shneidman and Maltsberger. More than other theorists, these two writers believe that suicidal events are provoked by extreme pain, but both believe that suicide does not happen unless, in addition, the victim performs certain voluntary and cognitive operations. Shneidman states, " ... the common stimulus of suicide is unendurable psychological pain,". (1985, p. 215) Shneidman, however, is not using "unendurable" in its literal sense: he states, "In general, we can assert that an unbearable pain is a great pain about which the individual makes a qualitative judgment: This far and no farther." (p. 125, see also p. 134) Shneidman uses "unendurable" and "unbearable" in hyperbolic senses, as in, to use an example from ordinary life, "Her behavior at the party was simply unbearable." Pains that are literally unbearable do not get borne no matter what mental operations one performs. For Shneidman, the sequence of events leading to suicide is great pain, followed by a judgment of "No farther," followed by (see Chapter 2) the mental operations of intending and willing.

Maltsberger also uses the mental and moral framework and is even closer to the line between voluntarism and involuntarism.

> The subjective experience of despair has two parts. First, the patient finds himself in an intolerable affective state, flooded with emotional pain so intense and unrelenting that it can no longer be endured. Second, the patient recognizes his condition, and gives up on himself. This recognition is not merely a cognitive surrender, even though most hopeless patients probably have thought about their circumstances and reach conscious, cognitive conclusions to give up. A more important aspect of the recognition I am describing is an unconscious precognitive operation in which the self is abandoned as being unworthy of further concern. First of all, let me address three affect states that may rapidly become unendurable; often they force the patient to commit suicide. These are *aloneness, self-contempt,* and *murderous rage.* (1986, p. 2.)

Maltsberger's position on despair is confusing. It seems to have three parts, not two. The first is intolerable pain. Since additional conditions must be met for suicide to occur, he seems to be using "intolerable" in Shneidman's hyperbolic sense. The second condition uses the language of cognition and volition: "the patient recognizes his condition and gives up on himself." The third condition is the obscurely described unconscious precognitive operation. (The obscurity is how an operation can be both *precognitive* and an act of *recognition*.) This seems to be involuntary, but we are not told if it happens in all cases, most, or some. Can we unconsciously (or preconsciously?) give up and consciously not give up? Or vice versa? Maltsberger follows Shneidman in using strong language — "force" — to describe the pain, and in using clearly volitional terminology elsewhere: "Yet giving up on oneself at last can be a relief. The patient who decides to abandon his wretched life may feel his spirits lift, especially if he trusts something better is waiting for him on the other side of the grave." (p. 85, see also p. 123) Since Maltsberger repeatedly characterizes the suicide as someone who gives up on himself and uses the concept of intention (pp. 62, 63, 86) we must assume that he joins with the other theorists in regarding pain as a necessary but not sufficient condition for suicide.

2. (*p. 4*) Only one writer mentions the possibility of impaired volition, "In all psychiatric disorders, of course, there can be impairment of perception, volition, and cognition." (Litman, 1987, p. 89) However, Litman's discussion concludes, "In summary, experience indicates that a person must have a certain minimal degree of intact volition and thinking ability, and understanding of cause and effect, in order to produce fatal self-inflicted injuries." (P. 90. see also Litman, 1984, p. 94)

CHAPTER TWO

1. (*p. 22*) "Permanent solution to temporary problems," is a phrase worth avoiding in suicide prevention work. Some problems, in part at least, are permanent. This slogan does nothing to deter suicide in such cases. While the slogan may be helpful to people who are able to conceptualize their problems as temporary, many suicidal people — rightly or wrongly — are unable to view their problems as anything but permanent. "Permanent solution to temporary problems," belittles; as with other forms of belittlement, this expression is something that the non-suicidal use to protect their own emotional equilibrium. Most uses of the phrase are just less crude ways of saying, "stupid, foolish."

2. (*p. 23*) The one maneuver that *sometimes* brings a change in thinking is the gross-out technique: "Does that method always work? Doesn't it sometimes just leave the person paralyzed?" But increasing the level of fear someone has about a particular means is not the same as changing his thinking about the rationality of suicide.

3. (*p. 29*) In a paper on how therapists can cope with their own anger toward their suicidal patients, (Maltsberger and Buie, 1980, p. 632) the authors say that for the therapist, "The best protection from antitherapeutic acting out is the ability to keep such impulses in consciousness. Full protection, however, requires that the therapist also gain comfort with his countertransference hate through the process of acknowledging it, bearing it, and putting it into perspective."

4. (*p. 35*) A 1987 nationwide survey of more than 11,000 eighth- and tenth-grade students found that

> Twenty-five percent of the boys and 42% of the girls reported they had, at some time during their lives, seriously considered committing suicide. Eighteen percent of the girls and 11% of the boys reported they had actually tried to injure themselves in a way that might have resulted in their death. (Centers for Disease Control, 1989, p. 2025)

If one-third of us have had suicidal thoughts by age 16, it is not unreasonable to assume that one-half of us have these thoughts at some time during the entirety of our lives.

5. (*p. 36*) Hillman, unlike many of his followers, consistently applies his views on the virtues of brinkmanship to social issues:

> The point is: *the more immanent the death experience, the more possibility for transformation.* The world is closer to a collective suicide, yes; that this suicide must actually occur, no. What must occur if the actual suicide does not come is a transformation in the collective psyche. The Bomb may thus be God's dark hand which He has shown before to Noah and the peoples of the Cities of the Plain, urging not death, but a radical transformation in our souls. (p.70)

The arms race is a good thing: an opportunity for radical transformation, self-knowledge, and the discovery of collective individuality. On this latter point Hillman is correct. A species that relishes the plutonium lining of the cloud of nuclear holocaust is decidedly individual.

6. (*p. 38*) As Shneidman does in his explication of his definition of suicide, " ... we can be certain that such human disorders as malaria, syphilis, and tuberculosis are not accurate paradigms of suicide. In this sense suicide is more akin to delinquency or prostitution or craziness." (1985, p. 207)

CHAPTER FOUR

1. (*p. 61*) Fears of involuntary detention and institutionalization involve much more than the fear of loss of liberty. In New York City adults and children who express thoughts of suicide are liable to be handcuffed by police officers and taken to city hospitals. This may happen in situations where the measures are plainly not needed, and the authorities are following self-protective policies. A number of counselors have told me about situations in which children were taken out of school in handcuffs by uniformed officers in front of other children. The suicidal child nearly always changes schools or becomes a dropout; the other children are effectively deterred from seeking help for themselves or a classmate. City hospitals often have occupancy rates of greater than 100 percent. This means that the hospitals have admitted more patients than they have beds. The procedure for many adult psychiatric patients in this situation is to handcuff them to wheelchairs and have them sit for several days in the emergency room until a bed is available, or until they persuade the physicians that they are no longer at risk of suicide and may be safely discharged. During the days (up to a week) that patients remain without a bed in the emergency room, they are often refused permission to make a phone call, and they may receive such necessities as food, clothing, and bathing opportunities on a very irregular basis. Personal security in city hospitals is poor; patients often become crime victims. Adult suicide attempters who are taken to hospitals are not always given an opportunity to secure their homes. After release from the institution, they find out that their apartments have been burglarized.

CHAPTER SIX

1. (*p. 87*) Freud speaks of the "... initial envy with which the elder child receives the younger one." (1960, p. 65-6) This is not the only type of reduction that might be suggested. Someone with a background in biology might suggest that all forms of envy are reducible not to envy of being loved by one's parents, but to envy of reproductive fitness: we envy

people things that we lack and that we believe will give them an advantage in furthering the survival of their genes. This reduction is not committed to the additional step required by psychoanalysis: reducing envy to anger. Many forms of envy, such as envy of health, may be more plausibly and directly reduced to envy of reproductive fitness than to envy of parental love in early childhood. Reductionist analyses often yield insights; sociobiology and psychoanalysis are certainly capable of providing their share. But the reduction comes at a price, it causes us to miss insights that can be derived from analyses that move in the opposite direction. Instead of reducing the many to the one, it may be more helpful for the purposes of recovery to decompose the one to the many. Envy of health is envy of freedom from pain, envy of normal and restful sleep, envy of freedom from anxiety, envy of normal functioning at work, school, and play, envy of being able to go outdoors, envy of unimpaired emotional and cognitive capacities. Envy of health has constituents, and its constituents have constituents.

2. (p. 90) An excellent book on shame and family therapy is *Facing Shame: Families in Recovery*, by Merle A. Fossum and Marilyn J. Mason. The authors do not discuss depression and suicide, but their definition of shame captures some of the pain:

> Shame is an inner sense of being completely diminished or insufficient as a person. It is the self judging the self. A moment of shame may be humiliation so painful or an indignity so profound that one feels one has been robbed of her or his dignity; or exposed as basically inadequate, bad, or worthy of rejection. A pervasive sense of shame is the ongoing premise that one is fundamentally bad, inadequate, defective, unworthy, or not fully valid as a human being. (p.5)

3. (p. 108) Hendin (1964, p. 14) and other psychoanalysts follow Rado in adding guilt to anger as a cause of depression. Hendin, using intentional language, writes: "Just as retroflexed anger can at times be the motivating force in suicidal patients, so can suicide be an act of expiation." Guilt is of course a common component of suicidal pain, but on the aggregate pain theory it is a mistake to regard it, or anger, or both together, as *the* cause of suicide.

CHAPTER SEVEN

1. (p. 115) The most recent North American study of the incidence of attempts and suicidal ideation in the general population found that 10

percent of 679 Calgary adults self-reported suicide attempts of low or greater lethality and that more than 30 percent had had periods of suicidal thoughts. (Ramsey and Bagley, 1985) The authors cite earlier studies that found lower rates. In studies that ask, "Have you ever thought about or attempted suicide?" it is something of a curiosity that populations of young people (see Centers For Disease Control, 1989) often self-report *higher* rates than are self-reported by populations of older people.

2. (*p. 141*) The review by Lazarus and Folkman (1984) surveys a vast academic literature on stress and coping. Unfortunately, this area of inquiry has little material on the problem of coping with suicidal pain, or even on the broader problem of coping with social oppression. A basic difficulty with this field is that it employs conceptions of coping that exclude "ride it out," and other coping strategies of the suicidal. Lazarus and Folkman discuss three conceptions of coping:

> The concept of coping is found in two very different theoretical/research literatures, one derived from the tradition of animal experimentation, the other from psychoanalytic ego psychology. ... Within the animal model, coping is frequently defined as acts that control aversive environmental conditions, thereby lowering the psychophysiological disturbance. ... In the psychoanalytic ego psychology model, coping is defined as realistic and flexible thoughts and acts that solve problems and thereby reduce stress. (pp. 117-8)

They argue that these two definitions make coping " ... tantamount to solving problems by acting effectively to obviate them," (p. 138) and, consequently, are too restrictive: some problems in life, such as natural disasters and aging, cannot be solved, but are things with which people can cope. Lazarus and Folkman offer a broader definition:

> We define coping as constantly changing cognitive and behavioral efforts to manage specific external and/or internal demands that are appraised as taxing or exceeding the resources of the person. (p. 141)

Their definition, however, is also excessively restrictive. The "constantly changing" and "cognitive and behavioral efforts" clauses exclude "resist change," "do nothing," "make no effort," "continue to avoid people," and even "The meek shall inherit the earth," as forms of coping. The acutely suicidal and the profoundly depressed often strike counselors as being extremely rigid and inflexible. It is natural that they should be this way. They believe — consciously or unconsciously, correctly or incorrectly — that any change will bring them more pain. And, to be suicidal is to be in a situation where more pain may cause death. In this horrible situation, "Do nothing. Try to ride it out," must be regarded as a form of coping. For the suicidal, coping is *anything* that is done to try to manage pain. Acute suicidal pain can be chaotic and full of turmoil; people in this situation are liable to grasp at anything that gives them a sense of stability. It is extremely unfair for their counselors to use "rigid" and "inflexible" as derogatory expressions. Many suicidal people, like many of the elderly, who also employ conservative and passive coping strategies, see change as making things worse, and consequently they resist change. Though neglected by academic theory, conservative, change-resisting strategies are very basic parts of human nature. In the elderly, the suicidal — and, perhaps, in all of us — they may be used in efforts to preserve conceptions of personal identity. In extreme situations, if "Put all your effort into resisting change," does not succeed, some people revert to "Make no effort at all."

Lazarus and Folkman write:

> It is difficult to see how the unfolding nature of most stressful encounters, and the concomitant changes in coping, could be adequately described by a *static* measure of a general trait or personality disposition. ... The dynamics and change that characterize coping as a process are not random; they are a function of continuous appraisals and reappraisals of the shifting person-environment relationship. Shifts may be the result of coping efforts directed at changing the environment, or coping directed inward that changes the meaning of the event or increases understanding. (p. 142)

Riding it out, however, *is* a coping strategy. It does not try to change the environment, or change the meaning of the event or situation, or increase understanding. It is a response to stress, but it is not an effort that is directed at change. "Tell no one about how bad it is," or "Don't talk about it. You'll give people ideas," are strategies to cope with fear; they need not undergo change over time, or evolve in a way that could be characterized as a process.

CHAPTER NINE

1. (*p. 171*) This was prepared by a member of Compassionate Friends, a support group for parents who have lost a child by any means. Two

privately published books that have helped a great many survivors of a suicide victim are Wrobleski, 1984, and Bolton, 1983. Dunne, 1987, contains four chapters that are accounts by survivors. The literature by and for survivors is in its embryonic stage, and the many gaps include caregivers other than mental health professionals, friends, and heterosexual and homosexual lovers. Filling these gaps would be a contribution toward breaking down the silence and isolation that exist after a suicide.

2. (*p. 177*) The rejection theory is sometimes extended beyond the immediate survivors: the suicide saw what the world had to offer and found it wanting. Behind this position are literary and philosophical views about the meaninglessness of life. It is sometimes also claimed that some or all suicides reject themselves. Evidence for this is the self-reviling verbal behavior of many suicidal people. The arguments against the view that suicide is a rejection of the immediate survivors can be adapted to these positions. Prior to the onset of the pain that led to their deaths, most suicides do not have marked hatred for themselves or for the world in general. Pain can involuntarily cause anger at the self or the world in the same way it can cause anger toward loved ones.

3. (*p. 178*) Lukas 1988, pp. 31, 56, & 94. See also Lindemann, 1972, p. 68: "To be bereft by self-imposed death is to be rejected." The view that the suicide is a family hater is standard in psychoanalysis. For a technical discussion of "the hate aspects of suicide", see Maltsberger and Buie, 1980, p. 62. The authors support their views by reference to an early paper of Menninger's:

> Menninger (1933) has pointed out that to destroy something dear to another person is an effective means of attack, and that the greatest hurt a mother can endure is to see her child tortured or killed. He points out that when a child, piqued at some reproach or denial, takes his own life, he takes it also from his parents. 'He robs them of their dearest possession knowing that no other injury could possibly be so painful to them.'

CHAPTER TEN

1. (*p. 210*) It might be argued that this provides a counterexample to the claims that suicide is involuntary, or that all suicidal behavior, short of highly lethal attempts, is a cry for help. In the first place, we need to note that in some of these rare cases, the person is not suicidal,

but simply an extortionist. He privately does not expect to die, regardless of the outcome of his situation. The behavior of this non-suicidal person is not a basis for negative attitudes toward the suicidal. The meaning of the cry for help presentation is, "If I don't get custody of my children, my pain will be overwhelming and I will die." This is simply a prediction of what its speaker believes will happen, not a statement of intention, and not an attempt at extortion. The suicidal extortionist, whose pain is not approaching intolerable proportions, does express intention: "If I don't get custody of my children, I will take my life with the purpose of causing pain and harm to others." This really is a threat, and, if it happens, is an instance of voluntary suicide. The behavior of volitional suicides, such as extortionists, terrorists, patriots, or religious martyrs, may well be intentional, and not follow the model of the aggregate pain theory.

CHAPTER ELEVEN

1. (p. 279) There are a number of reasons why suicide statistics are inaccurately low. In some cases, such as victim precipitated homicides and highway accidents, suicides are unknowingly certified as other types of death. Examples of a second factor are in Chapter 9: physicians who were family friends knowingly certified the deaths of Miss A's mother and Miss B's father as other than suicide. When the body of a drowning victim is recovered, the authorities may never be able to collect enough evidence to determine if the death was suicide, homicide, or accident. Such deaths are recorded in a separate category: "Deaths from injury undetermined whether accidentally or purposely inflicted." A fourth factor — delays in certification procedure — is less well known. It is a major source of undercounting in New York City. I do not know the extent to which this problem occurs in other communities. Each March the New York City Department of Health Bureau of Vital Statistics compiles its figures for the preceding calendar year. In March of 1987, for example, the Bureau of Vital Statistics totalled all 1986 deaths that had been reported as suicides. This figure, which was 593, was published as the official number of New York City suicides for that year, and was the figure used in the compilation of the total number of suicides for that year in the entire United States. However, because of the length of time necessary to complete laboratory tests, delays in collecting police evidence, and paperwork delays, reports of deaths as suicides for a given calendar year continue to be made after March of the following year. Some 1986 deaths, for example, may not be reported as suicides until 1988 or 1989, or even later. Although it is then too late to make corrections in the published figures, the Bureau

has maintained a "Scientific File" of corrected results since 1983. The Bureau of Vital Statistics kindly provided me with a printout of the corrected (as of July 24, 1990) scientific file.

New York City Deaths Due To Suicide

Year	Published Totals	Scientific File
1983	570	734
1984	585	751
1985	594	790
1986	593	783
1987	502	716

The death certification process for suicide takes longer than it does for other types of death. Since we want health statistics to be timely, this means that published figures for suicide are undercounts for the final number of certified suicides. In 1986, the published figures for the city, and for the United States, were low by at least 190.

CHAPTER TWELVE

1. (p. 301) The notes were written by white Protestant males between the ages of 25 and 59. They were selected from 721 notes left by completed suicides in Los Angeles County during the period 1945-1954. Shneidman and Farberow estimate that 12 percent to 15 percent of the Los Angeles suicides during this period left notes.

2. (p. 308) The definition of suicide proposed in Rosenberg, 1988 ("... death arising from an act inflicted upon oneself with the intent to kill oneself."), is true of only a tiny percentage of all suicides, and should be converted to a disjunction: "death arising from an act inflicted upon oneself with the intent to kill oneself, or, death arising from a self-inflicted injury by someone in overwhelming pain." The disjunction should be regarded as inclusive, rather than exclusive. Theoretically it is not nececessarily the case that all suicides are either voluntary or involuntary, but not both. Death is an event that can be overdetermined; it need not always fall into a single category. It may be impossible for an autopsy to determine whether a heart attack victim died of cardiac arrest or died because he was crushed in an automobile accident. It is possible that both occurred simultaneously. Similarly, a suicide may simultaneously suffer a self-inflicted gunshot

and a gunshot inflicted by someone else. I do not know how we could decide if this is suicide or homicide; it seems to be both. We could further imagine cases in which someone suffers both types of suicide simultaneously. A spy may voluntarily take slow acting poison, and then suffer misfortunes that increase his personal despair to overwhelming proportions. If this caused a second attempt, and death by both means occurred simultaneously, then this suicide would be both voluntary and involuntary.

3. (p. 326) The position of psychoanalysis is that anger, and in some cases and to some extent guilt, is the cause of depression and suicide. By equating depression with cognitively distorted sadness, Beck moves to the opposite extreme and gives anger no significant role at all. The aggregate pain approach regards both these views on anger as one-sided. The principle that one emotion, either cognitively distorted or unconsciously repressed, is the root of depression, is extremely dubious, and itself a cause of lack of progress in the theory and treatment of depression. As was argued in Chapter 6, the superficial theoretical economy provided by this principle cannot help but exact a heavy cost in our efforts to assist suffering individuals.

4. (p. 329) Beck uses "pessimism", a more cognitive concept, as a synonym for hopelessness. ("The Measurement of Pessimism: The Hopelessness Scale", 1974b, and 1977, pp. 116-20.) When Maltsberger refers to Beck's work, and in his own account of the suicidal state, he uses "despair", a less cognitive concept. (1986, pp. 84 & 2)

5. (p. 333) For a discussion and bibliography of issues in contagion, and a report of some the results of this study, which was announced in the news media but is still in the process of publication in academic journals, see Gould, 1989.

6. (p. 335) If there is a contagion element in suicide, it is likely to be a factor in suicide among immediate survivors, which presumably would be a fairly stable part of the normally stable overall suicide rate, and would not be considered by the statistical efforts to study clusters. Increased risk for survivors, however, is due to much more than contagion, even if the contagion effect is stronger because of proximity. Survivors are directly harmed by suicide in many ways that are not factors when someone is affected by a suicide of a celebrity, fictional character, or fellow resident of one's community.

BIBLIOGRAPHY

Alcoholics Anonymous, Alcoholics Anonymous World Services, 1976. (Originally published in 1939.)

Allport, Gordon W., *The Nature of Prejudice*, Addison-Wesley, 1954.

Alvarez, A., *The Savage God*: A Study of Suicide, Random House, 1971.

"An Introduction to Sex and Love Addicts Anonymous", The Augustine Fellowship, P.O. Box 119, Newtown Branch, Boston MA 02258.

Beck, Aaron T., *Cognitive Therapy and the Emotional Disorders*, Meridian, 1977.

Beck, Aaron T., Dean Schuyler, and Ira Herman, "Development of Suicidal Intent Scales", in *The Prediction of Suicide*, edited by A. T. Beck, H. L. P. Resnik, D. J. Lettieri, Charles Press, 1974. (1974a)

Beck, Aaron T., Maria Kovacs, and Arlene Weissman, "Hopelessness and Suicidal Behavior", *Journal of the American Medical Association*, Vol. 234, No. 11, pp. 1146-9, 1975.

Beck, Aaron T., A. Weissman, D. Lester, and others, "The Measurement of Pessimism: The Hopelessness Scale", *Journal of Clinical Consulting Psychologist*, Vol. 42, pp. 861-5, 1974. (1974b)

Bolton, Iris, *My Son ... My Son ... A Guide to Healing After Death, Loss, or Suicide*, 1983, The Bolton Press, 1325 Belmore Way, N.E. Atlanta, GA 30338.

Cain, A. C., and I. Fast, "Children's Disturbed Reactions to Parental Suicide: Distortions of Guilt, Communication, and Identification", in *Survivors of Suicide*, edited by A. C. Cain, Charles C. Thomas, 1972.

Centers for Disease Control, "CDC Recommendations for a Community Plan for the Prevention and Containment of Suicide Clusters", *Morbidity and Mortality Weekly Report: Supplement*, Vol. 37, No. S-6, August 19, 1988.

Centers for Disease Control, "Results from the National Adolescent Student Health Survey", *Journal of the American Medical Association*, Vol. 261, No. 14, pp. 2025, 1989.

City School District of The City of New York, "Suicide Prevention", Regulation of the Chancellor No. A-755, 1986.

Cooke, Gerald, "Training Police Officers to Handle Suicidal Persons", *Journal of Forensic Science*, January, 1979.

Dunne, Edward J., John L. McIntosh, and Karen Dunne-Maxim, (eds.), *Suicide and its Aftermath: Understanding and Counseling the Survivors*, Norton, 1987.

Dunne-Maxim, Karen, Edward J. Dunne, and Marilyn J. Hauser, "When Children are Suicide Survivors", in Dunne, 1987.

Durkheim, Emile, *Suicide*, Macmillan Publishing, 1951.

Farberow, Norman, "Crisis, Disaster, Suicide: Theory and Therapy", in *Essays in Self-Destruction*, edited by E. S. Shneidman, Science House, 1967.

Fossum, Merle A., and Marilyn J. Mason, *Facing Shame: Families in Recovery*, Norton, 1986.

Freud, Sigmund, *Group Psychology and the Analysis of the Ego*, Bantam Books, 1960. (Originally published in 1921.)

Freud, Sigmund, "Mourning and Melancholia", in *A General Selection from the Works of Sigmund Freud*, Doubleday Anchor, 1957. (Originally published in 1917.)

Freud, Sigmund, *An Outline of Psychoanalysis*, Norton, 1949. (Originally published in 1940.)

Freud, Sigmund, "The Psychogenesis of a Case of Homosexuality in a Woman", in *Sexuality and the Psychology of Love*, Collier Books, 1970. (Originally published in 1920.)

Freud, Sigmund, *Totem and Taboo*, Norton, 1950. (Originally published in 1913.)

Goffman, Erving, *Stigma*, Prentice Hall, 1963.

Gould, Madelyn S., Sylvan Wallenstein, and Lucy Davidson, "Suicide Clusters: A Critical Review", *Suicide and Life-Threatening Behavior*, Vol. 19(1), 1989.

Gould, Madelyn S., "Suicide Clusters and Media Exposure", forthcoming in *Suicide Over the Life Cycle*, edited by S. J. Blumenthal and D. J. Kupfer, American Psychiatric Press.

Heller, Agnes, *The Power of Shame*, Routledge & Kegan Paul, 1985.

Hendin, Herbert, *Suicide in America*, Norton, 1982.

Hendin, Herbert, *Suicide and Scandinavia*, Doubleday Anchor Books, 1965.

Hillman, James, *Suicide and the Soul*, Spring Publications, 1964.

Kellerman, Arthur L., and Donald T. Reay, "Protection or Peril? An Analysis of Firearm-Related Deaths in the Home", *The New England Journal of Medicine*, Vol. 314, No. 24, pp. 1557-60, 1986.

Kubler-Ross, Elisabeth, *On Death and Dying*, Macmillan Publishing Co., 1969.

Lazarus, Richard S., and Susan Folkman, *Stress, Appraisal, and Coping*, Springer, 1984.

Lester, David, "Genetics, Twin Studies, and Suicide", *Suicide and Life-Threatening Behavior*, Vol. 16(2), 1986.

Lifton, Robert Jay, *The Broken Connection*, Simon & Schuster, 1979.

Lifton, Robert Jay, *The Future of Immortality and Other Essays for a Nuclear Age*, Basic Books, 1987.

Lifton, Robert Jay, and Eric Olson, *Living and Dying*, Praeger, 1974.

Lindemann, Erich, and Ina May Greer, "A Study in Grief: Emotional Responses to Suicide", in *Survivors of Suicide*, edited by A. C. Cain, Charles C. Thomas, 1972.

Litman, Robert E., "Mental Disorders and Suicidal Intention", *Suicide and Life-Threatening Behavior*, Vol. 17(2), 1987.

Litman, Robert E., and Norman Tabachnick, "Psychoanalytic Theories of Suicide" in *Suicide Behaviors*, edited by H. L. P. Resnik, Little-Brown, 1968.

Litman, Robert E., "Psychological Autopsies in Court", *Suicide and Life-Threatening Behavior*, Vol. 14(2), 1984.

Litman, Robert E., "Sigmund Freud on Suicide" in *Essays in Self-Destruction*, edited by E. S. Shneidman, Science Books, 1967.

Lukas, Christopher, and Henry M. Seiden, *Silent Grief: Living in the Wake of Suicide*, Scribners, 1988.

Maltsberger, John T., and Dan H. Buie, "Countertransference Hate in the Treatment of Suicidal Patients", *Archives of General Psychiatry*, Vol. 30, May 1974.

Maltsberger, John T., and Dan H. Buie, "The Devices of Suicide: Revenge, Riddance, and Rebirth", *International Review of Psychoanalysis*, Vol. 7, 1980.

Maltsberger, John T., *Suicide Risk: The Formulation of Clinical Judgment*, New York University Press, 1986.

Maris, Ronald, (ed.), *Biology of Suicide*, Guilford Press, 1986.

Maris, Ronald, *Pathways to Suicide*, Johns Hopkins University Press, 1981.

Menninger, Karl, *Man Against Himself*, Harcourt, Brace, Jovanovich, 1966. (Originally published in 1938.)

Menninger, Karl, "Psychoanalytic Aspects of Suicide", *International Journal of Psychoanalysis*, Vol. 14, 1933.

Miller, Alice, *The Drama of the Gifted Child*, Basic Books, 1981.

Miller, Alice, *Thou Shalt Not Be Aware*, Farrar, Straus, Giroux, 1984.

Miller, Marv, *Suicide After Sixty: The Final Alternative*, Springer, 1979.

New York City Commission on Human Rights: Report on "The Physically Handicapped Citizen: A Human Rights Issue", 1972.

New York City Department of Health: Bureau of Health Statistics and Analysis, "Summary of Vital Statistics", 1983-1988, 125 Worth Street, New York, NY 10013.

New York City Department of Health: Bureau of School Children and Adolescent Health, "Suicide Risk Protocol", 1985.

New York State Commission on Quality of Care for the Mentally Disabled: Report on "Outpatient Mental Health Services", July 1989.

O'Carroll, Patrick W., "A Consideration of the Validity and Reliability of Suicide Mortality Data", *Suicide and Life-Threatening Behavior*, Vol. 19(1), 1989.

Pfeffer, Cynthia, *The Suicidal Child*, Guilford Press, 1986.

Ramsey, Richard, and Christopher Bagley, "The Prevalence of Suicide Behaviors, Attitudes, and Associated Social Experiences in an Urban Population", *Suicide and Life-Threatening Behavior*, Vol. 15(3), 1985.

Rich, Charles L., Deborah Young, and Richard C. Fowler, "San Diego Suicide Study", *Archives of General Psychiatry*, Vol. 43, June 1986.

Rofes, Eric E., *I Thought People Like That Killed Themselves*, Grey Fox Press, 1983.

Rosenberg, Mark L., and others, "Operational Criteria for the Determination of Suicide", *Journal of Forensic Sciences*, Vol. 33, November 1988.

Sartre, Jean-Paul, "Portrait of the Antisemite", in *Existentialism from Dostoevsky to Sartre*, edited by W. Kaufmann, Meridian Books, 1972. (Originally published in 1946.)

Schneider, Carl D., *Shame, Exposure, and Privacy*, Beacon Press, Boston, 1977.

Shneidman, Edwin S., and Norman Farberow, (eds.), *Clues to Suicide*, McGraw-Hill, 1957.

Shneidman, Edwin S., *Definition of Suicide*, John Wiley & Sons, 1985.

Statistical Abstract of The United States for 1989, United States Government Printing Office, 109th Edition.

Stengel, Erwin, *Suicide & Attempted Suicide*, Penguin Books, 1964.

Struve, Frederick A., "Clinical Electroencephalography and the Study of Suicide Behavior", in *Biology of Suicide*, edited by R. Maris, Guilford Press, 1986.

Sudak, H. A., M. B. Ford, and N. B. Rushforth, (eds.), *Suicide in the Young*, John Wright/PSG Inc., 1984.

Walsh, Mary Ellen, *Schizophrenia: Straight Talk for Family and Friends*, Warner Books, 1986.

Welu, Thomas C., "Psychological Reactions of Emergency Room Staff to Suicide Attempters", in *Proceedings, Sixth Annual Conference for Suicide Prevention*, edited by R. E. Litman, International Association for Suicide Prevention, 1971.

Wickett, Ann, *Double Exit*, The Hemlock Society, 1989.

Wolfgang, Marvin, E., "Suicide by Means of Victim-Precipitated Homicide", *The Journal of Clinical and Experimental Psychopathology*, December 1959.

Wrobleski, Adina, *Suicide: Your Child Has Died: For ALL Parents*, 1984, 5124 Grove St., Minneapolis MN 55436-2481.

INDEX

fear (continued), 247, 264-5, 267, 272-3, 278 287-8, 291-3, 295, 297-8, 300, 308, 313, 321-2, 332, 336, 339, 343, 347
fear, least fear theory of the means, 65-6, 180, 192, 200-1, 203-4, 338
fear, of death, 7, 63-4
fear, of suicidal death, 35, 42, 63-6, 296, 336-7
fears of counselors, 122, 135, 208-14, 290
fears of the suicidal enumerated, 59-63, 344
fears, nameless, 62
flirting with getting help, 138
Folkman, Susan, 346-7
Fossum, Merle A., 345
Freud, Sigmund, 28, 31, 65, 68-70, 83-4, 122, 176, 325-6, 344

Gay and Lesbian Switchboard, 271
gays and lesbians, homosexuality, 210, 277, 314, 316, 348
Gould, Madelyn S., 334-5, 351
grandiosity, 28, 103-7, 113, 126, 128, 145, 163, 293
guilt, 95, 108, 111-3, 169-70, 176, 194, 196, 199-200, 254, 274, 314-5, 324, 345, 351

Heller, Agnes, 158-9
Hendin, Herbert, 19, 27-9, 65-6, 270, 345
Hillman, James, 25, 28, 31, 35, 94, 107, 343
HIV, 29, 48, 74, 297-8, 332
Holmes, Thomas W., 257
homicide, 116, 169, 182, 191, 255, 267, 274-5, 279, 321, 339, 349, 351
hopelessness, 5-6, 30, 62, 91, 126, 131, 159-60, 163, 192, 221, 229, 254, 273, 296, 300, 321, 324, 328-32, 337, 339, 351
Hussey, Maria, 256
hypochondria, 77-8

imitation, 337-8
immaturity, 60, 93
inaccurate views of the self, 122-7, 145
infantile, 7, 53, 217
inner light, myth of, 133-5, 227, 301, 303
intention, 7, 11, 14, 17, 178, 306-8, 320, 323, 331-2, 338, 341, 345, 349-50
interruptions, 121, 156, 218, 301

Jungian perspective, 28
just wants attention, myth of, 7, 12, 21, 50-2, 56, 59, 88, 116, 137, 152, 209, 212, 225, 227, 229-30, 238, 256, 265, 281, 301-2

Kellerman, Arthur L., 274
King, Martin Luther, 198
Kubler-Ross, Elisabeth, 101, 174

language, of suicide, 12-5, 217-8, 259, 263-4, 301, 303
Lazarus, Richard, 346-7
legislation, 212, 271-6, 290, 302
Lester, David, 190
Lifton, Robert J., 26
Lindemann, Erich, 348
listening, 215-21, 224, 232, 239, 262-4, 297
Litman, Robert E., 19-20, 22, 31, 37, 69, 307-8, 314-6, 342
loneliness, 46, 91, 107, 113, 119, 146-7, 163, 206, 209, 219, 224, 240, 247, 260-2, 300, 309-13, 322
Lowell, Robert, 274
Lukas, Christopher, 186, 348

Maltsberger, John T., 19, 28, 75-7, 80, 84, 309-13, 341-3, 348, 351
Manes, Donald, 334-5
manipulativeness, myth of, 56-7, 59, 116, 121, 125, 137, 207-11, 214, 225, 268, 301, 327
Maris, Ronald, 19, 22, 25, 28, 94
Mason, Marilyn J., 345

The Author

David L. Conroy is a graduate of the Woodstock Country School, Claremont Men's College, and the University of Massachusetts at Amherst. The title of his dissertation was *Plato's Early Theory of Knowledge*. He is the Executive Director of a New York City non-profit organization that does public education work in the prevention of suicide.